UNDOCUMENTED LIVES

UNDOCUMENTED LIVES

....

The Untold Story of Mexican Migration

ANA RAQUEL MINIAN

Harvard University Press

Cambridge, Massachusetts

London, England

2018

First printing

Library of Congress Cataloging-in-Publication Data

Names: Minian, Ana Raquel, 1983– author.
Title: Undocumented lives : the untold story of Mexican migration /
Ana Raquel Minian.
Description: Cambridge, Massachusetts : Harvard University Press, 2018. |
Includes bibliographical references and index.
Identifiers: LCCN 2017039421 | ISBN 9780674737037 (hardcover : alk. paper)
Subjects: LCSH: Mexican Americans—Ethnic identity. | Mexico—Emigration
and immigration—Economic aspects. | United States—Emigration and
immigration—Economic aspects. | Mexico—Economic conditions—1918– |
Mexico—Social conditions—1970– | United States—Emigration and
immigration—Government policy. | Foreign workers, Mexican—
United States—History.
Classification: LCC E184.M5 M5496 2018 | DDC 973/.046872—dc23
LC record available at https://lccn.loc.gov/2017039421

For my parents and for those in migrant communities
on both sides of the border

CONTENTS

Introduction: From Neither Here nor There   *1*

1. An Excess of Citizens   *14*

2. "A Population without a Country"   *47*

3. The Intimate World of Migrants   *77*

4. Normalizing Migration   *104*

5. Supporting the Hometown from Abroad   *125*

6. The Rights of the People   *157*

7. A Law to Curtail Undocumented Migration   *183*

8. The Cage of Gold   *208*

   Afterword   *233*

Appendix A: Note on Sources   *239*
Appendix B: Queer Migration   *247*
Notes   *251*
Acknowledgments   *313*
Index   *317*

INTRODUCTION

From Neither Here nor There

T HE NIGHT OF MAY 3, 1980, was cold and foggy in southern San Diego.[1] Not foggy enough, however, to hide the hundreds of Mexican migrants who were being chased from the south by Mexican police officers and from the north by U.S. immigration agents.

Earlier that spring, migrant smugglers had taken control of a small piece of land on the northern side of the U.S.-Mexico border and had been using it as a launching pad to help migrants enter farther into California.[2] Although technically within the United States, the area was south of the Tijuana River, immediately next to Mexico. Every day, hundreds of migrants crossed through the then-dilapidated gate that separated the two countries and congregated on this sliver of land by the river's south levee. Then, in the late hours of the night, the smugglers would start throwing rocks at the Border Patrol officials policing the north side of the river's levee. While the officials were distracted, the migrants would wade through the river, run north, and try to evade the Border Patrol. Immigration officials had desisted from reclaiming the area, which had come to be known as No Man's Land, because they were far outnumbered by the migrants and feared that if they tried to regain control, it would "almost certainly mean injuries, possibly someone's life."[3] Behind closed doors, however, immigration officials began plotting.

On that foggy night in early May, they launched what they described as their "largest joint operation" with Mexican officials. As the smugglers waited for the right moment to start their nightly rock throwing, three Border Patrol Ram Chargers that had been outfitted with heavy wire mesh over the windows to brace against rocks forded the shallow river and headed directly toward the crowd. The migrants turned and ran south toward Mexico. But they faced an unexpected reception: waiting for them, on the other side of the dilapidated gate, were police officers from Tijuana who had been instructed to apprehend the migrants and arrest the known smugglers in the group.[4]

No one could have predicted what happened next. When the police officers saw these migrants running toward them, they decided to go against their orders and forced those they caught back into the United States en masse.[5] Although the officers' motivation is unknown, their actions meant that when the migrants tried to return home, fleeing the Ram Chargers speeding toward them, they were instead forced to cross the border once more—this time against their will. Not only did the actions of these police officers violate Mexico's constitution but they also delivered the migrants right into the hands of U.S. authorities. That night, over 250 migrants were apprehended by U.S. agents.[6]

U.S. officers responded to the migrants they caught with particular severity. In a departure from usual procedures, they charged, convicted, and incarcerated the apprehended migrants before sending them back. Arraigning, detaining, trying, and deporting migrants involved a huge expense and required a cumbersome bureaucratic process that immigration officials typically avoided, instead offering those caught "voluntary departure" by which the migrants avoided going to court. Migrants seized in the joint operation were not given this option.

Though atypical for the period, the episode captures the dilemma that millions of Mexican migrants began to face in the 1970s. Even as they struggled creatively and courageously against their poverty in Mexico and their unauthorized status in the United States, migrants remained a people without a place, whose presence could be denied by those in power in both countries. As the defense lawyers of those captured in this operation argued, "These persons, although they were forced into the United States by Mexican officials as part of the 'sweep' have also been charged with illegal entry."[7]

Even as the exclusion of undocumented migrants from the United States has been explained and normalized through the idea that they broke U.S. law, little attention has been paid to the exclusion of Mexican migrants from Mexico. In the United States, citizens and lawmakers have long debated whether those who crossed the border without proper

authorization should be legalized, deported, criminalized, or simply ignored. Underlying the debate is the assumption that "illegal migrants"
have full inclusion in Mexico. As the episode in Tijuana shows—and as
this book elaborates—that assumption is not always correct.

The actions of the Tijuana police on that spring night in 1980 might
have provoked protest in Mexico. Mexican police officers had pushed
citizens out of their own country without their consent. Yet those at the
highest levels of the Mexican government remained silent and did not
demand an explanation for what had occurred.[8] By then, Mexico's top
politicians had come to believe that the departure of those whom they
considered "surplus workers" could alleviate the socioeconomic problems Mexico faced. Migrants were pushed out of all the places through
which they moved, even a place deemed No Man's Land.

This book explores how, for more than twenty years, migrants sought to
establish a sense of local and national belonging, even as they were denied the ability to reside in any one place on a permanent basis. As they
struggled to belong, and as they were pushed from place to place, migrants described a life defined by being "from neither here nor there"
("Ni de aquí ni de allá"). The story takes place between 1965 and 1986,
a period when many of the current dilemmas around unauthorized
migration were born. It tells of how Mexican migrants went from being
a population that was pushed out of all the places they resided and
pressed to engage in circular migration, to a population that felt trapped
and pressured to settle permanently in the United States. It was during
these two decades that officials from both countries helped create a
permanent class of displaced, undesired people; that migrant activists rose up to insist that they deserved rights despite their lack of documentation; and that migrant communities forged and solidified the
structures required to sustain and propel the migratory flow for decades
to come.

In 1964, the United States ended the Bracero Program, a series of
bilateral agreements with Mexico. During its twenty-two years in operation, the program issued over 4.5 million guest-worker contracts to
Mexican men to labor temporarily in the United States.[9] Mexican workers
who had become accustomed to working in *El Norte*, even if just for short
periods of time, were dealt a huge blow by the program's termination.
The impact was compounded by the passage of the Immigration and

Nationality Act of 1965, which imposed for the first time a numerical limit on the number of Latin American immigrants to the United States.[10]

Those who sought work in *El Norte* after 1965 realized that if they wanted to keep crossing the border, they had to do so without papers. Unauthorized entries multiplied. The number of Mexican citizens apprehended in the United States—an imperfect but suggestive measure of Mexican undocumented migration—rose enormously in the two decades after the Bracero Program's end: from 55,340 in 1965 to 277,377 in 1970, to a peak of 1,671,458 in 1986, a 3,000 percent overall increase.[11] According to some estimates, approximately 28 million Mexicans en-

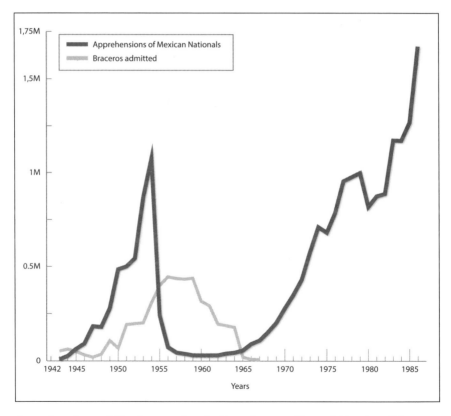

Apprehensions of Mexican nationals. Data Source: Manuel García y Griego and Mónica Verea Campos, *México y Estados Unidos frente a la migración de indocumentados* (México: Coordinación de Humanidades, Universidad Nacional Autónoma de México (UNAM) and Miguel Angel Porrúa Editor, 1988): 118–121, Table 2.

tered the United States without papers between 1965 and 1986, compared to 1.3 million legal immigrants and a mere 46,000 contract workers.[12] Before 1965, even those who crossed the border illegally typically viewed their migration within the context of the Bracero Program. It was only after no other real avenue existed for Mexicans to migrate north legally that illegality became the primary way in which they understood their journeys north.

Though the way migrants thought of their cross-border movement changed after 1965, another essential feature of migrant life remained the same for the next two decades: Mexican migration continued to be characterized by its circularity. Even though no longer bound to return to Mexico by the Bracero Program, the overwhelming majority of migrants chose to cross back and forth across the border rather than settling permanently in either country. Circularity meant that the overall number of Mexicans living without papers in the United States did not rise nearly as much as the number of individuals who migrated illegally. Indeed, 86 percent of all entries were offset by departures.[13] Circular migration counters the popular stereotype of Mexican migrants as forever desirous of living permanently in the United States.[14]

Migrants' continual cross-border movement in the absence of a formal program that encouraged them to do so raises questions about how migrants and others understood and negotiated their geographic movement and sense of belonging. In the 1970s, Mexican policymakers, U.S. authorities, large segments of U.S. society, and Mexican communities of high out-migration came to reject the long-term presence of working-class Mexican men of reproductive age. In Mexico, the country's top politicians reversed their long-standing opposition to unauthorized and long-term migration and began to view undocumented departures not as a depletion of the country's labor force, but instead as a way of alleviating unemployment. At the same time, in the United States, migrants found themselves classified as "illegal aliens," accused of taking jobs away from deserving citizens during a time of recession, and regularly deported. Their permanent residence was also denied at the local level. When they lived in their hometowns in Mexico, their families and communities pressured them to head north to make money and when they resided in their new cities and towns in the United States, their loved ones insisted that they return home. Increasingly, migrants found that they could belong nowhere, "neither here nor there."

Migrants tried to make the best of this circular, undocumented life and conceived ways to assert their own cartographies of belonging. The world they sought to create defied their triple exclusion (from Mexico, from the United States, and from their local communities) and instead established migrants as welcomed and even indispensable actors in all three spaces. Migrants resisted the idea that they were superfluous in Mexico by becoming vital economic agents in their home country through the money they sent from the United States. They countered their illegality north of the border by claiming rights. They diminished the pressures that their families and communities placed on them to engage in circular migration by reconfiguring the very meanings of hometown, family, and community life to include a transnational dimension. These efforts, some intentional, some not, provided migrants with at least partial inclusion in the multiple locales in which they lived; however, that inclusion was only possible because they resided, at least part of their time, in the United States. Thus, even as the actions migrants took challenged their various exclusions, they also bound them to the migratory process and to the United States.

In 1986, the U.S. Congress passed the Immigration Reform and Control Act, which made it more difficult for Mexicans to cross the border back and forth without papers. To avoid detection while entering the United States, migrants started having to pay much higher fees to their smugglers and to trek across hazardous terrains that were less patrolled. But by then, undocumented migration had already become a self-perpetuating phenomenon, and undocumented life had become normalized. In light of the new hardships of migration, many Mexicans settled permanently in the United States and dared not return to Mexico for fear that they would not be able to reenter the United States. Their presence was still rejected north of the border because of their undocumented status, and their own government representatives in Mexico still did not want them back permanently. But now, rather than feeling "pushed" from all these spaces, they found themselves trapped in the United States, which they referred to as the *Jaula de Oro*, or Cage of Gold.

The story of how migrants went from being ousted from the multiple spaces where they lived to being confined in the United States creates multiple subplots, exposes common assumptions about migration, and disrupts traditional narratives on the topic.

This book brings together two very different worlds that rarely interacted with one another—and that are rarely examined together—but that are crucial to understanding the history of Mexican undocumented migration. One story focuses on how Mexican and U.S. policymakers deliberated about how to deal with migration. It reveals how laws were written, how organizations lobbied government officials, and how the media shaped popular understandings of migration. But this is not the only story to be told. Mexican citizens experienced migration on a more intimate plane. It shaped how they thought about "home," how they were treated, what they could afford, and the ways in which they raised their children, sustained romantic relationships, and supported their aging parents. Migrants' personal stories seem so distant from the realm of congressional debates and bilateral meetings that, on the surface, they appear to be two distinct narratives. But it is only by examining these separate worlds together that we can understand each of them fully. After all, multiple decades of policies failed because lawmakers ignored the complicated social spheres of migrants; in turn, migrants had to restructure the lives they built in response to new laws.

The world of migrants did not just encompass migrants themselves, but also nonmigrants—all those who remained in Mexico.[15] Both are central to the narrative that follows. In the years between 1965 and 1986, approximately 80 percent of border crossers were men who left their families behind when they departed for the United States.[16] Even while examining the experiences of the women who did cross the border, the story of Mexican migrants is primarily a story about men. But the story of Mexican migration is not. Men migrated, in part, because their wives, parents, and friends pressured them to head to *El Norte*, making these nonmigrants central actors in migratory decisions. Moreover, those who did not cross the border experienced the vicissitudes of migration just as keenly as those who did. Women and other family members anxiously awaited news from those they loved, wondered when the men would return home, raised children without fathers, and depended on the money migrants remitted home.

Attending to the stories of nonmigrants sheds light on how factors such as sexual and gender norms, rather than economics alone, determined who migrated and who remained at home. In Mexico, not only women but also gay men tended to refrain from going to the United States. Women's decision to remain home and raise their children in

Mexico counters the stereotype of deceitful Mexican women giving birth north of the border in order to acquire U.S. citizenship—what would come to be known as the "anchor baby" phenomenon. Similarly, gay men's preference to remain in Mexico counters the assumption that queer people in small-town, Catholic Mexico would jump at the opportunity to head to the seemingly liberal United States. Examining the movement of women and gay men, as well as their ability to remain in their home country, reveals as much about the forces behind transnational migration as do the border crossings of migrants themselves.

Exploring the mobility of nonmigrants expands the history of unauthorized migration beyond a singular emphasis on the act of crossing the national border. This is not only a national or transnational story; it is also a local one. People's cross-border movement was deeply connected to their understanding of local mobility and spaces. For example, from the United States many men tried to limit their wives' movement back in their hometowns, as they believed that women's presence in public spaces signified marital infidelity. Women often felt imprisoned in their own houses, knowing that their husbands would get jealous if they heard that their wives were socializing outside the home and would stop sending money as a result.[17]

International migration is generally understood as a force that promotes cosmopolitanism and extends a person's sense of space. Yet Mexican migration in these decades sometimes prompted the opposite, shrinking the capacity of many people—both migrants and nonmigrants—to reside in local and national spaces. It is undeniable that migration extended people's lives and social networks across national borders. But a more nuanced analysis reveals that for many, including the women who were confined to their homes, migration also produced a significant contraction of space.

Even those who got to experience a new country saw the constriction of many of the spaces through which they moved. Mexican officials' growing support of the out-migration of citizens combined with increasing rates of deportation from the United States effectively constructed the territory that spanned between the two nation-states as one in which Mexican men's long-term presence was denied. Migrants experienced their own hometowns as shrinking in on them and pushing them out—a direct result of the pressure their families and communities placed on them to head north to make money. Once in the United States they found further restrictions on their mobility, as they sought to evade immigration officials. Many migrants constructed "movement maps" that helped them to circumvent streets they knew to be policed by these officials. They sometimes took jobs that allowed them to hide from the public eye. In Tempe, Arizona, for example, migrants preferred to pick lower-paying citrus fruits rather than onions, because the thick foliage in lemon and orange groves provided cover when immigration officials passed through the area. Until 1986, migrants continuously moved transnationally, but they regularly experienced local spaces as sites of confinement.

Some migrants responded to the exigencies of their situation through local, binational, and translocal activism. It was during this period that migrants first rallied around the idea that "illegal aliens" deserved rights in the United States. Such battles were complicated. In seeking benefits for undocumented people, activists risked reinforcing their categorization as "illegal." But through their efforts, migrants improved their working conditions, safeguarded their right to unionize, and ensured that unauthorized children could attend public school. These struggles are part of a long trajectory of undocumented migrant activism that continues to this day.

Migrant activists in the United States also built a type of extraterritorial welfare state by providing aid to those in need in many Mexican communities. Given that the Mexican government's economic restructuring plans during these two decades regularly overlooked communities of high out-migration, many of those who left for the United States sent money back not just to support their families, but also to support their hometowns. Unlike private remittances, the funds that migrant activists sent home provided assistance to entire communities. Migrants paid for doctor visits and medication for those who were sick, they gave a monthly allowance to the poorest members of the community, and in some towns, they even built basic infrastructure, including paving streets, erecting health clinics, and introducing potable water and electric power lines.[18]

These multiple subplots show how, in the years between 1965 and 1986, migrants and their multiple communities negotiated questions of unemployment, welfare, family arrangements, and sexuality in a way that led men to engage in circular migration between the two countries. Rather than attending to what was happening on the ground, however,

U.S. and Mexican policymakers simply repeated stereotypes about migrants' relationship to the welfare state, about their families and "excessive" fertility rates, and about the effects of migration on unemployment rates. Policymakers' failure to attend to migrants' lived experience limited their ability to implement workable solutions and to curtail the growth of undocumented migration.

Denied the ability to reside in any one place on a permanent basis, migrants yearned for a sense of belonging—both to a specific city or town and to a country. For them, a sense of belonging was simple, yet elusive. Migrants, like most people, wanted to reside in a place that was familiar, safe, and welcoming; they wanted to live there without feeling forced to leave, whether because of economic necessity, community pressure, alienation, or deportation.

While migrants rarely spoke of feeling like they could claim full belonging to either nation, they always upheld their Mexican citizenship. Scholars have long argued that individuals can hold formal citizenship even while lacking substantive citizenship. In the United States, women and racial, ethnic, sexual, and religious minorities, for example, are often described as holding second-class citizenship: they are citizens but they are still excluded from full rights. Yet this is not how migrants viewed their position in the world or understood the ideal of citizenship.[19] Even though Mexican officials favored their departure from Mexico, migrants' Mexican citizenship safeguarded them from being deported from their country of birth—a form of protection they treasured because of their experiences in the United States.

The particular pressures migrants felt in the years between 1965 and 1986, which prevented them from belonging in either country, were not experienced by them alone. Indeed, these pressures arose at a time when all working-class men and women, in both the United States and Mexico, saw their socioeconomic standing in their respective countries become diluted. During the 1970s and 1980s, the United States saw growing levels of inequality, unemployment, and inflation; accelerating deindustrialization; and intensifying attacks on unions and the welfare state. During these same years, Mexico experienced a rise in inequality, inflation, unemployment, and foreign debt, as well as a shift toward free trade. These economic trends expanded the number of economically displaced people, who lived in the precarious, liminal condition of nonbe-longing even while remaining in their place of residence.

Few issues in contemporary U.S. politics cause as much commotion as undocumented migration. Yet established archives are largely silent about the lives of undocumented migrants and those of their family and community members who remained in Mexico. Undocumented migration has touched all aspects of life in both the United States and Mexico, from popular culture to economics, from the mundane, daily struggles of individuals to the broad canvas of public policy and law. The story told in this book is as much a social history as it is a political, cultural, economic, and legal one. The people at the center of this story include the migrants themselves and their families and communities, as well as Mexican American and white activists, labor unionists, and U.S. and Mexican government officials. Tracing these different narra-tives, actions, and experiences requires using different types of sources.

The positions and actions of lobby groups, government officials, and the public at large can be traced using conventional sources—everything from government memoranda, letters, and action plans, to Gallup re-ports, newspaper articles, and TV shows—but uncovering the history of migrants themselves requires the discovery of a different set of ar-chives. Those who desired to go north illegally left their hometowns without notifying Mexican government officials, tried to cross the border without being detected, and lived in the United States in the shadow of public view. Their active efforts to remain invisible and live "undocu-mented lives" make it hard to trace their history. Even when migrants did leave footprints in traditional archives, those sources don't tell us much about their worlds.

To explore the lives of migrants and their communities, historians have to mine unconventional archives, such as privately held orga-nizational records, personal collections, newspapers, pamphlets, and other unpublished and even uncataloged ephemera. Some migrants and their spouses wrote love letters to each other across borders and kept them. Migrant activists saved the diplomas they earned, the minutes of their meetings, and the literature of their organizations. Almost everyone collected photographs of key moments in their lives, such as weddings. Because people do not have much physical space to store the documents they value, they often kept them in small closets. By keeping them, however, they helped preserve this history.

To supplement these documents, I conducted over 250 oral history interviews on both sides of the border. Some of these interviews were brief and haunted by hesitations; others were long and continued for days. In Mexico, most of my interviews took place in Michoacán and Zacatecas, two of the states from which migrants left in the highest numbers between 1965 and 1986. I focused in particular on some of the *ranchos* (hamlets) and towns with the highest levels of emigration. In the United States, I conducted most of my oral histories in the Los Angeles metropolitan area, the most popular destination for undocumented workers in the post-Bracero period, but also in other parts of California, as well

Places where oral histories were conducted.

as in Illinois, Arizona, and New Mexico. Given that oral histories often disclose more about people's memories than about their actual experiences, I focused on the types of stories that were repeated by many migrants, and wherever possible, corroborated these experiences with other available sources.[20] This method does not solve all the problems inherent in oral history, including that it often tells us only the stories that people remember and want to share.[21] But it does provide one of the few inroads into a relatively undocumented history.

The rise of undocumented migration from Mexico has left millions of people without a place to call home. It is only by bringing together a wide range of multifaceted stories and by exploring the silences in the archives that we can understand why laws fell short and migration came to change the nature of both U.S. and Mexican societies.

1

....

AN EXCESS OF CITIZENS

J OSÉ GARDOÑO HAD LITTLE energy to help the old man who was
struggling to keep up with the pace of the smugglers. It was 1979,
and although the U.S.-Mexico border was much easier to cross than it
would later become, Mexicans still experienced it as dangerous. Gardoño had already tried to enter California the day before but had only made
it seven miles in before being apprehended by the Border Patrol and
deported back to Mexico. "Without having eaten, without anything,
[immigration officers] threw us out [to Tijuana] at dawn, where I didn't
know anyone," he recalled.[1] Feeling lost, he started "roaming, roaming,
roaming" the city streets until he finally encountered some smugglers
who were leading a group of migrants across the border that same day.
It was these *coyotes* who were now ready to abandon the old man to his
fate. "Move you sons of . . . move!" the smugglers yelled at the group.
The elderly man finally shouted back, "You should leave already. I'll stay
here. I will only make it up to this point." Despite his hunger and ex-
haustion, Gardoño knew that he could not leave this stranger to cross
the border by himself. He and another migrant went back for the man,
held him up, and forced him to continue walking, while the rest of the
group left them far behind. After hours of walking without guidance,
trying not to get lost in the hills, the three finally made it to the United
States. Their success, however, was tainted by the hardships they faced
north of the border. Far away from their homes, families, and communities they now arrived in a place where they were viewed primarily as
"illegal aliens."

That same year, Mexico's secretary of foreign affairs, Jorge Castañeda
y Álvarez de la Rosa, met privately with U.S. officials to discuss the ques-

tion of undocumented Mexican migration. He explained that it was essential for the Mexican economy that the United States allow migrants to continue crossing the border, even if they were doing so without authorization. The "800,000 Mexicans [who] manage to cross the border annually and stay in the United States at least for a temporary job," Castañeda explained, helped his government "to partially solve the problem of unemployment in Mexico."[2] Castañeda was so invested in this issue that he even warned U.S. officials: "There are limits to the restrictive policies you can adopt. We are both conscious that massive deportation could have grave results in Mexico," which would then spill over to the United States. Castañeda knew about the adversity and exclusions that migrants faced crossing the border and living in the United States without papers but still considered undocumented migration an acceptable, partial solution to Mexico's problems.

While Gardoño's cross-border movement was part of a long trend of Mexican migration to the United States, the secretary's position on the topic was relatively new. In the first half of the twentieth century, Mexico's leaders spoke strongly against emigration. During those years, most high-ranking Mexican policymakers believed that a large population residing in Mexico was indispensable for economic growth. They thus opposed long-term departures from the country and actively supported the repatriation and deportation of those who had already migrated.[3] In the context of this history, Castañeda's insistence that the United States turn a blind eye to undocumented migration and limit deportations for the sake of Mexico's economic well-being represented a sea change among top Mexican government officials.

The years between 1965 and 1986 saw a seismic shift in Mexico's political culture with regard to emigration, which had deep ramifications for Mexicans' right to reside on a permanent basis in their home country. A series of economic crises combined with new economic models led Mexico's top government officials, including presidents, their cabinets, and those in Congress, to reverse their long-standing position on migration. While policymakers had previously held that a large population was beneficial to the nation's economy, by the mid-1970s they blamed the country's economic troubles on the large number of inhabitants residing in Mexico.[4] Castañeda's word choice at the 1979 briefing with U.S. officials reveals the way in which he and other policymakers had come to view undocumented migrants. He claimed that "the United

States will continue to be, to a greater or lesser extent, the safety valve for our surplus labor force."[5] This increasingly popular perspective over-looked migrants' humanity and cast them as a "surplus" and unwanted population that should not live in Mexico.

Existing government archives contain limited explicit evidence in which policymakers openly acknowledge changing their views on emigration as a means of alleviating Mexico's economic problems. Speaking of such a change would have meant recognizing that the ruling political party, the Institutional Revolutionary Party (PRI), was giving up on the Mexican Revolution's goal of providing Mexicans with the means of residing with humane living standards and economic opportunities in their country of birth. Despite the paucity of such explicit evidence, the multiple and jumbled changes in state practices and rhetoric that occurred between the mid-1960s and the mid-1980s elucidate officials' shifting position. These changes can be seen in politicians' modification of the Ley General de Población (General Population Law); in the increased attention they paid to undocumented migrants' human rights; in their attempts to convince U.S. officials to allow Mexicans to cross the border without papers; and in their introduction of new administrative practices that made it easier for migrants to head north. When analyzed together, these actions expose a broad shift in the way that those at the highest levels of the government conceived of citizens' departures to the United States.

Policymakers' silence on the issue of emigration is in and of itself revealing of officials' growing belief that undocumented migration could benefit Mexico.[6] Between 1965 and 1986, the number of Mexicans apprehended by the U.S. Border Patrol relative to the overall population of Mexico jumped from a rate slightly above 1 per 1,000 to 21 per 1,000.[7] Despite the magnitude of these rates, the question of migration did not create a national public outcry, nor did it become a central topic of concern among Mexico's politicians. The 1970s saw the rapid growth of public investment and social development programs in Mexico, but for the most part the government's economic and social policies ignored the issue of migration and failed to acknowledge the changes needed for citizens to be able to remain in their home country. Policymakers' omission effectively worked to ensure the continuing rates of out-migration.

The political culture that acquiesced to and even supported citizens' emigration flourished during the 1970s in spite of its implications. It implied that government officials had concluded that thousands of citizens, like José Gardoño, should be absent from Mexico and should reside instead in a country that viewed them as illegal.

From Mexico's independence in 1821 to the early 1970s, the country's policymakers tended to cast population growth as essential for economic growth and nation building.[8] Rather than regarding Mexico's workers as a "surplus population" during these earlier years, they considered them indispensable to the nation-state. Given these beliefs, when Mexican citizens started heading to the United States in increasing numbers at the turn of the twentieth century, representatives worried that their movement would damage state efforts to increase the size of the population.[9] Mexican consul Enrique Santibáñez called the presence of almost half a million Mexicans in the United States "a veritable hemorrhage suffered by the country."[10] Another government official went as far as to claim that he wished he could "build a Chinese wall clear across our northern border to keep laborers at home."[11] In 1926, the government enacted a migration law that sought to encourage immigration to regions with short labor supplies and increased restrictions on Mexicans' emigration to foreign countries.[12] Ten years later, Mexican officials designed the first Ley General de Población, the authoritative law dictating the nation's demography. It instituted three different means to achieve a larger population: promoting natural growth (increasing the birth rate and decreasing the death rate), repatriating nationals who were abroad, and to a lesser degree, encouraging the immigration of those deemed racially and ethnically assimilable.[13]

Calls to increase population growth by restricting emigration did not always receive unequivocal support because they challenged another one of the government's stated goals: achieving maximum labor efficiency. During the 1920s and 1930s, some policymakers came to believe that short-term migration improved the productivity of returned workers and established labor peace. Manuel Gamio, a preeminent anthropologist who advised the federal government on questions of migration, argued that "contact with American civilization" would transform natives or "mestizos" into "modern citizens" with the most updated "material culture."[14] Migration also allowed workers who could not support their families to make money in the United States and send remittances back home.[15] The economic security this afforded reduced the threat of rebellions in the countryside, a particularly important issue given that, between 1926 and 1929 and then again during the mid-1930s, a group of rebels, known as Cristeros, had led an armed conflict against the government in the name of the Catholic Church. Their protest took place in states from the Central Plateau region in Mexico, which contributed 60 percent of emigrants.[16] Many local officials responded by holding that the crisis could be eased by encouraging people to leave the area and go to the United States.[17]

While sympathizing with Gamio's claims, most policymakers believed that out-migration was not truly uplifting the country because it was taking place illegally.[18] When migrants crossed the border without authorization, they risked being deported back to Mexico without having learned occupational skills or acquired resources in the United States.[19] According to officials, illegality turned migrants into criminals instead of imbuing them with a sense of diligence and converting them into modern citizens.[20] This idea disregarded the fact that many migrants had crossed the border illegally in order to avoid Mexico's violence and criminality. Gamio's work itself documented how many Mexicans living in the United States in the late 1920s had originally emigrated to avoid Mexico's revolutionary violence. Pablo Mares, who Gamio interviewed in the mid-1920s, reported, "I had to come to the United States, because it was impossible to live down there with so many revolutions. Once even I was at the point of being killed by some revolutionists."[21] According to Mexican officials, however, undocumented migration meant that rather than being "admitted like workers" to the United States, Mexicans were "persecuted like criminals."[22] Workers should instead remain in Mexico.

The dual belief that more workers were needed to promote economic growth in Mexico and that undocumented migration led to the criminalization of Mexicans meant that during the 1920s and 1930s most policymakers insisted that the government needed to focus on curtailing long-term, undocumented migration even though they recognized the potential benefits of short-term and legal migration. Officials did not need to do much to encourage temporary migration; Mexicans were already going to the United States by themselves in large numbers. But they did need to restrict long-term and undocumented departures. The two federal government agencies in charge of handling out-migration—the Secretariat of Foreign Affairs and the Mexican Department of Migration, which was part of the Secretariat of the Interior—took this stance.

In 1928, Mexico's Secretariat of Foreign Affairs published a report claiming that "the disproportionate and illegal emigration of our nationals to the United States is harmful both to our country and to Mexican workers."[23] Similarly, in 1930, the director of the Mexican Department of Migration pinpointed undocumented border crossings as "the most important problem" he sought to address.[24] Even Gamio acknowledged that the prevailing position within the federal government went against his vision of migration. "The Mexican government," he recognized, "does not like to see the emigration, particular that of a permanent character, become extensive, since this means a step backward in the progress of Mexico and a definite loss in useful energy for the development of the country."[25]

The Great Depression opened the path for Mexican officials to repatriate those who were living north of the border. Policymakers hoped that through this measure they would achieve their dual goals: on the one hand, they would ensure that "modernized" workers returned home, and on the other, they would increase the number of people residing in Mexico.[26] The plan would also help migrants who had been hit hard by the growing rates of unemployment and the resulting anti-foreign sentiments in the United States. As part of the repatriation program, Mexican consuls provided approximately 100,000 Mexican migrants with food and free transportation to return to the interior of Mexico.[27] Once in Mexico, however, most migrants felt incapable of using any of their skills to improve their lives, much less to modernize their country of origin. One repatriated woman said, "How can we do anything? We are so poor. Surely many have learned useful skills there [in the United States], but what good does that do here [in Mexico] when they come back without anything, no tools, no work, nothing at all, not even to eat. What help can *repatriados* like that be?"[28] Despite their incapacity to absorb the returned migrants, Mexican officials continued to insist that citizens living in the United States ought to return.

A few years later, in 1942, another opportunity presented itself for Mexican officials to restrict out-migration and ensure that migrants returned to Mexico. The U.S. ambassador to Mexico, George Messersmith, proposed a plan to Mexican president Manuel Ávila Camacho by which Mexican men would be able to head to the United States legally to work for short periods of time and then return to Mexico. This plan would not only help Mexican workers, Messersmith explained, but would also help to curb the labor shortages that the United States was experiencing as a result of its participation in the Second World War. When deliberating on this proposal, Mexico's leaders initially feared that the plan would simply encourage more Mexicans to reside abroad permanently.[29] On further consideration and pressure from the United States, however, President Ávila Camacho and his cabinet determined that the proposal actually offered them the perfect means to achieve their goals.[30] The program restricted contracting to agricultural workers who were male, over eighteen years old, and could obtain recommendations from local authorities. It also limited the number of slots available. Rather than heading north illegally and potentially staying there permanently, under the program only a limited and controlled number of Mexicans would migrate with proper authorization, acquire modern skills in the United States, and then return to their home country. Not only did the Mexican government accept the proposal but it continued to renew it for over two decades in a series of agreements known as the Bracero Program.

During the Bracero Program, which lasted between 1942 and 1964, Mexican policymakers continued to oppose undocumented migration. In 1954, Mexican and U.S. migratory officials implemented Operation Wetback to intensify the already existing binational measures used to curtail unauthorized migration.[31] During the operation, the U.S. Border Patrol swept through southwestern states detaining those it found in the United States without papers and turned over the apprehended migrants to Mexican migration officials. Mexican authorities then forcibly relocated the deportees to the interior of Mexico, having learned from experience that if the detainees were released near the border region they would immediately attempt to reenter the United States.[32] The Mexican secretary of the interior boasted that "Mexico and the United States were carrying out the repatriation of thousands . . . in perfect coordination."[33]

Even though the participation of Mexican authorities in Operation Wetback violated the Mexican Constitution, which protected the right of citizens to enter and exit the country at will, officials held that they were simply helping the deportees get back home.[34] After all, a large proportion of undocumented migrants came from the Central Plateau, a region in the interior of Mexico that encompasses the states of Guanajuato, Michoacán, Jalisco, Zacatecas, Colima, Nayarit, and Aguascalientes.

While officials cast unauthorized migration as harmful to Mexico, the Bracero Program was portrayed as the perfect way to modernize the country. The Alianza de Braceros Nacionales de México en los Estados

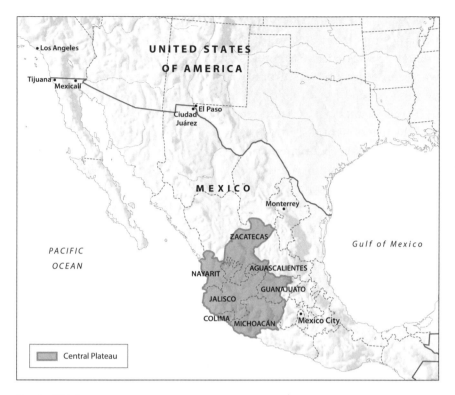

Central Plateau.

Unidos de Norteamérica, an organization that struggled to defend Mexican contract workers, announced in its membership cards: "With the knowledge and experience gained in the U.S.A. [these braceros] will return [to] their country to become the new farmers of Mexico. Please try to understand that they are eager and willing to work and learn. Please help them to obtain a fair and honest wage in order that when they return to their country they will be in a position to apply the newly gained knowledge and experience for the good of Mexico."[35] There is no reason to believe that U.S. growers cared about Mexico's development, yet the Alianza's stance speaks loudly to the idea that Mexicans viewed braceros as a means to progress. Scholars agreed with this view. In 1953, Verne Baker published an article entitled "Braceros Farm for Mexico," which credited the rapid agricultural development of the states of Sonora and Sinaloa to the efforts of guest workers who had returned from abroad with more efficient laboring practices.[36]

For policymakers, the return of modernized workers seemed particularly important during the Bracero period because of the implementation of Mexico's "Green Revolution"—an economic strategy that was itself guided by U.S. initiative. The endeavor, carried out jointly by the Rockefeller Foundation and the Mexican government, sought to introduce modern agrarian techniques in Mexico, such as irrigation and the use of hybrid seed stock that was specifically developed for its responsiveness to petrochemical fertilizers.[37] The mostly U.S.-educated Mexican scientists and the Rockefeller Foundation specialists who implemented the program did not attend to the ways in which Mexico's agrarian structure differed from that of the United States and simply assumed that U.S. farming technologies could be transferred to Mexico.[38] They thus maintained that returned migrants could play a key role in the Green Revolution by importing U.S. labor norms to Mexico's farms. For instance, Manuel Gamio, who remained influential in government circles, held that Mexico could maximize the state's investments in agriculture if its workers had already been in contact with Green Revolution technologies by working in the United States. For him, migrants constituted the ideal candidates to lead Mexico's Green Revolution. In 1952, he claimed that the success of the Valle Bajo Río Bravo irrigation project was based on "the bodies, work habits, and knowledge of Mexicans who had migrated to the United States."[39]

Dissenting voices, however, insisted that even short-term and legal migration hurt the country. Many agribusiness leaders held that braceros' experience in the United States was not always worth the reduction in the size of the Mexican labor force that resulted from migration. According to them, the Bracero Program had made it so hard to find men to work in the fields that their produce was rotting.[40] Paradoxically, many of the landholders making these claims came from the Mexicali Valley of Baja California and the Matamoros / Reynosa region in Tamaulipas, not only Mexico's most profitable and productive cotton farming areas but also the ones that Gamio's 1952 study claimed were benefiting from migrants' modernization. The Catholic Church also opposed the outflow of Mexican workers north. The Church's position stemmed, in part, from its fears that migration would expose its constituents to Protestantism.[41] The then-existing rift between the Mexican government and the Catholic Church meant that Mexican officials could disregard the Church's stance, but they took to heart the interests of growers and entrepreneurs.

Mexico's top policymakers agreed with employers that out-migration could hurt agriculture, but they insisted that the Bracero Program could be used as a tool to restrict labor flows. The Central Plateau was the area that was most at risk of facing labor shortages in its farms. Not only was it the part of the country from which most workers left to go to the United States, but it was also an area where an inordinately high number of people labored in agriculture.[42] To ensure that growers in the Central Plateau had enough access to workers, federal policymakers sometimes allowed the state governments in the region to pull out of the binational program. From 1943 to 1944, the governors of Michoacán, Jalisco, and Guanajuato banned individuals from their states from contracting as braceros by claiming that workers were required in the Central Plateau. According to Jalisco's governor, the ban prevented "the immoderate flow of Jalisciense braceros, with the purpose of protecting the productive activities of the State."[43] Other state governments, including those of Coahuila, Baja California, and the State of Mexico, followed suit and sought to restrict bracero contracting to preclude a shortage of workers.[44] These exceptions supported the perception that the Mexican government could prevent too many people from leaving the countryside through the Bracero Program.

Restricting emigration also seemed indispensable for the development of Mexico's cities. In the 1940s, Mexico's government, like that of many other Latin American nations, implemented the model of import substitution industrialization (ISI).[45] This policy called for a closed economy through the use of high tariffs and direct import controls. It allowed national and transnational corporations to produce manufactured goods in Mexico and sell them in the domestic market without having to compete with foreign-produced goods.[46] As industrial production increased, more jobs and higher wages became available in cities, encouraging many people to move there. Between 1940 and 1970, the number of people living in urban areas increased from 4 to 22 million.[47] During those same years, Mexico's labor force transitioned from working primarily in agriculture to working primarily in nonagricultural activities. The case of Lorenzo Ramírez is illustrative.[48] Ramírez grew up working in sugarcane presses in a small town in the highlands of Puebla. When he became unemployed in the 1960s, he decided to head to Mexico City—a place he had never seen before—searching for work. He had heard much about the city's flourishing factories and hoped to get a manufacturing job. Soon after his arrival, his brother-in-law, who lived in the city and was an industrial worker himself, helped Ramírez attain such a job.[49] For government officials, men like Ramírez seemed essential to develop Mexico's industries. Policymakers could not let these individuals emigrate to the United States instead of going to the nation's burgeoning urban centers.

The claim that transnational migration was cutting into the much-needed urban labor force gained particular strength in Mexico's northern borderlands, which had a large manufacturing base. In Nuevo León, a northern state that bordered the United States, 25 percent of people worked in manufacturing in 1960, mostly in the city of Monterrey, while in Mexico as a whole only 13 percent of people did so.[50] In 1961, President Adolfo López Mateos ordered the creation of the Programa Nacional Fronterizo (PRONAF) to develop the rest of northern Mexico by subsidizing Mexican industrial producers in the area and trying to attract tourists.[51] Under the tight reins of the program's director, Antonio Bermúdez, the PRONAF called for a closed border to both people and trade. "We must strive to consolidate our economy, consuming what we produce, investing in Mexico what we earn in Mexico," Bermúdez insisted.[52] The PRONAF's literature stressed the importance of curtailing border crossings to the United States to increase the number of people working in the borderlands. A program report explained that even though Tijuana's population had increased by 155 percent between 1950 and 1960, this growth had not helped to develop the city because "farm and industrial workers residing in Tijuana cross[ed] the border every day to work outside the country."[53] According to the PRONAF, even though Tijuana was experiencing population growth, its economy remained stagnant because people's cross-border movement had limited the size of the labor force.

Despite their intentions, Mexico's top government officials, including PRONAF leaders, state governors, and the secretaries of the interior and foreign affairs, failed in their goal of retaining workers in Mexico. Even while they forbade bracero contracting from areas with labor shortages, many men who aspired to work as braceros circumvented these bans by paying *mordidas,* or bribes, to local public servants.[54] Similarly, workers regularly managed to deceive authorities in order to join the program. For instance, although officials sometimes sought to ascertain that prospective braceros were agricultural workers in Mexico by checking to see if they had calluses on their hands, men found ways around this by roughening their hands at the time of contracting. Hipólito Burrola Ruiz who migrated as a bracero, recalls that people in his town who had not worked in agriculture before would "grab the pick and spade and would start making holes [in the earth] so they could acquire callouses."[55] Even more significant, the Bracero Program itself increased unsanctioned border crossings. More men wanted to join the Bracero Program than the number of slots available; many of those who could not become official braceros simply migrated without papers. The Immigration and Naturalization Service (INS) reported that the apprehension of Mexican nationals rose from 91,456 in 1946 to 1,075,168 in 1954.[56] Still, the political culture that disapproved of long-term and undocumented migration to the United States remained uninterrupted until years later.

At the national level, policymakers reversed their views that a large population was beneficial and that emigration ought to be limited during the course of the 1970s. In Mexico's northern borderlands, however, this shift took place earlier. In 1964, the U.S. government unilaterally terminated bracero contracting as a response to the demands of U.S. civil rights activists and labor unionists who denounced the program as exploitative. As the Bracero Program dwindled to an end, the number of contract workers hired fell from 177,736 in 1964, to 20,236 in 1965, and to 8,647 in 1966.[57] For the thousands of Mexican men who had become accustomed to working in the United States over the past decades, the termination of the Bracero Program meant a sudden end to their source of employment. A quarter million braceros who had been in the United States flooded into Mexico's border cities.[58] Many of them elected to remain in the northern borderlands instead of returning to their hometowns in the interior of the country because they believed that the program would be renewed. Even if it was not, jobs in northern Mexico tended to pay higher wages than those in their hometowns. Unfortunately, there was simply not enough work for all returning braceros in the region. Unemployment rates mushroomed in borderland cities including Ciudad Juárez, Tijuana, and Mexicali, reaching almost 50 percent of the population.[59]

Unemployed workers in Mexico's northern borderlands sent hundreds of desperate letters to President Gustavo Díaz Ordaz requesting help. Thirty-three-year-old Pedro Barraza Ríos, who resided in Tijuana, petitioned:

"My current situation is critical, economic hardship is the biggest enemy in my home; I am contacting you for help, I am not requesting money, rather I am attentively begging you for a job within the federal government."[60] Barraza Ríos claimed that he would welcome any job the president could give him. Hundreds of other men went directly to government officials to ask them for permission to work legally in the United States. For instance, Daniel Muñoz H., from Mexicali, headed to the Secretariat of the Interior in Mexico City to beseech aid so that he could work legally in the United States.[61] On occasion, workers congregated outside government buildings in northern cities demanding a renewal of the Bracero Program.[62]

Those in charge of migration in Mexico did not immediately react to the demographic growth and unemployment rates in northern Mexico by encouraging Mexicans to ignore the border and head to the United States illegally. Even though officials from the Secretariat of Foreign Affairs could deduce that unemployment rates in the area would decrease if returned braceros went back to the United States, now without papers, the agency continued to disapprove of unauthorized migration. The Secretariat issued a statement appealing to agricultural laborers to "remain at home rather than attempting to enter surreptitiously to the United States."[63]

Conversely, the agencies in charge of industrial and economic development, which had previously advocated for a closed border to trade, changed their stance. The secretary of industry and commerce, Octaviano Campos Salas, called for a new development model to encourage foreign firms, mostly from the United States, to build assembly plants (*maquiladoras*) in Mexico's northern region. The area within twenty kilometers of the border would become a special free trade zone, where foreign companies could import unfinished materials into Mexico without paying tariffs, assemble them into final goods—using cheap Mexican labor—and then reexport them back to the United States.[64]

While foreign investment had a long-standing history in Mexico, this plan represented a vast departure from the government's protectionist policies based on high tariffs. Before 1965, multinational corporations manufactured goods in Mexico and then sold most of their products there in order to take advantage of Mexico's protected domestic market.[65] In contrast, under Campos Salas's program, foreign corporations in northern Mexico were able to import production inputs and avoid paying tariffs as long as they exported the final goods. Campos Salas declared that this model would attract more foreign companies to Mexico and provide employment to returned braceros. He held, "We are sure that very shortly many companies will emerge throughout the border between Mexico and the United States that will produce goods of the best quality and employ no fewer than three hundred thousand Mexicans that used to emigrate to the United States year in and year out."[66]

The name of the free trade zone's program was itself indicative of officials' changing perception on the nation's labor force; it was called Program for the Use of the Surplus Labor Force along the Border with the United States.[67] While policymakers had previously portrayed a large laboring population as the ideal means to development, they now spoke of a ruinous "surplus labor force." The program, which soon changed its name to Border Industrialization Program (BIP), was led by Antonio Bermúdez, who had previously used the PRONAF to promote a closed economy and population growth.

Even though most government officials still did not openly support citizens' unauthorized relocation to the United States, the BIP "exported" Mexican laborers to foreign-owned assembly plants inside Mexico. If workers could not cross the border to work in the United States as braceros, they could simply work for U.S. industries in Mexico. In the words of James Givens, secretary of the Central Labor Union in El Paso, the BIP was "a Bracero Program in reverse. . . . Where we used to bring low-pay Mexican labor to our country . . . we now take the work to them."[68] Yet unlike the Bracero Program, which had not been considered a solution to overpopulation but a means to control the outflow of workers and modernize the nation, Mexican government officials now spoke of the BIP as a solution to the nation's surplus population.

Officials' hopes for the BIP did not last long. The plan that maquiladoras would help solve the unemployment crisis for returning braceros was ill-conceived because it overlooked gender dynamics in the industry. While braceros were all male, maquiladora plants preferred to hire women. A representative of the maquiladora industry in Mexicali explained, "[Women] are hired because of their finesse, because a man adapts less to that type of work."[69] Maquila employers also preferred that the women be single, around nineteen years of age, and without children, as they believed that this made them more compliant.[70]

By hiring young women, maquiladoras not only failed to employ job-less braceros; they actually expanded the region's labor pool and with it the levels of unemployment. Many women migrated to northern Mexico searching for jobs in the maquila sector. The industry's age hiring poli-cies, however, meant that a lot of women who had migrated to the northern borderlands searching for work found themselves unemployed after a few years. As a female worker protested, "Our laboring life within the industry lasts approximately 10 years. What are we going to do when this ends if they don't recognize our experience in any other maquila plants or in any other sector of production or service industries?"[71] The failure of the BIP to provide stable employment as officials had imagined meant that unemployment in northern Mexico continued to soar. In the 1970s, Ciudad Juárez had an unemployment rate of 14 percent, as 60,000 individuals sought jobs.[72]

In the 1970s, Mexico's economic problems began to spread far beyond the northern borderlands, leading to a wholehearted national change in the way officials thought about Mexico's workers and whether they should remain in the country. Early in the decade, the strategy of import substitution industrialization wore down as further industrial develop-ment required the incorporation of new and expensive capital.[73] Foreign debt, inflation, and unemployment increased. During Luis Echeverría's presidency, which lasted from 1970 to 1976, consumer prices doubled, and Mexico's balance of payment ran a huge deficit. In part, this was the result of the high costs of imported capital goods, many of which came from the United States, which was itself experiencing high rates of inflation.[74] Before leaving office, Echeverría was forced to devalue the peso, ask for assistance from the International Monetary Fund, and accept its austerity package.[75] Mexico's economy briefly recovered fol-lowing the discovery of new petroleum reserves in 1977, but with the collapse of world oil prices in 1982, the Mexican economy plummeted. That year, total employment fell by 0.3 percent and then again by 2.3 percent in 1983.[76] Whereas in the thirty years before 1970 govern-ment officials and scholars had pronounced a "Mexican miracle," the years between 1970 and 1982 saw so many difficulties that Mexicans refer to them as the "tragic dozen."[77]

As the economic recession mounted during the 1970s, citizens and policymakers came to see the country's growing population size as detrimental. The rapid rise in internal migration in Mexico meant that more people now resided in cities than the number of available jobs and housing. Between 1952 and 1970, the share of Mexico City's population that lived in urban squatter settlements rose from 14 to 50 percent.[78] Even activists from the Alianza de Braceros protested the rates of overpopulation in Mexico's cities and tried to convince its members to "stop the emigration to Mexico City."[79] The national availability of food relative to the number of people living in Mexico also became a problem. In 1970, Mexican farmers ceased to be able to produce enough food staples to feed the country's growing population, and Mexico had to start importing grains.[80]

International appeals for population control intensified the notion that there were too many people in Mexico. In a summit held in 1972, President Richard Nixon told President Luis Echeverría, "The biggest problem in Latin America at this time is population growth, unemployment, and the tensions provoked by international communism."[81] International agencies, such as the United Nations, insisted that Mexico and other less-developed countries lower fertility rates in order to curb population growth.[82]

While a large population unquestionably strained existing resources and services, the heightened focus on population as the source of the country's economic troubles masked the increasing inequality in income and resource distribution. Import substitution industrialization and the Green Revolution had hurt small agricultural landholders with rain-fed lands while benefiting large, commercial agricultural proprietors with irrigated lands as well as industrial entrepreneurs. This disparity was compounded by the fact that the government was enforcing below-market prices for agricultural goods to aid urban development. In 1958, the wealthiest 5 percent of Mexicans had incomes that were twenty-two times higher than those of the poorest 10 percent; by 1980, the disparity had more than doubled with the richest Mexicans earning fifty times more than the poorest ones.[83] For Mexico's leaders, it was easier to speak of population growth than income distribution.

Supporters of population control measures focused primarily on curtailing birth rates, but they also altered the political discourse on out-migration. Policymakers realized that by leaving the country, migrants lowered the levels of unemployment and underemployment. As U.S. economist Vernon Briggs noted, "[Migration] is especially beneficial to

the political leaders of Mexico. For without the outflow of a considerable portion of its surplus population, it would have the impossible task
of trying to provide jobs and some measure of community services for
these persons."[84] Similarly, Jorge Bustamante, one of the preeminent
Mexican scholars of migration and an adviser to the government, argued in a 1978 study that if Mexicans returned to their home country
and emigration levels fell, Mexico would suffer from "a potentially ex-
plosive situation in border cities," as there would be "a rapid rise in the
number of unemployed." Together "unemployment and overpopulation
would result in the rupture of the social order."[85] His statement stands
in stark contrast to those of scholar Manuel Gamio, who, in the 1930s,
had advised the government to repatriate those who had moved to the
United States.

During the 1970s, the idea that there were too many people in Mexico
played a larger role in political discussions about the benefits of out-
migration than did remittances and modernization. The question of
remittances was partially sidelined because of the way these were understood. Most studies published in the 1970s and 1980s regarded "migradollars" as a source of money that improved the material comfort of
individual families but did not promote productive investment or economic growth in sending communities.[86] Some even claimed that the
use of remittances for consumption meant that the money migrants
sent contributed to Mexico's economic dependency and undermined
development efforts.[87] By the mid-1970s, the question of repatriating
modernized workers from the United States ceased to be a major factor
influencing the views of those in charge of regulating migration. With
no work available for returned migrants, their potential to act as modernizing forces became irrelevant. These views did not lead policymakers
to completely overlook the value of remittances on local communities
or to stop speaking about workers' modernization while abroad, but they
did lead them to focus most of their attention on the agreed upon
beneficial effects of migration on unemployment.

The primary way Mexican officials supported undocumented migration was simply by allowing it to happen. The end of the Bracero Program and the increasing restrictions on legal immigration to the United
States meant that, independent of the actions of the Mexican government, more Mexicans were heading to the United States illegally. Between 1970 and 1977, the number of Mexicans apprehended by the INS

more than tripled, rising from 277,377 in 1970 to almost 1 million in 1977.[88] Mexican officials only had to step aside and watch their citizens head north, knowing that even though many would be apprehended, many others would be able to enter and reside, at least temporarily, in the United States.[89]

Although most men did not feel pressure from state officials to head north, they also found little encouragement to remain in Mexico. Antonio Córdoba from the town of Tzintzuntzan, Michoacán, migrated multiple times between Mexico and the United States. He recalled that when citizens attempted to meet with government representatives, the officials would generally just try to "push them" out of their offices. The representatives "would just say 'go! I'll examine your case on this date or that date,'" but "they never did anything."[90] According to Córdoba, in Tzintzuntzan, people's main demand was that the government help them acquire the resources they needed to work effectively in the fields, such as buying oxen. When officials ignored their requests, many workers were unable to compete in the market. Without prospects for jobs and nowhere to turn for help, many felt forced to leave their hometowns.

Even as unauthorized migration was increasing at staggering rates, government officials did not try to address its root causes through their development strategies. This was the case even though during this same period, President Echeverría's administration initiated several welfare policy programs to support poor Mexicans as part of a new model called Shared Development.[91] The plans the administration implemented failed to address, and often entirely disregarded, questions related to migration.

Although the exodus of workers could be traced directly to unemployment and underemployment in Mexico, many of the programs that the government introduced to create more jobs during the 1970s overlooked communities of high out-migration. In 1973, government officials used financing from the World Bank to launch the Programa de Inversiones Públicas para el Desarrollo Rural (Public Investment Program for Rural Development, PIDER). The program was meant to promote agricultural development and curb rural unemployment.[92] However, the government did not use PIDER investments to attend to the issue of emigration. Even though Zacatecas was one of the states receiving the most PIDER resources, the two communities with the highest number of emigrants in the state, the Juchipila Canyon and Jerez regions, did not receive any support.[93]

Other government programs introduced during these years also over-looked migration. In 1972, Echeverría's administration implemented the National Workers' Housing Fund Institute (INFONAVIT) to help Mexican workers finance new homes. Like PIDER, the program bypassed areas of high out-migration, including the Juchipila Canyon and Jerez regions, even while providing support to other parts of Zacatecas.[94] In 1974, the Echeverría administration initiated another program that failed to address Mexicans' departures to the United States: the National Social Solidarity Program. This program sought to expand the medical coverage of the Mexican Social Security Institute (IMSS) to the most impoverished people in the countryside. The offices in charge of the program reported that between 1974 and 1976, over 1.9 million people, many of whom had never had access to proper medical care, benefited from the expanded care.[95] Despite its importance, the Solidarity Program was not designed to cut migration, as medical care was not one of the principal reasons people headed to the United States. Moreover, the government soon had to reduce the funds of the Solidarity Program, as critics insisted that it was appropriating too many funds from the system's retirement and social security program. By 1976, the only medical services that were provided freely were emergency care and, tellingly, family planning—a service that supported government officials' goal of curbing population growth.[96]

Policymakers ignored the ways in which Mexico's development model was itself pushing those they now viewed as a surplus population to leave. Since the 1940s, the government had steadily withdrawn support for government-sponsored communal lands (ejidos). For peasants, ejidos constituted a great victory from the Mexican Revolution, and many of them were economically dependent on these lands. But the government had started to redirect the funds available to ejidos to large, commercial agricultural proprietors with irrigated lands.[97] Unable to borrow from the state, many ejidatarios were forced to take loans at high rates from private sources. Paying these loans back was hard, in part because the government mandated that agricultural goods be sold at below-market prices to support the country's industrialization efforts. For ejidatarios, small landholders, and farmworkers, it was often more profitable to stop producing altogether and migrate, either internally to Mexican cities or to the United States. A worker from Nochistlán, Zacatecas, described his situation in a local newspaper: "I have wanted to sow the fields here but

I have not been motivated to do it because, with the high costs of fertil-izers and the low prices paid for corn, it's no longer profitable, that is why I no longer work the fields, it's much better to go over there [to the United States]."[98]

Mexico's high-ranking officials could afford to ignore the relation-ship between the government's development model and out-migration because migrants lacked the needed political or economic power to make their demands heard in Mexico City. Reflecting on the general aware-ness on the issue of migration, scholar Jorge Bustamante noted in 1978 that "there exists a low level of conscience on the part of the Mexican public, particularly in urban areas, over the implications of undocu-mented migration. . . . The population of [these] areas don't see any link between their life and interests and the situation of the undocumented emigrant."[99]

Migrants had long insisted that the government provide them with the means to incorporate themselves fully into the legal and economic structures of either nation-state. Manuel Cusul Ávila, a day laborer, had written to President Díaz Ordaz asking that he assist him "in any way" he could. Cusul Ávila suggested that the president loan him a plot of land to work in Mexico or give him a "permit to work on the other side [meaning in the United States]."[100] These suggestions would have given Cusul Ávila the right to reside legally and economically in either country. Rather than seeking ways to include everyone in Mexico's development plans, government officials accepted the premise that some citizens would mi-grate illegally and belong nowhere.

Not only did Mexico's leaders fail to recognize and address the exodus of Mexicans to the United States through their development plans but, during the 1970s, they also started taking more active steps to facilitate undocumented migration. Their first change was to modify the Ley General de Población. In the early 1970s, President Echeverría joined the flurry of voices insisting that there were too many people in Mexico. While up to 1969 his slogan had been "To govern is to populate," in 1972 he declared a full-fledged war against population growth with the slogan "The small family lives better."[101] A year later, his nephew, Con-gressman Rodolfo Echeverría, proposed changing the Ley General de Población. With little opposition, the new law went into effect in 1974. Because it constituted the main law intended to regulate Mexico's demography, it both reflected and directed the government's discourse on who the government considered worthy of residing in the nation. The law attempted to reduce Mexico's "surplus" population in three main ways. It encouraged women to have fewer children, it lifted restrictions on undocumented emigration, and it imposed stricter bans on the immigration of workers to Mexico.

When designing the new law, policymakers focused primarily on slashing birth rates. Rodolfo Echeverría maintained that the project would fail "if it lacked the presence of women" and insisted that to "transform living conditions and Mexican demography," politicians had to alter "some models and some patterns of behavior based on the submission and absolute dependence of women."[102] Through the new law, women's rights became intrinsically linked to population control programs. The final version of the law mandated the creation of the National Population Council (CONAPO), which would encourage women to have fewer children.[103]

Catholicism posed one of the biggest challenges to reducing fertility levels. Authorities worried that rural, working-class, and indigenous women would reject birth control methods because they were practicing Catholics.[104] Not only did the Catholic Church and the government have a tense relationship, but in 1968 Pope Paul VI had promulgated the *Humanae Vitae* on the regulation of birth, prohibiting "any action" that was "specifically intended to prevent procreation."[105] Despite officials' fears, in December 1972 Mexican bishops released a pastoral letter supporting family planning. The letter asserted that "the population explosion" had produced "a very real and excruciating emergency for most Mexican families" and said that family planning was "for spouses to decide . . . loyally following the dictates of their conscience" without having any "reason for feeling cut off from God's friendship."[106] By not opposing the new family planning programs, the Catholic Church in Mexico in effect offered its support for the government's plans.[107] With this backing, Mexican officials bypassed an important obstacle to lowering the nation's birth rate.

Within Congress there was almost no opposition to the idea that birth rates ought to be reduced, although self-declared leftist congressmen claimed that the new law should be disassociated from what they referred to as U.S. pharmaceutical imperialism. These policymakers were most likely alluding to the case of Puerto Rico, where U.S. scientists had coercively sterilized women and tested oral contraceptives on them. These practices had been legitimized through arguments that population control would diminish the island's endemic poverty.[108] When discussing the new Ley General de Población, Representative Pánfilo Orozco Álvarez of the Popular Socialist Party claimed that although he supported the law, his party rejected "the neo-Malthusian social doctrine that north American imperialism . . . tries to implant in underdeveloped countries, and that attributes all the social ills and injustices to population growth, presenting birth control, through men or women's sterilization, as the only remedy to overcome the very contradictions that are generated within the capitalist system."[109]

Despite these assertions, after the new Ley General passed, some medical authorities in public health care institutions responded to the growing pressures to lower birth rates by forcibly sterilizing working-class women immediately after they delivered via cesarean section.[110] Because most of these cases went undetected and undenounced, their exact number is unknown. However, a governmental study performed in 1987 found staggering results. Ten percent of the women in the national sample claimed to have been sterilized without having been asked; 25 percent affirmed they were not informed that sterilization was an irreversible method of birth control or that other options existed; and 70 percent declared that they had been sterilized immediately after giving birth or having an abortion, meaning that not enough time had passed for them to recover and be able to make an unpressured, well-thought-out decision.[111]

More important for present purposes, the new Ley General de Población sought to reduce the number of people in the country by facilitating emigration. These changes were intended for men from the Central Plateau region, who politicians knew were the main people leaving the country in high numbers. The modifications Congress introduced to the law represented a restrained but concrete change in the way politicians discussed the departures of citizens. The 1947 Ley General de Población that preceded the 1974 law had established that the Secretariat of the Interior was responsible for the "investigation of the causes that give or may give origin to emigration and means to *prevent and avoid it*."[112] Instead, the 1974 law provided that the Secretariat was to "investigate the causes that give or could give origin to the emigration of nationals and dictate measures to *regulate it*."[113] This slight change in language was significant. "Regulating" emigration, as the 1974 law established, was a much more lenient order than "preventing" and "avoiding" it. The only reference that the 1974 law kept concerning any type of prevention of emigration stated that the government would take the "necessary measures . . . to restrict the emigration of nationals when the national interest so demands it."[114] Through this insertion, the law revealed that according to politicians, limiting emigration was no longer considered automatically good for Mexico.

Like the previous law, the 1974 one stated that emigrants were required to "fulfill all the requisites to enter the country where they [were] heading" so as not to be "fugitive[s] from justice." But it also removed a previously existing provision that had helped achieve this goal. The 1947 law had mandated the Secretariat of the Interior to "compile the facts about the working conditions and the required documentation abroad to provide this information to Mexican emigrants in order to help them avoid difficulties."[115] By taking this provision away, the 1974 law eliminated the only stipulation that ensured that the government informed prospective migrants of the hardships of heading north. The removal of this clause was particularly significant because, since 1926, the Secretariat of the Interior had tried to discourage workers from leaving Mexico by dispersing information on the costs of migrating to the United States.[116] Through radio advertisements, newspapers, and flyers, the Secretaría had informed citizens of the discrimination Mexicans faced in the United States, listed the difficulties of legal migration, and provided explicit details of the dangers of migrating without papers.

The 1974 law also introduced harsher penalties against human smugglers, known as *coyotes*. On the surface, this change seems designed to make it more difficult for Mexicans to migrate. However, policymakers actually proposed bolstering penalties against *coyotes* as a means to protect migrants.[117] The new clause in the 1974 law increased the penalties against smugglers by up to 50 percent if they dealt with minors or if their activities placed in danger "the health, integrity, or life of the undocumented."[118] The notion that *coyotes* harmed undocumented workers was widespread. In 1979, for example, Roberto de la Madrid, the governor of Baja California Norte, interpreted the massive sweep he conducted against "smugglers and border bandits who rob undocumented workers" as a way to defend migrants.[119]

Finally, the 1974 Ley General deemed the presence of unskilled and semiskilled immigrants in Mexico superfluous. The new law reflected the changing position of the Mexican government from one that encouraged immigration to Mexico to one that set strong limits on it. The 1947 law had stated that one of the ways to achieve population growth was through immigration.[120] The 1974 law removed this clause and added in its place one declaring that the Secretariat of the Interior would "fix . . . the number of foreigners whose admission in the country could be allowed."[121] An additional clause asserted that the Secretariat of the Interior could deny entry to foreigners when "the national demographic equilibrium demands it" or when such migration was "considered harmful to national economic interests."[122] This is not to say that up until 1974 Mexican officials had encouraged all immigration. On the contrary, the 1936 Ley General de Población had put strong limits on the immigration of those considered racially, ethnically, and culturally inassimilable.[123] But up to 1974, immigration was still seen as a way to promote population growth and thus help develop the nation. In contrast, in the 1974 law government officials indicated that they no longer considered large numbers of uneducated laborers residing in Mexico as supporting the nation's "economic interests" but, rather, as potentially harmful. The new law aimed instead to "facilitate the incorporation of the foreigners in Mexico . . . whose activity is of notorious utility to the country [while imposing] restrictions on the entrance to the country of foreigners . . . when they did not follow the requirements recommended for national convenience."[124] As established by the 1974 law, "desirable immigrants" were investors, technicians, scientists, and researchers who focused on disciplines that were insufficiently studied in Mexico.

Mexico's Congress was not alone in introducing a preference system for immigrants based on skills. The United States had instituted a similar system for countries from the "Eastern Hemisphere" (constituting those from Europe, Asia, and Africa) under the 1952 McCarran-Walter Act. Notions about what "types" of immigrants ought to be restricted from particular nation-states circulated freely between the United States and Mexico and influenced the rewriting of the new immigration clauses of the 1974 law. The new Ley General de Población, for example, established that "in the same way" that state officials punished those who smuggled Mexicans into the United States, they would impose a fine and a prison sentence on anyone who introduced "without the required documentation . . . one or various foreigners into Mexican territory" as well as on those who "with the purpose of traffic" sheltered or transported individuals "through national territory with the goal of evading migratory checks."[125] Mexican politicians learned how to deal with migrants and smugglers on the country's southern border from the experience of undocumented Mexicans heading to the United States.

The new immigration clauses of the law targeted Central Americans and particularly Guatemalans. Throughout the nineteenth and twentieth centuries, Guatemalans had entered easily into Mexico to live, work, and trade.[126] The Mexico-Guatemala border had historically been poorly guarded, and Mexican employers had often relied on Guatemalan migration to increase Mexico's labor supply. Although the restrictions on Guatemalan immigration were not enforced until 1980, when refugee migration rose exponentially, the 1974 law set the legal stage for Mexico to restrict immigration in its southern border.

The 1974 Ley General de Población reveals the understandings of high-ranking officials about who was worthy of residing in Mexico and who had no place there. The new law established that the children of "overly fertile" women would hurt the nation; it made it harder for working-class immigrants—who came primarily from Guatemala—to enter Mexico; and it facilitated undocumented emigration at a time when working-class men from the Central Plateau region were the primary migrants. The new law signaled that government representatives would no longer work to ensure that all Mexican citizens could reside in Mexico.

If the Ley General de Población introduced subtle changes that facilitated emigration, the five years following its passage saw Mexico's political culture openly switch from one that opposed undocumented and long-term emigration to one that accepted it as necessary. The new law warned of the perils of having so many people reside in Mexico. It also set the directive for the agencies in charge of dealing with migration—the Secretariat of the Interior and the Secretariat of Foreign Affairs—to follow. While the two ministries could have interpreted the new law differently, as they did other issues, they both realized that they could benefit from supporting undocumented migration.[127] Reducing the number of people searching for work in Mexico could prevent a social crisis, which was important for the Secretariat of the Interior. For its part, by defending migrants in the United States, the Secretariat of Foreign Affairs could present itself as a champion of the increasingly popular doctrine of international human rights.[128] Other government agencies also profited from supporting emigration. The Secretariat of Agriculture and Livestock issued a statement holding that the government should "not put shackles" on émigrés, as it was better for citizens to depart than to engage "in unnecessary agitations" if they faced unemployment.[129] Thus in the years after 1974, government officials and agencies began introducing new measures that supported out-migration.

In private, Mexico's leaders admitted that they were revising their stance. In a meeting held with officials from the U.S. Department of State in 1975, the Mexican deputy legal adviser of the Secretariat of Foreign Affairs openly discussed the "evolution in the Mexican viewpoint" on questions of out-migration.[130] He explained that, for the Mexican government, the "emphasis [was] now on the plight or fate of Mexican migrants now residing in the U.S., rather than the question of their illegal entrance."[131] Mexico's leaders would now defend undocumented migrants rather than oppose their unauthorized departures from their home country.

During the mid-1970s, Mexico's politicians addressed their "evolving" perspectives on emigration by implementing significant changes in state practices that facilitated the out-migration of those they viewed as a surplus population. They first altered the state's repatriation and deportation practices. While Mexico's Secretariat of Foreign Affairs had previously pursued the return of migrants from the United States, even by supporting deportations, by the late 1970s the Secretariat requested that the United States not return Mexicans to Mexico. At the 1983 Mexico-U.S. Bilateral Conference, representatives from the Secretariat of Foreign Affairs attempted to convince U.S. officials not to impose greater restrictions on immigration or increase the rate of deportations.[132] By the mid-1970s, the Secretariat no longer supported repatriation campaigns, as it had done earlier. Gregorio Casillas, a Mexican migrant in Los Angeles who dedicated his life to helping Mexican communities, recalled that "consuls did absolutely nothing. . . . If somebody came [to the consulate] and wished to return to his homeland, for instance, they gave him nothing."[133] These actions, or inactions, contrast sharply with previous government efforts to return citizens to Mexico, such as those carried out during the Great Depression and Operation Wetback.

In the mid-1970s, Mexico's leaders also ended their decades-long co-operation with U.S. officials on forcibly transporting deportees to the interior of the country rather than releasing them in northern Mexico. This practice was meant to make it harder for deported migrants to cross the border back to the United States immediately after being released. Even though relocating migrants against their will violated the Mexican constitution, Mexican officials regularly engaged in this practice until 1976. That year, U.S. officials wanted to sign a $2 million contract with private companies to airlift deportees into Mexico's interior. Mexican state representatives refused to give these companies permission to land. An official from Mexico's Secretariat of Foreign Affairs replied that his government could not "provide any facilities, nor collaborate in this type of activity."[134] In the end, Mexico's Secretariat of Foreign Affairs allowed the United States to send up to 15,000 workers to the interior of Mexico, but only if the migrants offered their consent and left no dependent family members in the United States.[135] These requirements ensured the airlift's slow death, as few migrants willingly signed up to be taken away from the border. Mexican officials instituted similar requirements in August 1983, when the INS proposed to "start busing captured aliens who volunteer[ed] for the ride hundreds of miles into the interior of Mexico."[136] This program failed within a month of its start. The change in the position of Mexican authorities was apparent. They had gone from forcibly transporting migrants themselves to allowing only those who volunteered and left no dependents in the United States to be returned to the interior of the country.

Mexican politicians also reversed their position on whether the United States should impose penalties on employers who knowingly hired "illegal aliens." Known as employer sanctions, these penalties discouraged employers from hiring undocumented workers. With fewer jobs available to them, unauthorized migrants would be less likely to head to and remain in the United States. Before the mid-1970s, Mexican authorities insisted that restricting out-migration was indispensable to Mexico, in part, by supporting employer sanctions. In October 1969, for instance, top officers from the Secretariat of Foreign Affairs and the Office of Migration told U.S. officials that "perhaps if there were some penalty against the employer who hires workers illegally in the country this would discourage employers from hiring such workers, which in turn would discourage Mexicans from entering the country illegally."[137] Mexican officials continued to uphold this position in the United Nations conference on the Human Rights of Undocumented Workers that was held in Tunisia in 1975.[138] By 1977, however, Mexican authorities came out strongly against employer sanctions, explaining that these would cause a massive return of poor people to Mexico.[139] Then, in 1983, the Mexican embassy in Washington claimed that the Mexican government opposed the introduction of employer sanctions, as these would harm the Mexican economy by limiting "the possibilities that [migrants] get hired in the U.S. labor market."[140] Without access to jobs, many workers who were in the United States would return to Mexico, weakening its economy.

Another change in the stance of policymakers occurred during the mid-1970s when officials claimed that they no longer favored the renewal of the guest-worker program as a means to curtail undocumented migration. Since 1964, when the United States unilaterally ended the Bracero Program, Mexican representatives had attempted to renew it as a means to control both the number of migrants who headed north and the duration of their stay in the United States. In a 1968 meeting with U.S. officials on contract workers, for example, Mexican authorities from the Secretariat of Foreign Affairs emphasized their concern with the "large numbers of Mexican workers [experiencing] illegality" and stressed that the U.S. government could reduce those numbers by devising a means for employers to hire those workers legally.[141] In October 1974, however, President Echeverría announced that the Mexican government no longer sought to re-establish the guest-worker program.[142] His administration even refused a proposal made by Henry Kissinger in which the U.S. government agreed to a new guest-worker agreement if Mexican authorities renewed their efforts to curtail illegal crossings.[143] Mexico's top officials were no longer trying to restrict undocumented migration.

During the mid-1970s, Mexican authorities also started defending the rights of undocumented workers. Although consulates had occasionally defended unauthorized migrants in earlier periods, they did so less frequently and with less fanfare than they advocated for legal border crossers. In all of the archives of the Mexican consulate in El Paso, Texas, ranging from the 1950s onward, there is no mention of the rights of the undocumented until the early 1980s.[144] Silence is also in the Migratory Workers Archives, which document the instances in which consuls assisted Mexican individuals. All of the currently stored files from 1965 to 1970 focus on the aid provided to legally contracted braceros. This is particularly surprising because, although some braceros were hired until 1967, the program officially ended in 1964, and by then, many more migrants were heading north without papers than as braceros.[145]

Before the mid-1970s, officials explicitly told Mexicans that they would lose their right to protection if they headed to the United States illegally. This can be seen in their correspondence with Epifanio Quintín, whose son died from asphyxiation in Houston in 1968 after being abandoned by his smugglers in an airless U-Haul truck with forty-six other Mexicans. For Quintín's family, the tragedy was compounded by poverty. As Epifanio Quintín explained to the Mexican consul in San Antonio, he could not support his son's wife and children with the "$5 daily pesos" he made as an ice cream vendor.[146] Quintín requested that the Mexican government "allow one of [his] other sons to cross over to the United States to work as a bracero" to prevent his "grandsons from becoming homeless."[147] The director of the agency on migrant workers in the Secretariat of Foreign Affairs replied that he could not authorize the departure of Quintín's other sons because the Bracero Program had officially ended. He added that he "considered it convenient" to emphasize that Quintín's sons "not abandon their residence without the existence of a legally authorized work contract," as they would otherwise expose themselves to leaving the country "without the protection of the law."[148]

In contrast, after the mid-1970s, state representatives repeatedly publicized their intent to protect the rights of undocumented migrants.[149] In 1978, the Secretariat of Foreign Affairs announced the opening of the "first office for the protection of undocumented Mexicans in the United States."[150] Then, in 1982, the government announced it would publish the *Basic Guide of Services for the Public* in English and Spanish and that it would distribute it on both sides of the border.[151] The guide contained information about government services, including consular assistance, and affirmed that consuls would defend all Mexicans abroad, including those who were in migratory detention centers.[152] Through these efforts, officials strove to inform citizens that the government would protect them if they decided to migrate to the United States, even if they did so without proper documentation.

The increasing concern for the human rights of undocumented migrants stemmed, at least in part, from officials' new perception of migrants as a surplus population whose presence was unwelcome in Mexico. Policymakers sometimes admitted that their new interest in human rights derived from their inability to deal with the nation's economic problems. In a 1979 conference on migration, government representatives and scholars acknowledged that, upon "careful examination," they had concluded that "the causes of Mexican migration to the U.S." were "traceable to Mexico's overall pattern of economic development." Because "the Mexican government [did] not see itself as being in a position to 'solve' the emigration problem in the short run," authorities had decided instead to attach higher priority to the problem of protecting the rights of Mexican migrants in the United States.[153]

Even as Mexican officials repeatedly proclaimed their concern with the rights of the Mexicans residing north of the border, they disregarded those of the citizens living in Mexico. As Human Rights Watch noted, since the late 1960s and early 1970s, "an array of abuses have become an institutionalized part of Mexican society," including killings, torture, abuses against independent unions, and violations of the freedom of the press.[154] In the government's discourse, some citizens only acquired the right to have rights after they migrated.

Another change that indicated policymakers' increasing support for the departure of Mexican workers can be seen in the attempts of the Secretary of Foreign Affairs to pressure the U.S. government to accept more Mexican migrants. In the same briefing he delivered to U.S. officials in 1979, Jorge Castañeda y Álvarez de la Rosa explained that even though in the past the Mexican government had believed that proximity to the United States created a "special relationship" between the two countries, Mexicans now knew that this was "a delusion."[155] Despite the fact that Mexico was "a neighboring country, with a long tradition of substantial emigration to the United States," it had not received "a more favorable consideration" than other countries when it came to immigration. The same was true in matters of trade. Given the absence of any "special relationship" between the two countries, Castañeda warned, Mexico would consider developing connections with the rest of Latin America, as well as with "Europe, Japan, the socialist countries."[156] In this not-so-veiled threat, Castañeda impressed upon U.S. representatives Mexico's interests. His warning carried weight because the growing instability in Latin America had increased Washington's fears that Mexico would become the Soviet bloc's "last domino."[157] Castañeda delivered his briefing the same year that the Sandinista rebels in Nicaragua overthrew the U.S.-supported government of Anastacio Somoza Debayle and that a military-civilian junta overthrew the government of General Carlos Humberto Romero in El Salvador. Despite Castañeda's threats, Mexican officials were, in fact, scared of the inflow of Central Americans to their country because they feared that refugees would import radical ideas and expand Mexico's "surplus labor force." In 1981 and 1982, the Secretariat of Migration violated the principle of *non-refoulement*, the nonreturn of refugees, by deporting 5,500 Guatemalans, often handing them directly to the repressive hands of Guatemalan officials.[158]

The changes in the political culture supporting out-migration that took place in the 1970s were reinforced in the 1980s when a group of technocrats took control of the state apparatus. This new state elite sought to improve Mexico's economy by applying what they believed to be rational and efficient principles and techniques.[159] They had built their career through the bureaucracy, rather than by rising through the party ranks, and many were U.S.-educated. They had no reason to try to stop emigration, as they believed that modernization and growth could only be achieved by opening all markets, including the labor market, to competition from abroad. Rather than seeking to develop employment in areas of high out-migration through increased government spending, technocrats called for an open northern border for trade and workers.

In general, each individual modification to the state's emigration practices benefited migrants and was widely popular with the Mexican public. Forcibly transporting citizens to the interior of the country or supporting the implementation of employer sanctions harmed those who crossed the border without documents. Officials' reversal of these policies, as well as their calls for migrant rights, received a favorable response in Mexico. The only change that produced mixed reviews was the decision to stop calling for a new Bracero Program: migrants publicly defended contract-worker agreements because they allowed them to go to the United States legally, but many Mexican and American intellectuals argued that the program led to exploitation.[160] However, when taken together, the modifications of the existing emigration procedures revealed that government officials had gone from discouraging long-term, undocumented emigration to welcoming it as necessary. Because government officials could not admit that they now approved of their own citizens' departure from the national territory, they adopted a strategy of silence.

Mexico's presidents avoided dealing with the question of migration. President Echeverría and his successor, José López Portillo, seldom spoke about the issue.[161] When U.S. president Jimmy Carter proposed new immigration measures in 1977, López Portillo's cabinet claimed it could not take a stance before receiving data from the Mexican Department of Labor. In 1978 and 1979, Mexico's National Center for Information and Work Statistics released the *Survey on Emigration to the North and to the U.S.* The survey confirmed that migrants were not Mexico's poorest, they did not come from the most marginal states in Mexico, and their numbers were not as high as predicted by U.S. sources. The results allowed the governments of President López Portillo and his successor, Miguel de la Madrid, to defend their silence on the issue of migration.[162]

In 1984, advisers to President Miguel de la Madrid provided him with talking points on what he ought to include in the speeches that he presented at the annual meeting of the Binational U.S.-Mexico Commission. When it came to the topic of migratory workers, the aides advised that it "would be convenient to not deal with this issue in the speeches of the President; it could be touched upon only if some journalist asks him something about it."[163]

Just in case journalists did ask de la Madrid his opinion, his aides suggested that he respond to the question "What do you think in respect to the emigration of Mexicans?" by answering, "It is evident that no country benefits from the loss of its nationals, even though it is temporary. However, its capacity to formally impede it depends to a great extent on the applicable legal regime. The freedom of movement within Mexico and to other countries is a constitutional right, thus, the state must not impede the emigration with coercive measures."[164] The answer went on to assert that "the emigration of Mexicans to the United States of America does not respond to the national interest and, as such, the Mexican government must not encourage but discourage it."

Even though public statements maintained that emigration did not benefit the national interest, government officials' private correspondence stated otherwise. The previous year, the Mexican ambassador in the United States had suggested that Mexicans use the Binational Commission meeting to convey to the U.S. government the idea that "Mexico was going through economic hardships" and that both employer sanctions and deportations would "obviously translate into additional difficulties for Mexico."[165] In private, policymakers willingly accepted that emigration ameliorated Mexico's economic problems and that return migration would harm the country.

The U.S. press occasionally disclosed that Mexico's leaders welcomed out-migration. In August 1977, for instance, a *New York Times* article stated that "while the [Mexican] Government, at a closed-door meeting with American officials . . . expressed its dismay at Mr. Carter's Aug. 4 message to Congress on ways of curbing the influx of undocumented aliens, it has refused to make its opposition public, and officials will merely state for the record that the problem is still being studied."[166] Articles such as this one publicized both Mexican policymakers' desire for silence and their support for emigration.

Some Mexican politicians spoke out against the growing support for emigration and demanded that the government find a different route out of its economic problems. In 1984, Senator Miguel González Avelar, a member of the ruling PRI party, told Congress that it was not convenient for Mexico to use the emigration of workers as an "escape valve," as it was doing.[167] Instead of "trying to provide greater facilities to migrants," González Avelar argued, the government should pursue a more restrictive emigration policy. In a context in which most Mexican politicians followed the political opinions of the president, González Avelar's statement stands out. It reveals both his own stance on out-migration and the general belief among high-ranking politicians that undocumented migration be used as an "escape valve."

Policymakers' efforts to hide their new position on emigration disclose the implications of their views. The premise behind their changed perspective was that under the existing economic model, some citizens should not reside in Mexico, their country of birth, and should instead head to a country that considered them "illegal." During the same years when Mexican politicians started to rebuff migrants' residence in Mexico using economic explanations, there were growing denunciations against migrants' unlawful presence in the United States. Together, these positions left many Mexican citizens without a place in the world in which their belonging was fully recognized and guaranteed.[168] As migrants constantly repeated, they could reside "neither here nor there."

2

....

"A POPULATION WITHOUT A COUNTRY"

G O, MAN, GO," CHEERED June Wilson of Hemet, California, as she read the newspaper on the last day of October 1974. The U.S. attorney general, William B. Saxbe, had called for the deportation of "1 million illegal aliens—mostly Mexicans" the following year.[1] Wilson applauded this move because she believed that migrants were taking jobs that "rightfully" belonged "to longtime U.S. citizens." Her views reflected those of thousands of native-born citizens who thought that the U.S. economy could not produce enough jobs for both them and migrants. To make matters worse, these foreigners were not even in the United States legally. In Wilson's words, "Granted the illegal aliens need jobs, but must we deprive our own citizens to care for those from another country who enter illegally? Doesn't charity (or concern) really start at home?"

Even though by the mid-1970s Wilson's views that "illegal aliens" could not be absorbed into the United States were widely popular, they were strikingly different from the most commonly held perceptions about Mexican migrants less than a decade earlier. The robust economy of the mid-1960s, and the economic model that guided it, had encouraged U.S. citizens to believe that enough jobs and resources could be created for both citizens and foreigners. In contrast, starting in the 1970s and continuing into the 1980s, the United States saw the seemingly contradictory combination of mass unemployment and high inflation ("stagflation"). Union clout and membership declined, economic inequality increased, welfare policies came under attack, and the economy continued its long postwar shift from manufacturing to the service sector. In this context, U.S. citizenship no longer afforded the same benefits and securities that it had a few years earlier. Many U.S. citizens began to fear that *they* were becoming economically redundant and responded by positing "illegal aliens" as the truly superfluous.[2]

The swift change in the prevalent assessments of the nation's capacity to incorporate Latin American migrants is evident in the vastly different arguments presented to the U.S. Congress in the hearings of 1965 and those of 1976. In 1965, Congress passed the Hart-Celler Act. During the congressional debates that led to its passage, citizens and policymakers expressed the need to curtail immigration from the Americas despite acknowledging that immigrants from this region could be incorporated into the nation-state. Their main argument for introducing legal restrictions on immigration from Latin America and Canada was that the existing system discriminated against those from the Eastern Hemisphere. In 1976, Congress passed the Eilberg Bill, which further restricted immigration from countries in the Americas. But this time, congressional hearings focused primarily on the idea that Latin American immigrants displaced citizens by availing themselves of scarce resources and jobs.

Notions that migrants could not be incorporated into the country's socioeconomic fabric became intrinsically connected with the idea that they were in the United States illegally. From the 1970s onward, the belief that there were too many migrants in the country encouraged government officials to limit the number of Mexicans who could legally enter the United States, to fortify the border, and to conduct more raids in Latino communities. These measures did not reduce the number of undocumented individuals who resided in the United States, but they did reinforce the association between migrants and illegality. They did so at a time when focusing on migrants' status was particularly expedient. In the wake of the civil rights period, illegality provided a way to express racial animus while still extolling the virtues of multiculturalism.

This was not the first time that the United States had portrayed migrants as harmful to the nation or closed its door to immigrants based on the ebbs and flows of its economy. During the Great Depression, for example, Mexican migrants were accused of taking resources and jobs away from citizens and were forced to repatriate. But the image of "illegal" Mexican migrants that arose in the 1970s was specific to the decade and was infused with the notion that their presence was superfluous: migrants were dispensable because they took low-paying service-sector jobs that had been traditionally understood as unimportant "women's jobs"; they drained the nation's public coffers at a time when the country was in the middle of a "welfare mess"; and they increased the nation's population through their incessant entrance and irrepressible fertility. These images cast migrants as an excess population that could not be incorporated into the nation.

Undocumented Mexicans felt bewildered by these representations. Manuel Jiménez, who migrated during this period, recalled thinking that "Americans didn't want the jobs that Mexicans took," yet by taking those jobs, Mexicans helped boost the U.S. economy even while migrants themselves remained without access "to social security benefits."[3] Similarly, Wendy Rodríguez wondered, "Why do people care that other people are here [in the United States]? Why are they so selfish? . . . We don't take anything from anyone."[4]

Perhaps even more important, if less relevant to U.S. citizens, Mexicans knew that in Mexico they had few economic opportunities and that the Mexican government was doing little to enable them to remain back home. Even as people in the United States started to denounce the presence of migrants, Mexico's leaders began to view working-class male citizens as a surplus population and to encourage their emigration to the United States. They did so, thanks in part to ideas similar to those that encouraged U.S. officials and citizens to devalue the physical presence of Mexicans in the United States: women's fertility, welfare, unemployment, and the apparent overabundance of workers in the national territory. U.S. citizens and politicians were not as responsible for the well-being of migrants as Mexican policymakers were. But together with Mexico's leaders, they created a situation in which thousands of individuals ceased to be welcome in either of the two countries where they resided. Migrants were wanted "neither here nor there."

Up until the 1970s, U.S. immigration legislation, media representations, and people's general perceptions as evidenced by national surveys tended to overlook the issue of undocumented migration and rarely portrayed it as a problem.

In 1965, the U.S. Congress passed the Hart-Celler Act, which repealed the racist national origins quota system that had been in place since 1924. In its stead, it introduced a preference system based on immigrants' skills and family relationships with U.S. citizens and residents. It limited the visas of those originating from the Eastern Hemisphere (defined as Europe, Asia, and Africa) to 170,000 per year with a per-country quota of

20,000.[5] Spouses, minor children, and parents of American citizens were
exempted from these ceilings.

Although the Hart-Celler Act has often been considered symbolic of
the progressive politics of the 1960s for eliminating national origin quotas,
it also introduced a ceiling of 120,000 visas per year to immigrants from
the Western Hemisphere (defined as the Americas).[6] By doing so, it reversed the then-existing immigration system, which had not imposed
numerical caps on the Western Hemisphere in order to promote good
relations with U.S. continental neighbors and to satisfy the need for agricultural labor in the U.S. Southwest. Until 1965, U.S. officials had only
limited immigration from Latin America through administrative regulations rather than through legislation.

When passing the Hart-Celler Act, Congress ignored Mexico's long
migratory tradition and the fact that those in Mexico who already had
connections with the United States and sought to migrate were left with
no option other than to do so illegally. A common story among those
who migrated in the years between 1965 and 1986 is that they grew up
seeing their fathers migrate as braceros and hearing tales about how their
grandparents had fled to the United States during the Mexican Revolution. Even as children, many Mexicans had thus imagined heading north.
But when they grew up and tried to go to the United States, they realized
that there was no pathway for them to do so legally.

By disregarding the deep ties that many Mexicans had with the United
States, those in Congress were able to argue that limiting immigration
from the Western Hemisphere was the fair thing to do.[7] Senator Sam
Ervin (D-NC), one of the main advocates for introducing quotas for the
Americas, insisted that "a very good case could be made for the proposi-
tion that we are discriminating against all the world in that we favor the
people of the Western Hemisphere under the existing law and will continue to do so."[8] Even while defending ethno-racial equality in name, congressmen such as Ervin used blatantly racist arguments to pass the law.
Ervin maintained that he worried that without limits on migration from
the Western Hemisphere, there would be more immigrants from Trin-
idad and Tobago and from Jamaica. Under the previous law, both these
areas had been considered colonies rather than independent nations
and were thus not deemed countries of the Western Hemisphere. The
implication was that the independence and potential immigration of
black people to the United States called for new restrictions.

Legislators also debated whether introducing quotas on the Western Hemisphere would help prevent excessive population growth in the United States in the future. In the 1965 hearings, policymakers on both sides of the issue agreed that at that time the population of Latin Americans was small, both in Latin America itself and in the United States. Secretary of State Dean Rusk used this belief to argue that Congress should vote against the introduction of quotas on the Western Hemisphere "until there is a need to do it."[9] The matter of overpopulation in Latin America, he insisted, was not urgent, and immigration quotas could affect U.S. foreign diplomatic efforts. Representative Clark MacGregor (R-MN) resisted this notion, contending that it was wiser to change the law immediately rather than waiting until a population crisis developed later.[10] It is significant that even MacGregor and those who supported curtailing immigration from the Americas did not believe that population growth in Latin America posed an immediate threat to the United States.

U.S. politicians could overlook questions of population growth and immigration because of the near ubiquitous belief that the United States was capable of absorbing more people. At the Hart-Celler hearings, Senator Jacob Javits (R-NY) argued that the existing national origins quotas law needed to be replaced because it was racist and "was designed and administered not to admit as many immigrants as [the country could] readily absorb, but to exclude as many as possible."[11] Similarly, when Senator Philip Hart (D-MI) asked, "How many immigrants can be absorbed and assimilated in the United States in a year?" the attorney general replied, "I certainly could not answer that question, Senator, although I would think that the number would be many times the number that we actually admit."[12] Policymakers thus spoke of immigrants taking jobs and resources without hurting U.S. citizens.

The then-prevalent belief in demand-side economics and full employment undergirded the notion that more immigrants could be incorporated into the nation. In the postwar economy, most policymakers assumed that adding workers would increase the demand for products, which would in turn expand the need for workers. At the hearings, the attorney general reasoned: "The actual net increase in total immigration under this bill would be about 60,000. Of this total, all would be consumers but only about a third would be workers. The rest would be wives, children, and elderly parents. Since the ratio of consumers to workers is somewhat higher than our present ratio, the net effect would be to create rather than absorb jobs."[13] Even the AFL-CIO, generally considered a bastion of anti-immigrant sentiment, maintained that immigrants could increase jobs through their consumption. Immigrants, union leaders asserted, were "buying shoes and milk and television sets and are going to the movies and eating in restaurants and sending their laundry out."[14]

Congress might also have been willing to gloss over the potential effects of immigration on unemployment because of the existing idea that joblessness did not affect white individuals who were in their prime working age. When deliberating the immigration law, Senator Paul Douglas (D-IL) explained that "unemployment is concentrated among young people, old people, and Negroes, and if you are unfortunate enough to be a Negro in both the young group or the very old group, you have a double handicap."[15] Because at the Hart-Celler Act hearings policymakers were primarily concerned with defending workers of European heritage, they centered their efforts on repealing the preferential treatment that western and northern European immigrants received over those from eastern and southern Europe. The AFL-CIO itself focused on how the quota system reflected the inferior status of southern and eastern European descendants in the United States rather than on calling attention to the existing unemployment among African Americans, the young, and the elderly.

Most Americans agreed with Congress that the number of immigrants in the United States was not a cause for concern. A 1965 Gallup poll revealed that 39 percent of respondents believed that immigration should be kept at the present level, 8 percent that it should be increased, and 20 percent had no opinion on whether it should be increased or decreased, which probably meant that they did not consider migration rates a serious quandary.[16] The poll did not ask about undocumented migration in particular, perhaps reflecting the little attention paid to the issue during the mid-1960s.

In 1965, politicians made no serious efforts to restrict unauthorized border crossings. The previous year, Congress had terminated the Bracero Program and policymakers knew that Mexicans would try to head to the United States without papers, especially if they introduced new immigration quotas on the Western Hemisphere. However, the topic of undocumented migration was scantly mentioned at the Hart-Celler Act hearings, and behind the scenes, James Eastland (D-MS), chair of the Subcommittee on Immigration of the Senate Judiciary Committee, sought to keep the border open to undocumented workers. A plantation owner himself, Eastland lobbied to limit the power of the Immigration and Naturalization Service (INS).[17] Between 1963 and 1969, the INS budget did not even keep up with inflation, and the number of permanent staff positions declined.[18]

During these years, the media also tended to overlook undocumented migration and rarely presented it as a problem. In 1968 the TV show *Adam-12* broadcast an episode in which police officers Malloy and Reed come across a truck full of undocumented Mexican children.[19] The children had entered the country illegally to follow a U.S. citizen who had been in Mexico and was returning back to the United States. They had done so out of pure naïveté: believing that the U.S. tourist in Mexico was the U.S. president, the children had decided to trail behind him and organize a celebration in his name. When the U.S. citizen explains the situation to the officers, the cops smile kindly and agree to allow the Mexican children to remain in the United States for a day while they hold the party they had organized to honor "*el presidente.*" Far from threatening, the border crossers were presented as guileless and innocuous.

Even though in the 1960s most white U.S. citizens did not fear that Mexicans were taking their jobs and resources, many still considered them to be racially inferior. The people of Tulare, California, for instance, made it clear that town residents despised having undocumented workers and braceros going into town to dine, shop, or socialize. According to Renato Sandoval, who worked as a bracero in Tulare, the town's residents viewed him and other Mexican workers as racially "inferior single men" who were "unworthy of enjoying or interacting in family-oriented venues catering to town resident families on weekends."[20] This does not mean that all U.S. citizens denigrated Mexicans. Jesús Hernández Medrano, who migrated from Guanajuato during the mid-1960s, recalled that white Americans treated him and the other migrants he worked with "very well . . . they were very good with me."[21] He said that on the occasions when he and his friends walked from the fields to the town, his employers would meet up with them and "send them on a taxi," and if townspeople saw them walking, they would drive them to the town themselves. On the numerous occasions when U.S. citizens did belittle Mexicans, however, they generally did so—as they did with Sandoval— because they disparaged migrants' race, gender, and assumed marital status; not because they believed that these migrants were taking up scarce resources or jobs.

While in the mid-1960s most citizens viewed migrants as economically absorbable, if racially inferior, Mexican American organizations differed, holding that migrants could not be incorporated into the United States. Mexican Americans—who were U.S. citizens of Mexican descent— maintained that Mexican migrants increased the discrimination they faced, took jobs, and reduced wages.[22] Groups such as the United Farm Workers (UFW), the G.I. Forum, and the League of United Latin American Citizens (LULAC) called for the state to do more to restrict Mexican migration. A cartoon published in 1965 in the UFW's newspaper, El Malcriado, depicts a Mexican American farmworker who is being squashed by a rancher who profits from hiring braceros instead of local workers. The government representative with whom the farmworker is negotiating is blind to the farmworker's struggles and even to his existence. The cartoon stressed that Mexican migrants were taking jobs away from U.S. residents and citizens.

After the 1960s, however, Mexican American organizations would retreat from the idea that migrants were unfairly taking U.S. jobs, but most U.S. citizens would come to believe it.

The 1965 immigration law was approved during a period characterized by rapid economic growth and low unemployment and inflation levels, but by the 1970s, the United States faced a severe economic recession. Inflation, which had averaged only 1.6 percent annually between 1948 and 1965, surpassed 12 percent in 1974.[23] Between 1973 and 1975, unemployment nearly doubled, reaching 8.3 percent and then remaining high through the 1970s, only to peak again in 1982 at 9.5 percent.[24] Unemployment hit workers in industrial communities particularly hard. Between 1975 and 1979, Philadelphia lost one in six (128,000) jobs, and places like Detroit and Cleveland were almost brought to bankruptcy.[25] Unlike in the mid-1960s, when economic woes were held to affect only the very young, the old, and African Americans, by the 1970s the recession had clearly hit white male workers as well. In this changing economic environment, the idea that migrants did not pose

Cartoon by and courtesy of Andy Zermeño, published in *El Malcriado*, No. 19 (Delano, California: Farm Worker Press, February 1965): 8–9. Reproduction from the Farmworker Movement Documentation Project, University of California San Diego Library.

an imminent threat to the nation and the assumptions that buttressed this position changed dramatically. In contrast to the frequently expressed beliefs in 1965 that immigrants could be absorbed into the country, during the 1970s popular sentiments echoed those expressed by Bill Clark from the Texas House of Representatives who maintained, "The resources of a state are finite. Our boundaries are finite; there are limits to our ability to produce food and jobs; there are limits on overcrowding in relation to our physical and mental health."[26]

Whereas in 1965 Congress spoke of Latin America as having a small population size, by the 1970s the media and government institutions spoke of Mexico's population as overflowing and seeping into the United States. An article in the *Christian Science Monitor* with the title "U.S.-Mexico Alien Problem Increases" began, "U.S. annual population growth— 0.9 percent. . . . Mexican annual population growth—3.2 percent."[27] The *Baltimore Sun* published an article entitled "Too Many Mexicans."[28] The title's lack of geographic definition matched the argument that "too many Mexicans" in Mexico led to "too many Mexicans" crossing the border to the United States. For its part, in 1972, the Commission on Population Growth and the American Future, an agency established by Congress, stressed that "illegal immigrants" were multiplying the number of people residing in the United States.[29]

During the 1970s, Mexican migrants became much more visible on city streets, which added to the sense that there were too many of them. Between the start of the Second World War and 1980, Los Angeles went from having one of the whitest and most U.S.-born populations of any major U.S. metropolitan area to having the second highest percentage of foreign-born residents.[30] In part, this change resulted from the increasing number of undocumented migrants entering the United States. Between 1965 and 1979, INS apprehensions of Mexican nationals rose from 55,340 to 99,883.[31] Additionally, more Mexicans started heading to cities rather than to rural communities. The Bracero Program had recruited workers primarily in agriculture. After 1964, when the program ended, migrants had few incentives to move to rural communities rather than to cities. Urban jobs provided them with work that tended to be less strenuous, was more stable, and paid higher wages. Through the Bracero Program, migrants had become familiar with U.S. social and labor practices, learned English, and developed networks north of the border that allowed them to take these urban jobs more easily. Los Angeles became migrants' primary destination.[32]

The experiences of Manuel Jiménez illustrate migrants' move to cities. Jiménez first crossed the border as a bracero and worked in the town of Esparto, California, picking tomatoes. As a contract worker, he recalled, he and his fellow braceros "had to pay for lodging . . . to feed ourselves, but the pay wasn't enough for that. [Additionally] one had families [in Mexico] and had to send money there."[33] Despite the low wages he received, Jiménez continued enrolling in the Bracero Program and then worked in the fields as an undocumented migrant until he learned through friends that life and work in the city were easier. A few years after the Bracero Program ended, he decided to go to South San Francisco, where he already had friends. There, he worked as a dishwasher and then as a cook in a Hyatt House hotel. His experience was similar to that of thousands of other migrants. While in 1965, 45 percent of Mexican workers in the United States labored in agriculture, by 1985 the rate had fallen to 25 percent.[34]

Migrants' move away from agriculture alarmed urban workers and state officials who worried that Mexicans were taking the jobs of white, blue-collar citizens. In 1975, the INS commissioner asserted, "Illegally employed aliens . . . take jobs normally filled by American workers; not only agricultural jobs in the Southwest, but high-paying jobs in metropolitan areas where the illegal alien is harder to apprehend."[35]

Politicians and lobbyists stressed that undocumented migrants were responsible for the high rate of unemployment among citizens. In 1979, Secretary of Labor F. Ray Marshall insisted, "One of the lowest estimates of the number of illegal workers in the United States is 4 million. If only half, or 2 million, of them are in jobs that would otherwise be held by U.S. workers, eliminating this displacement would bring unemployment to 3.7%, which is below the 4% full-employment target."[36] For his part, the director of legislation of the AFL-CIO sent a letter to the federation's members maintaining that "the House Judiciary Committee concluded recently that illegal aliens 'take jobs which could be filled by American workers.'"[37]

Changing economic theories bolstered the perception that the economy could not incorporate more workers. The simultaneous rise in unemployment and inflation in 1970 contradicted the prevailing beliefs about how the economy was supposed to work. Up until that point, the dominant economic model was based on the Phillips curve, which established an inverse relationship between the rates of unemployment and inflation. According to A. W. Phillips, reducing the rates of unemployment would increase wages and prices; conversely, increasing unemployment rates would slow down inflation. The concurrent rise in unemployment and inflation in the 1970s produced consternation. Some economists tried to explain what was happening by focusing on how increasing costs of production, caused primarily by the oil embargo by Arab countries, had driven up prices. Other economists took the opportunity to promote their critiques of the Phillips curve. Milton Friedman had long claimed that the Phillips curve was only a short-run phenomenon; in the long run, workers would attempt to anticipate inflation and negotiate for higher pay raises. These wage increases would eventually fuel unemployment back to its previous level, but now with higher inflation.

Friedman's increasingly popularized logic challenged the definition of "full employment" and the idea that all workers could be economically absorbed. A growing number of economists came to agree that government spending did not reduce unemployment as much as it raised prices, which would "sooner or later [make] a more extensive unemployment inevitable than that which that policy was intended to prevent."[38] In the face of such changing orthodoxy, the federal government started to back away from the idea that unemployment could be eradicated. In 1974, the Nixon administration determined that full employment consisted of an unemployment rate that ranged between 4.5 and 4.8 percent.[39] By 1978, economists were arguing that an unemployment rate that varied between 5.5 and 6.2 percent was most efficient for the economy.[40] Not everyone embraced this trend. Senator Hubert Humphrey (D-MN) and Congressman Augustus Hawkins (D-CA) designed a plan that defined full employment as attaining a 3 percent unemployment rate and that made the availability of jobs for all Americans a federal mandate.[41] Although the bill passed in 1978, it was by then so weakened that it was almost meaningless.[42] Policymakers had largely given up on the idea that the government had to intervene to lower unemployment levels. Some people were, in the words of Friedman, "naturally" unemployed.

In this new economic climate, many Americans began worrying that undocumented migrants were taking the limited jobs available away from citizens. A 1976 Gallup poll revealed that when asked, "What problems, if any, result from the presence of illegal aliens in this country?" 51 percent of respondents mentioned that migrants took jobs away from residents, and another 20 percent said that they were used for cheap labor.[43] The numbers were even higher among residents of states bordering Mexico, where 61 percent claimed that undocumented workers took jobs and 34 percent held that they were used as cheap labor.[44] Gallup polls also revealed that a growing number of people in the United States had come to believe that there were too many immigrants coming to the country. While in the 1965 poll only 33 percent of respondents had favored decreasing the current levels of immigration, a 1977 Gallup survey revealed that 42 percent of respondents had come to support such measure.[45]

In contrast, Mexican American organizations that had previously rallied against undocumented workers started to view these migrants as part of their community.[46] Such was the growing support of Mexican American activists toward migrants in the mid-1970s that some of them even spoke out against the UFW's anti-immigrant position. These critiques were remarkable given how popular the union was among Mexican Americans.[47] Knowing that he could not lose the support of the Mexican American constituency, the union's president, César Chávez, slightly altered the UFW's position. While in 1965 the union was still publishing anti-migrant cartoons in its newspaper, in 1974 Chávez wrote a letter to the editor of the *San Francisco Examiner* in which he promised to advocate for "amnesty for illegal aliens" even while reiterating that undocumented workers acted as strikebreakers.[48]

For their part, many black organizations and individuals expressed increasing concerns that undocumented workers were replacing them. The NAACP continuously demanded that policymakers curtail undocumented migration. *Ebony,* a magazine that reached a primarily black audience, published articles claiming that "illegal aliens" were a "big threat to black workers" because they took jobs.[49] Given the popularity of such views, some black organizers felt impelled to speak out against them. Bayard Rustin wrote in the *Oakland Post* that he found it "very disappointing" to discover that even "some of the most sensitive and decent leaders of the black community" were advocating for the increasing deportations of undocumented workers.[50] Instead of turning against unauthorized migrants as they were doing, Rustin insisted, black people ought to make them their allies.

Even white, blue-collar workers who regularly blamed people of color for the nation's economic problems sometimes used civil rights arguments to contend that undocumented migration had to be restricted. The palpable resentment of many white people toward minorities was captured in *All in the Family,* the most popular sitcom of the decade. The show's main character, Archie, embodied the bigoted blue-collar worker who begrudged the advancement of women and black people but was loyal to his union. The AFL-CIO, which was composed primarily of white people, depended on the membership of workers who held such views. Its newspaper nonetheless published an article that held: "Millions of unemployed American workers of all races—but particularly blacks, Asians, and Hispanics—feel today that they are the victims of reverse discrimination because employers prefer to hire the undocumented worker who will work for less, who is ignorant of the labor laws and who can be easily intimidated with threats of deportation."[51]

While sometimes attending to questions of race, the AFL-CIO's lead-ership generally promoted the view that unauthorized migration was hurting all workers. The federation insisted that the main problem re-garding undocumented migration was that those who were coming to the country without papers were taking the jobs of citizens who were already experiencing high levels of unemployment. Focusing on the de-clining number of industrial jobs, the federation's literature painted a grim scenario: not only were U.S. jobs being relocated to Mexico, but Mexican workers were coming to the United States and taking the avail-able jobs that remained.[52]

Migrants' movement into the United States and the movement of capital out of it were, in fact, interconnected phenomena. When U.S. assembly plants relocated to northern Mexico with the Border Industri-alization Program (BIP), they attracted a large number of geographically mobile people from central and southern Mexico to the area. But the unstable nature of the work these plants provided often led people to continue moving north, now to the United States. As José Juárez, who grew up in Mexico's border state of Chihuahua, noted, the BIP program attracted many individuals to northern Mexico, and although "many people remained" in the area, many others decided to cross the border illegally to the United States "because [BIP] jobs were very poorly paid."[53] Moreover, the same processes that stimulated emigration from Mexico also encouraged immigration to particular areas of the United States.[54] As U.S. corporations transferred their manufacturing operations abroad, they started to expand corporate centralized management within U.S. cities to oversee these operations. Such activities increased the demand for highly paid white-collar workers as well as for low-paid service-sector workers. Low-paid laborers, who were often migrants, worked as jani-tors, building attendants, domestic workers, dishwashers, and other such positions serving highly paid professionals.[55]

The case of Fairchild, a pioneering electronics company, shines light on the various connections between the moves of U.S. capital to Mexico and those of Mexican workers to the United States. In 1966, Fairchild opened a plant in Tijuana and soon thereafter relocated its headquar-ters to what would soon become known as Silicon Valley.[56] These relo-cations had significant consequences. By producing components abroad, Fairchild avoided hiring workers in the United States who would have had to receive higher wages. By relocating to Tijuana, Fairchild was one of the corporations that encouraged Mexican workers to migrate to northern Mexico, putting them in greater proximity to the United States. The later expansion of companies such as Fairchild in the United States increased the demand for both highly paid professionals and poorly paid service-sector workers in U.S. cities, which in turn encouraged Mexican migrants to head farther north. The Latino population in San Jose, not far from Fairchild's new headquarters in Mountain View, increased from 14 to 22 percent of the total population between 1960 and 1980. A large number of these migrants worked in low-paying service jobs within the booming electronics industry in the area.[57]

The service jobs migrants took were often seen as feminized and inconsequential, undercutting Mexicans' contributions to the U.S. economy.[58] When individuals hired a nanny or a babysitter, stayed in a hotel and had their rooms cleaned by the service staff, used bathrooms cleaned by janitors, or ate out at restaurants, the people who served them were often undocumented Mexicans, especially in California. These everyday encounters shaped the way citizens perceived and interacted with migrants. Cleaning, serving, and cooking were traditionally considered to be in the domestic sphere and within the purview of women. These jobs had been previously unpaid and continued to be paid poorly. Even within the feminized service world, migrants were seen as being secondary to white women. When patrons ate at restaurants, for example, they were served by white women working at undervalued "women's jobs," but these very women were in charge of the even-more-demeaned Mexican busboys.

The perception that Mexican laborers performed feminized work that was subsidiary to that of white women was reinforced by the fact that as Anglo women started taking more jobs outside their homes, they employed the services of lower-paid workers to carry out the labor that they had traditionally performed. A report submitted at the congressional hearings on the service industries explained, "As women moved into the labor force in large numbers, many tasks once done at home have been transferred into the market economy: demand has multiplied for day care centers, convenience food and fast-food restaurants, laundromats and dry cleaning services."[59] To make money by working outside the home, white women needed to pay less for these services than the money they earned in their own generally poorly paid jobs. As a result, women's domestic work was often taken by undocumented migrants.

In areas such as El Paso, it was automatically assumed that if white women worked outside the home, the household's domestic chores would be carried out by lower-paid Mexican workers. In 1984, Robert Lyons, a U.S. citizen who lived in El Paso, was interviewed by the University of Texas at El Paso Institute of Oral History. He told his interviewer that if he had a child, he would gladly stay at home so that his wife could continue working. He explained, "We don't really like the idea of leaving the baby at home with a maid . . . for the simple reason if [the maid is] Mexican, [the child may] assume that Mexican is its mother [sic]."[60] Beyond the pejorative views that Lyons demonstrates toward Mexicans, his answer also reveals that he assumed that if he was going to hire a domestic worker, "she" would most probably be a Mexican woman.

Accusations that undocumented migrants were stealing citizens' jobs ignored the fact that many native-born workers rejected the "feminized," low-paying service jobs that Mexicans were taking. The experience of David Phelps provides a perfect example. In 1974, thirty-two-year-old Phelps joined the ranks of the unemployed alongside 46,563 other workers in metropolitan Buffalo, New York. The unemployment rate for the area reached 8.5 percent that year.[61] After searching for other positions, Phelps realized that the demand for workers in the area was restricted to low-paying service jobs, such as busboys. These positions paid so little that he refused to take them. Instead, like other unemployed workers around him, Phelps cut back on essential needs, increased his debt, and signed up for unemployment insurance. Even while Phelps and other citizens refused to take the jobs Mexicans were generally hired to do, many of them still resented migrants and blamed them for their troubles. To them it seemed that the undocumented workers who labored in the service sector were replacing the white, male, blue-collar workers of the rust belt.[62]

Undocumented migrants were willing to take the jobs that U.S. citizens refused. Migrants had already left their families and hometowns for work, they had risked their lives at the border, they were ineligible for public welfare, and they had labored for even lower wages in Mexico. Manuel Jiménez recalled that when he was looking for a job in South San Francisco, an employer told him, "Look, I can give you work. The only thing is that now there are no positions that are sort of good." The boss offered Jiménez a dishwasher position.[63] "What do you want?" the employer asked him. "To be useless or to be washing dishes?" For

Jiménez the answer was obvious. He took the job and worked there for five or six years. He explained, "We [migrants] came to work, seeking to sustain our family." In contrast, he believed, U.S. citizens were not "going to work washing dishes . . . or in the fields." Jiménez recalled that on one occasion an American came to his job site and complained to the employer for hiring undocumented migrants when citizens like him could not find work. To pacify him, the employer hired him, but the man rapidly realized that the job was too hard and quit soon after starting.

The notion that Mexicans took citizens' jobs did not save migrants from also being portrayed as lazy welfare abusers who drained the state's limited resources. During these years, the welfare system became increasingly maligned as the percentage of Americans on welfare rose from approximately 2 percent in the mid-1960s to about 6 percent in the mid-1970s and as aggregate spending on welfare more than doubled.[64] People started blaming the "welfare mess" on the black "profligate, promiscuous, Cadillac-driving welfare queen."[65] But alongside the black "welfare queen," throughout the U.S. Southwest, Mexican undocumented migrants were cast as culprits draining the state's public resources. A 1976 Gallup national poll revealed that 57 percent of Americans believed that "illegal immigrants" receiving "unemployment payments or welfare" were a "serious problem" as they were "a drain on the taxpayer."[66] Newspaper headlines announced: "Illegal Aliens Here on Welfare Said to Cost Millions" and "Aliens' Abuse of Welfare Cited: Cost Is $72 Million Yearly in Five States."[67]

Despite these widespread beliefs, most researchers showed that undocumented migrants did not, in fact, drain welfare. At least six different field studies found that undocumented Mexicans barely utilized tax-supported programs such as unemployment compensation, welfare assistance, food stamps, and public education—usually in the 1 to 3 percent range.[68] According to federal regulations, only citizens and legal residents had access to public assistance programs, Aid to Families with Dependent Children, Supplemental Security Income, Medicaid, and food stamps. Undocumented workers feared identifying themselves by applying for welfare or unemployment compensation. Although unauthorized migrants paid for social services such as social security and taxes, few filed for benefits or tax refunds even when money was due to them because of fear of apprehension. The difficulty of crossing the border illegally also meant that most migrants were young, productive, and healthy workers who did not require much public support. A 1977 report of San Diego County asserted that undocumented migrants contributed approximately $48.8 million in taxes on wages earned locally each year, while the total cost of the social services they consumed only reached $2 million.[69]

Local governments from counties in California with high numbers of undocumented migrants acknowledged that migrants benefited national public coffers but insisted that they drained local coffers.[70] Some county supervisors explained that even though undocumented migrants were ineligible for most federal and state-funded social service programs, their counties were nonetheless required to provide them with emergency health care. Many counties offered them nonemergency health care services as well.[71] School districts also had to provide undocumented migrants with free K–12 education. In July 1977, Los Angeles County supervisors voted to sue the federal government to recover the cost of providing services to unauthorized migrants. The evidence they used, however, showed the biases of their assumptions. The board of supervisors urged legal action by citing a county Department of Health Services survey that estimated the annual cost of providing care to undocumented migrants at $50.7 million. Yet as the supervisors later recognized, the department's estimate included county overhead costs that would have existed even without migrants.[72] In fact, while most county studies determined that those without papers did cost counties money, they also asserted that "the impact" of migrants' use of "social service areas such as health care, welfare, and education" was probably "less than originally perceived by the general public."[73]

Mexican migrants tried hard to disassociate themselves from notions that they abused the state's welfare system and vilified those who did. Agapito Rodríguez, who migrated from Zacatecas, recalled that Mexicans believed that it was Mexican Americans who were the true welfare abusers. In his view, Mexican Americans were "lazy people. . . . We [migrants] would go to work . . . but those people generally did not work but instead survived from welfare."[74] Even migrants who managed to legalize their status insisted that they did not like relying on the state. Anaberta Reinaga, who migrated without authorization from Mexicali, recalled that after she became a legal resident some employers offered her a low-paying, part-time job, which she refused to take. Instead, she applied for unemployment insurance.[75] At the office, she was told that employers in the area were used to paying low wages because most workers couldn't turn jobs down and rely on welfare because they "did not have papers." Reinaga added quickly that even though she did seek aid from the state, she soon told herself, "I am not one of those who can be on welfare, I am not one to be waiting on a check," and immediately sought other work.

Rather than relying on the state for support, Mexican migrants, like other immigrant groups, tended to form mutual aid societies that provided members with economic relief during difficult times. Migrants living in Los Angeles established the Comité de Beneficencia Mexicana, often referred to in English as the Mexican Welfare Committee. This organization was originally formed in 1931 by a group of merchants and professionals under the direction of the consul to aid "poor or needy Mexicans."[76] By the 1970s, the most powerful members of the organization continued to come from affluent Mexican families, but migrants from all socioeconomic backgrounds belonged to it and contributed to its welfare projects. On December 5, 1967, Juan Franco, who barely knew how to write, donated $20 dollars to the Comité to help "the most needy people."[77] Franco realized that this quantity was not much but noted that it was all he could afford with his limited income. He hoped that "it could perhaps help somewhat."

Hundreds of migrants relied on the Comité during times of crisis, often seeking help to return to Mexico. For instance, in October 1970, María de los Ríos left her hometown for California, where her husband had just passed away. After the burial, she had no way of returning home.[78] After all, this had not been a well-planned trip for which she had saved resources. Significantly, her request for aid was not to *stay* in the United States, as most portrayals of Mexican migrants would have had it, but rather to *leave*. She was not alone. In 1970, approximately 25 percent of all aid requests to the Comité were from individuals who wanted to return to Mexico.[79] Most U.S. citizens and public officials overlooked these experiences and focused instead on stereotypes that undocumented migrants sought to come to the United States to use its welfare resources.

Even government officials who recognized that undocumented migrants avoided applying illegally for welfare sometimes insisted that migrants managed to access state resources through their citizen children. Keith Comrie, the director of the Department of Public Social Services in Los Angeles County, asserted that undocumented migration was "a time bomb waiting to go off."[80] Although he recognized that the cost of welfare to undocumented migrants was at the time "insignificant," he saw "a much greater threat in the number of children born to illegals in this country who, as citizens, are eligible to collect welfare." A study published by San Diego State University's Institute for Regional Studies of the Californias concluded that "children who were born in the United States, and hence eligible for AFDC and food stamps, may be embedded in families who are largely undocumented."[81] These accusations implied that simply by belonging to "undocumented families," native-born children did not deserve citizenship rights. They also contrasted starkly with the assertions of migrant rights organizations. The Immigration Coalition, for instance, reported that "some members of a family are eligible for food stamps, public assistance and medical care, while others are ineligible, resulting in most parents' being afraid to apply for benefits on behalf of their citizen children because they might be deemed 'questionable' and subjected to interrogations."[82]

Representations of migrants as welfare abusers were closely linked to ones that portrayed them as having too many children, which added to the sense that migrants were a surplus population. An article published in the *Los Angeles Times*, for instance, told the story of Hilda Tovar, a thirty-two-year-old "Mexican woman who . . . received welfare and had eight children while illegally in the United States."[83] The article described how Tovar had acknowledged depending on federally subsidized housing, welfare, and food stamps and presented her as promiscuous for her "overt" fertility and for not having married the father of her first five children.

The notion that migrant women were draining the country's welfare coffers through their excessive fertility sometimes had grim repercussions. In California, between 1971 and 1974 ten working-class migrant women of Mexican origin were coerced into sterilization immediately after delivering via cesarean section. Karen Benker, a medical student who worked at the Los Angeles County Medical Center where the women were sterilized, testified that doctors viewed their Mexican patients as women who had "come from Mexico pregnant on the bus just so that they could have their baby born a U.S. Citizen. . . . It was frequently expressed that the poor bred like rabbits and ate up money on welfare."[84]

Beyond welfare, many started to believe that women had children to acquire citizenship for themselves, thus laying the foundation of the "anchor baby" canard. Prominent news publications, including the *New York Times* and the *Los Angeles Times,* continually published stories of Mexican women who crossed the border to have children in the United States to gain legal residence.[85] One *New York Times* article told the story of "Ilda Leal, a small, shy, 27-year-old woman." An undocumented migrant, Leal had convinced her husband to have a baby to "fix the papers, to get a visa and perhaps eventually apply for United States citizenship themselves."[86] The article insisted that she was not unique.

In fact, Mexican women regularly left their children south of the border. Although the number of women who did this is unknown, Mexicans tended to believe that people in the United States had few family values, making it an unfit place to raise children. In 1973, María Suárez Oliva became pregnant while working in the United States. From the beginning, she knew that she did not want to raise a child there because she didn't like the "way of living" in the United States.[87] In particular, she worried that U.S. citizens thought it was "normal to live together without getting married" and that children "grew up addicted to drugs [and alcohol]." Although she wanted to raise her child in Mexico, Suárez Oliva figured that she could not travel alone while pregnant and was forced to stay in the United States. During the pregnancy, she saw a private doctor whom she and her husband paid for out of pocket, even though they both had full-time jobs that should have provided them with health insurance benefits. They did so because they feared that a public hospital might refer them to immigration services.

Oblivious to the realities of migrants' experience, many U.S. citizens came to see Mexicans as taking what was supposed to be theirs. Manufacturing jobs were being exported outside the country. A service sector staffed largely by undocumented workers was replacing the old industrial world manned primarily by white citizens. They also held that migrants were draining the state's welfare coffers because of their laziness and then using their irrepressible fertility to gain access to citizenship. Such people had no place in the nation.

At a time when racial prejudice was being denounced and a multicultural and post-racist society celebrated, many citizens and state officials denounced migrants' illegal status rather than focusing on their race and ethnicity. Illegality thus became a proxy for the racial hostility many Americans felt. Portrayals of Mexican migrants as "illegals" had existed since the 1920s, but the label regained strength in the 1970s and justified the most vituperative rhetoric. In the period between the 1950s and the 1970s, the most commonly used term to refer to undocumented workers switched from "wetbacks" to "illegals" and "illegal immigrants." This linguistic switch was symbolic of the changing politics of the period: while the word "wetback" essentialized the bodies (specifically the backs) of the Mexican workers who waded through the Rio Grande to enter the United States, the term "illegal" seemed to refer only to their legal status. However, the new usage actually inscribed illegality onto migrants' personhood. Even though unauthorized border crossings were generally not even considered misdemeanors, the term "illegal alien" ascribed criminality to workers' very existence.

Representations of migrants as illegal aliens were intertwined with those that cast them as a surplus population and bolstered the push for a legislative change to the 1965 law. While the debates over the Hart-Celler Act had for the most part overlooked the question of undocumented entry, the debates over the new law, which came to be known as the Western Hemisphere Act of 1976 (or the Eilberg Bill) were haunted by the spectre of the "illegal alien."

As in 1965, politicians in 1976 stressed hemispheric and country equity, asserting that changing the immigration law was important so as not to give preference to particular countries or hemispheres. Out of this reasoning arose the proposal that Congress ought to limit migration from the Western Hemisphere, just as it did from the Eastern Hemisphere. The 1965 act had placed a limitation of 120,000 visas on the Western Hemisphere, but it had not introduced per-country limitations or the preference system as existed for the Eastern Hemisphere. In the 1976 hearings, policymakers argued that this was unfair and suggested introducing both of these measures on the Western Hemisphere. Congressman B. F. Sisk (D-CA) claimed it was important to remove "the inequity which currently exists in the Immigration and Nationality Act and accord the same treatment to Western Hemisphere natives, including those from Canada and Mexico, as we now accord to Eastern Hemisphere natives."[88]

Even when putting these proposals forward in the name of equity, politicians were aware that the new law would affect countries differently. The Select Commission on Western Hemisphere Immigration had warned that limiting countries of the Americas to 20,000 immigrants would be failing to "recognize the traditional hemispheric pattern of immigration."[89] A limitation of 20,000 would hit Mexico more than any other country, as it was the only Western Hemisphere nation that used substantially more than 20,000 visas annually. Although estimates varied, at least 45,000 individuals entered from Mexico each year who did not have "immediate relatives" in the United States.[90] In contrast, by 1976, Canadian migration had fallen to approximately 8,000 immigrants per year.[91]

While the appeals to fairness and "equality" were seemingly similar in 1965 and 1976, the concerns Congress expressed in the two hearings were vastly different. During the 1965 Hart-Celler Act hearings, the question of immigration from the Americas had been secondary, only an addendum to the primary issue of national origins quotas. A decade later, it was the sole focus in the discussions over the passage of the Western Hemisphere Act. Immigration from the Americas had become an explicit problem in U.S. politics.

Participants in the 1976 debate routinely appealed to stereotypes of migrants as a surplus population that could not be absorbed. Senator Strom Thurmond (R-SC) asserted, "America is, in reality, still a land of opportunity and the most generous Nation in the world. However, our wealth is not boundless, and the current unacceptably high level of domestic unemployment clearly shows that we do not have a general excess of available jobs."[92] He also claimed that, "in many cases, these illegal entrants and their families soon become a welfare burden on our society, supported in one way or another by American taxpayers."[93] The AFL-CIO, speaking in support of the proposed restriction, declared: "Illegal immigrants have for years been taking jobs from American citizens and legal immigrants in increasing numbers, [they] often work for substandard wages and accept substandard working and living conditions, . . . and are all too frequently a drain on the welfare resources of the communities where they live."[94] One particularly vociferous group, Zero Population Growth (ZPG), asserted that "the population pressures in the less-developed world are so enormous that even by opening our doors we are not going to alleviate the situation in those countries."[95] As such, the group insisted, propositions to allow Mexico to have a higher quota than 20,000 were useless.

Determined to address both Latin American migrants' illegality and their seemingly surplus numbers, policymakers suggested repealing the existing exemption from labor certification enjoyed by parents of minor U.S. citizens and permanent resident aliens. The labor certification requirement sought to ensure that immigrant applicants did not displace citizens in employment by checking that there were no citizens or legal residents who were willing to accept the jobs that these migrants would take. Up to 1976, however, the parents of U.S. citizen children could waive this requirement. While debating the passage of the Western Hemisphere Act, many in Congress sought to terminate this exemption, arguing that it encouraged Latin American migrants to have children in the country to avoid having to acquire labor certification. Representative Paul Sarbanes (D-MD) maintained that laws that allowed couples to have a child in order "to stay in the United States" created "an opportunity to circumvent what otherwise may well be a fairly well balanced and constructed immigration law."[96]

Policymakers understood that the annulment of parents' exemption from labor certification would have acute repercussions, given that 25 to 35 percent of all Western Hemisphere immigration to the United States resulted from it.[97] Because Mexican workers found it virtually impossible to get certified, eliminating this exception meant that the parents of U.S. citizens who did not have papers would no longer have a legal path to remain in the United States. Congress hoped that this would prompt the parents to return home. It also meant that their citizen children would be forced either to leave their country of birth with their parents or to live apart from their families. Legislators disregarded these concerns and focused instead on the image of conniving, undocumented migrant women who birthed children in the United States to acquire citizenship.

The final version of the Eilberg Bill established a quota of 20,000 entrants per nation per year without giving a higher quota to Mexico. It introduced a preference system based on skills and family relationships and repealed the exemption from labor certification for parents of U.S. citizens who were under twenty-one years of age.[98] Through these combined measures, Congress ensured that most Mexican migrants would only be able to reside in the United States without proper authorization. Mexicans would continue to migrate but would have no path to become permanent residents or citizens.[99]

Even as it became more difficult for migrants to gain legal status, life without papers became harder. The perception that migrants were a surplus population led U.S. authorities to increase the crackdowns against them. As early as 1973, immigration agents decided to "step up" their drives against migrants in response to the growing media attention on the issue. Donald T. Williams, acting director of the INS, explained the necessity of such action by appealing to the existing stereotypes. Undocumented migrants, he explained, "attend schools at taxpayers' expense, they take jobs that normally would go to Americans, and many of them go on welfare and use other public social services."[100] That same year, President Nixon selected former Marine Corps General Leonard Chapman as commissioner of the INS in order to bring a militaristic approach to the organization.[101] Chapman stoked the growing sense of urgency, insisting that the number of unauthorized workers was so high that it constituted a "silent invasion."[102] By increasing deportation rates, Chapman held, he could help open up a million jobs to U.S. citizens "virtually overnight."[103] In 1975, the Border Patrol dramatically increased the number of "linewatch-hours" at the border, and between 1978 and 1988, total INS funding jumped 185 percent.[104]

Despite the expansion in INS enforcement, migrants did not actually experience a higher risk of apprehension or deportation. Between 1965 and 1980, the probability of apprehension for individual migrants remained between 35 and 45 percent.[105] Proportionally, the number of migrants entering the United States without papers grew faster than the number of Border Patrol agents. Migrants also adapted to the new border regime. More and more Mexicans hired smugglers, or *coyotes,* to help them cross the border.[106] Whereas in 1965 only 40 percent of all migrants used *coyotes,* a decade later over 70 percent used them.[107] Still, while INS efforts did not reduce the number of unauthorized workers in the United States, they did make a clear public statement that Mexicans were not wanted in the country.

Beyond seeking to close the border, the INS conducted raids in the country. Migrants often claimed that they were being racially targeted. For instance, Tiliberto Rodríguez recalled that the INS used to conduct a lot of raids in South San Francisco. "It was racism in those years," he held. "There were migration agents early in the morning, and they would stop people when they saw [any] Mexican features."[108]

INS agents conducted targeted raids on the sites that conformed to popular stereotypes of migrants. Portrayals of Mexicans as welfare abusers prompted INS directives and the U.S. attorney general to order a raid on El Concilio Manzo, a voluntary social service agency in Tucson, Arizona, that provided support to undocumented migrants.[109] The center offered many services, including health referrals, immigration counseling, job placement assistance, and legal aid.[110] During the raid, which took place in April 1976, INS officials confiscated the records of over eight hundred clients. They then arrested and subsequently deported 150 people who had sought immigration counseling at the center to adjust their status. Officials hoped to uncover evidence that the counselors were helping foreigners make illegal claims for welfare and food stamps. Ultimately, however, they found insufficient evidence to prosecute the agency's leaders.

Even as ideas about the problematic Mexican family and its use of welfare led immigration authorities to conduct more raids in migrant communities, the deportations that resulted from these raids sometimes split up migrant families and drove Mexicans to seek aid. In January 1971, Imelda Ortega approached the Comité de Beneficencia Mexicana because her husband, who had been the principal breadwinner of the family, had recently been deported to Mexico, leaving her and their five children without their main source of economic support.[111] Without her husband's income, Ortega could not afford to feed the children. The immigration system forced women like Ortega to become dependents—not of the state, as nativists feared, but of other migrants.

Violence during deportation ordeals also led some individuals to become dependent on their community. Although it is impossible to quantify how often this happened, we know that it did. In 1970, INS officials apprehended twenty-four-year-old Ubaldo Rosas and sent him to Mazatlán, Sinaloa. On the train ride south, migration agents beat up Rosas and took away his belongings. Fearing for his safety, Rosas jumped from the train, but he miscalculated the distance and fell on the rails.[112] The train cut off both his legs and two fingers from his left hand.[113] Neither U.S. nor Mexican migratory officials admitted responsibility for the accident, leaving Rosas to fend for himself with no government assistance. Because he could not afford the wheelchair he needed, his family, which remained in the United States, solicited help from the Comité. Border enforcement had separated Rosas from his family and created his need for welfare aid. Yet rather than resorting to U.S. state resources, Rosas depended on the support of other migrants. The Comité ultimately provided him with financial support and the wheelchair he needed.

The notion that migrants took jobs away from citizens led the INS to conduct targeted raids at worksites. In April 1982, the INS launched one of its largest sets of sweeps, officially known as Operation Jobs. During the operation, officers raided work sites that paid more than the minimum wage, deporting all those found without proper documentation so as to make these jobs available to citizens.[114] "The question is, can we cost-effectively apprehend illegals who are holding jobs that can be filled with U.S. citizens?" an immigration officer asked.[115] Acknowledging that U.S. citizens would not take low-paying service jobs, INS officials maintained, "We aren't going after the busboys but rather after those jobs where we believe there is a demand among legal workers."[116] In particular, Operation Jobs targeted factories. During the operation, officials rounded up 5,635 individuals in nine different cities and sent 75 percent of them back to their countries of origin. They then referred 5,065 of those jobs to employment agencies.[117]

To demonstrate the success of the operation, the INS broadcast that more than 1,600 citizens and legal residents had applied for fewer than 200 jobs in Chicago and 1,000 Americans had sought 82 jobs at a site in Los Angeles. Despite these assertions, a survey conducted by the *Los Angeles Times* three months after the raids found that 80 percent of the suspected undocumented workers apprehended in Los Angeles and Orange Counties were back at the worksite. Employers indicated that many U.S. citizens and documented residents who were originally hired to fill the vacancies did not stay on the job, because either the wage was too low or the working conditions too poor.[118] Notably, even if each of the jobs opened up by the sweeps had been taken by a U.S. citizen, the number would have been minimal when compared to the number of unemployed in the country.

The INS also targeted spaces geared toward the "Mexican family." During Operation Jobs, INS officers went to schools in Texas and asked teachers to identify the children whom they believed came from "undocumented families."[119] Migrants complained that officials detained pregnant women without providing them with proper care and refused to allow detainees to contact relatives.[120] When undocumented parents were deported, their children had to find other temporary caretakers.

In another operation, held in March 1984, INS officials apprehended Ms. Aguilar, a widowed mother of three children.[121] That day, the children's school nurse happened to call the mother's workplace and found that Aguilar had been taken into INS custody. The nurse immediately called officials to explain that Aguilar had three children, one who suffered from polio and another who was a U.S. citizen. She requested that the mother be allowed to stay in the United States. Despite the nurse's insistence, INS officials deported Aguilar to Tijuana. The kindergarten teacher of the youngest child—who took the children home with her for the weekend—wrote a letter to Congressman Tom Lantos protesting, "As a parent myself, I can imagine few circumstances more traumatic than being forcibly separated from my children and being unable to ensure either their safety or their maintenance. . . . Surely, we as a society, place a higher priority on the integrity of the family than we do on the undocumented status of certain workers."[122] In fact, popularized beliefs about migrant families and fertility had helped to produce the climate that led U.S. state officials to conduct such operations.

INS sweeps turned all Latinas / os, including permanent residents and citizens, into potentially deportable subjects, outside the boundaries of national belonging. On February 15, 1984, Mario Moreno López, a legal resident of Santa Ana, California, stood waiting for work with other day laborers when INS officials carried out a raid.[123] Upon seeing the officers, Moreno López's friends told him to run, but he refused as he had no legal reason to avoid immigration authorities. When the officials asked him for his identification, he explained that he had left his green card at home. If Moreno López had been white, this might not have been a problem.[124] As a Latino man, however, he was deported. INS officials refused to accompany him home for the card or to release him. Instead, they took him to Los Angeles for processing and insisted that he sign a voluntary return form. When he refused, INS officials slammed him against the wall. Under pressure and fear, Moreno López signed the form and was subsequently deported to Tijuana, Mexico.

Neither the state violence perpetuated against Moreno López nor the fact that officials viewed him as an "illegal alien" simply because he was brown was anomalous. The animus against undocumented workers tended to endanger documented Mexicans and Mexican Americans as well. As Angela Bean, an activist from the Mexican American Legal Defense and Educational Fund (MALDEF), argued, "Abusive treatment is . . . justified by the belief that since undocumented people don't belong here they may be treated in whatever manner the border patrol chooses. . . . In many communities, no distinction is made among the legal and illegal immigrants in the community since both legal and illegal immigrants share appearances, culture, language and other characteristics."[125] She then claimed that Mexicans were considered parasitic outsiders because they were "perceived to take jobs away from U.S. citizens, avail themselves of public services and otherwise drain the U.S. economy."[126]

Notions of hyper-fertile Mexican migrants who increased overpopulation, took away citizens' jobs, and drained state resources made it harder for Mexicans to live within the United States. Legislators reduced the number of legal immigrants allowed from the Americas, and the INS increased raids against undocumented migrants. While claiming to seek equality and free themselves of an "illegal" population, these policies were fraught with racist beliefs and fears that often affected U.S.-born Latinas/os as well. The message was powerful: Mexican migrants did not belong in the United States, even if they lived there.

In October 1977, more than two thousand people came together for the First National Chicano/Latino Conference on Immigration and Public Policy. A pamphlet circulated at the conference was addressed to friends of "the 'unwanted,'" those migrants who could not belong in either their home country or the United States.[127] The pamphlet asserted that "the unwanted" were being pushed out of both the United States and their native countries, unable to belong to either: "Driven here by intolerable conditions in their own countries, they are compelled to take the most miserable jobs and submit to abuse and exploitation at every turn. They are unable to assert the most basic human, social, economic or political rights for fear of deportation should they draw attention to themselves."

The pamphlet encapsulated how migrants' permanent residence had come to be rejected in both Mexico and the United States. Starting in the 1970s, Mexican government officials began to favor working-class men's out-migration from Mexico. Influenced by concerns about the nation's limited public resources, unemployment, and overpopulation, these policymakers espoused emigration as a potential solution to Mexico's problems. They did so knowing that unsanctioned border crossers would

be considered "illegal aliens" in the United States. During this same decade, impelled by similar concerns as those of Mexican representatives,
U.S. officials sought to make it harder for migrants to enter and stay in
the United States. The U.S. Congress limited the number of Mexicans
who could immigrate legally. Like Mexican policymakers, they did so
even when they knew that their actions would increase undocumented
migration. As Melanie Wirken, the political director of ZPG, admitted
in 1976, "It is unrealistic to think that this reduction [of legal immigrants
from Mexico] will not further add to already existing pressures to bypass the formal U.S. immigration process and enter the U.S. illegally significantly increasing our illegal alien population."[128] Soon after Congress
limited legal immigration from Mexico, the INS intensified the fortification of the border and escalated raids. Because these policies failed to
address the circumstances in Mexico that had led migrants to leave or
the continuing demand for their labor in the United States, they did not,
in fact, reduce unauthorized migration. But they did reinforce the notion that Mexicans were "illegal aliens" who could not be incorporated
into the nation as full members of society.

Together, the views about migrants in both Mexico and the United
States created an undesirable population that lived outside the borders
of national protection and belonging. Ben Burdetsky, the deputy assis-
tant secretary for manpower, said it best at a 1975 congressional hearing
on immigration when he described migrants as "a population without a
country or the benefits of permanent residence."[129]

But as migrants knew, it wasn't only U.S. or Mexican government
officials who prevented them from residing permanently in one place.
Far from government offices, union halls, and nativist lobbies, migrant
communities held their own ideas about who had a right to live where.
Their own notions about gender, sexuality, and the divisions of labor
within the family pushed some to cross the border to the United States
and then return back to their hometowns, others to head to Mexico's
larger cities, and yet others to remain in their own households. It is to
these houses, cities, and borderlands that we now turn.

3

·············

THE INTIMATE WORLD OF MIGRANTS

F IELDS OF MAIZE LINED the path leading into Santa Fe de la Laguna, a small Purépecha town in the state of Michoacán. Green mountain peaks, serene lagoon waters, and an imposing cross on the roof of a church dominated the horizon. The church itself opened the way to the town's central plaza—a space that had traditionally structured social life in the region. Townspeople used the square to engage in local commerce, walked through it to reach other parts of the village, and congregated there annually to celebrate the town's patron saint. As more men started heading to the United States, however, the sounds, movements, and socialization that occurred in the plaza began to change. During the men's stay in the United States, their absence from the square was noticeable; upon their return, they could be seen there fraternizing with friends, getting reacquainted with missed family members, seducing lovers, and flaunting the money they had earned while abroad.

The intimate world of migrants was far removed from that of the policymakers of both countries. The two had distinct textures that on the surface seem disjointed but in practice intersected to shape migratory patterns. During the 1970s and 1980s, migrants were not just discouraged or precluded from living permanently in the United States or Mexico by the governments of those nations. They were also denied the ability to settle in their local communities by their families and friends who were adamant that they engage in circular migration. When men spent time in their hometown plazas and saw the effects of migration everywhere they turned, they were reminded that they too were expected to go to *El Norte* to make money. Once men arrived and lived in their new cities and towns in the United States, the same individuals who had encouraged them to leave Mexico now insisted that they return home to be with their families. At the national level, migrants' permanent presence was not welcomed in Mexico or in the United States by the respective officials of each country. At the local level, their permanent settlement was denied by their loved ones. The exclusion migrants faced shaped their sense of not belonging anywhere.

Just as the policymakers of both nation-states used notions about migrants' families, sexuality, and relationship to welfare and unemployment to propel working-class Mexican men to leave their countries, Mexican communities encouraged men to engage in circular migration by focusing on these same issues. Considered the economic providers of their families, men of reproductive age rapidly learned that if they couldn't find a job in Mexico to ensure the well-being of their loved ones, they should go to the United States.

Understandings of gender and sexuality played an important role in the selection of who migrated and who remained in Mexico. During the 1970s and early 1980s, queer men could refrain from migrating because they did not experience the social or economic pressures to go to the United States that heterosexual men faced. Without these forces compelling them to go north, queer men abstained from risking their lives at the border. On the other side of the spectrum from heterosexual men, women were dissuaded from migrating by their own communities. Not only did women face many more dangers at the border than men but they were also supposed to raise children in their hometown. Queer men faced few social demands on their mobility and preferred to stay in Mexico, heterosexual men knew that they were expected to head to the United States, and women understood that they had to remain in their home country.

The phenomenon of international migration often suggests an idea of cosmopolitanism, in which people's worlds are opened as they move through new areas, expanding the territories they know and creating networks between faraway geographies. In some ways, the experience of Mexican migrants confirmed an expansion of vision, but in other ways it did not. Undocumented migration, in particular, tended not only to extend but also to constrain people's sense of space. When heterosexual men felt pressured to migrate, they experienced their communities as closing in on them and pushing them north. During their journey, they had to hide while crossing the border—a space designed to reject their presence. Once in the United States, migrants' sense of space expanded, as they encountered new cities and agricultural fields, but it also contracted as they had to limit their movements outside of their homes to avoid being deported. Many of those who stayed in Mexico also experienced the expansion and contraction of their worlds. On the one hand, they became linked to the United States through stories, letters, and international remittances. On the other, many married women saw their sense of space dwindle after their husbands migrated. Many men feared that when they were abroad, their wives would be unfaithful and thus sought ways to restrict the women from moving freely. In many towns, including in Santa Fe de la Laguna, married women began to abstain from socializing in public, including in the main plaza. Rather than opening spaces for women to be present in the public sphere and take on male roles, as one might have imagined, in the years between 1965 and 1986, male migration often confined women to their homes. Though generally overlooked, these restrictions on the quotidian and local movement of migrants and nonmigrants affected people's everyday lives as much as their international mobility.

Focusing on the cartographies of belonging and movement of migrant married men and nonmigrant women and queer men during the two decades following the end of the Bracero Program seems to imply that women and queer men never migrated. This was not the case. Scholars have already documented some of the migratory experiences of these two groups.[1] Yet almost nothing is known about the lives of the women and queer men who remained in towns of high out-migration, even though the majority of them did not migrate.[2] The fact that queer men migrated at lower rates than heterosexual men counters dominant gender and sexual stereotypes that establish that, if anything, queer men migrate in proportionally higher numbers in order to escape the discrimination they face at home. Everyday lore characterizes small, Catholic Mexican towns as conservative places in which the community aggressively frowns upon all forms of sexuality that take place outside heterosexual marriage. When contrasted with the image of a liberal United States, these places would seem to provide fewer opportunities for gay men to develop a community and to lead full lives. The notion that queer men are more prone to migrate has been supported by diverse studies.[3] These studies are extremely valuable as they offset the invisibility of queer people in migration. Yet the very premise of seeking out "homosexual

immigrants" that guided observers also led them to overlook the ways
in which men's same-sex desire and effeminacy allowed most of them
to remain in Mexico—a choice heterosexual men did not always have.
Examining where and how women and queer men moved and why they
generally refrained from heading to the United States provides an important window into their lives as well as a broader understanding of the
pressures to head north that married men faced.

The intimate world of migrants cannot be examined using traditional
sources. Those who headed north without papers purposefully attempted
to live in the shadows of society, leaving little documentation behind.
The sources that do exist rarely reveal much about migrants' private lives
and affective ties. To explore the experiences of migrants and those of
their community members in Mexico, this work uses representative examples from over 250 oral history interviews conducted on both sides
of the border. Oral histories often tell us more about people's memories
than about their actual lives, but they are one of the best ways to trace
migrants' hidden history.[4] In general, this work focuses on the types of
stories that were repeated by numerous individuals.[5] Together, these accounts illustrate how migrants' permanent settlement in any one place
was denied by their own communities as much as by policymakers, as
well as how migration did not always open up peoples' sense of space
but sometimes constricted it.

Married Migrant Men

Mexican migration to the United States increased rapidly between 1964
and 1986. During these years, undocumented entries rose from 87,000
to 3.8 million per year.[6] Approximately 98 percent of migrants were
married, and the great majority of these were men.[7] Between 50 and
60 percent of migrants originated from the Central Plateau region, particularly from the states of Guanajuato, Jalisco, Michoacán, and Zacatecas,
and 64 to 72 percent of them were born in towns with fewer than 15,000
inhabitants.[8] Most migrant men engaged in circular migration. By 1982,
some towns in Mexico had seen 20 percent of their migrants carry out
five or more trips to the United States.[9] Men engaged in circular migration in part because they felt that they could reside nowhere on a permanent basis.

During the 1970s and 1980s, many men felt pressured to leave their
hometowns because of the growing economic problems in Mexico. From

1970 to 1976, unemployment rose and consumer prices doubled, making it hard for many people to afford basic goods. The countryside faced its own set of problems that further propelled migration. The Green Revolution hurt small agricultural landholders while benefiting large commercial agricultural proprietors and industrial entrepreneurs.[10] Jorge Zavala recalled that he migrated to the United States from Churintzio, Michoacán, in 1970 because he "was working in the fields, and there wasn't too much work there."[11] Zavala's difficulties in finding work can be partially traced to the region's agricultural modernization. Since the late 1940s and early 1950s, a small group of entrepreneurs had started to introduce machines in the fields of Zamora, the municipality where many from Churintzio worked.[12] Mechanization turned workers like Zavala into unnecessary labor. Small farmers also found it increasingly hard to sell their products in the national market, as they had to compete with larger modernized farms that could outproduce and underprice them. Although Zavala would have preferred to find work in his hometown, he felt it could no longer sustain him.

Men's sense that they could not remain in their hometowns increased during times of emergency, when migration became an escape from destitution. Rodolfo Garza, who migrated continuously between Mexico and the United States, decided to go north for the first time "a year in which it didn't rain" and his crops died.[13] Similarly, Rosalía Laris Rodríguez, who lived in a town of high out-migration, recalled that men in the area started going to the United States in high numbers when the local lumbering industry collapsed in the early 1970s.[14]

For the workers who felt that they could no longer remain in their hometowns, heading to the United States seemed like the most obvious choice. The Bracero Program, which officially lasted between 1942 and 1964, promoted a vibrant migratory culture within Mexico. Millions of Mexicans migrated as contract workers, while many of those who could not find slots within the program crossed the border without papers. By the time the Bracero Program ended, migrating to the United States had come to constitute an important part of people's lives. Men thus turned to this option when they faced economic hardship in Mexico, as can be seen in the case of Clemente Lomelí. As a teen growing up in the late 1940s, he had seen his father come and go from Mexico as a bracero.[15] In the early 1960s, he joined him to work in the fields of Salinas, California. When the program ended in 1965, Lomelí tried to find a job in Mexico. After various unsuccessful attempts to find work, he decided to use his migratory experience to head to the United States without papers. Migration begat migration.

The pressure to migrate fell primarily on married men who were responsible for supporting their families. Divisions of labor within migrant communities meant that even though many women worked, both in their own homes and elsewhere, men were assumed to be the financial providers of their households. Garza's wife explained that she pressured her husband to migrate after they had children "because he had to make money to support us. . . . He had to work to be able to provide us with food . . . because in Mexico, life is very hard."[16]

The staggering rates of male migration left many men feeling inadequate if they did not go to the United States to provide for their families. Migrating became a way of establishing one's manhood. Not only did men's wives pressure them to head north but so did their entire social circle. Rafael Ruano recalled that like many other men, he migrated with three friends, who encouraged each other to take the journey and risk crossing the border through the desert. Had Ruano not migrated with them, he would have felt cowardly and would probably have been ridiculed.[17]

The experiences of the Hernández family illustrate the varying pressures to migrate that men felt at different stages of life. During the 1960s, Emanuel Hernández migrated continuously between Tangancícuaro, Michoacán, and the United States to support his family. By the mid-1970s, all his children had grown up, and he ceased to migrate. But his son, Rodrigo, soon took his place as family provider and in 1976, at the age of seventeen, departed to *El Norte* himself. Having seen his father migrate, Rodrigo knew that he should follow his example. Rodrigo dreamed of returning home with fancy clothes, a car, and money, but he also sought to help his parents. In fact, he remitted most of the money he made to them. Upon his return to Tangancícuaro, Rodrigo promised himself that he would not go back to the United States. "Life [in Los Angeles] was hard," he explained. "People treated you poorly, and you always had to hide" so as not to be deported.[18] But this promise to himself proved short-lived. Four years after he returned, Rodrigo married and had his own child. He felt that he could not remain at home but had to migrate to "search for a better life for [his] son."[19] This time he hoped to be able to buy clothes for his toddler and eventually to build a house for his family. Rodrigo's experiences were common. For the most part, active migration began among young unmarried men with a sense of adventure, declined immediately after marriage, rose again with the arrival of children, and ultimately fell as the children matured.[20]

Economic need, reinforced by family and social expectations, forced many men to migrate, even when they would have preferred to remain in Mexico. Their hometowns, it seemed to them, were shrinking around them and pushing them out. Staying was not an option.

Migrants also experienced a constricted sense of space in their new communities in the United States. Even though migration expanded both the actual space and the geographic vistas of many Mexicans, it also severely restricted migrants' spatial boundaries. Unlike in Mexico, in the United States, migrants' constricted sense of space did not generally arise out of economic reasons. While migrants left Mexico searching for jobs, they rarely returned home because they could not find work in *El Norte*. Even during the 1970s, when a fierce recession hit the United States, Mexican workers managed to obtain jobs, often in the growing service industry. Rather, migrants found it hard to remain in the United States permanently because of familial and legal reasons.

For men, migrating generally meant leaving behind wives, children, and parents, all of whom pressed them to return home after a long stay in the United States. Everardo Camacho recalled that his wife and daughter "reproached" him "for leaving" them "alone too much" during his stays abroad.[21] Even without this pressure, most men sought to return home to see their family members and friends. This was especially the case because in the United States they felt alienated from U.S. society. As a migrant recalled, "One finds himself in faraway lands, knowing nobody, with no friends and unable to trust the neighbor who lives right next door."[22] Most migrants arrived knowing little English, which made it hard for them to feel at home. They viewed the United States as a place to reside in temporarily while making enough money to take back to their home in Mexico. Equally important, undocumented migrants knew that at any moment immigration officials could apprehend and deport them, making it hard for them to imagine being able to remain permanently in the United States.

Apprehensions precluded undocumented migrants from living in the United States on a permanent basis and constricted their sense of space at the very local level. This can be seen in the case of the Animeño community. Many workers from Las Ánimas, Zacatecas, moved to South San Francisco and rented houses in a small, two-block street called Juniper Avenue. In the early 1970s, Border Patrol officials began roaming the area, searching for undocumented workers. Instead of detaining migrants in their homes, which required a search warrant, officers patrolled the neighborhood two to three times a week, stopping those whom they believed to be undocumented. In response to these searches, migrants refrained from leaving their homes as much as possible. Raúl Pérez, an Animeño living in South San Francisco, recalled that before he legalized his status, he "almost didn't leave [his] house."[23] Migrants would perform basic activities such as going to work and grocery shopping but would otherwise avoid spending much time outside.

Undocumented Animeños became acquainted with the places where Immigration and Naturalization Service (INS) officials lurked. With this information, they constructed mental maps of movement so as to avoid dangerous streets. Officials, they knew, often lingered in a park at the corner of Cypress and Pine Avenues or at the intersection of Juniper and Linden Avenues. "They were just there waiting to see who would come" so that they could apprehend him or her, Pérez recalled.[24] When returning home from work downtown, Animeños tried to walk around the officers by taking circuitous routes that required walking extra blocks.

Migrants were aware that their capacity to move through certain spaces changed at different times and on different days. A baseball-loving community, Animeños regularly gathered to play games in local parks. Those who were undocumented could attend the games because they took place on Sundays, when fewer INS officers worked. Some Animeños also gathered to play basketball in a nearby school "at night around 6:30 or 7:00 PM . . . because [INS officials] didn't work that late" unless they were searching for someone in particular.[25]

But even though migrants attempted to circumvent the INS, immigration officials would sometimes manage to apprehend them. Pérez worked at night as a janitor in the restaurant kitchen of a Hyatt House hotel. When leaving his shift one day at dawn, he and the other hotel workers realized that INS officers "were waiting outside the door" and had surrounded the building, "so there was no point in running."[26] Pérez was apprehended and sent back to Mexico.

Animeños were not alone in having to restrict their movements to avoid the INS or in trying to find moments of reprieve when they could

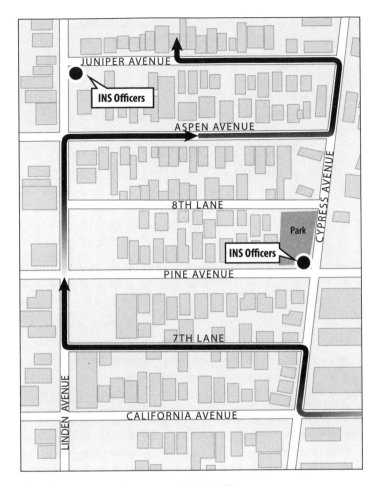

Circuitous route taken to avoid INS officers.

move more freely. Agustín Barragán, who moved from Jalisco to Santa Monica, California, in 1970, recalled that during those years "people lived practically in the shadows." Mexicans were afraid of *la migra* (the INS) even during periods when raids were not occurring, he said. On Sundays, when INS officers did not work, migrants would congregate in the Million Dollar Theatre to see their favorite Mexican bands play, but during the week, "fears" of apprehension made them go directly "from work to home and from home to work."[27]

Migrants' restricted geographic mobility often limited their economic mobility. Jorge Zavala, who migrated from Churintzio, Michoacán, to

Napa Valley, recalled that legalizing his status gave him freedom: "Once I had documents I only [lived] in apartment buildings" and no longer in the barracks within the fields. "I also started moving around more because I started feeling free. Before that, I was afraid of being caught by the INS and sent to Mexico."[28] This meant that he no longer had to work in agriculture but was able to seek construction jobs, which paid much higher wages.

Even though migrants faced acute constrictions on their movement at the local level in the United States, they were often forced to move from one locale to another. In particular, farmworkers moved from field to field during the course of the growing season. Some migrant streams extended between Mexico and the United States, others crossed state lines, while others simply followed crops within one state.[29] Urban undocumented workers also moved on a regular basis. Manuel Jiménez, another Animeño, recalled, "I lived like the pilgrims. First I arrived to Sacramento, then from Sacramento I went to Moorpark. . . . From there I went to Los Angeles, then the next time I [crossed the border] that is when I came here [to South San Francisco]."[30] Jiménez moved around so much because the work he found was often temporary in nature. If he lost his job in one place and heard of an opening in another city, he would simply move on. Even though migrants continuously relocated to different places, they could not move with freedom in any of them.

When migrants were actually apprehended, their mobility was further curtailed while they awaited deportation in detention centers. Migrants called the detention center in El Centro, California, "El Corralón" (the car pound). Jiménez recalled that it was "a large space. We would go outside by day. . . . We would not just stay hauled up in a room." Even though being outside gave migrants a certain sense of freedom, it also restricted their movement as they did not have the option of going back inside until sundown. During the day, he said, migrants would try to find refuge from the "tremendous heat" of the summer by congregating "in the little corners under the roofs, where there was a little bit of shade, that is where one would hang around."[31] Still, most migrants only spent a few days in these centers before being sent back to Mexico.

Deportations represented the most extreme form of evicting migrants from the place they resided. Apprehension often took individuals by surprise, catapulting them back to Mexico with little or no time to prepare or to make provision for responsibilities in the United States. While harvesting grapes in a field in Modesto, California, Antonio Córdoba suddenly heard officials yell, "Don't attempt to run," he looked around and "*la migra* was everywhere. They had surrounded the field . . . so there was really no way to escape."[32] Although he had intended to remain in the United States for another year or so, he knew that he would be sent back to Mexico that week. Similarly, Rafael Montañez was apprehended only two weeks after first entering into the United States in 1969.[33] This experience began a pattern in which he reentered the United States, lived there for a short period of time (although after the first time always longer than two weeks), and was then apprehended again and deported.

Migrants understood that they could not reside permanently in their hometowns or in their new communities in the United States. In Mexico, they faced severe economic hardships and could not provide for their families. But in the United States, they felt alienated, could not move freely, and were often deported. They missed their families in Mexico who, in turn, insisted that they come back home to visit them. In the end, most migrants returned to Mexico, either willfully or because they were deported. Between 55 and 60 percent of undocumented male migrants returned to Mexico within two years of their departure.[34] Because of the difficulties women faced when crossing the border, those who decided to migrate often did so without any clear expectation of returning to Mexico. The likelihood that they would head back within the first two years of departure ranged between just 30 and 40 percent.[35]

When migrants returned to Mexico from the United States, they faced the same economic and cultural pressures that had pushed them to leave in the first place. Thus, returning from the first trip only meant starting the migratory process again. From 1973 to 1983, the annual probability that a male household head would take a second trip to the United States was approximately twice as high as the probability that a Mexican male would head north for the first time.[36]

Comings and goings defined migrants' lives and relationships. Manuel Jiménez returned to Las Ánimas to marry his girlfriend, Feliciana Ramírez, who still resided in their hometown. They had dated for four years and were engaged before he left for the United States for the first time with the promise that he would soon return with money.[37] He fulfilled his promise and returned only a year and a half after he departed. However, he then migrated again soon after the wedding. This experience repeated itself as Jiménez moved back and forth between

Mexico and the United States. Over the years, the couple had ten children while Jiménez went north and returned.[38] Like him, millions of other migrants engaged in circular migration, feeling like no place could hold them permanently.

While U.S. immigration authorities sought to deport Mexicans, Mexico's changing emigration practices facilitated deportees' reentry to the United States. Up until the mid-1970s, Mexican officials forcibly relocated those who had been deported into the interior of Mexico to ensure that they would not simply cross the border again after being released in Mexico's northern borderlands. Being sent to their home states rather than released in the border region made it more costly for migrants to head north again. When the Mexican government changed its migratory policies and began releasing deportees in northern Mexico, many migrants decided to test their luck immediately and simply crossed the border again.

Even though the border constituted the most intensified area of danger for Mexican migrants, their willingness to engage in circular undocumented migration during the two decades following the Bracero Program reveals that the costs of remaining in either country permanently were greater than the risks of entering the United States illegally.

One of the safest ways to cross into the United States was by going through official INS checkpoints, known by migrants as *la línea*. In 1975, the INS reported that more than 20,000 Mexicans sought to enter through these points by making false claims of citizenship, and that 16,277 of them had presented fraudulent credentials.[39] Migrants also tried to go through *la línea* by using a border crosser permit. Officially known as Form I-186, this permit allowed residents of northern Mexico to enter legally into the United States but mandated that they had to remain within twenty-five miles of the border and leave the country within seventy-two hours of their entrance. Acquiring this "local passport," as it was known, was relatively easy. In 1970, 75,000 adult males in Ciudad Juárez alone possessed I-186 cards, and the El Paso INS office issued from 2,500 to 3,000 cards per month.[40] Because only residents of Mexico's northern borderlands could obtain local passports, migrants from the interior often moved there before applying. Those who managed to get hold of a local passport regularly broke the terms of their entrance and stayed in the United States for long periods of time in order to work.[41] Migrants who could not wait or sustain themselves in the northern borderlands to gain access to a local passport often paid to be smuggled surreptitiously through *la línea*. Smugglers, or *coyotes,* hid the migrants in trunks or other concealed compartments within cars and hoped that officers did not conduct detailed inspections. In these places, migrants felt that their allowed space had to contract temporarily for their world to open in the United States.

Many *coyotes* preferred to sneak migrants through unofficial points of entry, spaces that were meant to prevent migrants' very presence. According to estimates, approximately 85 percent of all undocumented migrants entered the United States through three narrow strips within the 2,000 miles of the border: the San Diego Sector, the El Paso Sector, and the San Antonio Sector (which includes Laredo).[42] Each border region posed distinct difficulties. Those who attempted to enter illegally through the Texas sectors had to wade through the Rio Grande. They often did so at night to avoid detection. The waters sometimes ran deep enough to reach their back (thus the term "wetback"). In the San Diego / Tijuana sector, smugglers often waited until nightfall to cross a group of six to eight migrants through the tattered remnants of a border fence into Otay Mesa.[43] Mild temperatures and chaparral brush under which to hide made it the easiest area to go through.[44] Once migrants had crossed the border, prearranged trucks or cars picked them up and drove them farther north.

During the 1970s, the INS increased its policing of the most popular crossing areas. These actions forced many migrants to seek other border crossing options. In 1977, for instance, the INS carried out a massive operation in the Tijuana / San Diego region.[45] In response, many migrants trudged eastward and crossed through the less heavily guarded mountain and desert terrains of El Centro, California, and Arizona. Going through these areas meant traversing a scorching desert full of rattlesnakes.

The hardships of the terrain left behind a trail of deaths. It is hard to know exactly how many people died throughout the years while trying to trek through the inhospitable land of the border. In one five-week period in 1985, the sheriff's office in Yuma County found ten bodies of suspected immigrants who had died in the desert.[46] On September 6, 1985, Border Patrol officials from El Centro reported that in the seventy-mile stretch of desert they patrolled, eight people had died from thirst and exposure in the course of the year.[47] The actual number of deaths was doubtless even higher, as many bodies were never found or reported. The Texas border had its own dangers. During the early 1970s, dozens of migrants drowned every month while trying to cross the Rio Grande.[48] For these migrants, the border constituted a space not only of constriction and rejection but of death.

On occasions, *coyotes* who were supposed to help migrants cross the border were instead responsible for their deaths. In July 1971, Jesús Ayala Domínguez and Delores Blanco hired a smuggler to drive them from San Ysidro to Salinas Valley for $250 each.[49] The *coyote* instructed them to get into his car trunk and locked them in for two days. Upon reaching Hollister, California, the smuggler opened the trunk to find that Ayala Domínguez had died from carbon monoxide poisoning and that Blanco lay unconscious. He threw their bodies into a roadside ditch.[50]

On other occasions, perverse violence prevented border crossers from concluding their journey. In 1976, in Douglas, Arizona, George Hannigan and his two sons kidnapped and tortured three undocumented Mexicans who were crossing through their ranch looking for work. One of the survivors reported, "First they tied our feet and hands; they cut our clothes until we were semi-naked. They took us next to a bonfire. After placing a rod in the fire they placed it on my feet. I heard an impressive sound that I will never forget: it was a *shhhhh* that made me scream until I became almost mute."[51] They then took one of the men and hanged him from a tree. After letting him drop, they dragged another across the floor, shooting him with buckshot. They later freed the men, naked and bleeding, and instructed them to run for their lives as they shot at them.[52]

While most migrants did not fear the border enough to refrain from engaging in circular migration, on occasion, some did. Manuel Jiménez did not dare to go back to his hometown to bury his mother because he did not know whether he would be able to reenter the United States, where his wife and children lived. He found out that his mother died on the same day that his wife was scheduled for surgery. When considering whether to return to his hometown for the funeral, he thought, "If I go [to Mexico] and then [my wife] gets sicker and I don't have the opportunity to come back, what will I do?" Jiménez concluded, "I can't go. . . . Let my mother forgive me."[53] That men like Jiménez refrained from going back to Mexico because of fears of crossing the border should have forewarned U.S. policymakers that increasing border enforcement would only encourage more Mexicans to settle in the United States without leaving.

During the years between 1965 and 1986, most migrants continued to engage in circular, undocumented migration. Their decision to cross the border multiple times despite the dangers they faced testifies to their inability to remain in either Mexico or the United States on a long-term basis. Migrants' limited ability to inhabit local spaces shaped their overall movement more than the act of crossing the border line.

Queer Men

Queer men's migratory patterns shed light on how ideas about gender and sexuality helped to shape Mexican migration to the United States in the years between 1965 and 1986. Mexicans had their own words to describe those they viewed as being different in terms of their gender and sexuality, such as *jotos* and *maricones* ("fags"). However, most of those who identified with the terms considered them pejorative and preferred that they not be used. As such, the terms "queer" and "gay" are used here instead. These terms are not used to refer to all men who engaged in same-sex relationships, but only those who openly identified as being different based on the gender and sexual paradigms of their communities. Mexicans who came from areas of high out-migration did not view the world as divided strictly between men and women. Instead, they believed that a small minority of people fell in between these two categories. Individuals who were considered to be males at birth but who then assumed the cultural roles ascribed to women and had sex with men were considered to be a mixture of both sexes; those who were deemed females at birth but who then displayed a male-like performance of gender and had sex with women were also considered queer. Conversely, those believed to be males at birth who played the active or assertive role in sex and performed hegemonic masculinity were considered "normal," even if they had sex with other men.[54] In a similar vein, feminine women could play the passive role in sex with other women without being viewed as odd.

In terms of migration, queer men headed to the United States at surprisingly low rates. This does not mean that all men who had sex with men migrated in fewer numbers but, rather, that men deemed "different" because they assumed a passive role in sex and were effeminate stayed in Mexico in higher numbers. Queer men's decision to stay in Mexico is rather surprising: everyday depictions of small-town Mexico as conservative and sexually repressive would suggest that queer men would jump at the opportunity of migrating to more liberal cities in the United States. Yet throughout the Central Plateau region from which most people migrated, queer men were more likely to remain in Mexico than their heterosexual counterparts. For instance, in the town of Nochistlán, Zacatecas, over 65 percent of all men who were older than fifteen years of age migrated at least once between 1965 and 1986.[55] In contrast, less than 15 percent of all known queer men of those ages who lived or had once lived in the town during this period migrated.[56] Beyond these figures, oral history interviews conducted throughout the Central Plateau region reveal that most people, whether queer or heterosexual, believed that queer men migrated less than heterosexual ones.

While heterosexual men felt pushed out of their hometowns because of economic need and their identities as providers, queer men saw their own towns as spaces where they could reside permanently. The most important reason why queer men did not migrate was because they could survive in Mexico with the money they made there.[57] Unlike married men, who needed to go to the United States to support their families, most queer men did not have wives and children to maintain and tended to live in their parents' home their whole lives. This difference highlights both the experiences of gay men as well as the importance of the gendered division of labor to migratory patterns that pushed many heterosexual men to go to *El Norte*.

Gay men also had access to employment that those viewed as "normal" found unattainable and unappealing. Enrique Plazas was born in 1963 in Santa Fe de la Laguna, Michoacán, and knew since he was a child that he was gay. So did all those around him. When Plazas reached his late teens and early twenties, his peers started migrating. Plazas, in contrast, stayed in his hometown and worked in restaurants—establishments whose owners preferred to hire him over a non-queer man. He explained, "A gay man had more doors open to him. People don't mistrust gays so much." While restaurant patrons could worry that heterosexual men would "do something . . . like raping or touching young ladies, or women," female clients knew that "we are not interested in them."[58] Plazas quickly added that queer men had already lost their male privilege and could thus engage in these types of "feminine" activities at no additional cost. Conversely, "real men" preferred to work in *"machín* [masculine]" jobs than to lose their gender privilege by cooking or engaging in occupations perceived as feminine. Heterosexual men would say, "I am a man. I don't have to be working in [domestic-type] jobs," Plazas explained, and they would work in the fields instead.[59] Because agricultural employment was seasonal and low paying in nature, this decision eventually led many to migrate. In other words, the existing division of labor meant that queer men could remain in town by working in service jobs while many heterosexual men felt the need to migrate.

Paradoxically, in the United States migrants worked increasingly in service-sector jobs. Although they were unwilling to lose their masculine privileges by performing "feminine" activities in their hometowns, in the United States they worked in jobs that Americans traditionally considered "women's work." Moreover, the growing number of men who migrated to work in U.S. service-sector jobs actually enlarged the demand for the service jobs that queer men performed at home. The remittances migrants sent allowed townspeople to spend more money on the sorts of services that gay men provided. They would buy more flower arrangements for *quinceañera* parties, get their hair done by professionals, and eat out more frequently.

Gay men could also refrain from migrating because of the wages they received. Not only did they have access to service-sector jobs but they were paid more than women for performing them. Queer men could reap male privilege, even while being feminized. While notions of their "inner female core" allowed gay men to work in jobs traditionally taken up by women, their male sex helped them raise their prices. David Aldame, a gay man from Tangancícuaro, Michoacán, recalled that all his friends were hairdressers, florists, and cooks.[60] Even though women engaged in similar occupations, people in town expected the work performed by gay men to be more creative and carefully done. As such, they were willing to pay more for it. Aldame explained, "People know us, people can distinguish us, can identify us. . . . If a woman puts a business similar to mine, as some women did, [customers still] came to my business instead of hers . . . because we give it an extra touch, we tend to make things more special, and to be more detail-oriented."[61] Angel Arias, another queer man from Tangancícuaro who benefited from this widely held stereotype, agreed: "A gay man has more imagination and can be more creative," allowing him to get paid more for his work.[62] The sexual ideologies in these towns constructed gay men as even more fit than women to carry out "women's jobs." These perceptions helped raise queer men's income enough that they did not feel the need to go to the United States.

Ill treatment in Mexico did not push queer men to migrate to the United States. For the most part, gay men lived in peace in their hometowns. On occasion they were called names in the street, and some even faced physical violence.[63] But few maintained that this treatment led them to consider going to the United States. In fact, many Mexican queer men claimed that their own country's gay lifestyle proved more enticing than that of the United States. Not only did they already understand the existing sexual practices in their hometowns but they could also move around more easily to meet men, as they did not have to fear being caught by the INS. The gay men who did go to the United States often believed that it was harder for them to "get men" north of the border than it was in Mexico. Diego Perea, who migrated without documents in the 1970s, recalled that even though he lived in Texas for approximately three years, he never had a sexual contact there.[64] In Mexico, he claimed, he always had sex. His lack of access to free sexual liaisons in the United States "obviously" played a role in his decision to return to Mexico.[65] Perhaps even more revealing, according to Perea, during the 1970s and 1980s, gay men who lived in migrant communities in the United States paid to be penetrated by those they called "normal men."[66] In contrast, in Michoacán, "normal men" paid to have sex with the queer villagers.[67]

While queer men did not experience the space of their hometowns as constricting, they knew that as undocumented migrants they would be suspect in the United States. Although most gay men did not have a full grasp of U.S. law, many of them sensed that because of their sexual and gender identities they would face even more legal dangers north of the border than did their heterosexual counterparts. Felipe Ramírez, a gay man from Santa Fe de la Laguna, explained, "There are people who don't like us [queer men]. If I went over there [to the United States] and I got to meet a guy and he didn't like me we would start having problems and fighting . . . and he could sue me."[68]

Gay men's belief that the U.S. legal system could bring them more trouble than the Mexican one was rooted in fact. The 1952 U.S. Immigration and Nationality Act excluded from naturalization "persons afflicted with psychopathic personality." This designation was "sufficiently broad to provide for the exclusion of homosexuals and sex perverts."[69] In 1967, the Supreme Court ruled this law constitutional in *Boutilier v. Immigration.* Perhaps even more significant, gay men in the United States could be arrested for solicitation for deviant sexual conduct, lewd vagrancy, or disorderly conduct, and many states still had sodomy laws even though they weren't consistently enforced. These multiple regulations on gay men could seriously impact the lives of queer migrants. Records on the numbers of male inmates released from the California prison system who had been paroled for the first time in 1975 show that thirty-seven men were arrested for "sex perversion."[70] They served an average of over four and a half years, with some serving over ten years. Four of these men were classified as being of "White, Mexican descent."[71] Conversely, in Mexico, consensual sex among adults of the same sex was not a crime, even though public "decency" laws were sometimes applied against homosexuals. In stark contrast to liberal perceptions, in the 1970s, gay men actually faced greater legal risks in the United States than in Mexico.

Queer men also claimed that the border zone posed more dangers and difficulties for them. Mario Melendrez, a queer man from Tzintzuntzan, Michoacán, claimed that like women, gay men were commonly sexually abused when crossing the border.[72] Because other migrants and *coyotes* thought of queer men as a sexual outlet similar to women, they did not refrain from abusing them. In 1980, INS Commissioner Leonel J. Castillo reported that the dangers for homosexual men in undocumented detention centers were so high that officers separated them for their "own protection."[73] Gay men also lacked the social networks needed to head north. Angel Arias explained, "If you had, for instance, an uncle [who lived in the United States] but all of his family was straight and he knew that you were gay, he was not going to tell you: 'Come here and I'll get you a job in the factory' because then you would be with all his sons."[74] Queer men also faced more dangers when crossing the border because of their gender and sexual identities.

The migratory patterns of queer women are harder to distinguish. No town studied had enough women who identified as being different in terms of gender and sexuality in the years between 1965 and 1986 to make a meaningful comparison between their migratory rates and those of women who identified as "normal." Moreover, while most people within communities of high out-migration, including gay men themselves, agreed that queer men migrated at lower rates than those they referred to as "normal" men, no such consensus or even opinion existed on the relationship between women's migration and gender and sexuality. Teresa Villarreal, a gay woman from Pátzcuaro, Michoacán, maintained that heterosexual women "were very scared of the crossing" while lesbians "were a bit more daring, they liked adrenaline a bit more," and so they were more likely to migrate.[75] Despite holding these stereotypes, she knew few lesbians who had migrated. Elena Arceo, a queer woman from Nochistlán, Zacatecas, provided equally gendered reasons to explain the opposing view, even though she migrated in 1986. She maintained that her desire to go north had nothing to do with gender or sexuality. If anything, lesbians were less likely to migrate because they "liked to work in the fields, to do hard work . . . and they were better at fieldwork than men."[76] Arceo made it seem as if queer women were so good at agricultural work that, unlike men, they could support themselves by working in Mexico's fields. Moreover, like straight women, lesbians faced high levels of sexual violence at the border, which generally deterred them from migrating. In fact, most people in the Central Plateau region insisted that there was no relationship between "lesbianism" and international migration.

Queer migratory patterns shed light on the migratory patterns of Mexicans in general. Gay men's capacity to remain in town because they could find jobs that paid a living wage indicates that more heterosexual men might have refrained from migrating if they did not experience their hometown spaces as limited; gay men's idea that their femininity implied that they ought to stay in Mexico illustrates the importance of gender ideologies in migratory patterns; and their preference to stay in their hometowns highlights that the United States was not necessarily a more liberal place for racialized sexual minorities.

Women

Like queer men, women tended to remain in their hometowns rather than migrating, but unlike queer men, they did not necessarily remain at home out of their own volition. While married men were compelled to leave for the United States to support their families, cultural norms and border policies pressured women to remain in Mexico. This reality stood in stark contrast with U.S. representations of Mexican women that depicted them entering the United States in inordinate numbers to birth children in the country. In fact, women were expected to remain in Mexico to take care of their children. Not only were they discouraged from heading north, but when their husbands migrated, many of them were even deterred from going outside their homes during their free time. The increasing rates of male migration left many women feeling imprisoned within the confines of their hometowns and within their own household walls.

Even though the Bracero Program only contracted men, its termination did not equalize gender migratory patterns. Men continued to go to the United States at much higher rates than women. The annual probability that a man aged fifteen or older migrated for the first time without papers increased by three times in the years between 1965 and 1975 (from 0.7 to 2.1 percent of the total population).[77] This probability then fell sharply again during the Mexican oil boom, which lasted from 1979 to 1982, but rose again at astonishing rates after the devaluation of the Mexican peso and the collapse of the Mexican economy in 1982.[78] In contrast, the migration of undocumented women did not fluctuate as much. Instead, the 1970s saw moderate growth in the likelihood of women's undocumented migration, with annual probabilities approximating 0.7 percent in 1980.[79] Still, the rate of male migration increased so rapidly that despite the growth of women's migration, men's migratory dominance actually increased from the early 1970s to the late 1980s.[80] These mobility patterns were reflected in the demographic compositions of towns of high out-migration. For instance, in the late 1970s, 39 percent of all individuals living in Las Ánimas who were between sixteen and thirty-nine years of age were men, while 61 percent were women.[81]

Sexual violence at the border constituted one of the main reasons why women abstained from going to the United States illegally. In addition to the dangers that all unauthorized migrants faced when crossing the border, such as dehydration and drowning, women were also at risk of sexual assault.[82] Horrifying stories of the dangers women faced circulated throughout towns, discouraging many from going on the journey. For instance, in the town of Ruiz Cortines, Michoacán, women warned each other against trying their luck in *El Norte* by gossiping about a female villager whose *coyote* had raped her.[83] After that, they held, "her life was no longer good."[84] For many women, the danger extended beyond their own safety to that of their daughters. Laura Mazos stayed with her children in Ruiz Cortines, she recalled, because she would "not give them to a *coyote*" who could sexually assault them.

Women also stayed in Mexico because of widespread beliefs about the division of labor within the family. When women migrated, they did so to Mexican cities, while they were still single, in order to support their parents and siblings.[85] In metropolitan areas, women labored as domestic workers, as street vendors, and in the service sector. With the growth of the Border Industrialization Program (BIP) in the late 1960s, many single women also started to migrate to northern Mexico to work in assembly plants. A study found that 40 percent of all women who worked in the BIP in Ciudad Juárez had migrated there alone in search of work.[86] Once women married, however, they were supposed to stay in their hometowns.

While married men felt the need to head north because they were considered the financial providers of their households, married women felt the need to remain in their hometowns because they were responsible for raising children. José Magaña, who first migrated as a bracero and then as an undocumented worker, recalled that his wife really wanted to live in the United States, but he "couldn't take her."[87] After all, he asked glibly, "With whom would the children have stayed?" Although Magaña could have considered staying at home while his wife migrated, his assessment that the whole family could not leave was not misguided. Going to the United States without authorization was an expensive endeavor. People often got into debt to pay *coyotes'* fees, which ranged between US$150 and US$250 per person.[88] It was hard enough to pay for one family member to migrate and almost impossible to pay for others to do so.

Given the mores of migration, it was understood that if someone were to leave the country for money it would be the man. When María Reyes married, her husband began to go back and forth between Mexico and the United States. She recalled, "I thought about migrating, but I couldn't because of my many children. I was tired of being alone, and I would tell my husband, 'Take me with you,' and he would say, 'How can I take you with me? First, where would we stay? We are too many. Second, how can I take you when it is so hard to cross children?' "[89] While Reyes wanted to head north, she never considered asking her husband to look after the children in Mexico while she migrated and remitted money for the family. Reyes was not alone in asking her husband to "take her" with him only to have him turn down the request. The majority of women interviewed explained why they never left Mexico through statements such as "My husband didn't invite me" or "He didn't take me." Talía Herrera recalled that when her husband started migrating in 1978, she would tell him, "Take me with you." But, she said, "he didn't want to. He just went," and she remained in Mexico.[90] Because it was understood that migration was primarily a male activity and that women were responsible for raising children in Mexico, most women ultimately accepted their husbands' decision.

Men also worried that in the United States their wives would engage in extramarital relationships. Herrera's husband claimed that when women went to the United States, they "left their husbands for others."[91] In Mexico, he explained, men could control their wives through physical violence, while in the United States they could not since "they had laws against that." Herrera's husband was not alone in his belief that protective laws gave women too much power in the United States. The *corrido* "Las Pollas de California" advised Mexican men: "If you are to go to California / I bid you pals, do not believe the chicks / better to live single / If the husband goes to the canteen / to sprees or the billiards / and his wife finds out / she is going to complain to the judge."[92] Many men believed that in the United States they would not be able to "control" their wives, which would lead the women to have extramarital affairs.

While men often limited the migration of their wives, parents discouraged single women from crossing the border because of the reigning sexual ideologies. Even though parents encouraged their daughters to work in Mexican cities, they frequently considered the United States to be too sexually liberal. They worried that if their daughters migrated transnationally, they would become promiscuous and lose their sexual respectability.

In the two decades following the end of the Bracero Program, representations of Mexican women as having an uncontrolled sexuality limited women's mobility on both sides of the border. In Mexican towns, families feared that migrant women would fall prey to sexual temptations; in the United States, the media, citizens, and government officials regularly depicted migrant women as sexually irrepressible and accused them of birthing too many children and burdening the state. Ultimately, both of these portrayals presented Mexican women's sexuality as intrinsically unrestrained and in need of regulation. They both also limited women's movement. U.S. officials used these notions to further fortify the border, which made border crossing increasingly dangerous; Mexican families used them to prohibit women from moving to the United States.

Perhaps even worse than feeling contained in their hometowns, many women started feeling constricted within them. After going to the United States, many men from towns of high out-migration in Michoacán prohibited their wives from socializing outside the home, which in their view signaled infidelity. Limiting their wives' movements allowed men to assert their presence in their hometowns and family lives even when they were far away. To be sure, women's mobility was not constrained in all towns of high out-migration. Few women from Zacatecas, where gender relations tended to be more equal in general, described facing the social control that Michoacanas experienced. But in Michoacán, a state that had one of the highest levels of out-migration, women remembered that when men started heading to the United States in increasing numbers, their own mobility at the local level declined.

International migration extended the practice of control that already existed in a more limited form beforehand. According to many women, men's fears that their wives would cheat on them increased after they migrated. Ana Beltrán, who lived in Santa Fe de la Laguna, Michoacán, recalled that after marrying, her husband would inquire about her "expeditions" in the village ad nauseam.[93] Such inquiries multiplied after his departure to the United States. He would only be satisfied if she remained at home and left the house only to conduct the household's business, such as selling crafts in the local market. Physical distance thus increased men's desire to control women's mobility. While the feminization of the population in towns of high out-migration could have furthered women's autonomy, in reality male migration deepened men's control over women's movement. The effects of migration on women's mobility warn against simplistic readings of Mexican machismo: men's control of women's mobility looked different after their departure.

Restrictions on women's movements occurred slowly and sometimes took place even as women became wage earners for the first time. Women who had not worked outside their homes before their husbands migrated sometimes had to take jobs to support their families while waiting for the first remittances to arrive.[94] This meant that they actually spent more time outside. Regularly, however, women quit these jobs after their husbands started sending money. But even the women who continued working outside their homes described that after men migrated, they stopped socializing in public. Women could go outside to labor but not to enjoy leisure time.

To prevent their wives from walking around town "more than necessary," migrants enlisted the help of those who remained in Mexico. When Raúl Mazos migrated from Ruiz Cortines, Michoacán, he began fearing that his wife was being unfaithful, so he called their son and interrogated him about who their mother saw when she left the house. He then instructed the child to never let her go by herself to Tangancícuaro, the town closest to the rancho.[95] More commonly, men's own parents were charged with policing and restricting women's movements. In the years between 1965 and 1986, women would regularly move in with their parents-in-law when their husbands migrated. Men's parents often also worried that their daughters-in-law would engage in extramarital affairs and thus habitually forbade the women from leaving the house. As a result, many women felt like prisoners while their husbands were in the United States. Eloísa Arroyo recalled that her parents-in-law "hit me, they would not give me food, [and they would] not let me out of the house because they feared that I would cheat on him."[96]

Even when women lived in their own houses, the town's gossip often served to restrict their movement. According to Ana Beltrán, people talked about women who socialized outdoors, accusing them of being unfaithful to their husbands. It was as if they believed that "women had to be locked in."[97] As a result, Beltrán recalled, most of them "barely went out" so as not to be accused of engaging in extramarital affairs. Gossip could do more than destroy women's reputations. Because rumors of infidelities often reached *El Norte*, wives also feared that if they spent too much time outdoors their husbands would find out and stop sending them remittances. Before heading north, Beltrán's husband warned her to "be careful" not to be seen in town too much; gossip about her behavior would reach him "all the way to the United States," he insisted. The potentially high price of moving throughout town meant that many women avoided leaving their house even for a few blocks for the purpose of socializing. Women's fear that others would gossip about them if they spent too much time outside led them to self-regulate their movements. Laura Mazos recalled that she didn't "like to go visit someone [*a la fulanita*] or to be outside, or to amuse [herself] by leaving the house, or to sit in the plaza or anything . . . because of gossip." She explained, "My husband has his family here, and I have a sister-in-law who doesn't like [me] and she . . . invented stuff."[98]

While women regulated their own comings and goings so as not to be accused of infidelity, they were also the primary enforcers of this type of surveillance-through-gossip. Women participated in policing each other's mobility because they did not consider such limitations abusive. Many Michoacanas even used the term *muy callejeras* to refer to other women.[99] This term classified women who spent a lot of time on the streets and was used to refer to "loose women." Women in Michoacán often considered the restriction on their movement as acceptable; simply a sign of the respect owed to their husbands. When a woman's husband migrated to the United States, townspeople's sense that she needed to stay indoors to signal her fidelity increased. After all, without him nearby, she could have more opportunities to cheat on him. Beltrán maintained that in Santa Fe de la Laguna, people would gossip: "Why does she dress like that? That is not correct. Oh! It's because her husband is not here."[100] Of course, women could not simultaneously chitchat about other women's movement within town and not leave their own house themselves. But they would go outside for "allowed" activities, such as shopping, and talk to other women on the way. As a result, women both suffered from and were responsible for enforcing the patriarchal rules that limited their mobility.

Even as women experienced consistent surveillance of their movement, they worried about their husband's affairs abroad but could do little about it. María Suárez Oliva recalled, "I was worried because many [migrants] didn't return; they remained with other women [in the United States]."[101] Yet there was nothing she could do to prevent him from cheating on her with other women. Fears that men would leave them for other women were compounded by the anxiety that if this happened, men would stop sending them remittances. Laura Mazos recalled that when her husband told her he would migrate, she constantly worried, "What if something happens to him on the crossing, and he leaves me with so many kids? Or what if he goes and he thinks differently, and he gets together with another woman and doesn't come back? If so, what am I going to do with his children here [to support them economically]?"[102] While men could restrict women's local movements, women had no control over where men went or how they spent their time.

In communities of high out-migration, ideas about gender, sexuality, family composition, and economic progress affected people's movement on an international scale. They drew a map in which heterosexual men of reproductive age felt pressured to go to the United States, women were prevented from doing so, and queer men could stay in Mexico. Of course, these differences were never absolute. Women and queer men sometimes headed to the United States; women in some areas of high out-migration could move within their towns with freedom after their husbands migrated; and many heterosexual men from the Central Plateau region never migrated. Still, for the most part, people's identities generally shaped their ability and desire to move across borders. The rising rates of the transnational migration of men, in turn, built new borders. In the United States, undocumented migrants had to live in hiding, and in Mexico their wives had to appear respectable by staying indoors. The rise of undocumented migration created new cartographies of movement that ranged from household confinement to transnational relocation.

During the years between 1965 and 1986, Mexican migrants found themselves in an overall impossible situation.[103] Mexico's leaders believed that they could not be economically incorporated into the nation and favored their emigration from Mexico, many U.S. citizens and officials began to call for their departure from the United States, and their own families and networks encouraged them to engage in circular migration. Migrants, however, challenged the multiple pressures they faced that forced them to be permanent residents of nowhere.

4

....

NORMALIZING MIGRATION

JOSÉ MINERO LEGASPI, one of the most famous public intellectuals of Nochistlán, Zacatecas, wrote a poem in 1976 about how his town had come to represent "the simplicity of friends / the hardworking nature of woodworkers, / the sadness of the migrant [*norteño*]."[1] In another he affirmed: "You [Nochistlán] are the flower / that adorns the farmworker / that provides dreams to those exiled from the nation [*despatriado*], / that shouts its history / that sows flowers together."[2] In poems such as these, Minero Legaspi conveyed the generalized perception that, just as migrants' dreams and sense of self were forged by their departure from the town, their comings and goings had come to define Nochistlán as a whole. Like Nochistlán, in the years between 1965 and 1986, hundreds of communities on both sides of the border came to be shaped by migrants' translocal movement.

The growth of circular migration reconfigured the ways in which many Mexicans organized their everyday lives and relationships. Love and intimacy began to take place across borders. Parental advice was handled via letters. Friendships thrived in an alien society. Translocal attachments and dependencies developed. Remittances allowed people to improve their homes. These changes had begun with the Bracero Program, but it was during the two decades after it ended that undocumented migration became inextricable from life in Mexican and U.S. communities.[3]

Those who headed north managed to acquire partial belonging in their local communities on both sides of the border even though they could not reside in any one place on a permanent basis. Starting in the

1970s, migrants came to experience that in Mexico, policymakers viewed them as economically superfluous and supported their departure from the country; in the United States, authorities and society declared them "illegal aliens"; and in their own communities, their families and friends pressured them to head north to make money and then to return to their hometowns. Although migrants agreed to engage in circular migration, in part because of family and community pressure, their cross-border movement redefined the very meaning of "family" and "community." For many Mexicans, these concepts ceased to be associated with home and proximity and instead came to include a transnational dimension.

The growing rates of migration in the years between 1965 and 1986 even altered the meaning of the spaces through which migrants moved.[4] The places from which migrants were "pushed" to leave on both sides of the border came to exist as they did only because of migrants' translocal movement. Migrants became both exiles from these locations and central figures within them. Not only did remittances change the infrastructure of Mexican towns but, as Minero Legaspi's poems illustrate, migration changed how people understood their hometowns. Migrants also altered how they related to space in their new locales in the United States. Through the networks they built, migrants found ways to live in spaces where they were generally considered outsiders.

By changing how individuals understood the world and their place within it, migration came to be seen as a normal and entrenched phenomenon. Men realized that their cross-border movement allowed them to gain partial inclusion in their hometown and in their new communities in the United States. For their part, their networks came to view their comings and goings as indispensable.

These developments can be seen by focusing on the community of Las Ánimas and offering comparisons and contrasts with other communities.[5] Las Ánimas belongs to the Nochistlán municipality of Zacatecas, a state in the Central Plateau region (see map in Introduction). The patterns of migration in Las Ánimas were usually similar to those of other communities in the region; when they were not, the differences are in themselves revealing of how migration became normalized throughout the area even while producing distinct changes in some towns.[6] It is only by examining how migration came to be an intrinsic part of life in Mexico and the United States that we can understand why efforts to curtail it by militarizing the border did not curb the migratory flow.

The growth of circular migration forced individuals to reconfigure their nuclear and extended family relationships. María Reyes recalled that her understanding of what being a parent and wife meant changed as a result of her husband's continuous movement between Las Ánimas and South San Francisco during the late 1960s and early 1970s.[7] Throughout the years, the couple conceived seven children, all of whom Reyes raised while her husband was away. "Everyone [in town] said that I was both the father and the mother of our children," she maintained. When talking about her children, people would never say that "they are his offspring; they would always say that they were mine." The kids themselves barely knew their father: "I would go to their school, I would go to their meetings," and he had to miss all those things. If the children had a problem they would automatically turn to her. For her part, Reyes relied on help from her mother-in-law in cases when she had to take on her husband's tasks. For instance, when one of her children got sick and had to be taken to the hospital, her mother-in-law would stay home to look after her other children.

Reyes experienced her husband's migration as particularly hard because it began before migration from Las Ánimas had become a fully established phenomenon. Even though many men were already heading north and had done so for many years, men's departures still cast a shadow on their wives' reputations. Reyes herself viewed mothers who did not have a husband by their side as "fallen women" and wondered what people said about her. She was not being unreasonable. During the Bracero period and the years that immediately followed, communities regularly regarded migrants' wives as debauched, shunned, and unwomanly for not having their husbands next to them.[8] Reyes didn't even know how to identify herself: "I was not married. I was not a widow. I was not abandoned. I was like a rotten thing."[9]

With the growth of circular, undocumented migration during the 1970s and early 1980s, long-distance partnerships in Las Ánimas became so common that women no longer questioned what their spouses' migration implied about them. When Esther Ortega decided to start dating Jorge Medina in the late 1970s, she knew that he engaged in circular migration, but neither she nor her parents had any qualms about his migrant life. Many of Ortega's female friends were also dating or married to men who worked in the United States. Ortega never feared that Medina's departure would lead people to view her as unwomanly simply because he wasn't around.

This does not mean that during the late 1970s and early 1980s all gossip and hardships dissipated from long-distance relationships. Fears of infidelity arose often. At one point, rumors reached Ortega that Medina was dating someone else in the United States. Her anger and fear could only be expressed and resolved through written correspondence. Medina tried to reassure her, writing, "I don't want to lose you only because of what people are saying [*por bocas de otra gente*]."[10] In another letter, Medina wrote, "I have come to think that I trust you more than you trust me. I ask you as a favor for the sake of both of us, for our happiness: trust me . . . even in the smallest stuff. . . . There is no one else in my mind or in the depth of my heart. Only you, Esther."[11]

Correspondence as a means of communication added to the complexity of relationships. Because some migrants and their family members had difficulty reading and writing, they had to find someone else to perform these tasks for them. Mail traveled slowly between South San Francisco and Las Ánimas, taking an average of two and a half weeks.[12] Although Medina and Ortega dated for a long time and corresponded frequently, there was much about each other that they did not know because they could not be together. As Medina explained in a letter, "I hope that one day I have the opportunity to tell you my whole life."[13] Communicating by mail made jumbled feelings hard to parse out and meant that big announcements could not be revealed in person. In one single letter, which reflects the realities and contradictions of forging love across borders, Medina expressed his love, fears, insecurities, and plans to marry Ortega. In July 1981 he wrote, "It gave me much joy to receive your letter as I had thought that you had forgotten about me."[14] He then expressed his wishes to get to know her better: "You tell me that you would like to know more about me; I also would like to be close to you." In this very letter in which he acknowledged that they did not know each other well and that he feared that she would leave him, he also indirectly proposed marriage to her. He wrote:

> I am planning a trip to the ranch in January at the beginning of 1982 and no one but you knows this, Esther. . . . You are the most special

person [to me]. And I am going to tell you this and I hope it is agreeable to you or otherwise you will let me know. You know I have thought a lot about this and this is why I would like to talk with you personally but because that is not possible right now I have no other recourse than to tell you via letter: you know I have thought and have made dreams—To Marry a very special person to me. You are that person.[15]

Once married, the couple decided that Ortega would head to *El Norte* to join Medina.[16] Aware of the risks of the trip for women, Medina made sure to help Ortega cross to the United States himself rather than "give her to anyone," like a *coyote,* to help her through.[17] After several failed attempts, the newlyweds finally managed to enter into the United States illegally. Their happiness did not last long, however. Soon after arriving, Ortega decided that she did not like life in the United States: "I was more comfortable here [in Las Ánimas]," she recalled. In South San Francisco, she said, "I didn't know the language so it was hard to make myself understood and any time that I went anywhere I had to take someone to translate for me and that was hard."[18] While Animeños expected Medina to migrate and make money, the same was not true for Ortega. She thus decided to go back to Mexico and, like many other spouses were doing, the couple went back to having a translocal relationship. Medina worked most of his time in South San Francisco and visited his wife in Las Ánimas for a couple of months every year.

As the comings and goings became routine, Medina and Ortega built a family life across borders, conceiving children whenever he returned to Mexico. By 1985, they had five children. That year, Medina sent Ortega a card for Mother's Day that said, "Mother of my children, happy Mothers' Day. My whole love is only for you."[19] Letters were now not only a means to communicate feelings but also to solve the practical problems of the family. In one letter Medina asked Ortega to go to the doctor: "Esther, please . . . go see someone [a doctor]" and reminded her "anything you need, if you don't have [money] or if you are scared about money running out, get some—my dad has money that belongs to me for when it is needed."[20] From sentimentality to everyday matters, Medina and Ortega formed a transnational family through letters and trips.

Like Ortega, thousands of families came to be dependent on the remittances migrants sent. From the early 1960s to the early 1980s, the percentage of migrants who sent money back home crept upward from 60 percent or less to over 70 percent (albeit there were some fluctuations).[21] During this same period, the percentage of migrants who returned with savings increased from a little over 50 percent to 65 percent.[22] This money had a huge impact on their families, often constituting over 80 percent of their monthly cash income. A season of wage labor in the United States could raise rural families' standard of living to that reached by professional workers in Mexican cities.[23] In Las Ánimas, only 13.6 percent of families had enough money from local earnings to live above the poverty line, but most of them lived fairly comfortably thanks to the money migrants sent from the United States.[24]

Migrants' income also reduced many of the practical problems people in Mexico faced. Rosario Montoya recalled that her house used to flood whenever it rained. The remittances her husband sent allowed them to buy the concrete needed to raise the floor level. Montoya explained that, thanks to her husband's departures, they were "poor but at least we are here" and a little better off than before.[25]

Mexican families' increasing reliance on the foreign income sent by migrants mirrored the Mexican economy's growing dependence on the United States as a whole. As Mexican government officials moved away from the goal of national economic independence during the 1970s and 1980s, migrants' families became more dependent on remittances. In a parallel process, as migrant men became indispensable to the economic welfare of their communities, Mexican officials began to view them as a surplus population.

Neither the normalization of migration in family life nor the economic benefits that it provided dissipated the uncertainties caused by migrants' unauthorized departures to the United States. Women whose husbands had migrated in earlier years through the Bracero Program had a sense of when they could expect the men to return. Sometimes they could even pressure their husbands into returning through official channels. Pedro Capica recalled that when his father left as a bracero, his mother and her friends whose husbands had also enrolled in the program would sit outside their homes and talk about them. Soon "the rumor spread that the men were there with American women."[26] Out of fear that their husbands would stay in the United States with their new lovers, the women complained to the Mexican Consul, who forced Capica's father and the other men to return to their homeland to see their wives before signing another contract.

After the Bracero Program ended, those who remained in Mexico had fewer recourses when they did not hear from their loved ones who had gone north. The silence could mean that the men were hiding from the INS, that they had been injured, that they had died while crossing the border, that they had been detained by U.S. officials, that they had lost their jobs, or that they had decided to leave their Mexican families behind and create new ones in the United States. Such fears haunted undocumented, transnational family life.

For some people, such as for María Acosta, the worst of these fears materialized. Her youngest son decided at age sixteen to join his brothers and his father in the United States.[27] Acosta did not want to let him go, insisting that he was too young to leave. But he paid no attention and left with the promise of only living in the United States for a short period of time. Years later, Acosta noted with pain that his promises proved true: he did not live in the United States for long, not because he returned home but because he drowned soon after leaving. Although Acosta never learned the details of his death, it is likely that her son drowned, like many other migrants, while attempting to cross the Rio Grande. For Acosta, the biggest source of pain was that she could not bury him: "He died and I never saw him again because they never brought [his body] back."[28]

Despite these calamities, in the years between 1965 and 1986, un-documented migration became a widespread phenomenon in many Mexican communities. People feared the migratory trajectory and missed their loved ones when they were abroad, but migration itself came to be seen as normal. For many, the family became a translocal institution in which members lived apart from one another.

The growth of circular, undocumented migration in the two decades following the end of the Bracero Program reshaped people's sense of community. Social networks proliferated in both countries, as did translocal connections between those who were abroad and those who remained in Mexico. Some of these changes were beneficial for those involved while others produced great pain. All, however, made migration appear normal by altering how people related to each other and how they understood their society. Even as migrants felt coerced by their social networks to engage in circular migration, which prevented them from residing permanently in locales on either side of the border, their very movement redefined the meaning of community and local space.

The growth of out-migration led many Mexicans to start thinking of their communities as existing in multiple locales and extending across national borders. Local churches in migrants' hometowns frequently spearheaded efforts to reinforce the ties between migrants and their home communities because they feared that once in the United States individuals would forget their people and flock. In 1983, local churches in Nochistlán established *El Sembrador,* a biweekly newspaper. In its second issue, the paper explained the importance of migrants to the community: "Because Our Parishes are rural they suffer from this phenomenon of Emigration and it is important to find solutions together . . . to this situation that affects us very much."[29] The newspaper hoped to act as a tool to help migrants remain in touch across national borders: "From this newspaper that will be released every 15 days we hope to communicate with people that find themselves there in *El Norte,* we invite them to communicate [with us] to tell us about their experiences and about how they find themselves."[30] The paper's attempts to promote community bonds between Mexico and the United States seem to have been successful. The January 1984 issue reported: "One of the preoccupations of this periodical is the communication with the ABSENT SONS of our communities. That is why we have inserted information directed at them throughout our broadcastings. We believe that the great majority of absent ones from Molino, Las Ánimas, Nochistlán, and San Pedro Apulco [communities in Zacatecas] receive our communication periodically."[31] Efforts such as these restructured the understanding of "community" held by those in towns of high out-migration so that it transcended territorial borders and included the diaspora.

To further strengthen migrants' ties to their home communities, many priests and local government officials started to organize festivities to honor those who had left. These events often took place on the Saint's Day of each town and came to be known as the "day of the absent sons." The term "absent sons" or *hijos austentes* originally referred only to those who migrated within Mexico, but as more individuals headed north, it also started encompassing transnational migrants. It indicated that communities thought of their migrants in terms of kinship and that they were willing to put much effort into celebrating them. In Nochistlán, the "day of the absent son" took place on the last Sunday of July. Over 15,000 Nochistlenses who had migrated within Mexico and to the United States returned to their hometown for the festivities.[32] In 1984, one of the town's local scholars, Pedro Rodríguez Lozano, wrote that the festivity created "a sense of fraternity and a reciprocal understanding among all the sons of this land, including those who . . . live abroad."[33]

In other words, the day increased the sense of community-as-family. The event began with a small procession to the local parish in which people carried religious standards, brought flowers, and played music. There, the priest gave a special mass for the absent sons. Afterward, the community congregated to eat and listen to mariachi bands. At nightfall, various groups staged dances, plays, and poems that paid homage to migrants.[34]

Beyond deliberately incorporating those who had departed from the hometown in their definition of community, those who remained behind reshaped their relationships to one another as a result of the high levels of out-migration. The process varied by region. In most towns and ranchos in Zacatecas, the wives of the men who had migrated supported one another emotionally. Although these emotional networks did not diminish the sense of absence women experienced, they did provide companionship. Commiserating with one another allowed women to forge close relationships among themselves. The women whose husbands had migrated did not form intimate friendships with other men, however, out of a sense of "respect" for their spouses.[35]

In many towns located in Michoacán, women even tried to abstain from forming attachments with other women, including with those who were undergoing similar experiences. In Michoacán, the control over women's movement was stricter than in Zacatecas, and women feared that female "friends" would gossip about their actions and portray them as unfaithful to their husbands who were in the United States. As Ana Beltrán from Santa Fe de la Laguna maintained, "There were friendships but without full trust among them. . . . You just say hello and goodbye."[36] Similarly, Laura Mazos, from Ruiz Cortines, claimed that she did not have intimate friendships in town: "Friends, friends no, I talked to everyone, they all answered with respect but I didn't like to have such intense friendships because I don't like to go to the streets, I don't like friendships all that much because that is where gossip comes from."[37] These experiences were so notable that anthropologists who worked in Michoacán in the years immediately following the end of the Bracero Program described towns of high out-migration as ones in which there was "a community of women who are alone, who stay silent, work, and wait."[38] The women experienced the silence as the deafening power of gossip.

The rising rates of migration further altered community relations in Mexico by creating new class divisions among women, allowing some to have a more leisurely life. Before men headed to the United States in such large numbers, women and children formed a vital part of the workforce. In Las Ánimas, they shopped, prepared food, delivered it to those working in the fields, weeded, harvested beans, embroidered and sold pillowcases, and, if their husbands owned businesses in town, helped run them.[39] With the growth of remittances, however, many women no longer had to perform these jobs to survive and decided to focus all their attention on domestic chores. Migrants' money even allowed some of them to purchase commodities ranging from stoves to disposable diapers that made domestic chores easier.[40] Because not all men went to the United States or sent equal amounts of remittances, some women became much richer, while others became relatively poorer when compared to the town's rising standard of living.

Even the physical space of the hometown changed as a result of migration. When walking around town, residents could easily point out which houses belonged to migrants who had made money in the United States based on their sizeable dimensions and U.S. architectural styles.[41] For instance, a family from the Tangancícuaro municipality of Michoacán that had all migrated renovated their home so that the front lawn resembled that of a suburban U.S. house.[42] Before their migration, the residence had a plot in front of it, where the family grew fruit trees and raised animals. After they remolded the house, they divided this front porch into two symmetric squares of grass with a stone pathway in between them that led to the house. Instead of providing the homeowners with food, this new front lawn provided them with prestige through its foreign style.

Hometowns also began to look different because land cultivation declined. During the 1970s, some Animeño migrants managed to legalize their status in the United States and moved there permanently. Legal status helped them get better jobs, which, in turn, allowed them to buy plots of land back in Las Ánimas. They cared about land ownership as a way of showing their status in their hometowns and their continued belonging there. While less than a third of Animeños residing in the village could afford a plot of land, over half of all legalized migrants who lived north of the border owned land in Las Ánimas.[43] These absentee landowners generally sent enough money for their land to produce food to support their close family members who still resided in the village, but they invested little money on its agricultural development.[44]

Other terrains stopped being cultivated because fewer men were available and willing to work them. In Las Ánimas in 1978 and 1979, only 33.7 percent of all men aged sixteen to fifty-four were present in the village.[45] Even those who remained found no reason to work for low wages when they had the option of heading to the United States. Manuel Jiménez recalled that during the early 1960s, when Animeños did not migrate in such high numbers, there "wasn't a single space remaining in Las Ánimas . . . that wasn't planted."[46] But once people started heading north, they thought: "Why am I going to sow? Why should we work the fields if one month [in the United States], or two, would give us enough money to pay for what we need for a year and with much less toil?"[47] When Jiménez first started migrating, he would still work the land when he returned to town, but, he said, "I started seeing that I didn't get much out of it." On his third return trip back from California he decided not to work in the village anymore. One month of U.S. wages allowed him to buy enough maize and beans for his family for a year; the money he made the rest of the year "allowed them to live a little bit better." In Las Ánimas, plots that were not highly fertile or near town were abandoned.[48]

Enraged by the situation, many landowners echoed U.S. tropes by claiming that laziness and a kind of welfare dependency on remittances were plaguing their communities. Even some landless villagers and migrants began to decry the situation by which migrants' family members refused to work. Jiménez, for example, reprovingly explained that people in Las Ánimas "became lazy. . . . They no longer wanted to work because they had children [in the United States] and their children sent them money . . . and as a result they no longer want to work." These parents, Jiménez remembered, "tried to have a cow or something like that [which was easy work] only for milk," and the land was no longer sowed.[49] Jiménez considered it acceptable for migrants not to work themselves during their return trips but viewed the refusal of the men who stayed in town to labor as a sign of indolence that was destroying community values. The reality was, in fact, more complicated. Villagers often snubbed work not only because of remittances but because the Mexican government's policies toward trade made agricultural production increasingly unprofitable.

Not only did migration alter the sense of space and community in people's hometown; it also created new networks across migrants' trajectory that extended all the way from their hometowns, to northern Mexico, to the United States. In the case of Las Ánimas, one of these communities developed in Mexico's northern city of Tijuana.[50] In 1981, approximately forty families from Las Ánimas lived there. They had no desire to move to the United States but preferred living in Mexico's northern borderlands because there were more jobs there than in their home community. These families regularly assisted prospective Animeño migrants. In particular, an old Animeño couple that had originally moved to Tijuana in the 1940s, Roberto and Adriana, ran a boardinghouse that migrants used as a springboard for border crossing.[51] Lucio Rodríguez, who stayed in the couple's house on multiple occasions on his way to the United States, said that at times up to twenty individuals would be there waiting for an opportunity to cross the border.[52] Eight or nine prospective migrants would sleep in a single room in the couple's house.[53] Roberto and Adriana would charge them only a small fee, cook them food, and help them find a smuggler.[54] The community that flourished in their home eased the stressful experience of entering the United States illegally. During the tense hours before heading to the border, Animeños congregated in the house and rooted for each other.[55] Afterward, those who failed to cross successfully would simply return to the house and start over again. In contrast, migrants from other areas who did not have this support system sometimes felt discouraged if they did not manage to cross the border after repeated attempts, and they returned to their hometowns.

The Animeño community in Tijuana tried to ensure that prospective Animeño migrants faced as few risks as possible while entering the United States illegally. In 1981, Trino González, who was fifteen years old at the time, set out from Las Ánimas to the United States. Those in Tijuana decided that he was too young to risk getting across through the hills and insisted that he go through *la línea* (an official checkpoint). After two months of housing him with multiple community members, including Roberto and Adriana, they found a *coyote* who assured them that Trino would be safe. The smuggler dressed Trino as a student and convinced Border Patrol officials that he was a rich Mexican boy who studied in a U.S. school. The officials let him though without giving him any problems.[56]

Migrants also created strong networks to help one another when they first arrived in the United States. Uriel Rojas, who moved to the United

States from the town of Moyahua, Zacatecas, recalled, "We were such a united community that when people originally came from Mexico, we would help them when they arrived, they would not have to pay food or rent for a month. Only after a month would they have to find the way to work to be able to pay for themselves."[57] The same was the case for Animeños who had an implicit two-month rule during which they would host their co-villagers.[58] When Trino's older brother, Francisco, first arrived in South San Francisco, he stayed in a basement room in the house of his aunt who already lived there. By the time Trino himself arrived in the United States, Francisco had moved into a three-bedroom house that he rented with approximately ten other Animeño migrants, and Trino joined them. At first, the group did not charge him rent and provided him with all his meals. After some days, they helped him find a job washing dishes. Once Trino started making money, he began paying for his own food and board. These networks eased and normalized the migratory process.[59]

Migrant communities in the United States varied by location. In agricultural settings, migrants lived in very close quarters. Because of the seasonal nature of the work, very few male farm laborers attempted to bring their wives and families with them from Mexico. As such, the communities they formed in the United States were markedly male-centered. In the late 1970s, 72.8 percent of Animeño workers residing in rural communities in the United States were male.[60] In the agricultural town of Bell Gardens, they all resided in a single apartment complex, where five men crowded into two-bedroom apartments.[61] These tight enclosures meant that the men would wake up, have meals, work, wash their clothes, and rest together. The same was true for migrants from other communities. Jorge Zavala, who migrated from Churintzio, Michoacán, recalls that when working on farms in California and Washington, he and the other male workers woke up early to have breakfast and arrive in the fields by 7 AM.[62] They then worked until 5 PM, when they returned home to cook. After eating they were too exhausted to do anything else. On Sundays, their only day off, they would generally stay in their quarters, "talking with others who lived there and doing laundry." Not only were they too tired to leave, but they were also far away from towns and afraid of encountering immigration officials. Approximately once every three months, however, when a band came from Mexico to play near where they resided, the men would garner energy and put fears aside to go see the performance. Once there, they would also try to "meet women and look for a girlfriend."[63] The infrequency of these outings, however, meant that migrants' social life typically revolved around each other. As they joked, suffered, and ate their meals together, they formed strong connections.

Urban undocumented workers tended to interact with more people than those in the countryside. Although most of them were also male, there were more undocumented women and children in cities than in agricultural settings. For example, in the late 1970s, 62 percent of Animeños in cities were men, and 38 percent were women.[64] As in rural areas, urban migrants tended to live close to others from their hometowns. Animeños who moved to East Los Angeles generally lived within a few blocks' radius of one another.[65] This allowed them to spend much time together. On weekends, when they knew immigration officials were not around, they organized gatherings and parties in their homes or at parks. Everyone brought food to share, which meant that those who could not afford healthy food could eat better than they did regularly.

Migrants often tried to stay connected with those from their hometown who lived in other parts of the United States. Because Animeños migrated to multiple locations in California, they all got together in either Los Angeles or South San Francisco, where most of them lived, on an annual or biannual basis to play baseball. Those who came from out of town stayed in the already crowded apartments of their friends and family members. Although baseball served as the official rallying call to get together, these trips were understood as true revelries by the community. These *pachangas,* or parties, lasted two or three days as Animeños got together, saw family members and friends, played baseball, and ate together in the park.[66] On Saturday night, they all headed to a nightclub to dance together. Through these activities, Animeños formed a solid community that spanned across multiple cities and agricultural areas in the United States.

Although many of the activities that Animeños performed during these get-togethers were divided by gender lines, both men and women recall them as establishing unity rather than division. Only men played baseball while women, children, and non-playing men watched; women did all the cooking and even formed teams to prepare food for all attendees. For most, these gender divisions seemed natural. They simply extended everyday practices to these particular occasions. What people remember from these get-togethers as being out of the ordinary was the sense that their community expanded, took care of everybody, and diminished their sense of being far away from home. Feliciana Ramírez's most powerful memory of these events was the feeling of sharing that she experienced when she and the other cooks brought out food for all to eat.[67]

Migrants also developed a broad community with those who originated from other parts of Mexico, which they would not have done if they had remained in their hometown. Because the Animeño community that was dispersed throughout California only got together once or twice a year to play baseball, Animeños in South San Francisco started to play more regularly with migrants who came from other parts of Mexico but who lived closer to them.[68] Animeños residing in South San Francisco played on an almost-weekly basis with a team of migrants who had migrated from Las Cañadas, Jalisco, and who lived only two miles away, in the city of San Bruno. Although migrants from these communities lived nearby, and Las Cañadas was close to Las Ánimas, the two sets of migrants didn't actually know one another until they began playing baseball in the United States. Eventually, migrants from other parts of Mexico who lived near South San Francisco also started playing. Together, they formed La Liga de la Amistad (The League of Friendship), which provided a space for those who came from towns in the states of Zacatecas, Jalisco, Sinaloa, and Veracruz to meet up to play on the weekends when INS officials were not around. After the games, they ate lunch together, conversed about their daily lives, and ultimately developed deep ties. Although migrants from the different hometowns competed against one another—and cared deeply about winning—their regular meetings also helped them build a single, broader, Mexican community out of their distinctive ones.

The solidarity and networks that Animeños formed in the name of baseball extended back to Las Ánimas proper. When visiting the rancho in the 1960s, Lucio Rodríguez realized that many young men in his hometown could not afford the balls, bats, and mitts they needed to play.[69] He decided to raise funds among the Animeños who lived in California to help those back home. Hundreds of villagers contributed significant donations, and others joined his organizing efforts. A group of girls in Los Angeles collected donations at rodeo events and sold food and aguas frescas. By the 1980s, migrants had raised enough money to

Las Ánimas baseball team. Lucio Rodríguez is the team manager. Photograph from the personal archives of Raúl Jiménez.

buy land and build a sports field in their hometown.[70] The interest and financial support of those in California changed the nature of baseball in Las Ánimas. It went from being a game played informally with old equipment in a rocky and muddy terrain to one played by an official town team, *Los Arrieros* [The Muleteers], with quality bats and mitts on a regulation baseball field. Playing styles also began to change. According to Rodríguez, the team in Las Ánimas played with a faster pitch than that of Animeños in California but would become slower when a lot of migrants returned home.

As with baseball, *charrería* (horsemanship) provided a space for migrants to form a distinct translocal and multi-local community and culture. Uriel Rojas, who migrated continuously between Zacatecas and California during the 1960s and 1970s, joined a group that practiced horsemanship during his stays in the United States. *Charrería* allowed men like Rojas to engage in a pastime that they had practiced in their hometown and to meet with Mexicans who had migrated from different parts of Mexico. "We were people that came from a ranch. My grandparents and parents had ranches and we were basically raised among horses and once one arrived here one missed that," Rojas explained. "So I informed myself of where there were horses or horsemanship events . . . to remember the times back there." Then, "Sunday after Sunday or on other days that we went to practice, we would build friendships there and soon one invited you here and someone else there," and a community was built.[71] The Los Angeles *charro* network to which Rojas belonged had connections to other *charro* communities in the United States and Mexico: "We were invited to *charrear* all the way from San Isidro, to Riverside . . . to Phoenix, to multiple locations in the interior of Mexico from Guadalajara to Zacatecas."[72]

Catholic Mass presented another opportunity for migrants to meet up and strengthen community ties, particularly for women. In general, women attended Church more regularly than men. According to Jorge Medina, most Animeño men living in South San Francisco would fraternize by "telling each other jokes, drinking a beer, and gossiping" while "women would go to Mass" and there they "would joke and talk to each other and then go to eat."[73] Even though in the United States men attended Church less regularly than in Mexico and some migrants converted to Protestantism, for many individuals, Catholicism remained a pillar of community building. It allowed them to practice their faith as they had back home and to meet up with friends and family members on a weekly basis. Their feeling of belonging to U.S. parishes increased in towns like South San Francisco, where they could attend mass in Spanish.

While engaging in these various quotidian social activities and meeting other Mexicans, migrants created a sense of *Mexicanidad* from the ground up that was detached from official state initiatives. Since at least the early 1930s, Mexican authorities had hoped that U.S.-bound migration would "create 'Mexicans' out of former mestizo villagers." Manuel Gamio, the preeminent Mexican anthropologist at the time, had argued that before migrating to the United States, "the natives or Mestizos" had "not much notion of their nationality or their country," knowing only about the particular town or region where they were born. Abroad, they learned "what their mother country means."[74] By the mid-1970s, the Mexican government had given up its attempts to use short-term migration to modernize citizens and build up their identification with the Mexican nation-state. In part, these efforts were no longer needed, as most of those who migrated in the post-Bracero period already identified with Mexico before heading north. Yet even in the 1970s, most migrants still identified with their hometowns, or *patrias chicas,* more than they did with the Mexican nation-state. Gregorio Casillas recalled, "One feels one hundred percent Mexican, particularly when one is outside of the country," but he also insisted that his primary geographic loyalty rested with his hometown, Guadalupe Victoria.[75] The affective community of Mexicans in the United States did not replace migrants' primary attachment to their hometowns, but it did increase their identification with Mexico as a whole.

Even though migrants' networks in the United States normalized the migratory experience and made the process easier for most individuals, migrant communities should not be romanticized. As in many social systems, migrant communities experienced fractures, practiced forms of exclusion, and enforced gender and racial norms. For example, a deep fissure developed in the migrant community of South San Francisco. Young migrants from Las Ánimas and those from Aguililla, Michoacán, both of whom lived in the area, regularly waged war against each other. "Almost every time we saw one another we would come to blows," recalled Epigmenio Jiménez.[76] The skirmishes even took place in church. On one occasion, the Catholic church in South San Francisco organized a dance to raise funds. Soon after the event began, migrants from Las Ánimas and those from Aguililla started calling each other names, which soon turned into punches. Approximately thirty men became engaged in the fight, and the police had to be called. Although the brawls began over women, as those from each group believed that the Latinas who lived in town should pay exclusive attention to them, racial issues probably also played a role. When explaining some of the clashes that occurred between migrants from Las Ánimas and those from Michoacán, Jiménez recalled that Michoacanos were "not as civilized as we were."[77] This belief was most likely grounded in the widely held notion that while Zacatecanos were primarily mestizos, Michoacanos were primarily indigenous. The colonially inherited ethno-racial system in Mexico ranked indigenous people below mestizos and cast them as "uncivilized."

Indigenous individuals regularly experienced exclusion in mestizo-dominated migrant communities. Because migrants found being a part of a strong network in the United States indispensable to their well-being, many indigenous people misrepresented themselves in order to fit in with the group. Purépecha workers who migrated from the town of San

Andrés, Michoacán, recall trying to pass as mestizo in the United States. In Mexico, they had not had to perform as mestizo because, up until the early 1980s, they only rarely encountered nonindigenous Mexicans. Most communities around San Andrés were also Purépecha, and San Andresinos found it too expensive to travel much farther. But once they headed to the United States, they consistently met Mexicans from other regions. When in front of them, they tried to hide their indigenous heritage and culture. Raúl Sánchez, who migrated in the early 1980s, recalled that when he and his friends crossed the border, they spoke in Spanish rather than in their native Tarascan language. This continued once they were living in the United States: "Nobody knew [that we were indigenous] because there we didn't talk [in our native language] like we do here [in San Ándres]."[78] According to Sánchez, they tried to hide their identities "because [mestizos] would immediately mock you" if they found out "we were Purépechas." To do this, he recalled, "We only spoke in Tarasco among ourselves."[79] Sometimes, however, their accent would reveal their background.

San Andresino migrants did not just attempt to "pass" from one unchanging culture to another. During the course of the 1970s and early 1980s, San Andresinos had increasing access to public education, which meant that more children learned Spanish as the Mexican government hoped to homogenize its citizens though public education. While in the United States indigenous migrants were trying to hide their identification with a culture that was considered backward and unchanging, the culture in their hometowns was in constant flux. Moreover, like mestizo migrants, indigenous ones altered some of their customs after spending time abroad. José Domingo Magaña explained that before migrating he only knew Tarascan; he learned Spanish in the United States after spending time with other migrants.[80] In other words, he learned Mexico's official language abroad. When he and other San Andresinos returned home, they taught Spanish to other villagers who hadn't learned it.

For their part, single women who migrated by themselves found it harder to belong in migrant communities in the United States because they regularly worked as domestic laborers in spaces where their employers could limit their social interactions.[81] On occasion, Mexican women who did not have the resources required to cross the border agreed to be transported into the United States by highly organized smuggling rings under the condition that they would pay for their "transportation fees" with their work in the United States. Once they were north of the border, *coyotes* would sell them to employers, who would then force them to work as indentured servants until they paid off their debt. According to migrant organizers and federal investigators and prosecutors, cases of women being sold and forced to work as domestic laborers happened "all too often."[82] A *New York Times* article published in 1980 reported that there were "uncounted thousands" of them.[83] The article told the story of a twenty-two-year-old Mexican woman who had been forced to become a live-in domestic worker for a wealthy Nevada family. "They held her in the house. . . . She worked from sun-up to way after dark. She requested that her wages be sent to her father in Mexico. No money was ever sent to her father. This went on for about a year and a half. Then she flipped—she became insane, broke out of the house and ran down the street. That's when the Border Patrol got her."[84]

Because domestic workers labored in their employer's house, they had restricted access to the social relationships that could help them leave exploitative situations. In the mid-1980s, the Magañas, a local family in San Andrés, approached Eva and Rafael Villalobos in their hometown and asked them to allow their daughter, Sara, to go to *El Norte*. The Magañas insisted that they would ensure Sara's safe passage to the United States and would then find her a job as a domestic worker in Oregon so that she could pay off her debt to them and send money back to her family. Eva recalled, "They came and asked us. They said you should let her go, she will send you dollars, we will pay her in dollars, and there she will be very happy."[85] Eva and Rafael needed the money, trusted that the Magañas would take care of their daughter, and knew of the extensive migrant community in the United States. However, even though Sara migrated with a local family, her position as a domestic worker separated her from the rest of the San Andresino community in the United States. Thus when she found herself in trouble, she did not turn to other migrants for help or contact her parents back home. A couple of months after her arrival in Oregon, Eva and Rafael found out that Sara's employers had fired her and that she was trying to pay off her debt to the Magañas by engaging in sex work. According to the rumors, she "was going to the canteens after men and took their money."[86] Her work and acquired reputation reinforced her exclusion from the community networks that could have helped her leave that world.

Despite its fractures and exclusions, migrant communities normalized migration and prompted many individuals to make the trip north. The new modes of emotional, practical, and financial support people developed assisted and nourished those who crossed the border as well as those who remained in Mexico. Unintentionally, these networks countered the pressures migrants felt at the local level. While migrants' own families and communities pushed them to leave and return to their hometowns on a regular basis, their migration reconstructed the very meanings of family, community, and local space. Migrants acquired partial inclusion and became central figures in the multiple places where they lived, but only as long as they spent some of their time working in the United States.

In a similar way, migrants found that living north of the border allowed them to challenge Mexican officials' perception that they were superfluous. Their migration bound them to the United States but cast them as economically indispensable actors in Mexico.

5

....

SUPPORTING THE HOMETOWN
FROM ABROAD

I N 1987, GREGORIO CASILLAS returned to Guadalupe Victoria, a small rancho in the state of Zacatecas, as he had done many times before.[1] He proudly noted how his long hours of work in the Club Social Guadalupe Victoria had made nearly unrecognizable the hometown he had left when he first migrated in 1948. The club, formed in 1962 by migrants residing in Los Angeles, aimed to send aid to improve the rancho. By 1987, it had paved the main street, built a clinic, fenced the school, installed benches in the church, erected electric power lines, provided potable water, and created a program that helped the town's elderly attain their basic needs.[2] Surveying the scene, Casillas could see how he was still a significant presence in Guadalupe Victoria, despite his frequent absence.

Like the Club Social Guadalupe Victoria, which so transformed the small hamlet in Zacatecas, many other clubs developed in Los Angeles from the 1960s onward around the idea of providing resources south of the border. During these years, migrants countered the sense of exclusion they experienced when their families and communities pressured them to head north by unwittingly redefining the meanings of "family," "hometown," and "community." In turn, through their club activism, migrants intentionally challenged the idea that they were economically superfluous to their country of origin.

Clubs turned migrants into indispensable economic agents in Mexico, thus defying Mexican policymakers' beliefs that working-class men from the Central Plateau region were a surplus population. Club activities also

countered policymakers' notion that migration represented a partial solution to Mexico's economic problems. Migrants hoped that the resources
they sent home would help address the poverty in Mexico that had originally led them to migrate, saving others from having to take that path.
By building up Mexico, migrants affirmed that Mexicans ought to be
able to attain a minimum standard of living in their country of origin
without having to go to the United States illegally.

Clubs further challenged Mexico's government by acting like an extraterritorial welfare state. After the Mexican Revolution, the ruling
party, the PRI (Institutional Revolutionary Party), established itself as
the promoter of a Mexican welfare state.[3] It aimed to follow the example
of President Lázaro Cardenas (1934–1940), who had instituted agrarian
reform, leftist education, and economic nationalism. The ideal of the
Mexican welfare state rested on the notion that all Mexicans ought to
have their basic necessities satisfied.[4] Yet despite the PRI's rhetoric, it often
failed to guarantee the fundamental necessities of life, forcing private
associations to assume some state duties. Of all the projects adopted by
the Club Social Guadalupe Victoria, for instance, only the restoration of
the church fell outside the purview of the state's recognized responsibilities. Taking care of the elderly, building clinics, fencing schools, paving
roads, and providing electricity and running water should have been—
according to the PRI's own credo—tasks performed by the government,
not by migrants.

Categorizing clubs as an extraterritorial welfare state defies traditional
definitions of the welfare state in two important ways. First, the welfare state is generally associated with government assistance, but clas-
sifying it only as a set of government programs obscures "the true size
and scope of [the] welfare state" because it "mistakenly excludes the vast
array of private activities that address economic security."[5] Second, many
club activities, including the construction of infrastructure, are not traditionally associated with the responsibilities of the welfare state. However, migrants and community members in Mexico understood these
projects as similar to providing medical assistance to the sick and aid
and insurance to the poor. In areas of Mexico that had been disregarded
by the government's development plans, club projects were conceived as
a means of ensuring the economic security and well-being of all members of society. Equally important, club members viewed their activities

as ones that they had to perform as a result of the Mexican government's inaction and lack of support to areas of high out-migration. They identified the work they were doing as the work that Mexico's supposed welfare state should have been performing.

Ironically, even as migrants sought to build up their hometowns so that Mexicans could live there with a decent standard of living, their activities ended up promoting the view that migrating was the best path to achieve partial inclusion in their communities. Not only did migrants' work in clubs provide them with political power in Mexico that they would not have had if they had remained in their home country, but it also helped them establish a sense of belonging north of the border. The social network migrants built allowed them to fight against the isolation they experienced in the United States. Equally important, the world that migrants built in Los Angeles was sometimes more inclusive than their world back in Mexico. Because club activists recruited members who came from marginalized groups, the club setting gave individuals who were traditionally discriminated against due to their class background, gender, legal status, or ethnicity the tools to insist on their inclusion and to assert political power in the United States.

The club activism that took place in the years between the early 1960s and the mid-1980s reveals how migrant activists challenged exclusionary notions of where they ought to reside. These clubs were not the first organizations formed by those in the United States to improve the lives of fellow ethnic Mexicans. Since at least the 1840s, Californios had developed mutual aid societies to assist one another.[6] These *mutualistas* helped members find jobs and provided them with loans, economic assistance, and medical insurance.[7] Some mutualistas engaged with political developments south of the border, and some, including the Alianza Hispano-Americana, even formed affiliate lodges in Mexico.[8] In their provision of aid, community-building efforts, and civic-mindedness, mutual aid societies resembled and paved the way for the clubs that developed later. But unlike the social clubs of the 1960s onward, the mutualistas prioritized helping their own members, while the primary goal of the clubs was to improve life in migrants' hometowns.

Club activity changed dramatically after the mid-1980s. By then, Mexican government officials realized that the clubs had become too powerful and sought to become involved in their projects by developing

plans to match the funds that clubs sent for the betterment of communities. State involvement markedly increased the influence of migrant
associations. As such, most scholarship on these clubs—which sociolo-
gists refer to by the contemporary terms hometown associations (HTAs)
or *clubes de oriundos*—focuses on the late 1980s onward.[9] However, as club
activists and many HTA scholars have argued, Mexican politicians used
their newly developed relationship with clubs to co-opt migrants' visions
of development and community.[10] After the mid-1980s, migrants could
no longer claim to be autonomous from state projects, but before then,
migrants used clubs to confront the displacement that they experienced
in both nation-states.

Gregorio Casillas's father, officially known as Gregorio Casillas Jaime,
grew up in Guadalupe Victoria, a small rancho in the state of Zacatecas,
in the early twentieth century.[11] In Guadalupe Victoria, Casillas Jaime
felt comfortable, safe, and at home—feelings that were particularly valued
in the aftermath of Mexico's revolutionary turmoil. Still, in the early
1920s, he opted to leave his hometown in search of better economic opportunities. He could have headed to one of Mexico's growing cities,
but Casillas Jaime did not have strong feelings of attachment to his
country. During this period, the Mexican nation-state had not yet fully
materialized, and individuals like Casillas Jaime identified with their
patrias chicas—in his case Guadalupe Victoria—rather than with Mexico.[12]
For Casillas Jaime, the choice was clear. If he was going to leave his
rancho, he would go to the place that provided him with the greatest
economic prospects: Los Angeles. Initially, the move seemed profitable.
Upon his arrival and settlement, Casillas Jaime started a grocery store,
and he markedly increased his standard of living. However, by the end
of the decade, with the start of the Great Depression, Casillas Jaime
could no longer support himself in the United States. Like thousands of
other Mexicans living in Los Angeles, he voluntarily repatriated with
the help of the Mexican consulate.[13]

In 1932, only a year after his father returned to Mexico, Gregorio
Casillas was born. During Gregorio's childhood, his father did not return to the United States, but like many other Mexicans, his family
continually relocated within Mexico. The rise of internal migration
during the early 1940s was so impressive that local churches worried it
would destroy their economic base and erode people's faith. In response,

they set out to organize migrants into domestic hometown associations in an attempt to keep them attached to their local churches.[14] Although Casillas's family did not partake in the activities of local HTAs, he grew up in a world in which migrants remained attached to their place of origin through voluntary associations.

In 1948, Gregorio Casillas decided that instead of continuing to migrate domestically, he would follow in his father's footsteps and head to the United States. During this time, many men migrated as part of the Bracero Program, but Casillas was still too young to become an official contract worker. Thus he decided to cross the border without papers. In the United States, he first labored in tomato, cotton, and plum fields, but after a couple of years he moved to Los Angeles, where he worked as a carpenter.[15] In both the fields and the city, Casillas felt estranged from American society, but as he explained, "there was much more work [there than in Mexico], and it was well paid," an opportunity that he could not let pass.

According to Casillas, it was migrants' sense of isolation and lack of belonging in the United States, rather than the example of domestic hometown associations, that led him and other migrants to form a *club social* in Los Angeles. Every Sunday, migrants from his hometown got together to have breakfast at Las Delicias, a restaurant owned by Jesús Durán, a Guadalupe Victoria native himself. The men often reminisced about their hometown, informing each other of any news they had heard. They would ask one another: "Hey did you hear that there were problems with that? The lack of water is such a problem," and they would remember "that old man who is sixty or seventy years old [and] cannot even afford food."[16] It was during one of these breakfast reunions that the idea to form one of the first clubs developed. On one Sunday in 1962, the members of the group decided to move beyond chatter and to pool their money to help the needy elders in the town. They called their new organization Club Social Guadalupe Victoria. The migrants hoped the group would make their hometown more economically inclusive while also providing those who were in the United States with more opportunities to meet and establish their sense of belonging north of the border.

Clubs of migrants from the state of Zacatecas were not new. By 1962, three other such clubs already existed in Los Angeles: Club Social Fresnillo, Club Zacatecanos, and Club Social Jalpense.[17] For the most part, however, these helped individuals in Los Angeles rather than sending resources back to Mexico. According to Casillas, although he knew about the Club Jalpense (Guadalupe Victoria is located in the Jalpa Municipality), he saw it primarily as a group that organized recreational activities. Antonio Galarza Viramontes, a member of the Club Social Jalpense, recalls that, during that period, the organization's activities generally consisted of helping needy Jalpenses living in Los Angeles. While extremely important for the well-being of migrants, these groups did not focus on helping communities in Mexico as the *clubes sociales* that came later did.

Sending money to Mexico was not new either. Migrants had remitted money to their families south of the border since the start of the twentieth century to increase their relatives' ability to purchase consumer goods.[18] This financial help radically improved many Mexicans' standard of living, but it was not designed to promote the development of communities as a whole.[19] The activists who created new organizations dedicated to providing aid to their hometowns did not have close relatives in Mexico to whom they needed to send remittances. They could use their resources to aid their home communities.

Clubs designed to send money back to Mexico had formed in other cities, and some did so even earlier than the 1960s, but it was the Angelino organizations that developed from the 1960s onward that first managed to introduce vast changes in Mexican hometowns and attain political power. Migratory patterns aided the development of clubs in Los Angeles. Clubs were composed almost strictly of Mexican-born individuals at a time when approximately 30 percent of all Mexican migrants moved to Los Angeles.[20] Within Los Angeles, most club activists lived and worked in the contiguous eastside enclaves of Boyle Heights, Lincoln Heights, and East Los Angeles.[21] This made it easier for them to meet and organize.

Boyle Heights had provided some club founders with powerful examples of community organizing. Although by the 1960s the neighborhood's diversity had declined, during the 1950s, Boyle Heights "became something of an ideological bunker," where residents remained committed to building a new multiracial community with a radical ideology.[22] In 1949, the Soto-Michigan Jewish Community Center organized the first Friendship Festival to "bring together Mexican, Japanese, Negro, and Jewish youth in a cooperative venture."[23] They also organized events with B'nai

B'rith, the American Jewish Congress, the Japanese American Citizens League (JACL), and the Community Services Organization (CSO), which primarily served ethnic Mexicans. Beyond the ethnic diversity, many minorities in Boyle Heights worked to remain attached to their perceived homelands. For instance, the Jewish people living in the neighborhood were often active Zionists.[24] In the 1960s and 1970s, Chicano/a activism erupted in the area with the East Los Angeles blowouts of 1968, the Chicano Moratorium of 1970, and the growth of the Brown Berets. Club members could also look at the rise of the United Farm Workers (UFW) and at the black civil rights movements for inspiration. But as foreigners who remained attached to Mexico and who feared protesting because they were often undocumented, club members sought other ways to bring about change.

When the Club Social Guadalupe Victoria first started, organizers attempted to raise funds to send to Mexico by coordinating small-scale social affairs, such as meals in a member's house or picnics in Lincoln Park, which was located near where most migrants lived and worked.[25] These activities were generally familial affairs because most of the individuals who formed part of the club world had already established deep roots in the United States. This meant that there were many more women and families among club activists than there were in the population of Mexican migrants at large. The family-friendly get-togethers that migrants organized were highly successful. Activists would donate and cook food and sell it at the gatherings to raise money. Casillas estimates that the amount collected ranged from US$200 to US$1,000 per event, a considerable sum in 1960s Mexico.[26]

Migrants from other communities in Mexico soon heard about the club's projects and started to create their own organizations to send money to their respective hometowns. In the mid-1960s, several groups started meeting at La Casa del Mexicano, an impressive building with fifty-foot ceilings and a cupola, which had been bought by the Comité de Beneficencia Mexicana, a Mexican charity organization. It was in La Casa that club culture developed, continuing a long tradition of activism in the neighborhood. As fledgling organizations, clubs appeared and disappeared rapidly, and membership fluctuated. Because of such variations, it is hard to trace their growth. During the late 1960s and early 1970s, the number of dues-paying affiliates in these clubs ranged from

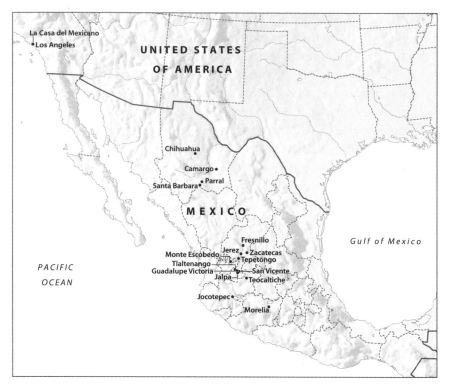

Hometowns represented in the *clubes sociales* of La Casa del Mexicano.

sixteen to sixty-five, with an average of thirty-five members.[27] At least twenty clubs met at La Casa del Mexicano in 1968.[28] By 1975, the number had risen to thirty-two, but eleven of the groups established in 1968 had either disappeared or ceased to be involved with La Casa. According to activists, the number of groups grew from the mid-1970s onward.[29]

Despite their instability, the surviving clubs organized a collegial and visible community that worked to support Mexican towns. The club culture that took shape in La Casa del Mexicano revolved around meetings and dances. At meetings, members of each club would gather to coordinate the everyday affairs of the organizations. Once a year they would elect club officers, including a president, vice president, secretary, treasurer, and multiple coordinators.[30] On the weekends, clubs organized lively parties at La Casa to raise funds. These were large family events with 200 to 350 attendees.[31] At a typical party, members from all Los

Angeles clubs showed up with their families and friends, creating a convivial atmosphere in which clubs supported one another. Members of the hosting club cooked and supplied food for free to all the guests, who paid for admission and for alcoholic beverages. The parties generally began at 8:00 PM and ended at 2:00 AM. Children would fall asleep on the chairs or under the tables as their parents laughed, danced, and conversed until the music ended.[32] Once they finished, migrants left with a renewed sense of community and belonging; the hosting club with a profit of as much as US$600.[33]

Clubs frequently donated the money they collected at these parties to preexisting organizations in Mexico, particularly to religious groups that offered social services. In 1968, for instance, multiple groups joined together in an effort to support an orphanage that was led by the Dominican Sisters in Tampico.[34] Other clubs made contributions to the Club de Leones (Lions Club).[35] Donating money to organizations that already operated in Mexico, and which migrants knew, made clubs' tasks easier, as they did not have to worry about the mechanics of aid distribution.

However, club members in Los Angeles sometimes wanted to have full control over the resources. They regularly created club branches in Mexico with local "agents" in charge of managing the funds sent from Los Angeles. For example, the Club Social Guadalupe Victoria sent checks to club agents residing in the rancho in Zacatecas. These agents then distributed it to the elderly on a weekly basis.[36] If the club in Los Angeles mailed more than expected, club agents in Guadalupe Victoria would make breakfasts or purchase clothes, blankets, and other items for the needy. If the elderly became sick, agents would take them to a doctor and buy their medicines. Migrants in the United States raised money, and club representatives in Mexico ensured that it was appropriately distributed. Together, they formed a welfare system that guaranteed that the basic necessities of the rancho's most vulnerable people were met.

No known records remain of how club agents in Mexico decided who to aid or if they imposed behavioral restrictions when making such decisions. Charity organizations, including some of those run by people of color in the United States, have a long history of policing the behavior of those they support and denying aid to those they consider "unfit."[37] But when asked how they chose which elderly individuals to support, Luciano Solís, who was in charge of the operations of the Club Guadalupe Victoria in Mexico, recalled that they would simply "see who was further behind, who could not work."[38] He insisted that they did not impose any requirements on them: "One would simply see if that person truly needed help." The things that they would "look at" were whether the person "had something to eat, or not, or whether the person was sick."[39] Nevertheless, this does not necessarily mean that the group dispensed aid without prejudice.

In fact, the way in which clubs elected representatives in Mexico reveals that they were well aware of notions of respectability. Rather than allowing town residents to choose local club agents, migrants selected those they considered most responsible and wealthy. In Guadalupe Victoria, they designated Asunción Miramontes as the first president of the club's local committee because, in the words of Luciano Solís, "he was a very serious man . . . very respectable."[40]

Even though clubs handpicked their agents, accusations of theft occurred often. Some villagers in Guadalupe Victoria accused Solís and the other agents of stealing money. Town residents would bicker: "They are there out of convenience; they keep some of the money."[41] The agents of the Club Teocaltiche, which ran a public dispensary in the town, faced similar quandaries. On October 9, 1968, they sent a letter to Luis Córdova, the president of the Club Social Teocaltiche in Los Angeles, explaining that some of the town's residents who sold medicines opposed the public dispensary because it took their business away and that others accused the committee of embezzlement.[42] In February 1970, the agents could no longer withstand the town's criticisms. Repeating concerns similar to those of Luciano Solís, the agents in Teocaltiche again wrote to Luis Córdova, telling him that they were handing over the administration of the public dispensary to the town's priest because they had "experienced that those who do something good only received criticism as payment."[43] Local communities' strong suspicion that individuals became club representatives to misappropriate resources dissuaded many from taking these jobs.

The suspicion cast on club members in Mexico meant that clubs did not develop into a powerful social movement south of the border. Beyond the frequent accusations against agents, many locals saw little reason to take a position because of the limited power that these conferred. Joining the board of a group in Los Angeles provided migrants with an aura of respectability and authority within the club culture; being one of its agents in Mexico, however, provided no such benefits.

In their 1968 letter to Luis Córdova, the members of the Teocaltiche public dispensary requested that club representatives in Los Angeles "come by the Dispensary [in Mexico] to get to know in depth its way of functioning, so that they can comment and even demand responsibilities from us."[44] In their 1970 letter, which announced that they were closing down, they reported that they had "archived everything, writing down everything until the last payment that we made, and would be ready to explain any misunderstanding."[45] While service as president of the Club Teocaltiche in Los Angeles provided Luis Córdova with the capacity to decide the club's actions, for Ernesto Ríos González, his tenure as the president of the public dispensary only placed him under others' authority and suspicions.[46]

Club members in Mexico possessed little power, even in cases in which they complained to those in Los Angeles. On June 14, 1972, for instance, Antonio Solanes wrote to Raúl Villarreal from Ciudad Jiménez in Chihuahua and protested that "some time ago I wrote to you asking about the matter of the ambulance of the Red Cross of Jiménez, since people here are already eating me alive . . . because I have not accomplished what was planned. . . . Today I am bothering you again to beg if we can still count on your spontaneous offering . . . for the Red Cross."[47] Even such a letter of protest reveals that club members in Mexico were fully dependent on the actions of migrants in Los Angeles for both their own activism and their reputation.

Serving as a club agent in Mexico lacked the social benefits of club membership in Los Angeles. Migrants in the United States used the clubs as an opportunity to socialize with others from their hometowns. In communities in Mexico, residents did not create a broad social movement because they did not experience the same solitude, discrimination, or need to remain attached to hometowns that had pushed those in Los Angeles to organize. They felt that it was the state's responsibility to improve the communities—and that there was little that they could do to pressure the government.[48] They relied on migrants because, with their money, those abroad were in a better position to influence state decisions.

In an unpublished memoir, Raúl Villarreal, who was one of the most visible participants in the club setting, presents a strong critique of the Mexican state, writing that his story is one "of a simple dishwasher" from a Los Angeles restaurant who, by working in clubs, ended up "helping the people" of Mexico "more than the government itself."[49] Through their activities, clubs took on some of the responsibilities of the Mexican government, becoming a kind of extraterritorial welfare state. In the 1970s, Mexico's top government officials began to take the view that Mexico's population was too large and sought to address this perceived surplus by encouraging out-migration; in Los Angeles, the very migrants deemed superfluous by this view organized to transform the structural socioeconomic problems they saw as the true roots of Mexico's difficulties—problems the Mexican government was ignoring.

The members of the club Unión de Mexicanos y Residentes en el Extranjero (UMRE) spoke clearly of their perception that the Mexican government was failing working-class communities and leaving men with few options other than migrating. In a letter sent to President Gustavo Díaz Ordaz, Jesús Ortega, the group's principal signatory, explained that he, "like thousands of Mexican citizens who reside in this side of the border," longed "to be able one day to save enough money with which to establish a business [in Mexico]."[50] They "aimed to return to their home country without having to lend [their] services as employees or factory workers" since in Mexico, unlike in the United States, laborers received "miserable wages, small insurance coverage, and few loans." Ortega asserted that most migrants who wished to return found themselves "in a pessimistic mood, caused by a sense of hopelessness" that was augmented by their "knowledge of the imbalances and injustices that dominate the governmental machinery and, more generally, all of Mexico's social environment."[51] Ortega claimed that the prevalence of these injustices not only forced Mexicans to remain abroad, despite their desire to return, but also pushed thousands of others to continue emigrating.

UMRE members suggested creating businesses in Mexico that would allow migrants to return to their home country. Specifically, they wanted to build a poultry farm in Tijuana that would provide club members with jobs. According to UMRE plans, migrant activists would invest half of the necessary money, and the federal government would provide the other half. Ortega described the many benefits that such a farm would bring to Mexico, including the creation of jobs and the entrance of foreign currency. He ended the letter by emphasizing that "uniting the government with this important mass of Mexicans [living in the United

States]—in order to give life to this project capable of amplifying . . . and generating a force that helps our people solve its economic and unemployment problems—would fulfill the greatest longing of my life."[52] Ortega and the other eighteen migrants who signed the letter dreamed of establishing a true democracy in which men like them were not viewed as a surplus population but were able to reside with economic dignity in their own country.

Most clubs did not have the creation of jobs as an explicit goal. Instead, they aimed to raise money in the United States to aid Mexican communities to provide all villagers with economic well-being and inclusion. For example, the Club Social Fresnillo sent Mex$40,000 (US$3,200) between 1968 and 1970 to support an orphanage.[53] Similarly, in 1968 the Club Social Teocaltiche donated money to fund a public dispensary to distribute medicine to the poor. That year, the club remitted Mex$20,698 (US$1,656) to buy all the medicines needed by the community.[54] In 1970, the Teocaltiche group also sought to fence the town's public kindergarten for the children's safety.[55]

In 1975, the Club Social Santa Rosalía Camargo, Chihuahua, started a campaign to aid Mexican citizen Antonio Leyva Ayala, from Camargo, Chihuahua. Leyva Ayala could not afford the orthopedic leg he needed.[56] The club raised enough funds for Leyva Ayala's surgery, his physical therapy, and his rent and food for two months. Responding to their service on his behalf, Leyva Ayala wrote to individual members of the club, expressing his deep gratitude for their efforts, along with a hint of the personal toll that charity took on him. He ended his letter by saying, "I can do nothing more apart from thanking you for the time you waste reading these lines that unfortunately are always a bother to you."[57]

Club members realized that they were taking on the roles of the state but argued that if they did not, the Mexican government would not either. As Gregorio Casillas explained when reflecting back on the clubs, "It is the government's obligation to provide what the people or the community . . . needs like electric light . . . clinics, schools, but unfortunately they don't do it, so we had to intervene."[58] When the Mexican government, despite raising taxes, failed to provide its citizens with their basic needs, migrants in the United States used their own income and funds that they managed to raise in order to carry out what they felt should have been state-funded projects.

Migrants did more than take on the government's fiscal responsibilities. Club functions also cast migrants themselves as the rightful successors of the Mexican Revolution, contradicting the history textbooks, murals, monuments, and speeches that provided legitimacy to the PRI by portraying it as the inheritor of the nation's revolution. On a regular basis, clubs would invite the famous actor and singer Antonio Aguilar to Los Angeles to perform at large, glamorous events. Aguilar played the traditional macho character in movies and had come to epitomize the type of men to which the PRI traced its mythological origins.[59] The PRI used characters such as his to push forward the idea that although the Mexican Revolution had been violent, it had forged a modern nation that was more stable and just than the previous regime.[60] Club events promoted a different vision: although they still portrayed Aguilar as the ultimate macho hero, they emphasized that migrants, rather than the state, continued the cause of building Mexico. At these events, Aguilar spoke about how clubs—especially those from Zacatecas where he was from—were developing Mexico and helping the poor.[61]

Even as clubs took on traditional government responsibilities challenging the PRI's status as the sole legitimate heir to the Mexican Revolution, they also had to deal with the official government. Through their investments, club members acquired a voice that had previously been denied to them in the operations of the Mexican state. This was a slow and complex process and, up to the mid-1980s, migrants mostly forged official relationships with municipal governments. To build its clinic, the Club Social Guadalupe Victoria bought land and paid for a workforce. But they then persuaded the municipal government to cover the costs of the materials.[62] Significantly, residents themselves did not have the power to exert such pressure. When residents of Guadalupe Victoria had asked the municipal and the state governments to construct a clinic, officials had replied with vague promises.[63] By guiding government investments, migrants acquired citizenship rights in Mexico greater than those of Mexican residents.

The Club Social Jocotepec also attracted the attention of the town's municipal government. In 1968 club members communicated their interest in building a hospital for the community to the municipal president, Arnulfo Vergara Ramírez. He immediately offered free *ejido* (communal) land for the purpose and commended migrants for their "laudable enterprise that will contribute to the benefit of our beloved Jocotepec."[64] In the same letter he informed club activists that his government was planning to construct "an edifice for a middle school and an athletic unit in our town" and asked the club to help fund the project. Vergara Ramírez supported migrants' vision of what the town needed, thus giving them a voice in the government, while also incorporating them into existing government projects.

Migrants could generally develop a close relationship with Mexican municipalities because they had grown up together with those who composed the local government. José Encarnación Bañuelos, who belonged to the Club Deportivo Tepetongo in Los Angeles, recalled that he "had always" known the municipal president in Tepetongo because it was "a small town."[65] Still, this does not mean that migrants always developed smooth relationships with municipal governments; these depended on who was in power.

In contrast to connections with local officials, up until the mid-1980s, the relationship between clubs and state governments was estranged. Members of the Club Social Teocaltiche tried to build a working relationship with both the town's municipal president and the governor of Jalisco, where Teocaltiche is located, by inviting them to Los Angeles. The group proposed that the officials visit them for the important Anniversary Dance held to celebrate the club's founding.[66] With complete insensitivity to migrants' traditions and activities, Jalisco officials informed the group that no representatives could attend on the club's proposed date and requested that the event not be a dance, even though this was the key event clubs organized. Instead, they suggested that the group organize a banquet to "give the visit a greater official character."[67] The state government attempted to impose its own vision of what "official" ceremonies consisted of, overlooking migrants' practices. More important, before 1985 no state governors developed a working relationship with the clubs, not even those who did attend dances.[68] For the most part, the governors attempted to increase their own popularity and to encourage Los Angeles migrants to travel to Zacatecas as tourists and spend money there.[69]

Clubs had even less contact with Mexico's federal government, and the contact they did have tended to be negative. According to migrants, from the 1960s to the early 1980s, Mexican consuls in Los Angeles did "absolutely nothing" to support club development, even when members requested their support.[70] Even worse, Mexican customs officials often tried to steal from migrants who were bringing aid to Mexican hometowns. On June 22, 1970, Natalia Villaseñor wrote to the president of the Comité de Beneficencia explaining that she had much trouble crossing the border with the wheelchair that the Comité had donated. Customs officials insisted that she could either pay high taxes to import the wheelchair or a bribe of Mex$500 (US$40). In the end, she "talked to them again and told them that [she] only had 10 dollars to give to them, and they agreed to that."[71] Despite hindrances from Mexican state officials, clubs managed to provide aid south of the border.

Clubs focused their attention on sending resources to Mexico and only developed superficial connections with U.S. officials. Most of this contact happened through their work with the Comité de Beneficencia by which the clubs helped transport the bodies of deceased Mexicans back to their hometowns, informed migrants about their legal rights, and helped them find work in the United States. For these efforts, Los Angeles officials, including Mayors Sam Yorty and Tom Bradley, bestowed multiple certificates of recognition upon migrant organizers. Although these awards were strictly symbolic, they increased activists' motivation to work and inspired other migrants to join clubs. Forty years later, organizers still carefully saved the certificates that the city had awarded them.[72]

Still, clubs were primarily concerned with producing structural changes in Mexico rather than with aiding individual migrants in the United States. As such, they were less interested in their relationship with U.S. officials. Many, like María Elena Serrano, realized that they would stay in the United States but still felt more obligated to help those "from the place where you are from. . . . It is a love and desire to do something for that place from where you came."[73] Many club members also consciously avoided placing demands on U.S. officials for the betterment of migrants because of their legal status. Rafael Hurtado, who joined a club from Zacatecas in 1985, recalled that, while living illegally in the United States during the 1970s, he never considered the possibility of protesting for better conditions north of the border "because of fear of the *migra* [the INS]."[74] Hurtado and other undocumented Mexicans found the idea of voicing opposition to U.S. policies through clubs inconceivable.[75]

Through their efforts, club members demonstrated that they deserved a role in the governance of Mexico and a place in the United States. While

Mexican and U.S. politicians viewed working-class Mexicans as surplus or "illegal" subjects, *clubes sociales* struggled to incorporate them into the social and economic structures of both nations. Through their work in clubs, migrants proved that they were indispensable to their hometowns and made that heading to the United States and partaking in club activism was a way to defy one's political and economic exclusion.

As activists engaged in the work of providing needed social services in Mexico, they formed a community of clubs that incorporated migrants who were marginalized because of their class, racial, and gender identities. During this period, Mexican and U.S. government officials excluded working-class Mexicans from full social belonging. Migrant communities themselves featured divisions among people of different class backgrounds, and women and indigenous people were frequently the target of abuse. In contrast, those who were part of the world of clubs created an inclusive welfare community—albeit sometimes for only brief periods—that did not discriminate on the basis of class, gender, legal status, or ethnicity.

Activists' very migration created a space for them to rethink their identities. Those who created the *clubes sociales* were, for the most part, married mestizo men who had migrated from the Central Plateau and had settled in the United States, often with their families. In the United States, they had to integrate their previous understandings of identity with those they found north of the border. Gradually, organizers began to incorporate their lived experiences in the United States and to include all migrants in order to create successful clubs.

At the most basic level, clubs blurred the boundaries between documented and undocumented workers. Activists estimate that approximately a quarter of all members were in the United States without proper authorization. According to both documented and undocumented members, legal status did not affect people's capacity to participate in club activities.[76] There was only one area in which clubs differentiated between migrants based on legal residence: they prohibited undocumented women from participating in beauty pageants. This decision was made out of practical rather than ideological considerations. Groups awarded their beauty queens with a trip to their hometown in Mexico. Thus they only allowed women who could legally travel across the border to participate in the contest. By fully including those without papers in the

groups, with the exception of the beauty pageant contestants, clubs provided these migrants with a sense of belonging. These feelings were particularly important given that the society at large considered them "illegals." The clubs' position was not altogether remarkable for migrant
communities. In Los Angeles, documented and unauthorized workers
interacted on a daily basis. Many of the club founders themselves had
crossed the border without papers and later managed to legalize their
status.

The club setting facilitated contact between those from different socioeconomic backgrounds. Activists' migratory experiences provided the
seeds to facilitate this cross-class interaction. Whereas south of the border,
migrants' "Mexicanness" had not set them apart, in the United States it
constructed them as "others" and encouraged them to come together as
Mexicans. Many of those who started the clubs were blue-collar workers
in the United States. They met Mexico's elite because they organized their
meetings at La Casa del Mexicano, where economically influential Mexicans also gathered. Migrants of different classes interacted harmoniously
with each other in *clubes sociales* and managed to overcome traditional
modes of cross-class interaction—to an extent that surprised even their
own members. For instance, Raúl Villarreal remembers being impressed
by other activists' socioeconomic status and by their kindness toward
him.[77] Although there were times when he experienced discomfort
because of differences in wealth between himself and other club organizers, he always felt that he was welcome and had a voice in the
group. Class did not always determine who was elected to positions of
authority, such as club president. Villarreal, who was often one of the
poorest members, was the president of many clubs. Club activity had the
potential to upend the relationship between economic and political power.

In the 1980s, club members started to resist notions that women did
not belong in clubs. Activist María Elena Serrano played an important
role in bringing about this change. Serrano was extremely charismatic
and strikingly beautiful. In 1980, she was crowned queen in the Señorita
México de Los Angeles beauty pageant, the most important of the con-
tests that the migrant community organized. Responding to her conspic-
uous popularity, some activists of the Federación de Clubs Mexicanos
Unidos suggested endorsing her as their leader to gain further visibility.[78]

Serrano's election represented a significant change in clubs' notions
of gender and belonging. Before her presidency, migrants regarded club

meetings as a male space. When Serrano began her presidency, approximately forty men and no women attended meetings of the Federación. According to Serrano, the typical "woman tended to be very shy," and "husbands did not allow those who were not shy to participate."[79] Husbands argued that club decisions ought to be made by men and would only allow their wives to accompany them to large club functions. As president, Serrano assumed not only a traditionally male office but also the most important job within the organization. Once elected, Serrano worked to incorporate more women into the Federación. She recruited many of them by asking them to bring "their famous *mole* or salsa" to meetings.[80] Through these requests, which conformed to traditional gender expectations, she slowly recruited more women to participate. But Serrano also insisted women share their opinions and have a good time at meetings. Through these tactics, she increased the Federación's female membership and altered the idea that women did not belong in social clubs.

Women's participation in the Federación, however, cannot be overestimated. According to Serrano, many men accepted her because they viewed her paternalistically "as a daughter or a niece, and that she was useful . . . as a secretary."[81] Equally important, no other woman since Serrano has served as president of the Federación. Sociologist Luin Goldring, who studied these groups in the period after 1992, argued that "on the whole, hometown organizations represent a privileged arena for men's homeland-oriented political activity . . . while marginalizing women by excluding them from positions of agency and power."[82] The period before the one that Goldring analyzed, when María Elena Serrano was president of the Federación, was one in which club activities and functioning provided a space for women and created an opening to reverse traditional gender norms.

In fact, during the early 1980s, clubs expanded gendered ideas of belonging not only by including women but also by organizing events that subverted the seemingly natural correlation between femininity and womanhood. Multiple clubs joined together to invite to an event Valentina Ramírez, a famous revolutionary hero who broke the traditional feminine and passive behavior expected of women. Most narratives emphasized her gender-bending feistiness and often depicted her in men's garb. The popular 1958 film *Pancho Villa y La Valentina* shows her firing on Villa's troops, successfully hitting two of his men.[83] Because of her

Members of the Comité de Benficencia, the Club Michoacano (including María Elena Serrano, *second left*), and Valentina Ramírez (*far right*) dressed in military attire. Photograph from the personal archives of María Elena Serrano.

extraordinary aim, the soldiers in the film speculate that Ramírez is a man and are surprised when the sharpshooter reveals herself to be female. The movie also provides a queer perspective on Ramírez. Surprised by her manly skills, Pancho Villa asks her, "What do you rope: colts or mares?" to which she responds, "Mules." She neither identifies as nor "ropes" males or females, but combines both.

Ramírez's gender bending extended beyond folklore. She showed up to the clubs' gathering in full male military attire with the proper recognitions for her actions during the Mexican Revolution. Through her posture, dark glasses, and clothes, she could easily pass for a man. She spoke about her actions in the Revolution and about her life as Pancho Villa's lover. Observers were impressed by her "unfeminine" strength and recall that she still "spoke very loudly."[84] Through such events, clubs, in effect, brought to light female masculinity and destabilized the "naturalness" of gender roles.

Clubs also created a setting in which migrants could redraw lines of racial and ethnic inclusion and exclusion. Because migrants came from states in Mexico that had diverse ethnic populations, clubs produced a multiethnic mosaic in which indigenous groups coexisted with mestizos. The members from the Zacatecas clubs, for instance, came from a mestizo background and promoted this culture at their events. The Club Michoacano, conversely, promoted an indigenous Tarascan way of life. Collectively, the clubs promoted both mestizo and indigenous cultures, propagating an expansive vision of racial belonging.

The idea that mestizos existed alongside Indians was particularly important given that, since the 1920s, the Mexican state had portrayed its indigenous population as residing in a distant, glorious past. The national narrative of *indigenismo* satisfied the nostalgia for national origins while also creating a temporal distance that rendered Indians "a thing of the past."[85] Unlike the government, the Club Michoacano organized events showing that its members practiced indigenous traditions. In July 1984, for instance, the club participated in the Plaza de La Raza Folk-Life Festival. In the event's pamphlet, the group claimed, "The members of this organization perform dances such as the *danza de los viejitos* (dance of the old men, a traditional dance of indigenous Tarascans) which they learned in Michoacán. The Club Michoacano actively seeks to preserve its customs so that even small children take part in the performances."[86] Through such assertions, the Club Michoacano maintained that Tarascan traditions still persisted and belonged to future generations.

The Club Michoacano's discourse on Mexican indigenous groups wavered uncomfortably between a need to speak about the existence of Mexico's non-mestizo population and Mexico's problematic racial rhetoric. Most of the club events focused entirely on creating appreciation for Tarascan culture but did not actively seek to change relations of power either in Mexico or within the club. Although members of the Club Michoacano had grown up living side by side with Tarascans, most of them were not actually indigenous themselves. Moreover, by focusing narrowly on Tarascan's culture, the group emphasized the "folkloric" dimensions of Mexico's indigenous populations, obscuring the massacres and socioeconomic injustices that these groups experienced. In 1982, the Club Michoacano chose to forget the genocidal aspects of Spanish colonization and participated in the "Discovery of America Parade."[87] Thus the club produced a complex discourse that both generated and fore-closed possibilities for indigenous belonging.

Clubs did not alter members' prejudiced views against black Ameri-cans. Migrants' racist notions of black people arose from the interplay between U.S. and Mexican racial ideologies. Whereas in Mexico, mi-grants understood their "Mexicanness" as an ethnicity, in the United States people often considered it a sign of their racial background.[88] Many migrants reacted to their new racial categorization by asserting that even though not white, they were, still, superior to blacks. Many of them adopted common stereotypes that portrayed black men as dangerous. María Suárez Oliva, who migrated from Nochistlán, Zacatecas, a town that had a *club social* in the 1960s, recalled that she did not trust African Americans. When she resided in Los Angeles in 1972, she "avoided leav-ing [her] apartment because there was a black man [*negrito*] living in the building across from [hers,]" and she was "scared of him."[89]

Migrants did not learn white supremacy in the United States. Not only did Mexicans privilege those with lighter skin, but many felt ani-mosity toward black Americans long before crossing the border. Gerardo Armas Domínguez, who also migrated from Nochistlán, recalled that "coexistence with blacks was not easy. . . . Mexicans did not get along well with them. First, there was a language barrier, which distanced us; second, that we had a concept that we were told that they were bad people . . . even before we left [Nochistlán]."[90] Despite living alongside and interacting with black Americans and being themselves subjected to a racial hierarchy that placed them under whites, migrants found it difficult to dispel transnational racial ideologies of white supremacy.

The antagonism many Mexicans felt toward blacks meant that they did not invite them to club events. Moreover, there were no reasons and few opportunities for club members to interact with black activists. Club members perceived black activists as unconcerned with Mexico's devel-opment. Because club activists did not focus on changing U.S. politics, they did not follow the examples of the black power and black civil rights movements in their own struggle (as many of the other U.S. social movements of the 1960s and 1970s did).

Similarly, migrant clubs did not incorporate Mexican Americans. Club members recall powerful divides between these communities. Despite the fact that *clubes sociales* were an important venue for migrant organizing, activists argue that Chicana/o groups did not seriously engage with them. Even the Centro de Acción Social Autónomo (CASA), which was one of the groups most engaged with undocumented migrants in Los Angeles, overlooked *clubes sociales*. María Elena Serrano recalled that CASA was "very distant" from them.[91] Similarly, Gregorio Casillas said that even though clubs often invited groups such as CASA and Movimiento Estudiantil Chicano de Aztlán (MEChA) to their events, members of these organizations generally did not show up or support club projects.[92]

Migrant activists derided much Chicana/o activism. Casillas attended Lincoln High School in the late 1960s and clearly remembers the Chicano Blowouts of March 1968, when more than 10,000 Chicana/o students at five area schools walked out in protest. The students demanded a revised curriculum that included Mexican and Chicana/o history and culture courses, the recruitment of more Mexican American teachers, an end to the process of tracking Chicana/o students into vocational education, and the removal of teachers considered to be racists.[93] Casillas thought this movement of "gangs" was "horrible."[94] Although this position ignored the real struggles that Chicanas/os faced in the educational system, for Casillas and other club activists the idea of protesting for a particular curriculum, especially when in Mexico they did not even have access to a primary school education, seemed like a luxury. The only Chicana/o group for which club activists showed any respect was the United Farm Workers. This is surprising given that from the 1960s to the early 1970s the UFW called for increasing restrictions on foreign migration. UFW activists argued that Mexican workers took jobs away from Mexican Americans. Yet many club activists—whether they were documented or not—remember the UFW as the only Chicana/o organization fighting for a legitimate cause.[95] In their minds, the UFW strove for workers' rights rather than what they viewed as more bourgeois concerns. By the late 1970s, the UFW switched its position on foreign migration and began to defend the rights of undocumented migrants.[96]

In clubs, migrants created an extraterritorial welfare state that provided ample possibilities for inclusion by eroding differences in legal status, class, gender, ethnicity, and race. This does not mean that they ultimately produced a perfect haven of social and economic belonging; clubs encouraged paternalistic attitudes toward women, celebrated the "Discovery of America," and did not truly alter migrants' negative perceptions of blacks and Chicanos. Still, through their acceptance of undocumented migrants, cross-class memberships, acceptance of indigenous peoples, and openness to having a female leader, clubs often produced capacious visions of civic citizenship.

Clubs extended visions of belonging by providing a space in which migrants could identify themselves with multiple local, state, national, and transnational communities simultaneously. The very existence of organizations in Los Angeles that represented small communities in Mexico reveals the power of the *patria chica* in people's imaginations. Through clubs, migrants remained attached to their hometowns, forming translocal communities that stretched beyond national borders. While migrants remained primarily attached to their *patria chica,* they also mapped their identities onto multiple geographies. From the 1960s to the mid-1980s, clubs' geographic attachments continually fluctuated. Such flux had material significance because it influenced clubs to send money to different locations.

Clubs fostered a community in which migrants could hold multiple geographic loyalties at once. At the scale of their hometown, club activities helped migrants express their attachment to their *patria chica,* which, as Mexicanist historians have emphasized, often "took precedence over loyalty to the nation."[97] The very fact that activists formed the Club Social Guadalupe Victoria, even though a Club Social Jalpense already existed, demonstrates the particularity of migrants' attachments. Both Jalpa and Guadalupe Victoria were in the same municipality and were located only ten kilometers apart from each other. Similarly, the songs that club members composed often described their love for their particular hometowns. At club events, Antonio Galarza Viramontes often sang the following verses he composed for Jalpa:

> *Aquí me pongo a cantar a orillas de una banqueta*
> *Los versos que le compuse a mi Jalpa Zacatecas*
> *Es mi Jalpa Zacatecas del Cañon de Juchipila*
> *Tierra de lindas regiones y de grandes tradiciones*
> *Es mi Jalpa Zacatecas una tierra sin igual*
> *Tierra de lindas mujeres su cielo es primaveral*
> *Ahí entra la fiesta del 19 es fiesta tradicional*
> *Me dejo muchos recuerdos que nunca puedo olvidar*
> *La fiesta del día primero de mi Jalpa tan sencillo*
> *Donde vamos por la noche a ver quemar su castillo*

Las muchachas de mi Jalpa todas de buen corazón
Van a rezarle a la virgen todas con gran devoción
La fiesta del día primero de mi Jalpa tan sencillo
Donde vamos a mirar quemar su castillo
En las fiestas del día primero con tapancos de a montones
Mariachis y tamborazos vienen de todas regiones
La fiesta del día primero con sus corridas de toros y carreras de caballos
Son fiestas por tradición también sus peleas de gallos
Las muchachas de mi Jalpa todas de buen corazón
Cuando es de dar su cariño no piensan en la traición
A mi Jalpa Zacatecas yo me quiero regresar
Quiero morir en mi pueblo
Porque es mi tierra natal

Here I begin to sing along the banks of a sidewalk
The verses that I composed to my Jalpa Zacatecas
It's my Jalpa Zacatecas of the Canyon of Juchipila
Land of pretty regions and of great traditions
It is my Jalpa Zacatecas, a land like no other
Land of beautiful women, with a spring-like sky
There goes the party of the 19th, it's a traditional party
It left me with many memories that I can never forget
The New Year's Day party of my so-simple Jalpa
Where we go at night to see fireworks
The girls of my Jalpa, all kindhearted,
Go to pray to the virgin all with great devotion
The New Year's Day party of my so-simple Jalpa
Where we go to see fireworks
On the celebrations of New Year's Day with piles of tapancos
Mariachis and drumming come from all regions
The party of the first day with its bullfights and horse races
Its cockfights are also parties by tradition
The girls of my Jalpa, all kindhearted
When showing affection they think not of betrayal
To my Jalpa Zacatecas, I want to return
I want to die in my village
Because it is my homeland

Galarza's song reflects his attachment to his hometown rather than to Mexico as a whole. Galarza missed Jalpa's particularities and wanted to die in his town.[98]

Even though most Mexicans adored their hometowns, their exact definition of "hometown" varied. Migrants did not simply relocate from their native communities to the United States. Many of them passed through multiple locales within Mexico before crossing the U.S.-Mexico border. Although Gregorio Casillas formed the Club Social Guadalupe Victoria, he was actually born in Rincón de Roma in the State of Aguascalientes.[99] However, because both of his parents had been born in Guadalupe Victoria and had family there, they moved back when Gregorio was two years old. Eight years later, the Casillas family relocated to Tlatenango, where Gregorio lived until he was sixteen years old and decided to migrate to the United States. Still, Gregorio Casillas did not join the Club Social de Tlatenango, even though he spent much of his childhood in that town. Similarly, Gregorio's attachment to Guadalupe Victoria did not "naturally" stem from the fact that his parents were rancho natives. Although José Encarnación Bañuelos and his parents were born in Monte Escobedo, Zacatecas, he never joined the Club Social Ranchos Unidos de Monte Escobedo, Zacatecas, but instead created the Club Deportivo Tepetongo. He considered himself to belong to Tepetongo because his family had migrated there when he was very young.[100] Migrants' multiple geographic loyalties, reflected in the clubs they formed, complicate straightforward definitions of the *patria chica*.

Even though migrants started social clubs because of their attachments to the place they considered home, the social networks they developed in the United States often proved even more important. Many migrants found that there were no clubs from their hometowns and joined those from other parts of Mexico in order to have a community in the United States. They later left them for clubs that fitted them better, or they created new clubs affiliated with their hometowns. Their capacity to remap their attachments to different Mexican hometowns indicates that their sense of belonging was deeply rooted in the "otherness" they experienced in the United States. Raúl Villarreal, who was born in Jerez, Zacatecas, originally joined the Club Social Avalos, Chihuahua, in the early 1970s. He then moved to the Club Social Independencia, and then to the Club Social Camargo, both of which also worked to send money to the State of Chihuahua.[101] Finally, in 1978, he left these groups and formed the Club Social Hermandad Latina, a Latin American mutual aid club. By allowing members from different places to join their club, activists created inclusive organizations in which members could express multiple and flexible loyalties.

Clubs themselves often changed their geographic attachments. Although most of the members of the Club Social Hermandad Latina were

Benefit poster, Sepulveda Litho Service, Los Angeles, California, 1968.
Reproduced from uncataloged archives, La Casa del Mexicano,
Los Angeles, California.

Mexican, some came from other Latin American countries. Its founding statutes asserted, "The object and goals of this club are to unify the Hispanic colony in Los Angeles and its surroundings with the end goal of presenting a united front to all our collective problems, be they moral or social."[102] Soon after its creation in 1978, however, the club started focusing on sending aid to Mexico and then specifically to the town of Jerez. Eventually, the group even changed its name to Club Social Hermandad Latina de Jerez Zacatecas.[103]

In this club world in which members switched clubs and clubs changed geographic loyalties, activists developed multiple visions of belonging simultaneously. This flexibility allowed them to work together and ultimately to create an extraterritorial welfare system in which neither the membership nor the destination of the aid were determined by singular, previously conceived borders. On August 3, 1968, the most "prestigious Club Sociales of Los Angeles" coordinated a dance to support the Dominican Sisters of Tampico, in the State of Tamaulipas. Two main bands played at the event: one specific to Chihuahua, Ray Rodriguez y su Romantica Orquesta de Solistas de Cd. Juarez, Chihuahua, and the other from Mexico's northern borderlands in general, Los Rebeldes del Norte. The event was sponsored (*apadrinado*) by Sam Yorty, the mayor of Los Angeles, and by the president of the Comité de Beneficencia

The words at the bottom of the club's logo read: "The effort for the good of our people." Logo, Club Social San Vicente, R. A., ca. 1967. Reproduced from uncataloged archives, La Casa del Mexicano, Los Angeles, California.

Mexicana, Luis Hermosillo. This event thus incorporated five different regions with which migrants affiliated: Tamaulipas, Chihuahua, the northern borderlands, Los Angeles, and all of Mexico.

Clubs that were committed to a particular rancho or town often adopted a broader, transnational perspective. The Club Social Guadalupe Victoria established in its 1963 statutes, "The reason to form this group is to create a fund for medical help to needy families who, because of their lack of resources, deserve our cooperation."[104] Those families could reside in "Guadalupe Victoria, Zac., or in any other place." Similarly, the statutes of the Club Social San Vicente asserted, "This society was funded for the benefit of families that lack economic resources, for medical assistance, and other needs of a first-degree in San Vicente and equally to extend our aid to all peoples [*pueblos*] which deserve our cooperation."[105] The logo of the San Vicente Club exemplified multiple conceptions of the *pueblos*. At the top, members wrote the name of the club, which directly referred to San Vicente. Beneath the writing the insignia depicted the flags of Mexico and the United States. Below them, two hands were shown clasped in a handshake, representing binational cooperation. Even though clubs sent aid to Mexico, the United States figured strongly in their iconography. Most migrants wanted to return to Mexico, but they lived and worked in Los Angeles. Rather than projecting an antagonistic relationship between the two countries, they sought a world in which the two coexisted and in which they could live in and contribute to both nation-states. Indeed, in the logo of the San Vicente club, the word "Zacatecas" is shown suspended between the two flags, as if the state itself helped unite both nations.

The Club Social Independencia, which identified with Chihuahua, also adopted a transnational perspective. It tried to create a more inclusive club setting and distributed aid outside of Mexico and the United States. In 1970, it began providing financial support to Peru after the country suffered a significant earthquake.[106] It organized an event to give the money it had raised to Peru's general consulate and invited the Mexican consul.[107] In other words, this club used its aid to bring Latin American officials and migrants closer together. Clubs increasingly tore down the borders between Mexican and other Latin American migrants. Individuals from Puerto Rico, El Salvador, and Nicaragua attended club dances, bringing Latin Americans in Los Angeles closer together.[108]

In the club setting, activists developed flexible and expansive geographic loyalties. Even though the clubs represented a space for people to continue to participate with their home villages, they provided membership to people from different geographic locations. Their welfare system sent aid to ranchos, to individual Mexican states, to Mexico as a whole, and to other Latin American countries. By developing expansive visions of social and geographic belonging migrants countered visions that restricted full membership to particular, bounded communities.

In the late 1960s, club activists decided to unite multiple clubs together in federations. Four clubs from different areas in the state of Chihuahua, in conjunction with the Club de Leones, formed an association called Fundación Humberto Gutiérrez.[109] Although state borders dictated the Fundación's membership, it did not impose geographic restrictions on its aid. If anything, its motto, "United clubs at the service of humanity," reflected a global conception. By 1969, clubs from multiple states joined the Fundación, including those from Zacatecas, Jalisco, and Nayarit, replacing state boundaries with national ones.[110]

Although the Fundación withered away shortly thereafter, club members created other federations.[111] In 1972, eight different clubs from the state of Zacatecas joined together to create the Federación de Clubs Sociales Zacatecanos.[112] Activists realized that by uniting they could increase the amount of money they made at events. Clubs invested approximately US$700 to US$800 per social function.[113] By throwing joint events, activists reasoned, the costs to each individual club would fall and the revenues would increase, as more people would attend. The federation's "Pilot Plan" claimed: "Given the current existing situation in [the] Los Angeles social ambience, in which fraternal clubs mutually compete against each other, it is imperative that the Clubs Zacatecanos unite in a more effective manner and manage to conduct social events that not only give prestige to the Zacatecana Colony but which also provide economic benefits to carry out the numerous economic responsibilities of beneficence that each organization has."[114] However, the Federación soon became Zacatecan in name only, as clubs from other states began to join it. Thus in 1980, when there were approximately twenty-five groups from different states working together, the Federación changed its name to Federación de Clubs Mexicanos Unidos (Federation of United Mexican Clubs). Through this change, the Federación ideologically switched from one that aligned itself with Zacatecas to one that endorsed a national perspective.

At its inception, the Federación de Clubs Mexicanos Unidos seemed extremely successful. By 1983, it represented thirty-four clubs and brought hundreds of migrants together.[115] It regularly held massive dances and organized meetings at La Casa del Mexicano every other Sunday. After the meetings, hundreds of club members and their families gathered to eat and spend time together, deepening their sense of solidarity.[116] The Federación de Clubs Mexicanos Unidos also increased the attention that clubs received from Mexican consuls. While the consulate in Los Angeles had previously ignored club activities, once the clubs came together as the Federación, it could no longer overlook them. In fact, the Federación became a "bridge" between the consulate and individual clubs that were trying to transport goods and funds across the U.S.-Mexico border.[117] On one occasion in the 1980s, Raúl Villarreal attempted to enter Mexico with the money that clubs had donated to Zacatecas. When customs officials insisted that he needed to pay them a bribe, Villarreal called the Federación, which in turn got the consulate in Los Angeles to force border officers to allow Villarreal through.[118] Because of the Federación, Villarreal's experience was very different from that of Natalia Villaseñor, who had paid custom officers US$10 to enter with a donated wheelchair in 1970.

Still, the Federación de Clubs Mexicanos Unidos faced representational problems from the start. Given their long organizational history and their numerical importance, groups from the State of Zacatecas dominated the sessions and the events. Out of the thirty-four clubs in the Federación in 1983, fifteen were from Zacatecas (44 percent), and two more were led by Zacatecanos (the Liga de Beisbol Baldwin Park and Hermandad Latina). As such, exactly 50 percent of all clubs in the Federación identified with Zacatecas.[119] Clubs from Chihuahua, Jalisco, Durango, Guerrero, Michoacán, and Mexico as a whole held the other 50 percent. This meant that, when voting, Zacatecan groups could silence competing interests. As a result, other clubs protested that the Federación did not represent them and regularly withdrew from it.[120]

By the mid-1980s, Zacatecan clubs themselves realized that separating from clubs that affiliated with other states could serve their political interests. In 1985, Genaro Borrego Estrada opted to propel his campaign to run for governor of Zacatecas by approaching migrants in Los Angeles. He urged them to join together in a statewide federation, insisting that an organization that united the multiple Zacatecan groups could truly pressure the state government. In 1986, Borrego, who was by then governor, agreed to develop a program by which the state government would match every dollar migrant organizations sent to Zacatecas for the betterment of communities.[121] This agreement marked the first time that clubs were granted official recognition by a state government. Migrants were unofficially incorporated into the state apparatus. Two years later, the federation changed its geographic borders again to become the Federación de Clubes de Zacatecanos del Sur de California.

Thereafter, club activism became increasingly attached to the state. The government launched the Programa Dos Por Uno (2X1) and then the Programa Tres Por Uno (3X1) in 1992 and 1999, respectively.[122] Through these programs, the federal and state governments—and then the municipal government as well—each contributed a dollar for every dollar that migrant organizations sent. Government interest and financial backing fostered migrants' visibility and gave them political power in Mexico but also curbed their ability to decide how their money was spent.[123]

From the 1960s to the mid-1980s, migrant leaders established the organizational framework necessary for Mexican politicians to recognize the clubs. The achievements of early club activists meant that state officials could not continue to disregard migrants' lives and efforts. Perhaps even more important, before the Mexican government became involved in club activities, migrant organizers created an autonomous extraterritorial welfare state that countered both the cultural and economic structures that excluded them from social membership in both countries. Migrants used their own capital and energy to take on government responsibilities because the state failed to do so. Through their work, migrants became part of an inclusive world of welfare provision that did not limit the distribution of aid to particular localities and that fostered a capacious sense of migrant identity.

Migrants' activism improved conditions in Mexico, it also revealed that migrating was a way to counter the economic and political exclusion that working-class individuals experienced in Mexico. Club activism also established that migrants could find social belonging in the United States. The club setting thus reinforced notions that migrating and engaging in club work were an effective way to achieve partial inclusion on both sides of the border.

Even as club activists defied the views held by Mexican officials that working-class people were an economically superfluous population, other migrants sought to achieve greater inclusion in *El Norte*. To do this, a coalition of groups set out to demand rights for those who were in the United States without proper authorization.

6

....

THE RIGHTS OF THE PEOPLE

LONG BEFORE DAWN ROSE on the sleepy town of Tyler, Texas, on September 9, 1977, José and Lidia López packed all of their belongings into their Dodge Monaco and drove their son, Alfredo, to the courthouse.[1] Only eight years old, Alfredo did not fully understand what was happening, but he knew that his family might have to leave the United States. His parents, however, had already carefully considered and prepared for the potential consequences of this moment. With the support of renowned lawyers from the Mexican American Legal Defense and Educational Fund (MALDEF), the López family, along with three other families, had decided to contest a law that prevented undocumented children from attending school in Tyler. José and Lidia knew that this decision meant that they might be deported that very day. They nonetheless drove to the courthouse. They did so not just for their son but for all undocumented children, who they believed deserved an education.

The members of the López family were part of a growing group of individuals who started to demand their rights as unauthorized migrants in the United States in the 1970s. Before that decade, migrant activists and their allies had fought to improve the conditions of Mexicans in the United States—many of whom were undocumented—but they had tended to refrain from identifying their struggle as one for unauthorized migrants explicitly.[2] Claiming rights for undocumented migrants had seemed politically ineffective. U.S. citizens across the political spectrum viewed those whose territorial presence in the country was unsanctioned as undeserving of civil rights. The idea that all individuals deserved extra-national rights based on their essential humanity had not yet become common.[3] Unauthorized migrants stood as a people "whose inclusion in the nation was at once a social reality and a legal impossibility."[4]

Claiming rights for undocumented migrants became imperative during the 1970s and early 1980s because of the growing surveillance that unauthorized individuals confronted. Schools, highways, factories, hotels, restaurants, and fields within the country began to be used as sites to regulate the boundaries of legality and to deny rights to those who did not possess papers. For Alfredo López, the surveillance meant that his status was policed not only at the border but also at his school's gates. Other migrants remember that during these years all places within the United States became sites of potential deportation. Mario Lazcano recalled that during this period people were apprehended everywhere: "Once I went shopping . . . and they caught me in the street. Because [at that time] *la migra* could catch you anywhere. In the streets . . . in the fields . . . in places where Mexicans worked outside of agriculture . . . the raids were huge."[5]

Because undocumented migrants had much to fear from protesting against this elastic geography of border regulation and exclusion, they did not always do it as visibly as the López family. Many migrants, such as those involved with *clubes sociales,* avoided U.S. politics altogether, preferring instead to place their energy on working to improve economic conditions in Mexico. But other migrants decided to put aside their anxiety and fight vocally for their rights north of the border.

Given the risks unauthorized migrants faced when they protested, the support of other communities was indispensable, but these alliances did not form easily. During the 1970s, Mexican American organizations went from blaming Mexican migrants for the discrimination Mexicans born in the United States faced to supporting migrants' struggles.[6] But the rapprochement between these communities was often difficult. Some Mexican American organizations took longer than others to change their position, and many continued to oppose undocumented migration. Even as Mexican American groups came to be at the forefront of many struggles for the rights of undocumented migrants, such as the support they provided to the López family, many Mexican nationals continued to distrust those born in the United States. The same was the case with white progressives. During the 1970s and early 1980s some white activists decided to splinter away from the mainstream union movement that continued to oppose unauthorized workers and to fight for those without papers. Despite their efforts, they could not always gain migrants' trust. Still, to be able to win rights in the United States, unauthorized migrants needed to build strong alliances with individuals and organizations from other communities.

The diverse group of activists that started demanding rights for undocumented migrants during the 1970s and early 1980s included unauthorized migrants themselves as well as legalized migrants, Mexican Americans, and white progressives. Like the black civil rights movement of earlier decades, the movement for undocumented migrants' rights adopted both grassroots and legal strategies, producing different types of struggles.[7] The work of the Maricopa County Organizing Project (MCOP) exemplifies some of the efforts performed by grassroots organizations. MCOP sought to unionize undocumented farmworkers in Arizona. It helped migrants attain a sense of political power and built an activist community, but its victories were limited to the specific locales where its struggles took place. In contrast, other migrant activists and legal advocates fought through the courts for those without papers to be able to unionize, go to school, and move freely on the highways. Legal battles did not build social movements, but if they reached the Supreme Court, they had implications for undocumented migrants throughout the United States.

No matter what strategy activists chose, they had to wrestle with the question of who to present as the legitimate bearers of rights. Although a few organizers considered their movement as one designed to attain rights for those without papers from the start, most initially conceived of their actions as being for "migrant workers," "children," or "ethnic Mexicans." Undocumented children, for instance, deserved to go to school not because undocumented migrants deserved rights but because children did. Ultimately, however, migrants and their allies concluded that labeling their struggles as being for the undocumented was inevitable because migrants were being denied protections primarily on the basis of their legal status.

Claiming rights for unauthorized migrants, however, had the unintended effect of reinforcing migrants' classification as "illegal." By fighting in the name of undocumented migrants, as if they were an identity group, activists reinforced a category that they rejected. Unlike many gay people, women, and ethnic and racial minorities, all of whom created identity-based movements during this period, few migrants wanted to embrace an undocumented identity, draw pride from it, or claim it as who they were.[8] Their presumed "illegality" did not stem from their own sense of self but rather from immigration laws drawn by legislators.

Even while strengthening migrants' categorization as undocumented, struggles for rights increased migrants' sense that they could belong in the United States and resist their exclusion there. By risking deportation, subjecting themselves to lengthy legal battles, and forming alliances with other communities, Mexicans asserted their rootedness north of the border. They concluded that improving their lives in the United States, where they resided for significant periods of time, was worth the effort.

In the burgeoning world of grassroots activism that started to flourish around the fight for undocumented migrants' rights, few movements attained as much success as the one that developed in Maricopa County, Arizona.[9] There, undocumented workers labored in citrus groves where the thick foliage of lemon, grapefruit, and orange trees allowed them to hide from the immigration authorities who patrolled the area.[10] Manuel Marín Bernal, who migrated from Nayarit, reported that when he first arrived to work, the foreman at the citrus orchard "explained to [him] that the majority of the workers stayed there in the groves . . . and didn't have any problems [with *la migra*]."[11]

Workers paid a high price for their ability to take cover from migration officials. The other work available in the area consisted of harvesting onions, which provided no cover under which to hide but paid higher wages and offered better conditions. In the citrus groves, pickers lived under the trees in cardboard boxes and had no access to toilets or medical care. Growers did not even provide workers with potable water, which meant that they drank ditch water.[12] In spite of the hardships migrants faced, the wages they received in Maricopa's groves were much higher than the money they could make in Mexico. Marín Bernal, for instance, had a small corn plantation in his hometown, but he could not support his wife and three children with it. His family worked his land but he still had to send "almost all of what [he] earned [in the United States] so that they could eat."[13]

Despite the appalling working conditions in Arizona's citrus groves, up to the mid-1970s most unions refused to organize undocumented migrants. Even the United Farm Workers (UFW), which was composed primarily of Mexican American and Filipino farmworkers, supported the deportation of those without papers. In 1974, for instance, the union's president, César Chávez, wrote to Congressman John Conyers calling for "immediate action from the Immigration and Naturalization Service" to apprehend unauthorized workers.[14] The UFW also implemented the "wet line" to remove undocumented migrants from the citrus fields of Yuma, Arizona. As part of the wet line, UFW members patrolled 125 miles of the border to prevent undocumented migrants from entering into the United States. Some migrants who sought to bypass the wet line reported that UFW organizers beat them with sticks and a battery cable, robbed them, stripped them, and then just left them in the desert.[15]

Lupe Sánchez, who previously had been undocumented himself, was one of the UFW organizers who worked in Arizona during this time. While a migrant farmworker, Sánchez had met UFW activist Gustavo Gutiérrez, who convinced him to join the union. As a UFW organizer, Sánchez attained significant upward mobility. He recalled, "One of the things that the union did for me was that it brought me out of the fields, trained me as an organizer, and I started going to college part-time— high school."[16] Despite the many opportunities the union provided him with, however, he felt uncomfortable partaking in the wet line.[17] Even though he had already managed to legalize his status, Sánchez fully understood the plight of undocumented workers.[18]

Sánchez became further disillusioned with the UFW in 1977, when Chávez decided to end one of the onion strikes in Arizona against the will of the striking workers in order to divert funds back to California and ensure that all union operations were controlled through the UFW's central offices.[19] Sánchez responded by forming a different union; one that was willing to organize undocumented migrants. He recruited a small but diverse group of people, including Gustavo Gutiérrez, who identified as Mexican American and Native American; Jesús Romo, who came from a middle-class family in Mexico and had migrated legally; and Don Devereux, a white journalist who had come to the area that year. They enlisted many other members, including women, who worked alongside this core group of men but did not receive much credit.[20]

The organizers understood that to win they needed media coverage, and thus they chose to strike at Arrowhead Ranch, which was partially owned by the brother of Senator Barry Goldwater. They also knew that in Arizona it would be best not to unionize workers per se. In 1972,

Arizona legislators had passed a law prohibiting farmworkers from organizing strikes and boycotts during the harvest season and allowing only those workers who had labored with the same employer in the preceding calendar year to vote in a union representation election.[21] Sánchez and his fellow activists circumvented this problem by calling themselves the Maricopa County Organizing Project and avoiding the term "union." Romo publicly declared, "We aren't interested in contracts and unions. We were founded . . . as a private organization designed to improve the wages and living conditions of field workers. We are a civil rights organization more than a labor union."[22] Rather than go on "strike," which was illegal, the group planned a "work stoppage" against Arrowhead Ranch.[23] These differences were primarily linguistic, but they allowed the group to organize within the boundaries of the law. Because organizers could not ask for union recognition or bargaining rights, they decided that their tactic ought to consist of causing enough havoc at the groves that the owners would want to sign long-term contracts to gain predictability.

The group's most shrewd strategy, however, consisted of adopting a transnational approach to counter the captivity workers experienced in the fields. In Maricopa County, the sweet scent of citrus that emanated from the groves could travel more freely than the undocumented workers who labored in them. Because the Border Patrol roamed continually through the region, undocumented migrants dared not wander beyond the orchards' boundaries. Workers lived in the groves, even though there were no houses there. They bought food from the store within the property, even though it was disproportionally expensive. While migrants could not leave the groves for fear of being apprehended, MCOP activists could not enter them, as they were private properties. Migrants' isolation posed a huge problem for MCOP organizers. Devereux explained, "When the workers . . . were on the ranches they were effectively isolated," making it impossible for activists to meet with them and have the "heartfelt conversations" needed to organize a strike.[24]

Sánchez decided to overcome migrants' seclusion in Arizona's groves by heading to Mexico and approaching workers in their hometowns.[25] The plan was viable because most of the Mexican migrants who worked in the citrus region in Arizona originated from particular towns in the states of San Luis Potosí, Sinaloa, Nayarit, Michoacán, Querétaro, Guanajuato, and Guerrero.[26] Once in workers' hometowns, Sánchez went door-to-door to migrants' houses trying to convince them to carry out a work stoppage. As he explained, it was important to meet with migrants themselves but also "to meet their families, establish a bond with the local priest, with the families, with the women, with the wives. Basically, eat and sleep in their homes [because] once you do that, you're no longer an outsider."[27] A former unauthorized, Mexican farmworker himself, Sánchez immediately gained the trust of those on whose doors he knocked. He always emphasized that if migrants really needed the money and could not afford to strike they should head to other ranches or fields in the United States rather than acting as scabs in Arrowhead. After meeting with families in each town, Sánchez identified the men who regularly crossed the border without papers and who were considered leaders in their respective communities. He encouraged these men to join MCOP and to organize a workers' committee that would inspire other migrants to carry out a work stoppage in Maricopa County.[28]

Regions of MCOP organizing.

The men who led MCOP's workers' committee in Mexico had a hard task in front of them. As undocumented migrants who worked in dire conditions in Arizona's groves, they fully understood the need for collective bargaining. But they also knew that migrants and their families depended on U.S. wages. Asking the men to strike meant encouraging them to head north, cross the border without papers, and make no money, since MCOP could not provide workers with any strike funds. The commitment involved a huge sacrifice. Still, men like Manuel Marín Bernal and Hilario Pacheco Suárez believed that the possibility of unionizing undocumented workers in Arizona was worth the high costs.[29] They set out to organize those in their villages to convince them to cross the border to strike the following harvest season. Their efforts paid off.

On October 3, 1977, nearly 300 undocumented Mexican workers declared a work stoppage at Arrowhead Ranch.[30] They demanded to be paid the minimum wage, access to safe drinking water, advance warning of insecticide spraying, an accurate method to account for the hours they worked and the bags of citrus they picked, and a means to purchase food that was not sold by the growers themselves, which was substantially more expensive. As MCOP organizers had predicted, the walkout received immense press coverage because of the grove's association with the Goldwater family. TV crews and newspaper reporters showed up at the ranch every day. Workers held press conferences showing the bleak conditions under which they lived and worked.

Arrowhead Ranch growers retaliated by calling the Border Patrol and asking officers to deport the striking workers. Without questioning their role as proxy strikebreakers, immigration officials sent men, helicopters, and vans to catch the undocumented migrants. Devereux recalled, "We had for over three weeks the biggest game of hide and seek you've ever seen. Six thousand acres of trees to hide in, 300 workers out there, and probably 50 Border Patrol people looking for them, chasing them around."[31] In turn, MCOP activists posted lookouts for *la migra* along the grove roads where workers were demonstrating to warn them when officials were coming. They also helped those who had been deported to re-enter the country and continue the strike. Twenty-two days after the strike started, the Goldwater family caved. Tired of the bad publicity they were receiving, the growers agreed to install toilets, showers, and clean drinking facilities and to raise the wage from 54 cents to 80 cents per bag.[32] They refused, however, to sign an actual labor contract.

While farm owners intended to silence further dissent through this agreement, MCOP's victory, in fact, reenergized the activists to continue fighting. Two months after the first stoppage ended, they declared a new one with a whole new set of demands. After winning that strike, they declared another one. Between October 1977 and January 1979, workers and organizers continually closed Arrowhead Ranch.[33] By the end of that stretch, the growers were ready for a long-term solution and agreed to sign an actual labor contract with MCOP. It provided workers with housing, health insurance, paid vacations and holidays, health and safety rules, clean water, grievance procedures, pay increases (including a 10 percent raise for piecework), and an agreement by the growers to fund job development in Mexico.[34]

The victory at Arrowhead Ranch represented the first known successful strike by undocumented workers who explicitly demanded their rights while asserting that they were in the country illegally. It seemed to signal that those without papers were no longer afraid to fight for their rights in the United States. After the 1979 victory, a *Washington Post* article reported, "Although thousands of illegal aliens are believed to be covered by labor contracts, [the labor contract at Arrowhead] is the first negotiated for a group that is almost exclusively composed of 'undocumented workers.'"[35] Migrants themselves had promoted this view. In April 1978 MCOP members held the National Workers Conference on the Undocumented in Washington, D.C. This was the first time that self-identified unauthorized workers went into the White House. There, they tried to remind President Jimmy Carter of his declared commitment to human rights.[36]

Despite migrants' decision to fight for their rights in the United States, they also remained invested in improving Mexico's economy so that they would have an alternative other than being undocumented workers in the United States. Activists' desire to produce viable economic opportunities for migrants to remain in their home country if they so desired led them to negotiate for the grower to help fund job development in Mexico. Some migrants were so invested in this project that they put money from their own salaries into the fund, beyond the growers' contributions.[37] To further increase the fund, MCOP members applied for grants from institutions such as the Ford Foundation, the Stern Foundation, and the Inter-American Foundation.[38] Activists knew that this meant accepting money from foundations that were known for promoting

U.S. global interests abroad, but they still thought it beneficial and used the money for projects requested by those living in Mexican communities.

To manage the fund, MCOP activists formed the Farmworkers' Economic Development Corporation (FEDC) in the United States with an auxiliary branch, the Cooperativa sin fronteras (Cooperative without Borders), in Mexico. By 1984, the FEDC could claim multiple successes. In the Ahuacatlán region in Querétaro, it funded an ambitious irrigation project after agronomists concluded that with a more reliable water supply the area would be ideally suited for peach growing.[39] In the community of La Caja, located in the state of Guanajuato, residents used the fund to purchase a drilling rig to build wells, while in a rural village in the state of Sinaloa the FEDC built houses after those in the community determined that was their main priority.[40] They also constructed a tortilla factory and formed cooperatives to process cheese, milk, and meat. All these projects led Mexican families, which had been completely dependent on wages earned by migrants in the United States, to begin dreaming about making their livelihoods together in Mexico.

These dreams never materialized. MCOP did not manage to create enough job opportunities south of the border to allow most migrants to remain in Mexico. On the contrary, if anything, MCOP's efforts drew more individuals to the United States as wages became more attractive, working conditions improved, and migrants felt committed to working in Arizona as a result of their struggles there. Rather than protesting in Mexico to change conditions, workers had put their energies into improving their lot in the United States and as a result become more invested there. Marín Bernal described the work stoppages of 1977 as a "rebellion" and an "uprising," modes of protest that the migrants who went to Arizona had not sought out in Mexico.[41] Although most migrants continued to engage in circular migration, some became so attached to their lives and struggles in the United States that by the 1980s, they decided to settle in Arizona permanently with their families rather than continue to migrate back and forth between the two countries.[42]

While the efforts of the FEDC did not create enough jobs to counter migrants' economic exclusion in Mexico, MCOP's efforts did counter the notion that migrants' legal status rendered them ineligible for rights in the United States. In the groves of Arizona, workers from different parts of Mexico came together to demand better conditions for all workers. When abusive incidents occurred, they gathered around "and had many

discussions of the matter" in order to decide what action to take.[43] After
the first work stoppage, Pacheco Suárez, who had directed the workers'
committee in his village, accused one of the foremen of undercounting
the number of citrus bags he had picked. When he related his experience to the other workers, many of them reported facing similar problems. Together they decided to contact Lupe Sánchez who, with the help
of Legal Aid, brought a lawsuit against the growers.[44] In his deposition
explaining why the workers had begun to talk about a lawsuit, Marín
Bernal said, "According to the case, according to our manner of thinking,
we were going along without any rights." For them, this was no longer
acceptable.

Assertions that undocumented migrants deserved labor rights, however, also worked to reinforce associations between migrants' personhood and illegality. An Arizona state political leader declared, "The aliens
are finally coming out of the closet."[45] His statement was premised on
the idea that migrants, like other identity groups and most notably gay
people, needed to come out and assert who they were in order to achieve
inclusion. The concept of "coming out" rested on an identity-based model
of seeking rights. But, if anything, migrants wanted to distance themselves from the notion that they were "illegal."

The fight for the labor rights of undocumented farmworkers in Arizona shines light on the activist landscape that Mexican migrants
encountered during the 1970s. Even as most Mexican American organizations were becoming increasingly supportive of undocumented migrants, others, such as the UFW, continued to demand their deportation
and refused to organize them. This led many Mexican migrants to turn
to groups like MCOP that had Mexican Americans as members but that
did not identify as Mexican American organizations. Even within these
groups, they often continued to view other migrants, such as Lupe Sánchez, as their closest allies and leaders. Once they engaged with these
organizations, they also faced an unavoidable paradox. Resisting the notion that unauthorized migrants lacked protection in the United States
was the best option they had to improve the exploitative conditions they
faced north of the border, but it also bolstered the very category they
were fighting against and further attached their lives to the United States.

Far from the fields and streets where grassroots activists organized, another struggle developed in the courts. In this setting, unauthorized
migrants were particularly dependent on pro-immigrant lawyers and

advocacy organizations. During the 1970s and early 1980s, lawyers from groups such as MALDEF, the Federal Defenders of San Diego, and the National Center for Human Rights started to take up the struggle for undocumented migrants' rights. Attorneys from these organizations tended to come from outside the world of social movement organizing, but they often followed its lead. Peter Schey, one of the main lawyers involved in defending migrants' rights during the 1970s, explained, "I always sort of took the position that we were much like a flag, and the community-based organizations were more like the wind. And so we would adjust our priorities based on inputs from the community organizations, the thinking being that the community organizations were the closest entities to the community and best informed about the significant legal problems and violations of rights being experienced by the immigrants/Latino communities."[46]

Even when attorneys followed the direction of grassroots organizations, they were not trying to build a movement but to win a case. The cases rarely received much attention in migrant communities. Few migrants other than those involved in the cases tended to know that these struggles were taking place. As such, legal cases seldom changed migrants' views of Mexican Americans or white progressives, even when members of those communities were heading the struggles in the courts. For instance, even though MALDEF fought many legal battles for undocumented Mexicans, most migrants never heard of this organization and, instead, continued to judge Mexican Americans based on their everyday interactions with them. Migrants expected ethnic Mexicans to be kinder to them than Anglos were. When Mexican Americans disrespected them, they remembered. Sandra Paiz, who migrated from Sonora, explained, "There are Latinos who speak English, who were born [in the United States], and sometimes they treat you even worse. . . . I have had that experience . . . and that is the saddest that someone from your own race treats you like that."[47] None of the migrants interviewed for this book mentioned the legal struggles Mexican American organizations led during the 1970s to improve the lives of migrants. Yet many recalled some form of animosity they experienced from Mexican Americans in their daily lives that made them resentful.

Legal victories and defeats, however, had major impacts on the lives of undocumented migrants. Given that migrants were sometimes absent from the hearings because they had already been deported and that they were always dependent on attorneys to speak for them in court, legal cases had a different voice and makeup than grassroots campaigns. They nonetheless constituted a fundamental part of the struggle for migrants' rights.

During the 1970s, several key legal cases reached the U.S. Supreme Court. Some addressed migrants' right to move freely on roads and highways, others their right to unionize, and yet others their right to attend public school. When litigating these Supreme Court cases, the attorneys who defended migrants initially tried to refrain from declaring their cases as being explicitly for, or at least solely about, the undocumented. On roads and highways, they claimed to be defending Mexican Americans; in workplaces, employees; and in schools, children. Declaring rights under these different identities delineated the borders and consequences of each struggle. Ultimately, however, the various cases ended up centering on migrants' unauthorized status.

In the 1970s and 1980s, the Immigration and Naturalization Service (INS) started converting roads into border-type checkpoints, making them key sites in the legal fight for the rights of undocumented migrants. José Guadalupe Rodríguez, who migrated with his wife to Santa Ana, California, recalled that in the 1970s, "the situation became very delicate [because] immigration roadblocks in the freeways increased."[48] For migrants like Rodríguez, the interior of the United States came to represent a fraught zone where legal status could be checked at any time. This made it risky for migrants to perform daily activities, including going to work. As the number of inspections grew, pro-immigrant lawyers, and particularly John J. Cleary and Charles M. Sevilla, who worked at the Federal Defenders of San Diego, started to question the constitutionality of the internal checkpoints.[49]

Cleary and Sevilla had several options in choosing which arguments to employ. The Fourth Amendment established "the right of the people to be secure in their persons, houses, papers, and effects, against unreasonable searches and seizures." Under this definition, the Federal Defenders of San Diego could have focused on how all people—undocumented migrants included—deserved to be protected from unreasonable searches. While they did pursue this argument, they also focused on how Mexican Americans in particular were being held subject to arbitrary searches, even though they were citizens.

One of the cases Cleary took on came to define how "Mexican-looking" people could travel on roads and highways.[50] It was the case of Felix Humberto Brignoni Ponce, a U.S. citizen of Puerto Rican descent.[51] On the evening of March 11, 1973, Brignoni Ponce was transporting Elsa Marina Hernández Serabia, a Guatemalan citizen, and José Núñez Ayala, a Mexican citizen, into the United States illegally by driving them north on Interstate Highway 5 in Southern California. Although little evidence survives detailing the voices and experiences of Hernández Serabia or Núñez Ayala, other undocumented migrants have described the fear they felt when they saw Border Patrol cars while they were driving. Sandra Paiz remembers feeling "extremely frightened" when driving because there were Border Patrol agents "just stopping cars randomly."[52] While Paiz was never pulled over and apprehended by immigration officials, Hernández Serabia and Núñez Ayala did not have the same luck. In what turned out not to be a "random" decision, immigration officials in a roving patrol car stopped Brignoni Ponce's car. Upon questioning the driver and passengers, the agents concluded that Hernández Serabia and Núñez Ayala were in the country illegally. They arrested all three and then charged Brignoni Ponce with transporting undocumented migrants. Cleary took this case, which eventually reached the Supreme Court.

Cleary argued that because the car was not at the border, officers had to have probable cause to stop it.[53] The Fourth Amendment protected people "against unreasonable searches and seizures" but the "reasonableness" of a search varied depending on how close to the border it occurred. Searches that took place at the border itself required no warrant, probable cause, or even degree of suspicion, but this was not so in the interior of the country. Immigration officials, Cleary held, should not treat points within the United States as border zones.

The officers testified that they did have a justifiable reason to stop the car: the three occupants in the automobile "appeared to be of Mexican descent."[54] Cleary rebutted this logic by holding that the agents had "applied the impermissible assumption that the pigmentation of the skin of the Defendant and his two passengers rendered them more likely to be engaged in immigration violations." As Cleary held, looking Mexican "described thousands of American citizens."[55] MALDEF submitted an amicus curiae brief in support of Brignoni Ponce, which critiqued the agents' association of Mexican appearance with illegality. MALDEF

lawyers argued, "It is not a crime to be of Mexican descent, nor is a
person's Mexican appearance a proper basis for arousing an officer's
suspicions. Those broad descriptions literally fit millions of law-abiding
American citizens and lawfully resident aliens."[56] They further contended
that "persons of Mexican descent or appearance enjoy the same constitutional right to travel on the public highways free of unreasonable searches
and seizures as do other United States citizens and lawful resident
aliens."[57]

Although powerful and understandable, MALDEF's and Cleary's emphasis on the ways in which these stops affected citizens and legal residents undermined the notion that the Fourth Amendment protected
everyone in the United States, not just citizens. By crafting U.S.-born
Mexican Americans as the rightful bearers of constitutional protections,
these lawyers diluted the idea that all people—including undocumented
migrants—ought to be free from unreasonable searches and seizures.

The government's lawyers responded that immigration officials
should, in fact, have the same authorization to stop, seize, and search
cars in the entire border region that they have at the border itself. They
also insisted that officers should be allowed to take Mexican appearance
into consideration, because they were dealing "with an immigration law
enforcement problem of immense proportions, and nearly all the viola-
tors in the Mexican border area [were] illegal entrants from Mexico."[58]
Under these circumstances, they argued, it was understandable that "a
northbound vehicle carrying three persons of apparent Mexican descent
might arouse the suspicions of the agents." "Those suspicions," they
added, "in this case were borne out." Of course, their argument ignored
the fact that out of the three passengers in Ponce's car, only one was
Mexican while one was a Guatemalan citizen and the other was a U.S.
citizen of Puerto Rican descent.

On June 30, 1975, Justice Lewis Powell delivered the Supreme Court's
decision. Technically, *United States v. Brignoni-Ponce* constituted a victory
for unauthorized migrants and a loss for the U.S. government. The Court
reversed Brignoni Ponce's criminal conviction after finding that the
officers had violated the Fourth Amendment by relying solely on the
Mexican appearance of the driver and passengers. But even though
the justices found that "looking Mexican" could not, by itself, amount
to reasonable suspicion, they concluded that it could be relevant alongside other factors.[59] The court reasoned, "The likelihood that any given

person of Mexican ancestry is an alien is high enough to make Mexican appearance a relevant factor, but standing alone it does not justify stopping all Mexican-Americans to ask if they are aliens."[60] The following year, the Supreme Court built on this decision in *United States v. Martinez-Fuerte* (1976), holding that immigration officials could refer cars to secondary inspection at permanent checkpoints if the occupants of the cars appeared to be of Mexican ancestry.[61]

The Supreme Court thus put an official stamp on the association between "Mexican appearance" and illegality.[62] Most of those living and moving throughout the Southwest who "looked Mexican" were, in fact, U.S. citizens. The ruling also presumed that there was such a thing as "Mexican appearance" when, of course, Mexican citizens had wide-ranging phenotypes. Even though Cleary and MALDEF lawyers presented citizens and legal residents of Mexican descent as the ones whose rights were being breached through these stops, they did not manage to halt the practice. If anything, the case resulted in the Supreme Court's legalization of discrimination against all people of "Mexican appearance."

Despite the Court's rulings, smugglers found other ways to transport migrants, sometimes using racial stereotypes to their advantage. José Juárez recalled that immediately after he crossed the border in 1986, his *coyotes* took him to a garage where a car was waiting for him and other migrants. The smugglers instructed him and two other individuals to lay on the back seat and floor of the car so that they would not be visible. An Anglo American man drove the car, probably to avoid suspicions of illegality. When they approached an internal checkpoint, Juárez recalled, the smuggler instructed the migrants to get into the car's trunk, telling them "when [I] turn the radio on is when [we] are crossing so don't make noise."[63] Border Patrol officials only saw a white man in the car and allowed the automobile to go through with no problems.

Even as the lawyers from the Federal Defenders of San Diego were losing the legal fight around migrants' right to move freely on roads and highways within the United States, another set of pro-immigrant lawyers started focusing on a second site where migrants' rights were being curtailed because of their status: the workplace. The lawyers and activists who became involved in this legal battle sought to establish migrants as "employees" who were entitled to U.S. labor protections, including the right to unionize.

The struggle began in Chicago in July 1976, when the Chicago Leather Workers Union started an organizing drive at a set of leather-processing firms, referred to collectively as Sure-Tan, Inc.[64] Approximately eleven workers, most of whom were undocumented Mexican nationals, labored at the firms.[65] They were excited about the possibility of improving their wages and working conditions through collective bargaining, but they knew that joining the union was risky. In October 1976, their boss, John Surak, approached Francisco Robles, one of the employees, and told him, "Union no good. Little work. . . . Company is good. A lot of work here." After insisting that Robles vote against the union, he said, "O.K. Francisco?" to which Robles simply replied, "O.K."[66] To avoid problems with their employer, the workers sometimes pretended not to understand that a unionization drive was happening. In August 1976, Surak asked a group of employees, "You all union?" to which Floriberto Rodríguez, one of the employees, responded that they knew nothing about the union. Discerning the guise, Surak called the group "mother fucking son of a bitches" and left the room.[67] Despite fears that unionization would cost them their jobs and might even get them deported, the workers at Sure-Tan decided that they could not tolerate Surak's intimidation.

On December 10, 1976, the workers voted in favor of the union. When Surak found out, he became furious. "Union why? Union why?" he screamed at the workers and demanded to know if they had valid immigration papers.[68] Robles responded that "nobody had papers there."[69] Surak immediately informed the National Labor Relations Board (NLRB) that many of the workers who had voted in the union elections were "illegal aliens" who should not have had the right to participate. To Surak's surprise, the board overruled his objection and maintained that undocumented workers were considered employees under the National Labor Relations Act (NLRA) and thus had the right to participate in union activities. The NLRA established: "Employees shall have the right to self-organization, to form, join, or assist labor organizations, to bargain collectively through representatives of their own choosing, and to engage in other concerted activities for the purpose of collective bargaining or other mutual aid or protection."[70] The NLRA made no mention of legal status in its definition of "employees."

Surak did not give up. To disrupt the unionization of the shop, he sent a letter to immigration officials asking them to check the status of the company's employees. Responding to his request, INS agents carried out an investigation and deported five workers who did not have proper authorization to be in the United States.[71] Surak's actions sent a clear message to all undocumented migrants that joining a union would cost them their jobs and residence in the United States.

Aware of the consequences of allowing those who unionized to be deported, NLRB personnel declared that Sure-Tan had engaged in unfair labor practices. According to the agency's lawyers, immigration authorities could not be called "solely because" of workers' support for a union. The Federal Court of Appeals agreed. It also determined that if Surak had not called immigration authorities, the apprehended workers might have kept their jobs for at least another six months and therefore awarded the employees back pay.[72]

Because the migrants themselves had been deported, it was hard for them to speak out and defend their rights. However, Francisco Robles returned to the United States and testified at the hearing.[73] He conveyed how Surak intimidated him and the other workers so that they would not unionize. He also spoke about the threats Surak issued after he learned that the workers had voted for the union. Three other workers, Aguiminio Ruiz, Ernesto Arreguín, and Sacramento Serrano, wrote affidavits describing what had happened.[74]

To be successful, however, the deported migrants needed the support of the NLRB and pro-immigrant advocacy groups. They received it.[75] Even members of organizations that wanted to curtail unauthorized migration—such as the AFL-CIO and the UFW—came out in support as they understood that if they did not protect the labor rights of undocumented migrants, they would be depressing the status of all workers because employers would have even more incentive to hire the most vulnerable rather than rights-bearing citizens. *Sure-Tan, Inc. v. NLRB* ultimately reached the Supreme Court. The NLRB's brief explained that the nation's labor laws, as dictated by "the terms and policies of the National Labor Relations Act fully support[ed] the coverage of undocumented aliens."[76] The application of these labor laws to undocumented migrants, it explained, was also "consistent with and further[ed] the purposes of the Immigration and Nationality Act."

In 1984, the Supreme Court ruled in *Sure-Tan, Inc. v. NLRB* that the company had violated the rights of the apprehended migrants. The Court determined that undocumented workers were, in fact, employees under the NLRA and as such were protected by domestic labor legislation. It also agreed with the NLRB that protecting the labor rights of undocumented workers did not contradict immigration law. On the contrary, allowing them to unionize decreased employers' incentive to hire them over citizens, which could in turn reduce illegal migration.[77]

Even though the Supreme Court ruled that undocumented workers were included in the NLRA's definition of "employee," the case did not establish any repercussions that would, in practice, dissuade employers from violating the law.[78] The Court held that the back pay award set by the Federal Court of Appeals was too "speculative" and that the discharged workers could not receive payment for "any period when they were not lawfully entitled to be present and employed in the United States."[79] Because back pay constituted the only material repercussion employers faced for calling the INS in response to workers' unionization efforts, the Court's ruling, in effect, opened the way for employers to violate the law.

By the time the Supreme Court ruled on the case, the migrants who had been deported for their actions at Sure-Tan were not expecting to receive back pay, nor did they seek to be reinstated at the leather firm. While their unionization had led to their deportation, they knew they could return to the United States if they so desired because the border remained relatively porous. They also knew that they had not left without a fight. By joining the union and organizing for their rights, the workers had staked a claim to their lives in the United States.

For migrants to be able to reside permanently in the United States, however, they needed to do more than avoid deportation when they moved through the streets or when they demanded labor rights. They also needed to be able to bring their family members north of the border and ensure that they too had rights. Migrants took up this issue by fighting for the rights of unauthorized children to attend public schools.

In 1975, the Texas Legislature enacted a state law that enabled public school districts to charge tuition or to deny admission to children who were in the country illegally.[80] Districts in Texas responded in varying ways to the passage of this law: some ignored it; others moved to bar undocumented children from attending schools; and others decided to charge the children tuition, knowing that their families would not be able to pay. The Tyler Independent School District, on which pro-immigrant groups would eventually focus their efforts, began charging undocumented children $1,000 annually to attend school, an amount that migrants could not afford.[81] As the father of one of the children explained, his "salary [did] not meet that quantity of money."[82]

Those affected by this law were generally not circular migrants but families that had already decided to settle in the United States.[83] Consequently, they were more invested in, if also more scared about, fighting for their rights north of the border. Lidia and José López, for instance, knew that most migrants were men who went back and forth between the two countries while their families stayed in Mexico, but they decided that this was not the best option for their family. They moved together to the United States with the hopes of settling there and having their children attain the education that they had not received in Mexico.[84] Their desire to belong in the United States made them more willing to engage in a court battle to achieve rights. The other parents who took part in the case had also settled in Tyler. They all had lived there between three and thirteen years, they all had car titles and either rented or owned a house, they all paid federal and Social Security taxes, and they all had at least one child who had been born in the United States.[85]

When the families first heard that they could no longer send their children to school they tried to understand what was happening, often to no avail. One of the mothers talked with school administrators, who informed her that "there was nothing that could be done."[86] Another disregarded the notice she had received and took her children to school, but they were sent home.[87] Yet another was told by school administrators that "they would not admit [the children] without papers or permission." She and her husband believed the administrators were referring to "the papers of immigration," but they weren't entirely sure.[88]

Confused about what to do, one of the families turned for help to Michael McAndrew, an outreach worker at the local Roman Catholic church. In turn, McAndrew contacted local civil rights and labor law attorney Larry Daves who reached out to MALDEF.[89] Leaders there took a strong interest in the case because, in light of the 1954 *Brown v. Board of Education* decision outlawing segregation in schools, they believed education to be a civil rights cause célèbre. MALDEF's lawyer, Peter Roos, and its president, Vilma Martínez, agreed that it made sense to bring the lawsuit in Tyler because the district was small enough that it would not receive much media attention, had a progressive judge, and had few undocumented students, which meant that the new tuition served more as a symbol of exclusion than as a way to raise money for the district.[90]

Initially, most pro-immigrant lawyers cheered MALDEF's work on the case.[91] But the more they studied it, the more they worried about the appropriateness of Tyler as the chosen school district. They feared that even if MALDEF won, Texas legislators would be able to argue that the particularity of Tyler meant that the ruling could not be applied to other districts. As pro-immigrant attorney Peter Schey recalled, progressive lawyers throughout Texas started filing other lawsuits thinking "this one case in Tyler is probably not going to help me in Austin, it's probably not going to help me in Houston, it's not going to help me in wherever—in San Antonio. We have a different situation. We got 10,000 times more undocumented people. The money situation is different—everything's different."[92] Ultimately, these different lawyers called Schey, who had an impressive record of defending migrants' rights, and together they decided that this was "a statewide issue [and, as such,] ought to be done as a statewide class action."[93] They filed *In re Alien Children* as a statewide suit. In 1981, the Supreme Court consolidated Schey's and MALDEF's case into *Plyler v. Doe.*

The children in the case appeared with placeholder initials and last names Doe, Loe, Boe, and Roe to hide their identities.[94] Using their actual names would have made them visible as undocumented migrants and placed them at risk of deportation. As it was, accusations flared up that the U.S. attorney general had instructed the INS to conduct immigration sweeps in Tyler to intimidate the children's families so that they would drop the suit.[95] Roos threatened to accuse the INS of tampering with the trial, and no such raids occurred. Still, at every stage, the parents of the children knew they could be sent back to Mexico, and moving forward took great courage. Sometimes, immigration agents even showed up at lower court hearings when the parents were testifying, interrupting the proceedings.[96]

Before the Supreme Court, Roos and Schey argued that the Texas law violated the equal protection clause of the Fourteenth Amendment, which held that no state could "deny to any person within its jurisdiction the equal protection of the laws." Like the Fourth Amendment, the Fourteenth Amendment spoke in terms of persons rather than citizens. Undocumented migrants, Roos told the Court, were protected by the equal protection clause "because they are indeed persons."[97] To further stress the point, Roos noted that "Representative Bingham, who was commonly acknowledged to be the author of Section One of the Fourteenth Amendment," had spoken "of the due process and equal protection clauses alike as protecting the citizen and the stranger."[98] Through these arguments, Roos and Schey advocated for the idea that just by being present in the United States, even if illegally, migrants deserved constitutional protections.

Beyond portraying undocumented migrants as persons to be protected under the Fourteenth Amendment, they also appealed to the children's youth and innocence. By doing so they moved away from defending all undocumented migrants as rightful bearers of equal rights protections to promoting undocumented children as bearing these rights. Before the case reached the Supreme Court, a nine-year-old girl testified that she had been expelled from school even though she had been brought to the United States by her parents when she was still a baby.[99] Her siblings, who were younger, had been born north of the border and were thus citizens who could attend school. With tears in her eyes, the girl described how she yearned to go back and receive an education.[100] The difference between her and her sisters' situation shed light on the arbitrariness of the Texas law.

In June 1982, the Supreme Court ruled on the case. It decided by a 5–4 margin to strike down the Texas statute. The justices reached their decision by appealing to an innocent child versus a guilty adult paradigm, a result of the legal strategy to focus on children as the apt bearers of rights.[101] The opinion of the Court stated that while the parents of undocumented children had "the ability to conform their conduct to societal norms, and presumably the ability to remove themselves from the State's jurisdiction," the children themselves "who are plaintiffs in these cases can affect neither their parents' conduct nor their own status."[102] Through these words, the justices popularized portrayals of adult migrants as criminal and guilty for their migration, without noting the broader socioeconomic forces at play that led adults to head north without proper authorization.

Still, *Plyler v. Doe* changed the lives of the children involved with the case, in particular, and also those of all undocumented children who gained access to a public education. In 2011, José López's living room still displayed photographs of his children's high school graduations. The fear he and his family experienced on September 9, 1977, when he had packed his family belongings in his car in case they were deported, was only a memory. Now his grandchildren were attending school in Tyler and dreamed of becoming pediatricians and music producers.[103] In schools all over the country, children who did not have legal status were receiving an education thanks in part to the efforts of López and the other families involved in the case.

The decision in *Plyler v. Doe* had another consequence for the history of Mexican immigration to the United States. As the border became harder to cross after the mid-1980s, the availability of education for un- documented children in the United States meant that more families could start questioning whether men should continue engaging in circular migration or whether the entire family should move north permanently.

Laws on the books meant little if migrants didn't know about their existence. As such, alongside the legal battles that took place, undocu- mented migrants, their communities, and their allies worked to inform individuals—both before they headed north and once they were already in the United States—that their lack of papers did not necessarily ex- clude them from basic rights. Spreading this information required them to acknowledge the undocumented as an apt category under which to organize. Their efforts reinforced notions that undocumented migrants could belong and reside permanently in the United States.

Communities in Mexico worked to disseminate the idea that unau- thorized individuals deserved rights in the United States before migrants left Mexico. Many of these efforts were spearheaded by churches. In Nochistlán, Zacatecas, the priest and a few parishioners published the biweekly newspaper, *El Sembrador,* which contained a whole section dedicated to the question of migration. One of the articles in the paper had the subheading "The Undocumented and Their Rights in the United States."[104] Through these articles *El Sembrador* reinforced the notion that unauthorized migrants could settle in the United States and gave indi- viduals the tools to actually be able to do so. For example, an article con- veyed to migrants that they needed to know their rights through the story of Samuel, who could have avoided being deported if he had known that he was entitled to seek legal aid.[105] It also provided the example of Irma, who had opened her door and allowed an INS officer into her house, even though he did not have a warrant. According to the article, Irma should have been aware that she could deny entry to the officer.

These examples detailed undocumented migrants' rights while simultaneously stressing the importance of knowing them in order to be
able to remain in *El Norte*.

Grassroots organizers in the United States also produced literature
to inform migrants about their rights. In 1980, Deb Preusch and Tom
Barry, who had been part of MCOP, published *El otro lado: Una guía para
los indocumentados* (The Other Side: A Guide for the Undocumented).[106]
The title itself brought the identity of the undocumented to the forefront.
Barry recalled that they were inspired to write this guide because, while
he was working for MCOP, undocumented workers would sometimes
ask him and the other organizers about their rights, "and we didn't always have answers."[107] The guide addressed the very topics that lawyers
were debating in the courts, including migrants' unionization, movement
on highways, and access to school. It also imparted cultural and practical knowledge that undocumented workers needed in order to understand everyday life north of the border and avoid being apprehended. It
provided information such as how they could send money to Mexico,
learn English, use public transit, and buy food and clothes.

El otro lado became an extremely popular guide. According to Preusch,
the first series of 10,000 copies were bought as soon as they were published, forcing the authors to do more runs.[108] Legal Aid offices were some
of the primary consumers of the booklet, as it was the only literature
they knew that talked about the rights of the undocumented.[109] At least
fourteen Mexican consulates situated in Arizona, California, Colorado,
Florida, Illinois, New Mexico, New York, and Texas advertised or distributed the guide. So did more than sixty churches from multiple
denominations located in twenty-nine states.[110]

By 1980, the disparate groups, activists, and lawyers fighting for
migrants' rights decided to take an even more vocal stance by coming
together at the International Conference for the Full Rights of Undocumented Workers, which was held in Mexico City. This was not the first
conference that activists had organized to defend migrants.[111] But it did
bring together a more diverse group of organizations from both countries, and unlike other conferences, it did so under the banner of defending not just migrants but undocumented ones. By the conference's
end, the participating delegations issued a "Bill of Rights for Immigrant
Workers," which asserted many of the rights that lawyers and activists

were fighting for, including access to public education and freedom of movement.[112]

While migrants and their allies had previously fought for the rights of the unauthorized under other categories, they now came together at this conference in the name of those who crossed the border without papers, while also advancing a view that benefited the entire working class. For example, Article 10 of their Bill of Rights declared "the right of immigrant workers to unionize." To fulfill this clause, it also established "the right of agricultural and domestic workers to a National Labor Relations Act that would guarantee the full right to organize and unionize."[113] This addition was indispensable for undocumented migrants, as many of them labored in agriculture and domestic work, neither of which was protected by the NLRA. An expanded NLRA, however, would not just protect undocumented workers, but the U.S. workforce as a whole.

The struggles to defend the rights of undocumented migrants fractured the unquestioned marginalization experienced by those who were in the United States without papers. Even while unauthorized migrants continued to be excluded from social, economic, and legal incorporation because of their status, these struggles pushed forward the notion that their mere presence north of the border ought to provide them with rights and that they could seek belonging there.

Despite its increasing visibility, the movement for undocumented migrants' rights rapidly declined in the mid-1980s. Even MCOP, which had come to be known as a symbol of successful migrant organizing, saw its multiple projects collapse in the years between 1984 and 1986. The group was forced to shut down operations after citrus growers decided to bulldoze their farms and turned them into subdivisions for housing and shopping centers, which could make more money than growing fruit. Even more devastating for those who sought rights for undocumented migrants: as nativist voices began to gain a stronghold in Congress during the Reagan administration, activists had to refocus their energies into fighting against the passage of anti-immigrant legislation. Up to the mid-1980s, pro-migrant organizers had managed to stand up to nativist groups and win many rights for undocumented workers. By the mid-1980s, they were losing much of the ground and momentum they had gained.

Still, by the mid-1980s, migrants had already learned that they could strive for inclusion north of the border and invest in their lives in the

United States. They knew that migrating was the best way to achieve partial belonging in Mexico, in the United States, and in their communities on both sides of the border. Some of the victories of earlier years, especially *Plyler v. Doe*, had even opened up the possibility for them to move to the United States permanently and bring their families with them if needed. This is exactly what would happen after the U.S. Congress passed the Immigration Reform and Control Act (IRCA) in 1986.

7

....

A LAW TO CURTAIL
UNDOCUMENTED MIGRATION

C LAPPING AND CHEERS erupted in the Roosevelt Room of the White House shortly after 10 AM on the chilly morning of November 6, 1986.[1] President Ronald Reagan had just signed the Immigration Reform and Control Act (IRCA), a law that had been winding through Washington since 1972.[2] Hailing it as "the most comprehensive reform of our immigration laws since 1952," Reagan added that "future generations of Americans will be thankful for our efforts to humanely regain control of our borders."[3] His statement accurately predicted the significance of IRCA: the law became the most important legislation regulating immigration to the United States for at least thirty years following its passage. But Reagan's claim that future generations would be thankful for it proved incorrect. Scholars, Mexican American activists, and U.S. politicians from both the left and the right of the political spectrum soon declared the law a failure. In 2006, even Representative Romano L. Mazzoli (D-KY) and Senator Alan K. Simpson (R-WY), the authors of the bill, recognized that "the 1986 Immigration Reform and Control Act— IRCA, or the Simpson-Mazzoli bill—is referred to frequently in today's high-decibel immigration debates—and rarely affectionately."[4]

Legislators passed IRCA to reduce the number of undocumented migrants living in the United States. But in the two decades following its passage, the number of unauthorized migrants grew faster than ever. Whereas in 1986 there were 3.2 million undocumented migrants, the number reached 5 million in 1996 and peaked at approximately 11 million in 2006.[5] The measures that Reagan hailed to take "control of our borders" multiplied the number of deaths and injuries of those who sought to enter the United States illegally but did not dissuade Mexicans from heading north.[6] If anything, the increased fortification of the border kept migrants trapped in the United States.[7] Fearful that if they returned to Mexico they would not be able to go back to *El Norte* again if they needed work, Mexicans stopped engaging in circular migration as earlier migrants had done and instead settled permanently in the United States. With Reagan's signature, the faraway world of lawmaking crashed into the world of migrants, reshaping them both: the passage of IRCA restructured the contours of migrant life, while migrants' response to IRCA ensured that the law failed in its intended goal.

In the two decades prior to the passage of IRCA, migrants tried to make sense of a life in which they could belong "neither here nor there." During those same years, U.S. politicians and lobbyists became involved in a parallel effort, trying to make sense of the role of Mexican migrants in the United States. But the way in which policymakers thought about migration was fundamentally different from the way migrants conceived of their lives and journeys north. The gap between these two perspectives partially explains why IRCA failed to curtail undocumented migration. To the key stakeholders at the hearings, the needs and lives of migrants were irrelevant and invisible. This meant that they overlooked how, in the years between 1965 and 1986, many Mexicans had concluded that living in the United States, whether permanently or temporarily, was the best option they had to challenge the various exclusions they faced. By not acknowledging that for migrant communities going to *El Norte* had become a part of life, policymakers failed to address the true roots of migration and proposed only fruitless solutions.

In order to understand the perspective of those involved in crafting this law, one source is especially revealing: congressional hearings. When debating the various immigration bills proposed between 1972 and 1986, members of Congress held multiday hearings and invited representatives of relevant business groups, Mexican American advocacy organizations, and labor unions to offer testimony. Although the hearings do not demonstrate the full spectrum of political opinions or reveal the actual negotiations that happened behind closed doors, they constitute the key source of formal political discourse. The hearings display the rhetoric that politicians thought would be most convincing, both to one another and to Americans at large.

Along the long and tortured road that culminated in the passage of IRCA, policymakers constantly questioned whether migrants drained the nation's welfare coffers, took jobs away from citizens, increased population growth through their excessive fertility rates, or blurred the nation's boundaries through their illegal entrances. Even though the hearings, to various degrees, all revolved around questions of welfare, unemployment, border permeability, kinship, and population control, policymakers overlooked how these very issues guided the migratory process and emboldened migrants to live in the United States. Sandra Paiz captured how most migrants experienced the need to cross the border when she reported, "We never came with the intention of taking advantage of the United States or the benefits that the United States has. We simply came with the . . . idea of having a better life, of excelling . . . of coming to . . . work and to help our families that were in Mexico . . . and to leave behind the life that existed in Mexico, of poverty, of . . . scarcities."[8] Far removed from the world of migrants, those inside the marble and sandstone walls of the U.S. Capitol disregarded how the very forces they were describing through clichés actually worked on the ground to compel Mexicans to head north.[9]

Between 1972, when the first employer sanctions bill was introduced, and 1986, when IRCA passed, the anti-immigrant rhetoric at the hearings changed from "left" to "right" in the political spectrum and from national to international in focus.[10] While calls to curtail undocumented migration would eventually become associated with the right, in the early 1970s it was labor unions and Mexican American organizations, groups generally branded as liberal, that demanded sanctions on employers who knowingly hired unauthorized migrants. For their part, employer lobbies that depended on undocumented workers, and that are generally considered conservative organizations, insisted that migrants were a needed labor force. It was only in the late 1970s and early 1980s that the appeals to curtail undocumented migration came to adopt a more conservative base and international vision. During these years, liberal groups started to support unauthorized workers while conservative ones decided to stop defending migrants and to instead use the debates to spread their international influence. While the positions of the various stakeholders changed over time, their focus on questions of welfare, unemployment, border permeability, kinship, and population control remained consistent, as did their lack of attention to how these issues actually worked on the ground.

Even though the belief that unauthorized migration has to be curbed has come to represent a bedrock conservative principle, the push to curtail undocumented migration first originated with the left. The seeds that grew into IRCA were planted by pro-union politicians who denounced migrants for taking jobs away from citizens and draining state and federal welfare coffers. In 1972, Representative Peter W. Rodino (D-NJ), a strong ally of the AFL-CIO and chair of the House Judiciary Committee's Subcommittee on Immigration, introduced the first bill to impose sanctions on employers who knowingly hired undocumented workers.[11] He argued that employer sanctions would reduce the demand for unauthorized labor, which would, in turn, discourage those who did not have papers from migrating. The following year, an almost identical bill was proposed that also contained ancillary measures that required the Department of Health, Education, and Welfare to disclose the names of undocumented migrants who received public assistance benefits and that amended federal law to prohibit the misuse of entry documents.[12] Pro-union Representative Joshua Eilberg (D-PA) came out in support of employer sanctions, declaring that unsanctioned migration "compromises labor conditions, depresses wages, and deprives Americans of jobs."[13] The AFL-CIO had a similar stance: "With more than 7,500,000 Americans unemployed and joblessness rising the presence of millions of illegal aliens in this country is an acute and growing problem."[14] The federation also condemned "the heavy need of these illegal immigrants for free medical care, unemployment compensation, welfare and social services," which put "heavy burdens on government at every level and on the taxpayers of the nation."[15]

During the early 1970s, mainstream Mexican American organizations—which, like unions, were considered liberal groups—upheld the view that undocumented migrants were contributing to the nation's unemployment rates and welfare problems. The stance of the United Farm Workers (UFW) was particularly strong, in part because it was an AFL-CIO union, but most mainstream Mexican American organizations also sought to increase restrictions against Mexican foreigners, whom they blamed for the denigration that Mexican Americans faced in the United States. In the hearings on the issue of unauthorized migration held in 1975, the National Congress of Hispanic-American Citizens, which was linked to some of the most important Mexican American organizations, defended employer sanctions, claiming that "if the purpose of immigration laws is to protect the domestic work force, it is logical to exercise the most stringent control at the place of work."[16] During these years, only radical Chicana/o organizations, which did not voice their position in Congress, argued against the idea that migrants stole jobs from citizens and drained welfare. The Centro de Acción Social Autónomo (CASA), one of these groups, declared in its pamphlets, "The Rodino bill is not the solution to the growing wave of problems which confront this society and manifest themselves in the growing numbers of unemployed or high prices."[17] In terms of welfare, CASA maintained that because workers were "not to blame for fewer jobs or lower salaries," it was the government's responsibility to provide them with income.[18]

Migrants' need to have basic welfare provisions and access to jobs did in fact influence migratory patterns, but the relationship between these various issues was much more complex than unions and Mexican American organizations depicted. Individuals migrated without authorization because of Mexico's high levels of unemployment and underemployment. In the United States, they took poorly paid jobs, often in the service industry, which most U.S. citizens did not want. Though migrants were lambasted for stealing welfare dollars, the reality was that they did not qualify for U.S. welfare aid and only a few dared to apply illegally. Their jobs in the United States, however meager, provided them and their families with a safety net that the Mexican government's "welfare state" failed to provide. Some of these migrants even built an extraterritorial welfare system that supported those in their home communities. As Adalberto Rodríguez recalled, even though he missed his family tremendously, he migrated continually between Mexico and the United States because in his hometown there was not enough work to sustain him. "There were times when one would think I'm not coming back [to the United States] because it was so hard. . . . I would even start shivering before my departures, but despite this pain, [economic] need was greater," he explained.[19] Unemployment in Mexico made him return to the fields of Coachella Valley every year. There, he was often paid below the minimum wage and lived in cardboard boxes under trees.

While these types of jobs were undesirable to U.S. citizens, for Rodrí-guez and other migrants they represented a source of income that al-lowed them to survive and send money back home without relying on state aid. As Rodríguez sneered in 2015, "In all the years I have [been] living here in the United States, the government has given me nothing, not even a smear of Vaseline."[20]

In the mid-1970s, unions and mainstream Mexican American organ-izations started tempering—and sometimes even reversing—their anti-immigrant position. The development of a Chicana/o identity, which was inherently political, led many Mexican Americans to start seeing Mexicans as their brethren and to insist that anti-immigrant sentiments and policies translated into discriminatory measures against anyone who looked brown.[21] A Mexican American labor union official articulated this increasingly common position when he claimed that Mexican Amer-icans who still favored anti-immigrant policies "should realize that they would not be here if their fathers had not been illegal aliens."[22] As a re-sult of the new perspective on undocumented migrants among Mexican Americans, the ever-visible "Hispanic lobby" composed of the National Council of La Raza (NCLR), the Mexican American Legal Defense and Educational Fund (MALDEF), the League of United Latin American Cit-izens (LULAC), and the UFW began to support Mexican migrants.[23] In 1977, the Hispanic lobby gained the backing of the newly created Con-gressional Hispanic Caucus, formed by Latino representatives in Con-gress. The caucus's small numbers meant that it had limited power (as late as 1984, there were only ten Latinos in Congress, and they were all in the House of Representatives, a small portion of the House's 435 total seats). Still, the caucus represented a part of the growing number of Mex-ican American groups that advocated for undocumented migrants.

As Mexican American organizations began to defend unauthorized workers, they changed their rhetoric on the impact migrants supposedly had on the nation's welfare coffers and unemployment rates. In his 1978 testimony before the United States Commission on Civil Rights, Michael Cortés, then vice president of the NCLR, claimed, "There is a growing body of research that concludes that certain jobs have traditionally been shunned by the domestic labor force. Those jobs have traditionally been filled by immigrants."[24] Cortés noted that the press and politicians falsely accused undocumented migrants of "illegally receiving welfare payments and otherwise burdening the public treasury." Instead, he claimed, "undocumented workers are subject to withholding taxes and social security taxes in most employment settings," but unlike citizens and permanent residents, they "typically do not receive publicly supported protections and services paid for by those taxes."[25] Mexican American organizations also insisted that employer sanctions would increase discriminatory employment practices against brown people. As Vilma Martínez, the president of MALDEF, argued at hearings on unauthorized migration held in 1981: "For Mexican Americans and other Americans who share the physical characteristics of persons thought to be undocumented, employer sanctions will exacerbate existing patterns of employment discrimination."[26]

During the late 1970s and early 1980s, several unions also changed their stance. The United Auto Workers, the Longshoremen's Union, the United Electrical Workers, the Hotel Employees and Restaurant Employees, and the International Ladies' Garment Workers' Union (ILGWU), came to realize that they could not survive in the long run without recruiting the growing population of Mexican nationals. The case of the ILGWU is illustrative. Between 1948 and 1979, ILGWU's membership fell from 67 percent to 10 percent of all the workers who labored in ladies' garments in Los Angeles.[27] This decline could be partially traced to the growing anti-union sentiments in the United States as well as to the ILGWU's failure to organize undocumented migrants, who were a growing proportion of the workers in the garment industry.[28] To counter these patterns, the ILGWU began to hire Mexican migrant organizers so that they would enroll undocumented workers in the union. ILGWU activist María Elena Salazar explained to fellow union members, "For our own survival we cannot adopt the perspective that it is impossible to unionize them [unauthorized laborers]."[29] The ILGWU expanded its recruitment efforts through various means, including by publishing a series of cartoons. One of them challenged Spanish-speaking employees to join the union by asking them, "What Type of Worker Are You?" In it, a janitor complains, "I can't join the union because I am 'illegal' and I don't have rights. . . . Besides I am already going to return to my home country and also I don't have time and blah, blah, blah and blah, blah, blah." In response, a garment worker scoffs, "It is not illegal to be a worker! We produce much wealth for this country and we have the right to a union. The exploitative employers that steal from us are the illegals. . . . I support the union!"[30]

Cartoon, "¿Que Tipo de Obrero es Usted?" published in *Boletín Informativo Sobre Asuntos Migratorios y Fronterizos* (Centro de Información para Asuntos Migratorios y Fronterizos del Comité de Servicios de los Amigos, August-September, 1980): 10. Reproduced from the Nettie Lee Benson Latin American Collection, University of Texas Libraries, The University of Texas at Austin.

Cartoons such as this one recognized the exploitation that migrants faced, contested their "illegality," and replaced the traditional union narrative that depicted migrants as draining the U.S. economy for one in which they "created much wealth" for the country. ILGWU organizers like Salazar openly discussed the fact that undocumented migrants were taking jobs that U.S. citizens refused to take. As she explained, employers "don't find [U.S. citizens] who come to work in the garment industry because they pay the minimum wage . . . and they greatly exploit the people. It is hard work."[31] The shift in attitudes could sometimes seem like a contradiction. At the congressional hearings, ILGWU continued to support employer sanctions and sometimes even offered pejorative stereotypes about the economic effects of undocumented migrants; yet it also began to favor the legalization of those who were already in the United States so that they could become legal permanent residents.[32]

After switching their position, some unions and Mexican American organizations started to argue that migrants who were already in the country should be allowed to become permanent residents. In the hearings held in 1981, the president of MALDEF insisted that lawmakers should adjust "the status of undocumented workers who have equities in our society" given that they worked "in our industries, [paid] taxes, and contribute[d] to our economic welfare."[33] Many undocumented migrants were elated by the possibility that the law being discussed could help them legalize their status and eventually be able to acquire a green card and even citizenship. Wendy Rodríguez, whose parents had brought her to the United States as a child, recalled that she and her high school classmates, who were "going through the same thing" she was because they were also undocumented, would regularly talk about how the new law might help them gain legal status.[34]

Under pressure from some of its own unions and Mexican American organizations, the AFL-CIO capitulated to calls for legalization, and even though it continued to call for employer sanctions, it started to insist that these include measures to prevent discrimination. In the 1985 hearings, the federation called for "the most generous, practical, legalization program."[35] That stance stood in stark contrast to its position just a decade earlier, when it had held that in "the matter of the so-called amnesty," it "opposed [measures that] would sweep into legalization for employment large numbers of aliens who came here illegally in the first place" even while it recognized that "a strong case" could "be made for permitting aliens with family and employment ties going back over a reasonable period of years to become eligible for permanent residency."[36]

This decade-long migration of attitudes placed Mexican American organizations and unions closer to the traditional stance of business lobbies. For many employers, unauthorized workers constituted a cheap and exploitable labor force. Research conducted by the Concentrated Enforcement Program, an agency initiated by the U.S. federal government to protect workers, found that in San Diego, 33 percent of the companies inspected did not pay undocumented migrants the minimum wage or overtime, while almost none of the farms and ranches in the area did so.[37] Some employers also benefited from deportations, as these allowed them to avoid paying migrants the wages they owed them. Rodolfo Rosales, who migrated from Zacatecas in 1978, described a particularly abusive, but not particularly unusual, tactic: one of his employers took him and a group of other workers to a remote place to harvest onions for a week. When the job was done, claimed Rosales, "[the boss] failed to pay me." Rosales could not complain, however, because, as he explained, his employer drove off and "just left me there . . . and immigration officials caught me."[38]

At the hearings, employers defended the practice of hiring undocumented workers by insisting that migrants took jobs that U.S. citizens didn't want. Although the United States was facing high unemployment levels, employers held, Americans refused to take hard jobs. This meant that unauthorized workers were needed. The U.S. Chamber of Commerce, for example, maintained, "When unemployment is high, the desire to exclude illegal aliens reaches frustrating levels," but "undocumented workers do not cause unemployment."[39]

Employers also reframed stereotypes about the relationship between migrants and welfare in a way that allowed them to critique federal welfare provisions more broadly. The Arizona Cattle Growers' Association explained that few American workers actually wanted to perform the hard jobs needed at ranches. At these sites, employers could not "find many so-called domestic Americans willing to fill this job description." Sarcastically, the association's representatives then asked: "Why should they, when [the] system provides a better life through the various and sundry programs available to American workers. Most unemployment and welfare programs in this country now reward an individual for not working as hard as he has to on an Arizona ranch."[40] The association thus repeated the oft-told link between idleness and welfare but with a particular twist: that state benefits were the actual cause of unemployment among Americans, and a reason why employers had no choice but to hire migrants.

Some businesses even upheld the argument posed by Mexican American organizations that employer sanctions would induce them to discriminate against brown people. In their statement, the Arizona Cattle Growers' Association asked, "How does a rancher, for instance, differentiate between a legal domestic worker of Mexican descent and a so-called illegal alien that has somehow managed to acquire a social security card or other identification? Is he supposed to avoid hiring anyone with a Mexican or Spanish name [sic]. I don't have to tell you the discrimination problems associated with this method of hiring."[41]

Although the position of the AFL-CIO and Mexican American organizations began to coalesce with that of growers in support of undocumented migrants, the two sides continued to hold very different views on temporary guest workers. After the Bracero Program ended, some employers continued to hire contract workers through the H-2 program. The allowed number of H-2 workers, however, was negligible when compared to the number of men that had been recruited during the Bracero Program. At the hearings, farmer lobbies and their supporters insisted that, because unauthorized migrants were taking jobs that citizens did not want, legislators should only introduce measures to curtail undocumented migration if they also expanded the H-2 visa category. In the 1985 hearings, the general manager of the Florida Fruit and Vegetable Association stated, "H-2 employers have maintained that effective control of illegal immigration would require continuing and improving the H-2 program if it were not to have a traumatic effect on U.S. agriculture."[42]

For their part, both the AFL-CIO and Mexican American organizations argued that contract workers would, in fact, replace domestic employees, reduce wages, and bust unions. At the hearings, the United Farm Workers maintained that in 1978, employers in Presidio, Texas, hired H-2 workers even when many domestic laborers had applied for the positions. The union stated, "Unemployment in this part of Texas at that time [in the Rio Grande Valley] was the highest in the State." Even though the UFW had "submitted 1,700 names, addresses, and telephone numbers of domestic farmworkers who were ready to pick crops in the Presidio area," union representatives said, "none of these workers were contacted and those who showed up on their own were denied work. Instead, Mexican H-2 workers were hired."[43] The UFW claimed that companies preferred H-2 workers because they could pay them wages lower than the prevailing rate.

Labor unions and Mexican American organizations insisted that the Bracero Program had increased undocumented migration. Peter Allstrom, the director of research for the Food and Beverage Trades Department of the AFL-CIO, held that "guestworker proponents tried to explain [the need for such] programs as some sort of alternative, or answer to illegal immigration. They were haunted, throughout, by a spectre: During the bracero program illegal immigration actually increased."[44] This argument failed to recognize that while the Bracero Program had initially encouraged Mexicans to go to the United States illegally, by the program's end in 1964, so many men had become accustomed to enrolling as braceros that it was the program's termination, not the program itself, which had actually increased unauthorized migration. In 1965, hundreds of men headed to the sites from which braceros had been contracted, hoping that the program would resume. One of those men, Antonio Hinojosa, claimed, "I can't go home because there is no work there. And there is no work in Mexico City. I simply must wait here until I get a job on the other side and can send money home."[45] Tired of waiting for the program to restart, most men simply went to the United States illegally. In other words, by the mid-1960s, it was the lack of a guest worker program, rather than the existence of one, that drove unauthorized migration. Apprehensions by the Immigration and Naturalization Service (INS) rose from 43,844 in 1964 to 348,178 in 1971.[46] The AFL-CIO and the other organizations that spoke against the H-2 program failed to address this after-history of the Bracero Program.

Even as groups associated with the left softened their anti-immigrant stance, and as those from the right—namely businesses and growers—continued to benefit from undocumented migration, the passage of employer sanctions became ever more likely. In 1981, Ronald Reagan, who had previously backed employers, decided that given his emphasis on "law and order" he could not be seen as defending those who were in the country illegally.[47] After some key staff members and a few Republicans in the Senate urged him to introduce measures to curb unauthorized migration, Reagan conceded.[48]

When employers came to realize that they were going to lose on employer sanctions, they sought to reframe the debate to one that at least served them on other fronts. They thus started to critique undocumented migration, but rather than focusing on the familiar tropes that migration increased unemployment and strained the welfare system in the United States, they adopted an international vision on the relationship between migration, unemployment, and welfare. They argued that supporting free trade, capital investment, and a smaller welfare state in Mexico—which they held was necessary to make the Mexican economy more competitive—would increase the number of jobs available south of the border and curb Mexicans' need to head north. Unions and Mexican American organizations did not respond to these new calls with a unified voice. Some remained quiet, others openly spoke out against international aid and trade, and others spoke in favor. Ultimately, from a stew of different ideas, one vision came to seem natural and inevitable: that national borders should exist to contain the flow of people but not of trade and political power.

As they had done with questions of domestic welfare and employment in the 1970s, policymakers in the 1980s overlooked what was actually happening on the ground. In the 1981 hearings, the U.S. Chamber of Commerce argued that the business community was already helping curtail immigration by reducing unemployment in Mexico through capital investment. As the chamber explained, "Over 600 companies have attempted to utilize the large labor force in Mexico by building 'twin plants' along the U.S.-Mexico border."[49] The chamber acknowledged that many of the workers at those *maquiladoras* (assembly plants) would eventually migrate to the United States. But it concealed that the assembly plants employed primarily women, while men were the primary migrants. It also failed to disclose that the plants themselves encouraged internal migration to northern Mexico, which, in turn, increased border crossings to the United Sates. Mario Lazcano, one of the men who had migrated to work in this female-dominated industry, described his factory's tantalizing proximity to the north: "I lived for a while working in the assembly plants in Nogales, Sonora. . . . that was exactly at the border between Mexico and the United States . . . and there was a small block right there," he said, describing the factory's surroundings, and "every time we went out to eat . . . we went to sit on the block."[50] From that concrete block, Lazcano and his coworkers could see how immigration officials worked. As Lazcano sat and ate his lunch, he figured out how to enter the United States illegally.

Business lobbies also condemned Mexico's economic policies while ignoring migrants' experiences with these policies. In 1980, Mexico's president, José López Portillo, defied expectations when he refused to join the General Agreement on Tariffs and Trade (GATT).[51] To the business community in the United States, this decision seemed to symbolize Mexico's insistence on protectionist and welfare-state policies. The U.S. Chamber of Commerce held that Congress should consider taking "a more international and visionary perspective toward the issue of immigration reform."[52] Migrants came to the United States, the chamber argued, because "true opportunity for advancement" existed there, unlike in their countries of origin where "high taxes, overregulation, oversized governments and lack of personal freedoms [had] smothered [people's] possibilities for advancement and self-betterment."[53] According to the chamber, the United States ought to try "convincing the nations of Latin America and elsewhere to free up their economies, respect private property rights, and sell inefficient government-owned companies."[54] The chamber failed to explain how such "convincing" ought to take place, but it did argue that this measure would "do more to slow immigration than any fence along the Rio Grande or any regulation of American hiring practices."[55]

The chamber's investment in curtailing Mexico's public spending meant that it ignored the fact that a larger—rather than smaller—welfare state in Mexico might be a more effective solution. Increasing government spending could diffuse migrants' need to go north to provide a safety net and basic resources to their families and communities. In towns of high out-migration, individuals regularly complained that government officials ignored their needs. Once in the United States, migrants built *clubes sociales* that performed some of the activities that Mexican government officials failed to carry out. They did so without government support. Gregorio Casillas, who helped build the clubs, reported, "We started [sending money to Mexico,] but unfortunately we didn't have the support of the government."[56] When the U.S. Chamber of Commerce held that Mexicans came to the United States because of the "high taxes, overregulation, [and] oversized governments" in their country of origin, it ignored migrants' actual desires and needs. By applying their own perspective of the world onto the realities of migrant life, members of the chamber failed to recognize the complex forces that drove Mexicans to the United States.

On the other side of the political spectrum, Mexican American groups began to disagree among themselves. Like employers, some Mexican American groups came to recognize that employer sanctions would pass and decided to use the hearings to ensure that their opinions were heard. On October 4, 1985, the NCLR's president issued a confidential memorandum to the Congressional Hispanic Caucus claiming that the organization had decided to espouse employer sanctions as the only "realistic strategy."[57] He explained: "It is widely acknowledged that some type of immigration reform bill is likely to pass—if not this year then next. . . . [I]t is further acknowledged by most observers that any bill that passes both Houses of Congress will contain some form of employer sanctions." According to the NCLR, rejecting the law would simply mean allowing it to pass without Mexican Americans' feedback. Not all Mexican American groups agreed, however. MALDEF continued to insist that employer penalties were indefensible, a position that contributed to the organization's reputation as being "purist" in its politics.[58]

The disagreement among mainstream Mexican American groups extended to their position on using trade, capital relocation, and aid as a means to lower unemployment in Mexico and thus to reduce undocumented migration. Up until the 1970s, only radical Chicana/o organizations, such as CASA, denounced sending aid to Mexico, insisting that "only the total economic independence of Mexico from U.S. [*Yanqui*] imperialism . . . can solve the causes behind the push of immigration."[59] In contrast, during those years most mainstream organizations—including MALDEF, the American G.I. Forum, LULAC, and the NCLR—held that the United States should provide aid to Mexico to curb its rates of unemployment and reduce people's need to migrate.[60] The position held by these mainstream Mexican American organizations during the 1970s overlooked how U.S. foreign aid had historically indebted countries and forced austerity programs on them that exacerbated unemployment (at least in the short term) and thus promoted out-migration. Even the aid that migrants sent back to Mexico through remittances and transnational welfare aid organizations, which was so beneficial to their home communities, ultimately sustained migratory patterns by fostering the belief that going to the United States increased migrants' capacity to belong in Mexico and by making Mexican towns dependent on migration. In the 1970s, mainstream Mexican American organizations had such an implicit faith in the beneficence of U.S. development and aid that they failed to question how U.S. involvement in Mexico would actually impact migrants' lives and need to go to the United States.

By the 1980s, however, some policy-oriented Mexican American groups began to doubt that U.S. economic involvement south of the border was helping Mexico, especially when it came to capital relocation and trade. In 1985, LULAC's executive director said, "LULAC suggests that at a minimum, the proposed Presidential commission be directed to review immigration trends to establish whether or not a correlation exists between U.S. foreign and trade policies vis-a-vis principal countries of origin and numbers of persons seeking entry into the United States."[61]

The NCLR, in contrast, continued to unquestioningly support U.S. economic intervention in Mexico as a means to reduce migration, even by overlooking how economic support was often accompanied by political control. In 1982, the organization's leaders held that "the most significant deficiency" of the proposals for immigration reform was the "lack of any substantial mention of cooperative economic development efforts with countries from which large numbers of immigrants enter the United States. Comprehensive immigration legislation cannot be successful without measures on the scale of the recent Caribbean Initiative."[62] The NCLR's statement disregarded the fact that the Caribbean Basin Initiative sought to use trade and aid to counter the possibility of a communist revolution in the Caribbean and Central America.[63] The NCLR was willing to ignore U.S. political interference in Latin America as long as it came with aid.

Even as the congressional hearings became increasingly absorbed with opening markets and sending international aid to Mexico, Mexican officials struggled to be heard. By the late 1970s, Mexico's leading politicians opposed employer sanctions because they considered out-migration a partial solution to Mexico's unemployment, but they did not have the political capital to interfere in the U.S. legislative process. They sought other ways to establish their opinion. In 1984, officials from Mexico's Secretariat of Foreign Relations wrote in internal documents, "Even though it has been our traditional position to not pronounce ourselves on the internal legislation of any country, including the United States, it is important to make evident that this does not mean that we support [the legislation], so as not to risk the interpretation that 'he who is quiet consents [*el que calla otorga*].'"[64] In the 1980s, top Mexican government representatives continually tried to express their opposition to the immigration bills at binational meetings and in press releases, often claiming that they were defending migrants' human rights. They did so to no avail. Those in the U.S. Congress barely discussed the views of Mexican government officials and, in the end, ignored them. It is not clear that IRCA would have been any different if Congress had entertained the opinions of Mexico's politicians. But the fact that the Mexican government had no input on the bill only furthered the notion that migrants' lives and home country were irrelevant to U.S. policymakers.

When passing IRCA in 1986, U.S. legislators did not have to think about how to convince the Mexican government to retreat from its protectionist policies as the U.S. Chamber of Commerce had suggested. Mexico had borrowed heavily from the United States with the expectation that it would pay off its debts in the future with profitable oil revenues. However, as the price of oil started to decline in the first half of the decade, and then plunged in 1986, the Mexican government found itself unable to repay. Mexican government officials thus had to accept U.S. trade remedy measures. In 1986, Mexico's new president, Miguel de la Madrid, agreed to a much less favorable GATT protocol than the one López Portillo had rejected six years earlier. The Mexican government further assented to the liberalization of international trade in 1994 when it joined the United States and Canada in signing the North American Free Trade Agreement (NAFTA). This treaty continued the drive for the integration of all markets, except for labor, across national borders.

While calls for a more porous border that allowed for the flow of capital and trade became increasingly audible in the U.S. Congress, so did calls for a more fortified border that stopped the flow of migrants. It was the same politicians and organizations, traditionally associated with the "right," who made both sets of demands. The new clamor for border fortification, which developed quite quickly and vociferously in the 1980s, made sense alongside Ronald Reagan's valorized vision of "law and order."[65] And yet the belief that fortification would solve the problem of unauthorized migration was shockingly blind to a key fact of migrant life: the existing permeability of the national boundary allowed Mexicans to engage in circular migration rather than having to immigrate and settle permanently in the United States. Indeed, the danger of border crossing was already altering the return patterns of many migrants. Migrant women, for instance, did not return to their hometowns at the same rate as men because crossing the border was more fraught for women, given the risk of sexual assault. Whereas in the years between 1965 and 1985, 55 to 60 percent of all migrant men went back to Mexico within two years of arriving in the United States, only 30 to 40 percent of women did.[66]

The case of Feliciana Ramírez is an indicative example. When her husband first started migrating, she stayed in Mexico because, as she explained, "the smugglers are not always to be trusted."[67] In her hometown, everyone knew that *coyotes* regularly raped women. Border bandits and Border Patrol agents were also known to assault women at border crossings.[68] After many years of seeing her husband come and go, however, Ramírez decided to risk the border and head north. The crossing was uneventful, but once she made it to South San Francisco she felt scared to leave again. Unlike her husband, a life in both countries seemed impossible to her, because of the uncertainty of the border in between.

She only went back to Mexico twice in the next twenty years: once because she was deported, and once because her mother died. Policymakers overlooked the fact that a dangerous border was already trapping migrants in the United States; their proposed solutions would only exacerbate that condition of entrapment.

The obliviousness of politicians is not surprising, since the demand for a more fortified border was originally set off not by unauthorized Mexican border crossings but by Cuban refugees fleeing by boat to Miami. In April 1980, Fidel Castro's government announced that anyone who desired to leave the island could do so. Cuban refugees immediately fled from the port of Mariel to the United States, where news soon spread that a significant number of them had been released from Cuban jails and mental health facilities. By October, when U.S. and Cuban officials agreed to end the Mariel boatlift, nearly 125,000 Cubans had already crossed the Florida Straits and arrived in the United States.[69] The Select Commission on Immigration and Refugee Policy, a congressional group that studied migration, reported, "Nothing about immigration—even widespread visa abuse and illegal border crossings—seems to have upset the American people more than the Cuban push-out of 1980. . . . Their presence brought home to most Americans the fact that U.S. immigration policy was out of control."[70] Policymakers used the sense of crisis that stemmed from the Mariel boatlift to insist on a more militarized border with Mexico.

Policing the national boundary had not been as prevalent a topic in the hearings held in the early 1970s as it became in the 1980s.[71] The focus of the earlier hearings rested on employer sanctions. The preoccupation with domestic employment by the AFL-CIO and its supporters meant that the main goal had been to ensure that migrants did not get jobs. As a result, border security was only of secondary importance at the initial hearings (despite the fact that there were a few politicians who made an adamant argument for greater policing).[72] During the hearings held in the 1970s, INS officers themselves believed that the solution to undocumented migration lay with employer sanctions rather than border militarization. In 1975, INS commissioner Leonard Chapman argued that there were three alternatives "in the face of this growing flood" of undocumented migrants.[73] The first option was to do nothing "and watch the flood grow into a torrent." The second choice was to "build a massive Immigration Service to deal with the problem [. . .] with an army of Border Patrolmen" and investigators working in cities. This course of action was "not only impractical" but also "abhorrent to the American conscience." The third alternative, Chapman held, was "to turn off the magnet that attracts these millions of persons to our country. That magnet, of course, is jobs. Employment of illegal aliens must be prohibited."[74] According to Chapman, this was the choice to pick.

In contrast, the hearings held during the 1980s reflected heightened concerns about the need to assert control over the nation's borders. The White House set the tone of this changing rhetoric. At the July 1981 hearings, Attorney General William French Smith, the mouthpiece of the White House, declared: "We have lost control of our borders."[75] After acquiescing to employer sanctions, President Reagan redirected the emphasis away from penalizing private employers and instead painted undocumented migration as a foreign policy issue that required policing the country's perimeter with Mexico.

This new rhetoric on border control fit well with U.S. citizens' growing concern that the United States had to reassert its geopolitical influence. Communists remained in control of Eastern Europe and China; the U.S. embassy in Tehran had been taken over by revolutionary Islamic students and U.S. State Department employees had been held hostage; and left-wing guerrilla movements were threatening U.S.-backed governments in Latin America and the Caribbean.[76] The need for strong, well-defined national borders seemed urgent. Senator Simpson declared in the 1985 hearings that the United States was unable "to fulfill that first test and duty of a sovereign nation—control of our own borders."[77] This posed a foreign policy quandary and was an international embarrassment, he said: "Not only the American people and the American Government are aware of it, but people all over the world are aware that the United States cannot, or does not, control its own borders."[78]

Employers readily backed this new emphasis. Even if penalties were to be imposed against them for hiring undocumented migrants, the focus of the hearings, they eagerly agreed, should be on the border rather than on jobsites. In the 1985 hearings, the Farm Labor Alliance, an umbrella organization representing the interests of growers, processors, and marketers of perishable commodities, embraced the White House's talking points: "The problem of illegal immigration has grown over the years and there is a need for this country to address the problem in a manner that will enable us to regain control of our borders."[79]

In contrast, groups deemed liberal, many of which had been the primary supporters of the Rodino bill in the early 1970s, were ambivalent or silent about increased border patrolling in the 1980s. Unlike most employer lobbies, both the AFL-CIO and most Mexican American groups (including LULAC and MALDEF) tried to avoid the issue in their statements at the 1985 Senate hearings. When they did tackle the question of border regulation, they provided different perspectives. The Arizona Farmworkers Union and the National Hispanic Leadership Conference held that their members were "extremely concerned" about an increase in "border enforcement."[80] For his part, Raúl Yzaguirre, the NCLR's president, did not bring up the topic himself, but when he was asked about it by Senator Simpson, he responded: "We have in the past and continue to believe that the most humane, the most cost effective way to deal with immigration control is to deal with it at the border."[81]

By the mid-1980s, even the INS had switched its stance. Whereas in 1975 Commissioner Chapman had noted the inadequacy of border control measures, in 1985 Commissioner Alan Nelson defended those same measures. Although he called employer sanctions the "cornerstone of this legislation," he also described the new law as "absolutely essential to gaining control of our borders."[82]

The new emphasis on border "control" that was constantly repeated in the hearings expunged migrants' humanity by casting Mexicans as a horde to be defended against. It denied migrants the possibility of belonging to the United States and erased their many contributions to the country. Despite its recurrent use at the hearings, the militarized language of control appears outlandish when placed alongside migrants' actual lives and desires. Mexicans tended to go to the United States to work and support their families; they returned home regularly to see their missed wives, children, parents, and friends; they built strong communities to support one another; and they longed to be able to reside in Mexico permanently one day. The geopolitical story that was told in Congress did not match up with the very humane stories happening on the ground.

Across the rapid shifts in emphasis that occurred between the 1970s and 1980s, one issue remained stable throughout the hearings: a concern about who migrants were and where they belonged. Calls to restrain undocumented migration rested on notions about safeguarding the population of the United States and, with it, the very meaning of being American. The AFL-CIO spoke of protecting U.S. laborers, environmentalists of preserving the nation's environment from outsiders, and political conservatives of upholding the nation's identity. To make these claims, policymakers relied on the notion that there was an intrinsic difference between U.S. citizens and undocumented migrants, as well as on the fear that the growing rates of illegal entry, and the purported high fertility rates of those migrants, would change the demographic composition of the United States.

When warning about the growth in the number of unauthorized migrants living in the United States, lobbyists typically described only the upward trend in the number of people entering the country but failed to note that most of those who entered the United States eventually left.[83] According to one of the most reliable studies, in the years between 1965 and 1986, 86 percent of all unauthorized entries were offset by departures.[84] As a result, fears of population growth rested on wildly high estimates about the number of migrants residing in the United States. For example, the Environmental Fund's strict focus on entrance led it to assert that "illegal immigration" was growing by "an unknown number, but 1 million a year is not an unreasonable guess."[85] This estimate was much higher than even the highest official numbers cited at the 1985 hearings, which held that the "illegal population" was growing by 250,000 to 500,000 per year.[86]

Those who believed that migrants did not belong in the nation had to contend with a commonly repeated narrative about the United States: that it was, first and foremost, a "nation of immigrants."[87] The apparent contradiction led to a lot of rhetorical gymnastics. The AFL-CIO, for example, used this enduring ideal to portray itself as sympathetic to the plight of migrants, but then it immediately sought to distance itself from the migrants themselves. The secretary treasurer of the AFL-CIO declared that "as members of a nation of immigrants . . . we deeply sympathize with those who seek a better life in our country."[88] The federation also said that the exploitation of undocumented workers was an "acute concern to the American labor movement which insists on safeguarding its hard-won standards of life and work."[89] To do so, however, organized labor chose to protect U.S. citizens, not migrant workers. Rather than fighting for better conditions for migrants, the AFL-CIO called for "a strong, fair U.S. immigration policy," which included employer sanctions.[90]

In the hearings held during Ronald Reagan's tenure, conservative politicians addressed the nation's immigrant past by insisting that the character of the nation now depended on protecting U.S. sovereignty. The assumed inclusiveness of the nation's origins was even invoked to reiterate the theme of control. Congressman Hank Brown (R-CO) offered one version of a sentiment echoed throughout the hearings, when he claimed, "We rightly pride ourselves on being what John F. Kennedy called 'a nation of immigrants.' . . . At the same time, we are a sovereign nation and, as a sovereign nation, we have the right—and we have a duty to our own citizens—to control our own borders."[91] Business lobbies claimed that undocumented migration was destroying the United States and the very meaning of being American. In its 1985 statement, the U.S. Chamber of Commerce described the country's border as "hemorrhaging."[92] This image depicted the influx of Mexicans as bloodying the territorial boundaries of the United States and thus effacing the definition of the country. The porous border, in turn, was often inextricably linked to fears of a porous American identity. The statement by the Chamber of Commerce made this link explicit: "Our Nation's ability to control its demographic future is key to retaining the economic and political liberties which we value." Its members feared that the nation's "currently permeable borders" were creating great "social, economic, political, environmental, and cultural" costs.[93]

For Mexican migrants, the rhetoric about their place in the nation was particularly painful because it failed to address their contributions to the United States. While not using the term "nation of immigrants," Mexicans insisted that they were an indispensable part of building the country. Reflecting the perspective held by most migrants, Manuel Jiménez exclaimed: "Mexicans have lifted the U.S. economy."[94] Another migrant wrote to his local newspaper in Jalisco scorning U.S. citizens for believing that there were too many Mexicans in the United States. He argued that migration was "the best business that our neighbors, the gringos, have done because it provides them with a cheap labor force."[95]

Stereotypes about "Mexican families" and their "excessive fertility" haunted the hearings and buttressed arguments that undocumented migration would alter the demographic composition of the United

States. In practice, most Mexican women remained in Mexico and raised their children there. Nonetheless, John Tanton, the head of the population control organization Zero Population Growth (ZPG), asserted in 1975 that the "fertility of immigrant women" would increase population growth in the United States.[96] Although ZPG had the reputation of being an extremist organization, others repeated these types of claims. For instance, in 1983, Martin Finn, the medical director for public health for the Department of Health Services of Los Angeles County, which was a part of the very medical system sued a few years earlier for forcibly sterilizing Mexican American women, told Congress, "I noted that 64 percent of the deliveries in our hospitals were in the undocumented population. This shows the extremely high fertility rate in this population."[97]

For their part, in the 1980s, Mexican American groups and their allies tried to reframe the debate around "the Mexican family" away from its pejorative connotations and to pursue family reunification policies. In the May 1981 hearings, for instance, MALDEF claimed that Mexican migrants should be allowed to bring their relatives because "family reunification" had "for several decades been an underlying theme of American immigration policy."[98] Clergy from a range of denominations— from Catholics and Jews to the African Methodist Episcopal Church— added to this chorus, maintaining that "family reunion has appropriately been the cornerstone of our immigration laws and polices since their beginning."[99]

When focusing on "the family," Mexican American organizations and the clergy emphasized that deportations and employer sanctions would separate families, ignoring that migration itself split Mexican families. After all, most migrants were married men who left their families behind in Mexico. In the 1975 hearings, the secretary for research of the U.S. Catholic Conference maintained that employer sanctions would lead to "the dismissal of untold numbers of workers from their jobs in a short period of time," which would cause "unbelievable havoc among their families and in the communities. . . . [I]n our judgment, it is unconscionable that our Government should even consider separating families by forcing a mass exodus or deportation of literally millions of men, women, and children."[100] By emphasizing the primacy of unbroken families, these groups attempted to protect migrants from deportation but disregarded the fact that for most migrants the family was a transnational institution.

Repeatedly, the representations of Mexican families presented at the congressional hearings aimed to convince policymakers about the need to ease or increase restrictions on migration, but they failed to recognize the intricacies of migrants' family lives. Men's cross-border movement meant that many Mexican families lived across borders and shaped their attachments through regular visits, love letters, remittances, extended family, and gossip. Neither the joys nor the hardships of a binational family were recognized. Without an adequate analysis of—or even an interest in—the messy complexity of lived experience, it is no surprise that the solutions policymakers proposed were similarly one-dimensional.

The voices heard least at these hearings were those of undocumented migrants themselves, although after the mid-1970s, Mexican American groups often claimed to speak in their name. In a sense, migrants had already spoken. They had expressed their desires—or their lack of alternatives—with their very movement. They borrowed money to make their first trip, promised their families they would return, and left their hometowns in Mexico with a heavy heart. They willingly put themselves in danger in order to cross the border. They agreed to work long hours in the worst-paid jobs and live in fear of apprehension in a country that viewed them only as "illegals." Mexicans chose this path because, despite the hardships of migration, no other trajectory offered them better hope. Through these actions, migrants spoke with their feet rather than their voices. But those in Congress failed to hear.

In the rare instances in which unauthorized migrants were allowed to address Congress, they articulated their hopes for a world in which Mexicans could migrate in order to work, make enough money to live decently, and then settle permanently in their home country. Ramón Andrada, an undocumented migrant from Nayarit and a member of the Maricopa County Organizing Project (MCOP), an organization that insisted that migrants be given time to testify at the hearings, held that all Mexicans who wanted to migrate for work should be allowed to do so "because the fact that we live [in Mexico] does not mean that we don't have the right to work. We have the right to work, to support our families."[101] His ultimate goal was to settle down in Mexico: "My solution is come to work here, on a temporary basis, if allowed, because I believe that, with that time that I would be allowed to work here, we can better afford to support our families there, and avoid coming here."[102] Andrada recognized how his settlement in Mexico depended on his continued ability to migrate and live, for the time being, north of the border.

Andrada's aspirations for a different future never came to fruition. Neither did those of the groups that rallied for more stringent immigration control through IRCA. The Simpson-Mazzoli bill passed by balancing the interests of the multiple groups concerned with the issue, but it ended up satisfying none of them. IRCA introduced employer sanctions and increased the INS enforcement budget with the goal of reducing the number of undocumented migrants who entered and resided in the country. It placated employers' demands to keep their access to laborers by expanding the H-2 program, which allowed for the temporary admission of foreign guest workers.[103] It also established the new Seasonal Agricultural Worker (SAW) program: migrants who could prove that they had been in the United States for a minimum of ninety days, during the year ending on May 1, 1986, were offered a path to legal residency.[104] Beyond SAW, the new law allowed those who could prove continuous residence in the United States since January 1, 1982, to become legal resident aliens.[105] Congress agreed to this measure to pacify Mexican American groups that had come to support migrants. The fundamental compromise of IRCA, by which legalization was granted in exchange for an increase in border enforcement, employer sanctions, and guest-worker programs, failed in its intended goals. Nonetheless, the paradigm it employed continued to be used in immigration reform proposals for at least thirty years following the passage of IRCA. Similarly, public debate and legislative arguments continued to focus on traditional clichés that linked migration to unemployment and welfare abuse and that portrayed migrants as lawbreakers who altered the nation's demography through their unauthorized entrance and overt fertility. As the lives of migrants in the years following the passage of IRCA reveal, however, laws backed by stereotypes sometimes come at a very high price.

8

....

THE CAGE OF GOLD

I N 2014, SEVENTEEN-YEAR-OLD junior Adriano found himself unable
to travel beyond the small strip of land that surrounded the town of
Anthony, Texas.[1] If he headed north, east, or west, he risked being stopped
by the immigration officials who roamed the roads nearby or at one of
the internal immigration checkpoints in the area. If he headed south, he
would be in Mexico, where there were fewer job opportunities and from
where he would find it hard to reenter the United States and complete
his high school education. He fantasized about seeing California, but the
travel was not worth the risk. Even more hurtful, he dreamed of seeing
his parents, who lived in Mexico after his father had been deported. "I
do miss them a lot," Junior said. "I wish I was with them or . . . we were
all back together, but yeah, it's going to be hard for that to happen ever
again."[2] Junior Adriano felt imprisoned within the United States at
large and within the small belt of land around Anthony, in particular.

In some ways, Junior's spatial constrictions resembled those faced by
the migrants caught in the joint operation carried out by Mexican and
U.S. officials in 1980. As described in the introduction to this book, those
migrants had found themselves in a position that made it impossible to
move in any direction. They had set up camp in a small strip of land
just north of the border that they called No Man's Land. Their plan was
to wait until the late hours of the night and then run further into California. As they waited, however, three Border Patrol Ram Chargers came
directly at them from the north; when they then dashed south into
Mexico, Tijuana's police officers forced them back into the United States
and into the hands of U.S. immigration officials.

Even though, like Junior, the migrants caught in 1980 had been left
with nowhere to move, their spatial dilemma was very different from

the one undocumented migrants faced in the years following the passage of the Immigration Reform and Control Act (IRCA) of 1986.[3] The migrants apprehended in the 1980 sweeps did not feel permanently imprisoned in the United States. Their entrapment resulted from a fleeting encounter at the border with officials from both nation-states. Even though crossing the national boundary was no walk in the park, before 1986 most migrants were willing to engage in circular migration, as they believed that they would be able to reenter the United States if they left. If anything, they felt "pushed" out of Mexico and the United States by the policymakers of each country and out of their local communities by their families and social networks. This was not the case for Junior and his contemporaries. In the years following the passage of IRCA, the border became more fortified and thus harder to cross. But by then, migrants had already learned that living in the United States, at least for short periods of time, allowed them to counter the sense of local and national exclusion they felt. Because they could no longer cross the border repeatedly between the two countries and live temporarily in both, they decided to settle permanently in the United States. They did not return to Mexico out of fear that they would be unable to cross the border north again. Feeling trapped in *El Norte*, they started calling the United States La Jaula de Oro, the Cage of Gold.

Migrants felt further rooted in the United States after the passage of IRCA because their families followed them there. Once men realized that circular migration was no longer an option, they encouraged their wives and children to head north with them. Since crossing the border was even more hazardous for women and minors, once they migrated they refrained from going back. This meant that thousands of children, like Junior, grew up without papers in the United States but without knowing Mexico. They had no intention of heading back south.

IRCA also encouraged Mexicans to settle in the United States by providing millions of migrants with a way to legalize their status. Acquiring papers let people escape one of the main forces that pushed them to migrate continually: deportation. Whereas in Mexico they still faced poverty, which for many became exacerbated with the liberalization of free trade during those years, in the United States they were now legal residents and could live there permanently. Eventually, they could even become citizens.

IRCA did create a group of workers who still engaged in circular migration: temporary guest workers who joined the expanded H-2 program.

Migrating as contract workers did not subject individuals to the dangerous and expensive process of illegal border crossing. Over time, an increasing number of Mexicans became H-2 laborers in order to be able to work in the United States and return to Mexico to see their families. But guest workers paid a hefty price for their decision to avoid La Jaula de Oro and migrate circularly between the two countries. Although they were supposed to be afforded basic rights in the United States, they often had to tolerate even more abuse from employers than undocumented migrants did so as not to be blacklisted from the program. Circular migration was now a privilege that came at high costs.

Gone were the days when Mexican migrants came and went between Mexico and the United States, but even after 1986 migrants still saw themselves as being "from neither here nor there." Even while living permanently north of the border, few legalized migrants felt they fully belonged in the "here" that was the United States. For their part, unauthorized migrants continued to experience a sense of impermanence north of the border, even while feeling entrapped there. Fears of deportation plagued their lives and prevented them from being able to incorporate themselves in their new society, no matter how long they had lived there or how diluted their connections were to Mexico. As Junior explained: "When I'm at school I feel somewhat American, [but] when I start thinking about it . . . I have nothing to feel American about really. Cuz I can't do nothing at all. Let's say I do something bad and the cops get me. . . . I'm going to get screwed over, and I'm going to get sent back . . . to Mexico or something. Get deported because I'm not from here."[4] The "here" of the United States was also complicated because of the way migrants experienced local space within the country. After 1986, legalized migrants could move freely throughout the nation, but undocumented migrants and H-2 workers could not.

Tracing the mobility, residence, and sense of national belonging of the different categories of migrants created by IRCA reveals how most Mexican migrants went from feeling that they were "from neither here nor there" because they had to engage in circular migration to feeling that they were "from neither here nor there" while living—and sometimes even feeling trapped—in the United States.

IRCA opened the way for 2.3 million Mexicans to legalize their status in the United States.[5] Those who did so were the only migrants who increased their geographic mobility and came closest to achieving a sense of belonging in the United States as a result of the law. Because acquiring papers offered people so many benefits, news of the law's passage spread widely in migrant communities. Anaberta Reinaga, who lived in Thermal, California, in 1986, remembered that when IRCA passed, "there was much talk" about the new law.[6] "On TV, on the radio, there were places that opened up centers like Catholic churches . . . where they would advise us and would fill our paperwork" to apply for residency, she recalled.[7] "Almost everyone" in the migrant community in the area tried to become a legal permanent resident.

Legalization encouraged Mexicans to move north permanently. To legalize their status migrants had to live in the country for over a year, while making only "brief temporary trips abroad" in the case of a family emergency "involving an occurrence such as the illness or death of a close relative."[8] This measure encouraged migrants to settle north of the border. Equally important, once migrants became legal residents, they were no longer apprehended and forced to return to Mexico.

Migrants who became permanent residents regularly sought to bring their families north with them. Once migrants became full permanent residents, they were able to apply to bring their spouses, minor children, and unmarried adult sons and daughters. The waiting time, however, was extremely long and painful. For instance, when Everardo Camacho managed to become a permanent resident after legalizing his status through IRCA, he applied for a visa for his wife, who remained in Mexico. The process took nine years, Everardo's wife recalled.[9]

Legalized migrants could eventually become citizens, a process that also took years but that then allowed them to bring their spouses, minor children, and parents to the United States with no restrictions and to sponsor their siblings. Many Mexicans who ultimately became U.S. citizens sponsored family members decades later. In 2015, for example, Sandra Paiz reported, "I acquired many benefits [by legalizing my status]. Now, thank God, I am fixing my two sisters' papers, since I already became a citizen."[10] IRCA's legalization measure produced successive waves of legalization and naturalization. The number of naturalized Mexicans rose from 13,000 in 1992 to 217,000 in 1996.[11] By 1997, 22 percent of foreign-born "Hispanics" were naturalized U.S. citizens.[12]

For most migrants, legalization meant that they could finally expand their mobility within the United States and feel more at ease there.[13]

Those who were in the country illegally had to find ways to avoid encountering immigration officials. Acquiring papers through IRCA opened up the world for these migrants. Not only could they now move freely but they could do so without concern. Marco Antonio Velarde recalled that after he and his family put in their application to legalize their status, they "no longer [had] any fear" when moving around. "Before fixing papers" he lived in trepidation, he said, "regularly [having] this nightmare [that he] was being chased by *la migra*."[14]

Migrants who had experienced the greatest control of their movement profited the most from legalization. Andrés Delgado maintained that before IRCA, he and his fellow workers lived on top of the branches of the trees in the grapefruit orchard where he worked. They preferred to sleep on the branches rather than on the ground to avoid snakes. "I had . . . my mattress tied there [on the tree] by its four corners," he recalled. They didn't dare leave the orchard itself and rent an apartment in town "because *la migra* would be looking out" for unauthorized migrants on the streets and would check people's status when they stopped "at [red] lights." Getting from the grove to the town was too risky. For workers like Delgado, legalizing their status meant that they could finally reside in an apartment. "As soon as I fixed my papers, I went to live in the town," he said.[15]

Increased spatial mobility improved living conditions. For Delgado, being able to live in an apartment allowed him to be healthier. When sleeping in the grove, he and his fellow workers would "bathe there in a reservoir. . . . We would cook there. We would make flour tortillas . . . with potatoes, beans. That's what we ate. There in the desert." But as soon as they legalized their status and rented apartments in town, they "were able to eat better . . . [and] could refrigerate meat." Their stress levels and fear also fell. "We were no longer afraid that a snake would bite us. Or of, of anything! That *la migra* would get us, we already had papers," he remembered. Legalizing his status allowed him to live decently, "like God mandates . . . because we no longer merited that fate."[16]

Settling in the United States without having to fear deportation improved migrants' socioeconomic mobility and allowed them to make long-term financial decisions. Marco Antonio Velarde explained that once he and his co-workers legalized their status, their wages increased: "We could start demanding that they pay us like they should, unlike before [when we didn't have papers and had to accept lower wages]."[17] Just knowing that they would not be deported allowed migrants to invest in their future. Mirella Amador recalled being able to consider buying a home only after her husband legalized his status. Before then, it was hard for them to think about making such an investment. "When [living] without papers," she explained, "[we] couldn't be 100 percent sure that we would establish ourselves here. At any, any minute, we could be deported" and lose the house "as had happened to many people."[18]

Despite their new permanency in the United States, legalized migrants found it hard to feel like they fully belonged in the United States because they were regularly treated as outsiders. Olga Juárez overheard a teacher at her children's school where she also worked saying to another staff member: "Tell the parents that they are not in their country."[19] Similarly, Héctor Rodríguez said that around the time when he was legalizing his status, he was part of the soccer team in his junior high school. Members of the opposing team, who were primarily white Americans, would try to intimidate him and his teammates by yelling "Go back to your country."[20] These everyday encounters exposed legalized migrants' continued exclusion.

The pain legalized migrants experienced when they were undocumented prevented many of them from feeling fully a part of and safe in the United States. In 2015, Wendy Rodríguez described how the fears she felt as a kid continued to haunt her even though she had become a permanent resident decades before through IRCA. When her family was still living in the United States without authorization, her mother left for Mexico and then couldn't return to the United States because she was constantly apprehended. The whole family was scared. "We suffered!" Rodríguez recalled. "I remember the fear, the stress. I could not understand why my mother couldn't come. It was very hard: it was tremors at night. I remember that I woke up crying. I didn't know what it was that I was scared of, but I knew that . . . something was wrong. That my mom couldn't come back." This experience continued to haunt Rodríguez for decades. "For me, fear started then," she explained in 2015 as she reexperienced the terror and frustration she felt as a kid. "I feel the nerves! I feel like I was again in that situation."[21] She was not alone. In the interviews conducted for this book, dozens of migrants shivered and wept while telling their stories.

Hearing about the hardships of present-day undocumented migrants often resurrects the memories and pain of those who legalized their status. In 2015, Sandra Paiz explained that she was infuriated by the adversities undocumented migrants were facing in part because they reminded her of her past, before she was able to gain legal status herself: "It angers me. So many people that had so many dreams, and I think it is so sad because I, I was like that, without papers. I know what it is to be here in the United States without papers. And with so many dreams that you have."[22] In her account Paiz took on the voice of those who were still in the country illegally. Similarly, Adalberto Rodríguez explained that even though he legalized his status under IRCA, he continued to feel anguished by the existing immigration restrictions: "Everybody suffers. Even though we already have papers and everything, we also suffer for other people because we also suffered much."[23]

All in all, the migrants who legalized their status through IRCA were able to increase their socioeconomic standards and move freely within the United States. Although most never felt that they fully belonged north of the border, in part because of the discrimination they continued to experience and the memories they had of being undocumented migrants, having papers allowed them to settle more safely in the United States. As the exclusion of undocumented migrants intensified over the years, the rights acquired by legalization increased. José Juárez, who crossed the border in the 1980s, remembered that at first, papers "were not so indispensable. They became more necessary as time went on" and undocumented life became harder.[24]

While legalized migrants achieved an increased sense of belonging in the United States as a result of IRCA, this was not the case for undocumented migrants—a group whose numbers continued to grow after 1986.

IRCA did not provide papers to all undocumented migrants who were living in the United States at the time. Although most politicians used the words "legalization" and "amnesty" interchangeably to describe this measure, and Mexicans still hail it as *la amnistía,* IRCA did not provide a true amnesty. Amnesty would have given legal status to all undocumented migrants, but legalization required them to "earn" their new standing through measures such as criminal and national security checks and demonstration of English competency. To legalize their status migrants also had to be able to prove that they had performed seasonal

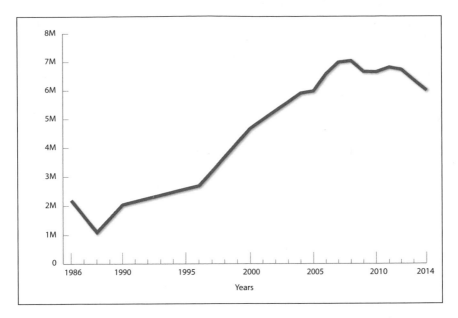

Estimated size of the undocumented Mexican population of the United States after 1986. Source: Douglas S. Massey and Kerstin Gentsch, "Undocumented Migration to the United States and the Wages of Mexican Immigrants," *International Migration Review* 48, no. 2 (Summer 2014): 482–499, Figure 1. © 2014 by the Center for Migration Studies of New York. Published by John Wiley & Sons.

agricultural labor in the United States for at least ninety days during the twelve-month period ending on May 1, 1986, or that they had resided in the United States since January 1, 1982.[25] Many undocumented migrants simply did not satisfy all these requirements.

Migrants who had greater access to financial resources and social networks often found ways to circumvent some of these restrictive clauses, but those who were less connected and poorer found it harder. Pedro Pérez managed to gain legal status even though he had not been in the United States before 1986 because his brother paid a corrupt grower for a letter that falsely certified that Pedro had worked for him for over ninety days.[26] More disadvantaged workers did not have this option. Josefina Cruz migrated in 1987. She could have bought a letter testifying to her residency before 1986, like other people did, but she did not know how to go about it. While she knew people who were acquiring fabricated letters from growers, she did not have access to such contacts. On one occasion, she recalled, a man "at work offered help . . . but I didn't feel

I could trust him. . . . He told me he would take me, to Sacramento, I believe, where they would sell me a letter [stating I had worked in the fields]." Cruz did not dare get into a car with him: "I was afraid because I was a woman."[27] Cruz's sex and lack of connections restricted her ability to legalize her status through fraud.

Other undocumented workers failed to recognize the importance of legalization and did not take advantage of the new law to become legal residents. Despite the difficulties of being undocumented before 1986, many people considered that the high costs and hassles of becoming legal residents were not worth the trouble. After all, before IRCA, the border was still not as fortified and there were no employer sanctions. Many migrants expected to return to Mexico shortly after the passage of the law and hoped to live there permanently. They figured that if they ever wanted to come back to the United States, they would simply cross the border illegally again. Such was the case of Fernando Gutiérrez. He and his brother submitted paperwork to legalize their status, but while his brother's went through without problems, Fernando was asked for further documentation. He could have provided the required paperwork, he said, but "the truth is that I didn't care because I had other plans of only being [in the United States] for a short period of time, gathering some money, and leaving to start my business" in Mexico, so he "didn't do anything." Years later, when he realized he was going to stay in the United States permanently, he tried to "reopen the case, but it was no longer possible." Without legal status, Fernando had fewer job opportunities than his brother, and his son had fewer educational opportunities than his nephews.[28]

Not only did IRCA fail to ensure that all those already living in the United States were doing so legally, but, more important, it also failed to curtail the continued rise of unauthorized entries. Despite the fortification of the border, migrants who wanted to enter the United States could still do so, as long as they were willing to go through more dangerous terrains that were not as heavily patrolled. By 1986, Mexicans from towns of high out-migration had already become accustomed to living in the United States without papers, and transnational migration was seen as a constitutive part of their identity and society. For many of them, residing permanently in Mexico was not an option. Millions of Mexicans decided to risk the border once and moved to the United States.

Mexico's growing economic problems exacerbated people's need to go north. Between 1980 and 1992, Mexico's GDP grew at an average rate of 2.2 percent, which stood in stark contrast to the 6.6 percent rate that took place between 1950 and 1970. In 1992, 53 percent of the population could not afford to purchase the basic food basket, housing, clothing, education, health services, and transportation; 21 percent of the population could not afford the basic food basket even if they spent all their income on it.[29] The numbers were even grimmer for those in the countryside, where 66.5 percent of people did not have access to all needed goods and services, while 34 percent could not afford the food they required even if they spent all their income on it.[30] The economic situation plummeted further after the precipitous fall of the peso, which plunged from 3.4 to 5.3 pesos per dollar from December 1994 to January 1995, and then continued to decline.[31] In this context, Mexican government officials continued to view migration as an escape valve, and even more Mexicans came to view it as an escape from destitution.

Increased trade and capital flows added to Mexicans' economic motivation to head north. The same year that the U.S. Congress passed IRCA, Mexican politicians signed onto the General Agreement on Tariffs and Trade (GATT) to facilitate international trade. Then, in 1994, Mexico, the United States, and Canada signed the North American Free Trade Agreement (NAFTA). Despite many protests, the economists who supported NAFTA predicted that the treaty would improve Mexico's economy and halt undocumented migration. Since wages in Mexico were the lowest of the three countries, they held, companies would relocate there to produce labor-intensive goods, thereby decreasing unemployment.[32] U.S. attorney general Janet Reno insisted on the benefits of signing onto NAFTA, declaring, "Our best chance to reduce illegal immigration is sustained, robust Mexican economic growth. That is why passage of the North American Free Trade Agreement will help me protect our borders. NAFTA will create jobs in both the United States and Mexico."[33] In reality, undocumented migration continued to grow after 1994 despite, and in many cases because of, NAFTA.

Trade liberalization accelerated the economic restructuring taking place in rural Mexico that was already pushing many to migrate. In the early 1990s, the administration of Mexican president Carlos Salinas de Gortari reduced input subsidies for farmers, stopped guaranteeing output prices, and introduced a constitutional change that allowed *ejidatarios* (communal land owners) to rent or sell their property—a measure that facilitated the movement of Mexicans off their lands and then to the

United States.[34] NAFTA hastened the changes in Mexican farms by eliminating tariffs from U.S. agricultural products, which were highly subsidized. Mexico's farms could not compete with U.S. imports. In 1994, most agricultural work in Mexico was dedicated to the production of corn and beans, yet the Mexican corn price per ton was more than double that of the United States. Importing cheaper U.S. corn helped Mexico's urban consumers but wrecked its farmers.

Some farmers switched to crops that the trade agreement made more profitable—such as avocados—and some migrated to work in Mexico's cities, but many headed to the United States. Not all corn producers could afford the high startup costs of profitable crops nor owned land that was suitable for such production.[35] Similarly, not all who sought jobs in Mexican cities found them. Despite the many predictions for NAFTA, between 1992 and 2007, Mexico's economy grew at an annual per capita rate of only 1.6 percent, one of the lowest growth rates in Latin America.[36] Griselda Mendoza, the daughter of a corn farmer from Mexico's southern state of Oaxaca who migrated to the United States after NAFTA, noted that the common lore of her hometown was that "before NAFTA, everybody . . . grew corn. People didn't make much money, but nobody went hungry," but as cheap corn came from the United States, farmers had to emigrate.[37] Corn growers were not the only ones who experienced this dilemma. A worker in the town of Jalpa, Zacatecas, explained that free trade policies had meant that it was "more expensive" for him "to raise and feed a chicken [in his hometown] than to buy one at the market that had already been cooked." This, he held, helped explain outmigration from Mexico: "Raising animals and agricultural work are more costly than profitable nowadays, which means many people go to the United States."[38]

While the border's increasing permeability to trade drove many people out of Mexico, the fortification of the border following the passage of IRCA encouraged migrants to settle permanently in the United States. Undocumented migrants feared that leaving the United States would mean an increasingly perilous border to return across. Many individuals decided to stay in *El Norte* instead. Before the passage of IRCA, approximately 76 percent of undocumented migrants who entered the United States every year returned home within five years.[39] By 1990, this figure had fallen to 40 percent. Gonzalo Bueno was one of the individuals who engaged in circular migration until the border became more policed.

On his last trip in 1997, he almost died when trying to return to the United States, and as of 2015 he had not gone back to Mexico.[40]

In turn, as Mexican men decided to settle north of the border, they encouraged their families to join them, which multiplied the number of undocumented migrants who headed to the United States.[41] Women had traditionally refrained from migrating because of their vulnerability, but now their husbands also faced much danger at the border. Rather than having men expose themselves to these hazards repeatedly, women started to risk the border once. Before 1986, women constituted only one-quarter of undocumented migrants; after the passage of the law, the figure rose to one-third.[42] Although there is no hard data on the migration rates of gay men after 1986, most individuals from communities of high out-migration, including queer men, believe that gay men continued to remain in Mexico at higher rates than heterosexual men. This might have been because the idea of the "gay family" in which queer partners followed each other was not as solidified as that of the heterosexual family, which led women to follow their husbands to the United States.

The movement of nuclear families to the United States further reinforced migrants' settlement north of the border. The risks women and children faced crossing the border meant that, once they migrated, they did not return to Mexico. The move away from male migration toward family migration was also a move toward permanence. The border had been fortified to keep unauthorized migrants outside of the United States, but in reality, it had served only to keep migrants *within* the country with their families and outside of Mexico.

Migrants who could not return to Mexico experienced their permanent residency in the United States as entrapment. In 1985, only a year before the passage of IRCA, the famous Mexican *norteño* band, Los Tigres del Norte, released its best-selling *corrido* (folk song), "Jaula de oro" ("Cage of Gold"). It tells the story of a migrant who has been in the United States for many years with his family but has been unable to gain legal status and longs to return to Mexico:

> *Tengo mi esposa y mis hijos,*
> *que me los traje muy chicos,*
> *y se han olvidado ya,*
> *de mi México querido,*
> *del que yo nunca me olvido,*
> *y no puedo regresar.*

¿De qué me sirve el dinero,
si estoy como prisionero,
dentro de esta gran nación?
Cuando me acuerdo hasta lloro,
que aunque la jaula sea de oro,
no deja de ser prisión.

I have my wife and my children
whom I brought when they were very young
and they have already forgotten
my beloved Mexico
the one that I never forget
and I cannot return

Of what use is money
if I am like a prisoner
within this great nation?
I even cry when I remember
that even if the cage is made of gold
it does not stop being a prison

As the border became more fortified, the image of the migrant caged in the United States proliferated in Mexican communities. To explain his life without papers, José Guadalupe Rodríguez said, "When one comes and establishes himself in a job, he becomes . . . like a prisoner" within the United States.[43]

The confinement migrants experienced north of the border placed a huge emotional toll on them and their loved ones. Josefina Cruz explained that she was not able to go back home when her mother and father passed away in Mexico, because she feared not being able to return to the United States, where she was raising her children. When her father died, the pain "was easier to bear," she recalled, "because my dad always told me on the phone that he didn't want me to come back [to Mexico]." But handling her mother's death without being able to go home to see her was much harder. Her mother suffered a slow death during which she kept asking Cruz to return to Mexico. During that period, Cruz said, "I had a crisis" and experienced "the desperation of sometimes saying 'I am going' and 'I don't care anymore if I am able to return again.'"[44] But then she would think through her options and realize that she couldn't take her children away from their lives in the United States or risk living without them. Her agony reflected that of thousands of undocumented migrants living in the United States and that of their parents who remained in Mexico knowing that they would probably die without being able to see their children again.

For migrants who could not return to Mexico, their capacity to belong to their country of birth and citizenship was attenuated. Even though most remembered Mexico fondly and sought to go back, they knew that they could not return to live there because they would encounter the same structural economic problems that originally led them to leave. In 2015, Gonzalo Bueno explained that if he were ever to go back to Mexico, he would no longer feel at home as he wouldn't know the country anymore. In the years he was away, he recalled, "everything changed . . . family, friends, life, all of that."[45] That same year, Fernando Gutiérrez said that in the United States he suffered a lot, but he did not feel like he could incorporate himself in Mexico again: "What would I do in Mexico? I've been here [in the United States], I have nothing there [in Mexico]."[46] Undocumented migrants experienced an impossible situation in terms of national belonging. As Bueno explained, "I don't feel like I am from here [the United States] because I don't have papers, and there [in Mexico] I am a stranger as well" after having spent so much time away.[47]

Unauthorized migrants not only felt entrapped in the United States but also constrained to certain areas within it. Immigration raids and stops had restricted their mobility inside the country long before IRCA. In the early 1990s, the limitations on migrants' movement saw an added twist as nineteen states established that those who were in the country illegally were ineligible for driver's licenses.[48] Gonzalo Bueno maintained that he was afraid every time he went away from his house without a license: "If the police asks me for an identification . . . and I don't have it and they call immigration? That is my fear." He thought that his odds of being stopped were relatively high because he was brown and believed that "cops [were] very prejudiced."[49]

Migrants regularly used prison metaphors to describe the constraint on their movement within the United States. José Gardoño, who originally migrated without papers from the state of Michoacán, claimed that legalizing his status changed his life "because at least one can move more freely wherever one wants without migration officials chasing you around. Because when one doesn't have papers one feels like confined

to a cage" and is always trying to avoid deportation.[50] Even the song by
Los Tigres del Norte, "Jaula de oro," holds that migrants are caged not
only in the United States as a whole but also in specific locales within
the country:

> De mi trabajo a mi casa
> Yo no se lo que me pasa
> Que aunque soy hombre de hogar
> Casi no salgo a la calle
> Pues tengo miedo que me hallen
> Y me puedan deportar

> From my house to my work
> I don't know what is happening to me
> Even though I am a family man[51]
> I almost don't go out to the street
> For I'm afraid that they will find me
> And might deport me

Undocumented migrants felt further excluded from national belonging in the United States because they were forced into the worst-
paying jobs and could not demand higher wages. Josefina Cruz explained:
"One would like to . . . find a more stable job," but for that one has to "be
able to say, yes I have documents."[52] The employer sanctions introduced
by IRCA meant that more employers started checking workers' legal
status. In 1996, the Illegal Immigration Reform and Immigrant Responsibility Act reinforced this measure by establishing a Basic Pilot program for
employers from California, Florida, Illinois, New York, and Texas to voluntarily check the identity documents of their employees against the Immigration and Naturalization Service and Social Security Administration
databases. In 2003, the program expanded to cover the entire nation.[53]

For Cruz, as for many other undocumented migrants, the hardest part
of living in the United States without proper authorization was not having
health insurance. Although she and her husband paid taxes in the United
States for most of their working lives, their inability to legalize their papers
meant that she could not receive treatment for lupus—a disease with which
she was diagnosed twenty-eight years after she first came to the United
States. Her husband's job was supposed to provide its workers with medical
coverage, but when the health insurance company discovered that Cruz
was using a false Social Security number, they denied her benefits.[54]

Even migrants who crossed the border illegally when they were children and lived most of their lives entrapped in La Jaula de Oro continued to face exclusion in the United States decades later. Fernando Gutiérrez brought his son across the border without papers when he was still a young child.[55] After finishing high school, his son wanted to attend university but found that he was ineligible for federal and most state-based financial aid, including loan programs, work-study jobs, and grants. He could, however, benefit from California's laws that allowed certain non-resident students to receive reduced in-state tuition at public colleges and universities.[56] At great personal cost, Fernando's son managed to attend California State University, Northridge. Because he could not afford to rent a room in an apartment or a dorm, he commuted by bus for two hours each way from his parents' house in Los Angeles. He could not drive to school because, as an undocumented migrant, he could not get a license. Once he graduated from college, he had to work part-time in a Mexican restaurant and as a parking lot attendant because no other jobs would take him. It was only after he managed to legalize his status by marrying a U.S. citizen that he was able to get a better-paying job. In contrast to Fernando's son, his daughter, who was born in the United States after the family migrated, had a much easier experience.[57] As a U.S. citizen, she was eligible for financial aid and scholarships. She attended University of California, Riverside, and used the aid money she received to rent a room in the area.

The rights that undocumented migrants did have in the United States had been won through the determined actions of activists in earlier years. For instance, while Fernando's son could not obtain aid to attend college, he could enroll in a public school in the United States. This had been ensured by migrants' 1982 victory in *Plyler v. Doe,* which had established that undocumented children had the right to attend public schools without having to pay tuition.

In the decades following the passage of IRCA, undocumented migrants continued to fight for inclusion. It would be impossible to narrate all their struggles, but even a sample of some of their most vociferous protests illustrates how they sought to resist their exclusion from Mexico and the United States. In the spring of 2006, hundreds of thousands of people declared "A Day without an Immigrant," a national economic boycott that was accompanied by multitudinous peaceful marches throughout the United States.[58] The protests targeted the Sensen-brenner bill, which had been passed by the U.S. House of Representa-tives in 2005 and made migrants' unauthorized status a felony subject to imprisonment. In response to the growing visibility of the immi-grant rights movement, the Republican Party abandoned the Sensen-brenner bill.

The movement for undocumented migrants' rights then continued to grow through the efforts of students. Many of them had been brought to the United States after 1986, when their parents decided that women and children should head north rather than having men engage in cir-cular migration. The activists who grew up in the United States tended to have different interests from those who migrated in the pre-IRCA years. While the migrants who came before 1986 sought belonging in both countries, those who grew up north of the border focused primarily on claiming rights in the United States. "DREAMers," as many in the student movement identified themselves, captured the nation's imagi-nation by writing eloquent editorial pages and blogs, holding protests and marches, engaging in nonviolent civil disobedience, and lobbying Congress and the White House.[59] In one blog, Julieta Garibay wrote, "For the past years and even decades, many of us have yearned to be accepted and recognized as part of this country—to no longer be rejected or de-nied. . . . I cannot continue to be living in fear; I cannot let my profes-sion and education go to waste. I will no longer tolerate injustice. We have dared to dream and we will not give up."[60] In 2012, President Barack Obama introduced the Deferred Action for Childhood Arrivals (DACA) program, which provided work permits to undocumented youth who came to the United States and prevented them from being deported.[61] Five years later, President Donald Trump revoked this administrative program, but by then, undocumented youth were already seen as more deserving of belonging in the United States than their parents.[62] Most U.S. citizens had come to view migrant youth as being in the country "through no fault of their own" even as they deemed their parents guilty and "illegal."[63] These perceptions paralleled the logic pronounced by the Supreme Court in *Plyler v. Doe*, which held that undocumented children could attend school because, unlike their parents, they were not respon-sible for their unauthorized migration.[64]

Even as undocumented and legalized migrants settled in *El Norte* after the passage of IRCA, they continued to fight for inclusion in Mexico. This

was especially true for those who migrated as adults. In 1988, Cuauhtémoc Cárdenas, the candidate of the center-left opposition party in
Mexico who later founded the Party of the Democratic Revolution
(PRD), lost the presidential bid in an election that most people believed
to be fraudulent. In response, immigrant rights organizations and
Mexican American groups in Chicago and Los Angeles mobilized for
the democratization of Mexico.[65] Leaders of *clubes sociales* in Los Angeles
became very involved in this movement. When Cárdenas was governor
of the state of Michoacán (between 1980 and 1986), he agreed to become the sponsor and honorary president of the Club Michoacano.
After the 1988 elections, club members vowed to rally for Cárdenas in
Mexico's next national elections. As club leader Salvador Vázquez recalled, "Even though there was still no [absentee] vote," migrants could
exert "pressure" from the United States by "informing people, their
families [back home] that there was a candidate" that they should support.[66] Vázquez remembered that members of the Club Michocano
would tell their Mexican friends living in Los Angeles, "We have a candidate now, Cuauhtémoc Cárdenas, write to your family [and ask them]
to vote for him." Because migrants were highly esteemed in their home
communities, they could sway how people voted. Noticing the potential
success of this strategy, other political parties in Mexico also began recruiting migrants. This gave Mexicans in the United States an unprece-
dented voice in Mexico's politics.[67]

The growing importance of migrants in Mexico's political life buttressed calls for their right to vote while abroad. In 2005, after determined demands from activists, migrants finally achieved absentee
voting.[68] For the next decade, however, this victory was only symbolic,
as migrants were required to hold a valid voter registration credential,
which was not issued outside of Mexico.[69] Those who did not already
hold a *credencial de elector* [voting card] did not dare to head back to Mexico
simply to get it and were thus effectively excluded from voting. A survey
conducted by the Pew Hispanic Center for the 2006 elections found that
only 31 percent of Mexicans in the United States had valid Mexican
voting credentials.[70] Other barriers to voting from abroad included the
lack of information about the process of voting.[71] As a result, the absentee
applications were trivial. In the 2006 elections, only 33,000 Mexicans
cast a ballot from the United States, and in the 2012 elections, only 45,478
Mexicans living in the United States requested a ballot.[72]

After 1986, undocumented migrants switched from being pushed to move back and forth between Mexico and the United States to being trapped north of the border. Despite their continued activism for inclusion in both countries, many undocumented migrants continued to feel that they were "from neither here nor there" and experienced that the spaces where they felt that they could belong shrank. In the words of José Juárez, it was after IRCA that "the fence" between Mexico and the United States "began encroaching" on everyone everywhere.[73]

While undocumented migrants felt trapped in the United States after 1986, those who joined the temporary guest-worker program that IRCA created could still engage in circular migration. The 1986 law created distinct programs (out of the then-existing H-2 visa category) to import unskilled temporary or seasonal workers.[74] Henceforth, agricultural workers migrated under the H-2A program, and nonagricultural laborers under the H-2B program. The hiring of these H-2 laborers increased dramatically after the late 1990s.

Mexican workers were interested in joining the H-2 program because it allowed them to cross the border back and forth without facing the risks and costs of migrating without documents.[75] Fernando Tapia, who headed to the United States approximately nine times as an H-2B worker between 1996 and 2010, said that he preferred to migrate as a contract worker "because when one goes illegally there is real suffering."[76] Unauthorized migration, he explained, involved "risking your life when crossing the river and then . . . risking your life also while crossing the hill," which was full of rattlesnakes. When walking through the hills, "tiredness beats [you down]," but if one succumbs and "lays down there for a while to rest . . . one of those animals can arrive." In contrast, he explained, "with a work visa, . . . one goes well, one goes legally. One doesn't go risking his life."[77]

Those who sought to work in the United States without having to risk their lives at the border or remain entrapped in La Jaula de Oro tried to join the H-2 program, but such a decision involved great sacrifice. While those without papers could look for other jobs if they faced unacceptable working conditions, H-2 workers were bound to the employers who brought them to the United States.[78] When exploited, H-2 workers had to decide whether to lose their legal status and switch employers, leave the program altogether and return to Mexico, or tolerate employer abuse. Many chose the latter option because the program allowed them

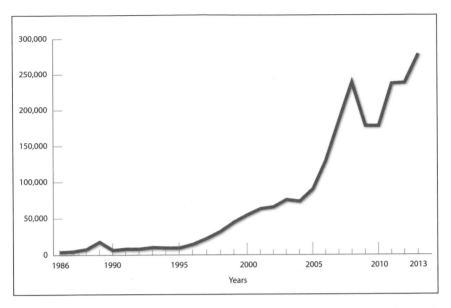

Mexican H-2 workers, 1986–2013. Data source: Lauren A. Apgar, "Authorized Status, Limited Returns: The Labor Market Outcomes of Temporary Mexican Workers," *EPI Briefing Paper*, #400 (May 21, 2015), Economic Policy Institute.

to go back and forth between Mexico and the United States. According to Adarely Hernández, the manager of the chocolate factory in Louisiana where she labored as an H-2B worker between 2003 and 2006 was very abusive. She considered "skipping" her contract, finding another job, and remaining in the country illegally. But she knew that if she did, she would never be able to get another H-2 visa again, and the program allowed her to migrate regularly between Mexico and the United States. When weighing her options, she would think to herself, "If I stay as an illegal, well, I have to give up, for example, my family." She would have to resign herself to "not seeing them, to being far." She explained her reasoning by recalling her cousins' situation. After they had migrated without papers, they had learned that their mother, who remained in Mexico, had become "very sick and . . . wanted to see them." The cousins "couldn't return [to Mexico] because they didn't want to leave their children there [in the United States]" and then not be able to cross the border north again. Their mother died, and they didn't come back [to see her in Mexico]," Hernández said. "In contrast," she added, "with the contract, one asks for permission from the boss [to return to Mexico]" and might then be able to come back to the United States with another H-2 visa "the following year."[79] Migrating as part of the program allowed guest workers to remain connected to Mexico in a way that undocumented workers could not.

The workers who did break their H-2 contracts and remained in the United States illegally generally did so because their closest family members were no longer in Mexico, so they didn't have to fear being trapped in the United States. When Raúl Pérez was hired as an H-2A laborer in August 2000, he was "determined to complete [his] contract," as it would give him "the opportunity to come and go" from Mexico to the United States.[80] But during the journey north from his hometown in Zacatecas to the tobacco fields in North Carolina, where he had been recruited to work, Pérez heard horror stories about the H-2 program from men who had already worked in it. They told him, "Working in tobacco can harm you. . . . Sometimes you just get sick."[81] Pérez decided to flee before he even reached the camp site and simply stayed in the United States without authorization. His choice was relatively easy because almost everyone in his family was already living north of the border and those who remained in Mexico had plans to migrate. But for individuals with families in Mexico, this decision was much harder, and most remained in the program despite its hardships.

Because the H-2 program bound workers to their employers, managers could keep tight control over every aspect of their laborers' lives. They could even control who the workers talked with. Conducting oral history interviews with current participants of the program, for instance, was much harder than interviewing undocumented migrants. One H-2B worker who labored in Minnesota felt compelled to ask her boss if she could be interviewed. Even though the worker had shown excitement and initiative in telling her story and the interview would have been conducted outside work hours, her boss did not give her permission. Because she labored for him from the early hours of the morning to the late hours of the night and then slept in housing he provided, she was scared of doing the interview without his permission.

H-2 workers regularly saw their movement and other activities policed and limited by their employers. According to Hernández, the owners of the factory where she labored had their H-2B workers live in a trailer park that was patrolled by security guards. Even though the workers paid rent, they were not given the opportunity to live elsewhere. Their employers restricted their movement outside the trailer park by saying that the workers "were under their responsibility and that if anything happened, then they would be blamed."[82] Hernández explained, "On the weekends we were just there, bored, because we couldn't . . . leave anywhere else or look for another job or anything like that." Guards also instituted other forms of regulation, including prohibiting the H-2B workers from receiving guests: "If someone arrived . . . the guards would throw them out." Sometimes the guards also went inside the trailers "to check" that "there were no alcoholic beverages in the fridges."

H-2 workers often faced geographic isolation. Some even used prison metaphors to describe their living situation. Raúl Pérez said that after he acquired an H-2A visa, those who had already been a part of the program in North Carolina would tell him that some workers "escaped from the ranch." Those ranches, he claimed, were too secluded: "It was like being *imprisoned*, because [the workers] were isolated, far from the city and everything."[83]

Many H-2 migrants experienced underemployment in the United States, as employers regularly over-recruited contract laborers and did not give them enough work after they arrived. This happened even to H-2A workers who were legally entitled to receive at least three-fourths of the total hours promised in their contract. In 2004, the Department of Labor's inspector general found that the North Carolina Growers Association sometimes refused to give H-2A laborers any work. For laborers, this meant that they were in the United States without pay and without the option of working for another employer.[84] H-2B migrants had an even harder experience than H-2A laborers when it came to getting enough hours of work because, up until 2015, the law did not establish how many hours of work they ought to receive. Fernando Tapia, who worked in landscaping in North Carolina, said that "[the employer] would send us home to rest because there was no work and we, well, had to pay rent."[85]

Under these conditions, some women engaged in sexual relations with their employers in exchange for more work. Jimena Herrera recalled that in her packaging job, "those who would go out with the employer or the son of the employer" would be favored in terms of the work hours made available to them. Once, Herrera claimed, she saw a mother take her two daughters, who were also H-2 workers, to "be alone in a trailer with the boss" so that they would "receive preference" and be given additional work.[86] As Herrera explained, this depicts the despair the women faced. "It is sad, right? . . . How far people have to go." She then asked rhetorically, "Why [did women do it]?" and answered, "To bring money, to make money, and because . . . we didn't know . . . how many rights we had."

H-2 workers sometimes spoke out and tried to defend themselves against employer abuses, but they did so at the risk of being fired and blacklisted from the guest worker program. Raúl Palafox had a fight with his employer when he complained to her that she was not giving him enough work and insisted that she at least lend him money to eat.[87] She paid him the outstanding amount that she owed him, fired him, and blacklisted him so that other employers would not hire him as an H-2 worker. Once in Mexico, he tried to get another H-2 position, but as soon as recruiters found out his name, they would say, "No, . . . I can't bring that person."[88] Palafox regretted his actions: "I dared to speak out . . . and now I don't have a job." Hernández and her coworkers also tried to dispute their living and working conditions and were, as a result, barred from the program. After they could no longer tolerate the conditions of the job, they went on strike. "The following day . . . the head of the company came. The very head [who was not even] in Louisiana," recalled Hernández.[89] The leaders of the strike, including Hernández, were blacklisted from the program, and all H-2 employers refused to hire them thereafter. With stories such as these circulating in migrant communities, it is not surprising that H-2 workers generally refrained from demanding their rights.

The limited number of H-2 slots available combined with the terrible working conditions those involved in the program experienced meant that most Mexicans continued to migrate without authorization. Although they would have preferred to engage in circular migration, as their fathers and grandfathers had often done, doing so was almost impossible and came at a very high cost.

IRCA created a new population of legalized migrants, settled undocumented migrants, and temporary contract workers. They could all strive for inclusion and a place to call home. By mandating the fortification of the border, however, IRCA also created another group: migrants who died, in much higher numbers than before, while trying to enter the United States. For them, national exclusion came to define both their lives and their deaths. In 1993 and 1994, U.S. state officials sought to

Fiscal year	Big Bend (formerly Marfa)	Del Rio	El Centro	El Paso	Laredo	Rio Grande Valley (formerly McAllen)	San Diego	Tucson	Yuma	Southwest border total
1998	3	28	90	24	20	26	44	11	17	263
1999	0	30	56	15	37	36	25	29	21	249
2000	3	48	72	26	47	40	34	74	36	380
2001	3	41	96	10	28	37	21	80	24	340
2002	4	29	64	8	15	30	24	134	12	320
2003	0	23	61	10	17	39	29	137	22	338
2004	0	21	36	18	22	35	15	142	39	328
2005	4	28	30	28	53	55	23	219	52	492
2006	4	34	21	33	36	81	36	169	40	454
2007	0	20	12	25	52	61	15	202	11	398
2008	3	22	20	8	32	92	32	171	5	385
2009	3	29	27	5	58	68	15	212	3	420
2010	0	23	14	4	35	29	8	251	1	365
2011	2	18	5	6	65	66	15	195	3	375
2012	1	29	11	1	91	144	5	180	9	471
2013	3	18	3	2	56	156	7	194	6	445
2014	5	17	6	0	49	115	5	107	3	307

Southwest Border Deaths by Fiscal Year (October 1 through September 30)

Source: "U.S. Border Patrol Fiscal Year Southwest Border Sector Deaths (FY 1998–FY 2014)," Statistics and Summaries, U.S. Customs and Border Protection (CBP), United States Department of Homeland Security.

fortify the border to make it harder for migrants to enter the country illegally by implementing Operation Blockade in Texas and Operation Gatekeeper in California. Migrating came to mean traversing through ever more treacherous routes to avoid being caught. Violent cartels developed to smuggle Mexicans and, increasingly, Central Americans. Smugglers would cross migrants through the arduous stretch of desert in Arizona, which is full of rattlesnakes and where dehydration is likely, or through the Rio Grande Valley sector in Texas, where drowning is a common occurrence. According to the United States Border Patrol, between 2005 and 2013, one person or more died every day on average while trying to cross the U.S.-Mexico border. The number is staggering but probably smaller than the actual number of deaths, as many bodies were most likely never found. The numbers elide the lives and humanity of the individuals involved. They do not capture their hopes and fears, their efforts to improve their situation, their kindness, their love and hatred, their human imperfections.

The history of fallen border crossers is also the history of their loved ones. The families of the migrants who were not found or could not be identified never learned what happened to their relatives. They didn't give up hope that those who headed north searching for a better future were still alive. This prospect made it hard for them to overcome the psychic pain of the loss.[90] In 2007, a woman in Tarímbaro, Michoacán, regularly went to the municipal palace to see if someone could help her find her son.[91] He had departed for the United States six months earlier, and she had not heard from him since. She did not know if he had been able to cross the national boundary but had no money to call, if he was still trying to cross the border, or if he had simply decided to maintain some distance from his family. The possibility that he could have died on the journey was too hard for her to consider, even though she had heard of many individuals who had died in the desert.

The remains of those who passed away while crossing the border and were never found or identified vividly capture the national deletion of migrants' lives and personhood. In Holtville, California, a small town less than an hour away from the Mexican border, the local cemetery contains dozens of anonymous graves marked by simple, mud-colored bricks with the names John or Jane Doe.[92] Most of these remains are of individuals who died while trying to enter the United States without papers. "The problem is that most of the time their bodies are found days, weeks, or years after they die. Sometimes authorities only find a femur or just a few bones," claimed Jesús Gutiérrez, head of the Legal Protection Department for the Mexican Consulate in Calexico.[93] Forever excluded from national belonging, fallen migrants also remain unacknowledged in death.

Migrants' struggles for a better life in a geopolitical context that did and does not recognize their belonging or cross-border movement are both haunting and inspiring. The post-IRCA period produced a vast change in migratory patterns. However, some aspects remained the same: the United States still considered migrants "illegal," Mexican government officials continued to favor their emigration, and migrants struggled to claim their belonging in both nation-states through their activism and "undocumented lives."

AFTERWORD

WHILE I WAS WRITING this history, the present kept intruding. With an estimated 11 million undocumented migrants residing in the United States, I always knew the importance of the stories I was telling. But I was not prepared for what happened next. As I was finishing editing this book, almost a decade after I first started my research in 2007, questions of migration came to the fore in U.S. and Mexican politics.

On June 16, 2015, Donald Trump announced that he was running for president and emphasized that he would make the question of undocumented migration one of his key issues: "When Mexico sends its people, they're not sending their best. . . . They're sending people that have lots of problems, and they're bringing those problems with us. They're bringing drugs. They're bringing crime. They're rapists. And some, I assume, are good people."[1] He continued this rhetoric throughout his turbulent campaign, portraying migrants as a group that stole jobs from citizens, drained the nation's welfare coffers, used its public resources, posed a threat to the country's sovereignty, and had so-called anchor babies in the United States.[2]

Trump blamed both U.S. and Mexican policymakers for undocumented migration and vowed to solve the problem: "The Mexican government is much smarter [than the U.S. government], much sharper, much more cunning, and they send the bad ones over because they don't want to pay for them, they don't want to take care of them. Why should they, when the stupid leaders of the United States will do it for them?"[3] Claiming that "illegal immigration is beyond belief," Trump promised to "build a great, great wall on our southern border. And . . . have Mexico pay for that wall."[4]

A year and a half after launching his candidacy, Trump became the forty-fifth president of the United States. Pejorative stereotypes about Mexican migrants had helped determine the U.S. presidency. Once Trump took power, it became clear that he had not just used this rhetoric to get elected. Within his first week, he took the first steps toward fulfilling his anti-immigrant campaign pledges by signing two executive orders that mandated the construction of a wall between Mexico and the United States and called for increased immigration enforcement efforts and deportations.

Although speaking in the present tense, Trump's view that "Mexico sends its people" to the United States was his interpretation of what had happened in the past, when undocumented migration had actually risen and shaped the situation of 2015. By the time Trump ran for president, net migration from Mexico was below zero, with more migrants returning to Mexico than heading to the United States.[5] The Great Recession of 2008 had limited the jobs available in the United States, making it less enticing for Mexicans to head north; the Obama administration had increased deportations; and the population-control policies that the Mexican government had adopted since the early 1970s had dramatically reduced Mexicans' fertility rate, which in turn lowered the number of prospective migrants.[6] When Trump claimed that undocumented migration was "beyond belief" and blamed Mexico for it, he did not acknowledge that since 2008 undocumented Mexican migration had ceased to grow. Instead, he attached himself to the historical narrative of surging and unceasing unauthorized migration that had existed since the end of the Bracero Program—a narrative that was far from accurate.

The notion that the Mexican government sent its citizens north and that U.S. leaders accepted them disregarded the fact that the rapid rise of undocumented migration that had occurred since the mid-1960s stemmed primarily from migrants' cartographies of belonging rather than from the whims of politicians. Notwithstanding the interest of Mexican and U.S. officials, Mexicans migrated to the United States as a means of defying their exclusion from Mexico, the United States, and their own communities. Rather than being "sent" north by state officials and being "taken care of" by the U.S. government, Mexicans were driven to migrate by the lack of jobs in Mexico, by U.S. labor demand, and by the cultural and familial pressures they felt on both sides of the border. Living abroad provided them with the best means to counter notions that they were economically superfluous in their home country, that they deserved no rights in the United States, and that they could not contribute to the well-being of their hometowns, families, and binational communities.

The actions of the top policymakers of both countries had influenced migration patterns, but in a much more nuanced way than the anti-immigrant narrative portrayed. Instead of contributing to undocumented migration by being too accommodating to Mexican border crossers, U.S. politicians had compelled unauthorized migrants to settle in the United States by enforcing stricter border control measures. Before 1986, the national boundary was sufficiently permeable that most migrants engaged in circular migration: they would go to the United States, work there for a short period of time, return to Mexico to be with their families, and then repeat the process. After the U.S. Congress passed the Immigration Reform and Control Act (IRCA), crossing the border became a much more expensive and dangerous enterprise, as migrants had to pay smugglers to help them get across hazardous terrains that were less heavily patrolled. Despite the new hardships of migration, relatively few Mexicans reconsidered their decision to head north. After all, the passage of IRCA did nothing to alter the economic factors that led individuals to leave Mexico, nor did it address the ways in which Mexicans acquired their sense of belonging by migrating. After 1986, most migrants decided to settle permanently in the United States and dared not return to Mexico. U.S. politicians' strong enforcement measures effectively created a cage of gold (*jaula de oro*) that prevented Mexicans from leaving the United States.

For their part, Mexican policymakers did not "send" migrants to the United States, but after the mid-1970s they stopped objecting to the departures of working-class citizens. Mexican officials' failure to attend to the question of migration through their development plans left millions of Mexicans with few options other than migrating. Individuals' willingness to head north despite the risks of crossing the border illegally and living in the United States without authorization attests to their deprivations in Mexico. Mexican officials did not see their suffering. For them, migrants' departures came to represent a partial solution to Mexico's socioeconomic problems. Mexico's leaders did not send "criminals" to the United States, but they did turn a blind eye to the exodus of those they deemed a "surplus" population.

Representations that portrayed Mexican migrants as abusing welfare, taking jobs away from U.S. citizens, and bearing children in the United States could have come directly from union representatives in the 1970s; notions that migrants dilute U.S. sovereignty and bring crime echo those of President Reagan and his supporters. Yet migrants were ineligible to apply for welfare, and few dared to do so illegally; they generally took jobs that U.S. citizens did not want; and they preferred to bear and raise their children in Mexico. Rather than bringing crime, they looked for work.

The greatest tragedy in the narrative that has been constructed about undocumented migrants, however, is that it obscures the lives and humanity of actual people—the very people whose stories this book has sought to document. How does the narrative of *bad hombres* accommodate the stories of Gregorio Casillas and individuals like him who, despite having poorly paid jobs, helped build an extraterritorial welfare system by raising funds in the United States to improve communities in Mexico? How does the narrative explain men like Rodolfo Garza, who wanted to stay in Mexico but was forced to go north after a drought killed his crops and the Mexican state offered no help? What about the pain of separation evidenced in the love letters exchanged between Jorge Medina and Esther Ortega? Where does this narrative leave the experience of Jorge Zavala, who had to migrate from Churintzio, Michoacán, after becoming unemployed because of the U.S.-guided Green Revolution? What about the stories of the thousands of children like Junior Adriano who grew up without legal papers in the United States but never knew Mexico?

The issue of unsanctioned migration should not be used as a scare tactic for politicians to rise to power or to mobilize nationalistic sentiments. It is a transnational issue that requires deep cross-border analysis and solutions. It affects millions of people. There are no conscionable reasons for workers to die in their search for work, for mothers to cry over absent sons who are trapped in *la jaula de oro* and cannot return, for children to grow up fearing deportation, or for people to live on the margins, not belonging in the place they reside.

APPENDIX A: NOTE ON SOURCES

APPENDIX B: QUEER MIGRATION

NOTES

ACKNOWLEDGMENTS

INDEX

APPENDIX A

Note on Sources

MIGRANTS' UNDOCUMENTED LEGAL STATUS in the United States accompanies their undocumented trail in the historical record. While one can track how Mexican and U.S. officials as well as the public at large viewed undocumented migration by using sources stored in established repositories, most archives do not contain much information pertaining to the world of unauthorized migrants. The evidence that does exist generally documents instances in which migrants were caught by U.S. officials and thus only captures a narrow sliver of their experiences. Documenting migrants' lives and communities requires the discovery and creation of a different set of sources and archives. Much of my research for this book took place in private individuals' closets, as well as in the storerooms of the migrant-led welfare institution, La Casa del Mexicano.

Migrants' experiences made it hard for them to preserve documents. When crossing the border illegally, they carried as little as possible; once in the United States, they relocated often and left many of their documents behind. Agricultural workers moved from field to field during the course of the growing season. Even migrants who lived in cities moved constantly as landlords evicted them from their apartments, they found cheaper places to live, or they were deported and forced to leave their belongings behind.

Nonetheless, many migrants I met had stored their correspondence, privately held organizational records, personal collections, photographs, pamphlets, and other unpublished ephemera. Even though only a

limited number of sources survived, the fact that some did is a testament
to the strength of migrants' networks and the importance migrant communities place on their own history. When migrants went to Mexico,
they often used the opportunity to store their memorabilia in the houses
of family members who still resided in their hometowns. Similarly, when
people were deported, their friends realized the importance of safeguarding their belongings and regularly picked them up and stored
them in their own homes. Migrants also sought other ways to preserve
their history for posterity, no matter how difficult the task. Raúl Villarreal, who had only a third grade education and had difficulty reading
and writing, collected boxes upon boxes of files documenting his life
and his many years of community activism and used them to draft his
memoirs.

To explore the social history of migrants, I also conducted 257 oral
history interviews on both sides of the border.[1] The methodology of oral
history is now well established and has been critical in reconstructing
the lives and communities of people who rarely left behind significant
written records or who were largely illegible to government officials. Most
of the questions I asked were open-ended, allowing interviewees to guide
the stories they told.[2] I also had categories of questions specific for different groups: I asked migrants about their journeys, family life, work
life, and social life in the United States. I asked nonmigrants about how
they experienced the migration of others. With activists, I asked questions about how they organized, why they did so, and how their groups
developed over time. The interviews generally lasted between one and
three hours, although a few lasted less than an hour and others were
over fifteen hours long and had to be conducted over the course of
several days. With the permission of my informants, I was able to record
almost all of the oral histories.

To attain a diverse range of experiences, I interviewed migrants and
nonmigrants of different sexes, sexual identities, and racial backgrounds.
Because many migrants took their first trip when they were as young
as fifteen and most migrated into their forties, I focused on people who
had been between fifteen and forty years old in the 1965–1986 period.[3]
Slightly over half of the interviews conducted were with the friends,
children, and (especially) wives of those who had gone north in the years
between 1965 and 1986, rather than with the migrants themselves. This

Characteristics of Interviewees

	Interviewed	Migrated	Migrated 1965–1986	Interviewed in Mexico	Interviewed in the United States	Identified as indigenous	Identified as queer
Men	136	94	89	81	55	23	32
Women	121	30	23	99	22	36	7
Total	257	124	112	180	77	59	39

Note: All indigenous people identified as Tarascans. "Queer" is defined as discussed in Chapter 3.

allowed me to capture how migration affected not only migrants but also other members of their communities. I carried out approximately one-quarter of the oral history interviews with Tarascan individuals from Michoacán and three-quarters with mestizo-identified individuals, who were the primary migrants before the passage of the Immigration Reform and Control Act.[4] I interviewed thirty-two men and seven women who identified as queer.

In Mexico, I conducted most oral histories in Michoacán and Zacatecas, two states that had especially high rates of emigration between 1965 and 1986, but I also conducted interviews in Aguascalientes, Guadalajara, and Mexico City. Within those locations, I focused on communities with particularly high emigration rates. In the United States, I conducted most of the interviews in California, which was the most popular destination for undocumented workers in the post-Bracero period, but I also conducted interviews with specific migrant activists in Illinois, Arizona, New Mexico, and Texas.

As with all sources, oral testimonies need to be analyzed with critical awareness. Oral history often tells us more about people's memories than about their actual experiences. These memories are shaped by what people wanted to do, believed or wished they were doing, and later considered that they had done. Moreover, interviews must be viewed as a complex product of the interaction between the informant and the researcher.[5] Aware of these issues, I brought surviving documents to the interview whenever possible to help refresh and corroborate people's recollections.[6] In writing this book, I focused on common themes that were repeated by many migrants even while underscoring idiosyncratic experiences. Still, this strategy did not address the fact that community

Interview Locations			
	Men	Women	Total
Mexico			
Aguascalientes, Aguascalientes	1	0	1
Guadalajara, Jalisco	0	1	1
Mexico City	1	0	1
Angahuan, Michoacán	1	5	6
Cañada del Herrero, Michoacán	0	2	2
Chavinda, Michoacán	0	3	3
Cucuchucho, Michoacán	1	1	2
Gómez Farías, Michoacán	0	1	1
Ihuatzio, Michoacán	1	0	1
Morelia, Michoacán	4	7	11
Pátzcuaro, Michoacán	3	4	7
Pichátaro, Michoacán	1	0	1
Quiroga, Michoacán	1	1	2
Ruiz Cortines, Michoacán	1	6	7
San Andrés, Michoacán	10	7	17
Santa Fe de La Laguna, Michoacán	10	15	25
Tangancícuaro, Michoacán	8	6	14
Tarímbaro, Michoacán	3	13	16
Tzintzuntzan, Michoacán	6	14	20
Zacán, Michoacán	0	3	3
Jalpa, Zacatecas	3	0	3
Jerez, Zacatecas	1	0	1
Las Ánimas, Zacatecas	10	7	17
Nochistlán, Zacatecas	16	3	19
USA			
Tempe, Arizona	2	0	2
Coachella Valley, California	8	8	16
Los Angeles Metropolitan Area, California	23	9	32
Napa Valley, California	4	2	6
Sacramento, California	1	0	1
South San Francisco, California	13	2	15
Chicago, Illinois	1	0	1
Pinos Altos, New Mexico	1	1	2
Anthony, Texas	1	0	1
Total	136	121	257

members often reproduce each other's scripts. Despite the many problems inherent in oral history, people's memories allowed me to trace more deeply than otherwise possible the social history of a group that purposefully hid and left little documentation behind.[7]

During the interviews, I was attuned to people's silences, which often spoke more than words. For instance, not long after I started the oral history with Eva Herrera in Angahuan, Michoacán, she was unable to talk and simply cried. I had just asked her to tell me about her experiences with her son, Francisco, who lived in the United States without papers. Although she never told me about her experiences with her son, she had already explained her pain: Francisco had migrated to the United States but could not return to Mexico for fear that he would not be able to go back north. Herrera, who was ill, knew she would probably die without seeing her son again. Despite her lack of words, Herrera's silence, her tears, and her facial expressions conveyed the agony of family separation, the emotional bonds that survived despite physical distance, and the human costs of the fortification of the border.

I was sometimes surprised at people's openness on certain topics. Individuals often brought up issues that I assumed they would have wanted to conceal. For instance, Michaocano husbands spoke openly about having threatened their wives to ensure that they were not unfaithful. It was clear that this practice was common enough that men saw it as normal and not as something they ought to hide. On the flip side, as with all oral histories, I am sure that in mine there were multiple issues that migrants and their families preferred not to discuss.

I met the individuals I interviewed in different ways. In many towns in Michoacán, I had close friends who were able to introduce me to members of their communities. In towns in Mexico where I had no contacts, priests often presented me at mass and asked the members of their congregations to approach me if they were interested in telling me their stories. I also met people in eateries, on buses, at small grocery stores, in plazas, and at the market in small towns. Because many of the areas in Mexico where I carried out research are not tourist destinations, people were surprised to see me and often approached me, rather than the other way around. I always asked those I had already interviewed to introduce me to others, a method known as snowball sampling. Most individuals were willing to introduce me to their family members, friends, and neighbors. Because snowball sampling only gave me the perspective of a particular network, I also continued to meet new people in public spaces. I kept conducting oral histories until I saw the similarities in people's experiences and could notice deviations from them.

Social networks facilitated the process of conducting interviews with the same community on both sides of the border. Because migrant towns in Mexico are linked to specific sites in the United States, I followed specific communities from one country to the other. For instance, because many migrants from the town of Las Ánimas, Zacatecas, headed to South San Francisco, after I had conducted interviews with individuals in Las Ánimas, I was able to get in touch with their family members in South San Francisco. The links that connected those in the United States with those in Mexico allowed me to trace migrant family histories at a very individual level.

Finding and talking to queer men proved slightly harder but was much easier than I had expected. Most community members in towns of high out-migration in Mexico knew who identified as "queer" in the years between 1965 and 1986. Reflecting the openness of individuals and communities around queer issues, on several occasions Catholic priests themselves introduced me to the men who identified as queer in the period under analysis. At other times, taxi drivers, who were acquainted with an extraordinary number of people because of the mobility of their job, introduced me to informants. After I met a few gay men in any particular town, I could easily meet others using snowball sampling. Meeting women who identified as queer in the years between 1965 and 1986 and who lived in towns of high out-migration proved much harder. I assume that this partially reflects women's dependence on men's remittances and their inability to lead full queer lives. As described in Chapter 3, the border was particularly dangerous for women, and many refrained from migrating. But unlike queer men, who could make more money in Mexico than straight men, queer women didn't seem to have had economic advantages over other women. Regardless of women's sexual preferences, if they wanted to avoid having to cross the border they depended on heterosexual marriage and remittances to improve their living standards. Future research is needed to be able to understand further queer women's lives in Mexican towns of high out-migration.

Finding particular club activists was the hardest part of the research. Community networks proved indispensable in identifying informants. I started examining the history of *clubes sociales,* now known as hometown associations (HTAs), by speaking to their current leaders in Los Angeles. They all insisted that I had to interview Gregorio Casillas, who they claimed had been the central figure in the formation of these organizations. The problem was that no one knew where Casillas resided, although one person thought he lived in the town of Jerez in Zacatecas. Determined to find him, I took a plane to Mexico City, boarded a bus heading to the city of Zacatecas, and then got on a smaller bus going to Jerez. As the bus pulled into the station, however, I realized that I was in a town of over fifty-seven thousand people where I knew absolutely nobody, and I was on a mission to find one man—who I wasn't even sure lived there. Without knowing what to do, I turned to the man next to me on the bus and asked him if he was acquainted with Casillas. He was not, but he did know all about hometown associations and sent me to the office of Encarnación Bañuelos, who was the main club activist in Jerez. Bañuelos knew Casillas but believed him to live in Jalpa, Zacatecas, which is approximately 100 miles away from Jerez. A day later, I hopped on another bus and headed to Jalpa. Once there, I approached a group of men talking outside a convenience store. They knew Casillas and his work. They informed me that Casillas had moved to Aguascalientes, but they had his contact information. I was finally able to reach him by phone and set an appointment.

That the first people I spoke to in both Jalpa and Jerez knew about *clubes sociales* and ultimately led me to Casillas speaks of an impressive migrant network that spans at least from Los Angeles to multiple towns in Zacatecas to Aguascalientes. These networks allowed migrants to gain partial inclusion in both Mexico and the United States. They also offer a way for scholars to document migrant histories despite the silences in traditional archives.

APPENDIX B

Queer Migration

I. TO CALCULATE WHETHER queer men migrated from Nochistlán in higher or lower numbers than their heterosexual counterparts, I first had to estimate the number of men who migrated from the town as a whole. To do this, I used three distinct methodologies, each of which had benefits and drawbacks. Using these methodologies I estimated that between 66.5 and 78 percent of men who were in their prime years to migrate headed to the United States between 1965 and 1986.

The first method consisted of taking the names of all the men born in the town of Nochistlán in the years 1940, 1950, 1960, and 1971 from the municipal records and tracking how many had migrated to the United States. I chose these years because between 1965 and 1986 men generally migrated when they were between fifteen and forty years old.[1] I began the data collection with the year 1940 because many men born in 1930 or earlier had already passed away by 2010, when I did this research. I also omitted the year 1970 (and used 1971 instead) because the municipal record for that year was illegible. I was able to trace 189 men (33.8 percent) out of a total of 558 registered men. I did this either by finding the men directly or by finding their family members. I then asked if the men had migrated. Out of the 189 men, 140 had migrated. This means that 74 percent of all the men I tracked in Nochistlán migrated at least once between 1965 and 1986.

The second methodology I used consisted of surveying people who went to the Catholic church in Nochistlán on Sunday, which is a common practice in the town. I interviewed individuals who had brothers who were born in the town between 1930 and 1971 and asked them if their brothers had ever migrated in the years between 1965 and 1986. If they had multiple brothers, I only asked about the eldest. Through this method, I tried to reduce the bias that could stem from church-goers versus non-church-goers, but I recognize a bias relating to the migration of older brothers. This method also failed to capture families that were not living in town. The results revealed a migration rate of 78 percent based on the finding that 196 men had migrated out of 250 men cited as brothers.

The third method I employed was the most traditional: counting 200 households in two neighborhoods to identify how many male household heads migrated in the years between 1965 and 1986. This is the approach employed by the Mexican Migration Project (MMP).[2] In the 1970s, Nochistlán was divided in sections according to the municipality, but town residents were not aware of these divisions. Instead, they understood the town's cartography based on *barrios* (neighborhoods). I picked the barrios of El Centro and Guerrero. (Richer people in the community generally lived in El Centro.) The main problem with this methodology was that, unlike the MMP, my project was a historical survey. Many people had moved, and their neighbors had no idea who had lived in a particular household between 1965 and 1986. For this reason, many deserted households (whose members had likely gone to the United States) went uncounted. With this methodology, I found that in 133 out of the 200 households (66.5 percent), the male head of household had migrated to the United States at least once in the two decades following the end of the Bracero Program.

The results of the three methods convey very high rates of migration and seem to be corroborated by data from the population census conducted by the INEGI (Instituto Nacional de Estadística, Geografía e Informática). Unfortunately, the census does not reveal where people migrated to (and many people migrated internally within Mexico); it only tracks people's residency at one point in time; and it considers the whole municipality of Nochistlán rather than the town alone. Still, the data are significant. In 1960 the municipality had 28,108 inhabitants, of which 14,001 were men and 14,107 women.[3] The similar gender ratio in town seems to signify a low level of out-migration. In 1970, conversely, the municipality's population was 30,606, of which 13,024 (43 percent) were men and 17,582, (57 percent) women.[4] The change in the gender ratio is consistent with the large out-migration rate of males from the municipality to the United States. Unfortunately, the 1980 census is mistrusted by academics, and its figures are considered corrupt. According to the census of 1990, the municipality had 32,327 inhabitants, of which 14,620 (45 percent) were men and 17,707 (55 percent) women.[5] The gender ratio had become more equal than that of 1970, which is consistent with the beginnings of higher migration rates by women.

II. To calculate the proportion of gay men who migrated, I asked the queer men I met in Nochistlán to name all the other gay men they knew from the town who were between fifteen and fifty years old during the years between 1965 and 1986. I insisted that the list should include the queer men who no longer lived in the town. Through this method, I created a "master list" of queer Nochistlense men. I then investigated whether they had migrated. Because Nochistlán is a small town, I could trace the migratory lives of everyone on my list. Overall, my master list included forty-one men, six of whom had migrated in the period under analysis. This reveals a rate of migration of 15 percent, which is much lower than the estimated 66.5 to 78 percent migratory rate of men from Nochistlán as a whole. Of course, there may be other factors (such as age, income, and education) that affect the decision to migrate and that are also correlated with people's identification as queer. However, the migratory differences between queer and heterosexual men are stark. Although the sample of queer men counted seems small, I limited my definition of "gay" to those who were classified as queer within the gender and sexual paradigms of their communities and who openly identified as such in the years between 1965 and 1986 (see Chapter 3). This means that I did not count all men who engaged in same-sex relationships. Given the small sample size, it is particularly important to note that the patterns found reflect the beliefs held by the vast majority of people in the region (whether gay or straight) that queer men migrated at lower rates than straight ones.

NOTES

Introduction

1. Weather history found in "Weather Almanac for KSDM—May, 1980," *Weather Underground*, accessed on June 26, 2017, https://english.wunder ground.com/history/airport/KSDM/1980/5/3/DailyHistory.html?req_city =San+Ysidro&req_state=CA&req_statename=&reqdb.zip=92143&reqdb .magic=1&reqdb.wmo=99999.
2. Evan Maxwell, "Aggressive Patrol Tactics Help Out Violence in 2 Border Trouble Zones," *Los Angeles Times*, June 14, 1980, A1; and "Cruel Cacería de 'Ilegales,'" *ABC*, May 5, 1980, Archivos de la Secretaría de Relaciones Exteriores, México, Topográfica: PAC-1-130-25. This translation, like all others in this book, was done by the author.
3. "Border Patrol under Siege in River," *Syracuse Post-Standard*, April 18, 1980, B8.
4. "Cruel Cacería de 'Ilegales.'"
5. Ibid. Also see Bill Ott, "Defense Plan for Aliens Falters," *San Diego Union*, May 9, 1980, continued from B-1, np; and "Memorandum of Points and Authorities in Support of Motion to Dismiss Pursuant to *United States v. Oscar*," Archivos de la Secretaría de Relaciones Exteriores, México, Topográ-fica: PAC-1-130-25.
6. Newspapers published differing accounts of the number of arrested migrants, though they were generally somewhere around 250. See, for instance, "U.S. 'War Wagons' Block Illegal Mexican Aliens' Calif. Path," *Chronicle Telegram*, May 7, 1980, 15; and "Cruel Cacería de 'Ilegales.'" How-ever, the official motion issued by migrants' attorneys stated that there were approximately 450. "Memorandum of Points and Authorities."
7. "Memorandum of Points and Authorities."
8. When the Mexican consul in San Diego reported the incidents to the head of Mexico's Foreign Affairs Ministry, he did not see the need to explain or ask for an explanation about how or why this had happened (Telegram

from General Consul Esteban Morales to Secretaría de Relaciones Exteriores, México, May 5, 1980, 2; and the letter that accompanies it with further information from General Consul Esteban Morales to Secretaría de Relaciones Exteriores, México, Archivos de la Secretaría de Relaciones Exteriores, México,Topográfica: PAC-1-130–25). Also see descriptions of Ernesto Viscaíno's report in a letter from A. Loza Amador to Secretario de Relaciones Exteriores, June 11, 1980, Archivos de la Secretaría de Relaciones Exteriores, México, Topográfica: PAC-1-130–25.

9. Mireya Loza, *Defiant Braceros: How Migrant Workers Fought for Racial, Sexual, and Political Freedom* (Chapel Hill: University of North Carolina Press, 2016), 2. Although the Bracero Program officially ended in 1964, contracts were actually issued until 1967. As such, the program unofficially lasted more than twenty-two years.

10. Mae Ngai, *Impossible Subjects: Illegal Aliens and the Making of Modern America* (Princeton, NJ: Princeton University Press, 2004), 227. The Immigration and Nationality Act of 1965 extended the quota system to the Western Hemisphere (Latin America, the Caribbean, and Canada), giving the region an overall quota of 120,000 visas starting in 1968. Douglas S. Massey, Jorge Durand, and Nolan J. Malone, *Beyond Smoke and Mirrors: Mexican Immigration in an Era of Economic Integration* (New York: Russell Sage Foundation, 2002), 40.

11. Calculated from Manuel García y Griego and Mónica Verea, *México y Estados Unidos frente a la migración de indocumentados* (Mexico City: Coordinación de Humanidades, M.A. Porrúa, 1988), cuadro (table) 2, pp. 118–121.

12. Massey, Durand, and Malone, *Beyond Smoke and Mirrors,* 45.

13. Douglas S. Massey and Audrey Singer, "New Estimates of Undocumented Mexican Migration and the Probability of Apprehension," *Demography* 32, no. 2 (1995): 210.

14. See Lauren Berlant, *The Queen of America Goes to Washington City: Essays on Sex and Citizenship* (Durham, NC: Duke University Press, 1997), 43.

15. Historians have only recently begun to pay attention to nonmigrants. See, for example, Ana Elizabeth Rosas, *Abrazando el Espíritu: Bracero Families Confront the US-Mexico Border* (Berkeley: University of California Press, 2014).

16. Jorge Durand, Douglas S. Massey, and Rene M. Zenteno, "Mexican Immigration to the United States: Continuities and Changes," *Latin American Research Review* 36, no. 1 (2001): 114–115.

17. Ana Beltrán (pseudonym), interview by author, July 14, 2005, Santa Fe de la Laguna, Michoacán, Mexico, digital recording.

18. Gregorio Casillas, interview by author, October 17, 2009, Jalpa, Zacatecas, Mexico, digital recording.

19. Even while refraining from using the lens of citizenship or statelessness, this book takes into account theories on statelessness, citizenship, and the biopolitical management of bodies and populations, including those of

Giorgio Agamben, *Homo Sacer: Sovereign Power and Bare Life* (Stanford, CA: Stanford University Press, 1998); Hannah Arendt, *Totalitarianism: Part Three of the Origins of Totalitarianism* (Orlando, FL: Harcourt, 1976); Hannah Arendt, *The Human Condition*, 2nd ed. (Chicago: University of Chicago Press, 1998); Michel Foucault, *The History of Sexuality*, vol. 1 (New York: Vintage Books, 1990); Natalia Molina, *How Race Is Made in America: Immigration, Citizenship, and the Historical Power of Racial Scripts* (Berkeley: University of California Press, 2013); and Ngai, *Impossible Subjects.*
20. See Appendix A for more on oral history methodology.
21. For more on my thoughts regarding the problematics of oral history, see Appendix A. Also see Daniel James, *Doña María's Story: Life History, Memory, and Political Identity* (Durham, NC: Duke University Press, 2000); Peter Winn, "Oral History and the Factory Study: New Approaches to Labor History," *Latin American Research Review* 14, no. 2 (1979): 130–140; Jeffrey L. Gould and Aldo A. Lauria-Santiago, *To Rise in Darkness: Revolution, Repression, and Memory in El Salvador, 1920–1932* (Durham, NC: Duke University Press, 2008); Alessandro Portelli, *The Death of Luigi Trastulli, and Other Stories: Form and Meaning in Oral History* (Albany: State University of New York Press, 1991); and Luisa Passerini, *Fascism in Popular Memory: The Cultural Experience of the Turin Working Class*, trans. Robert Lumley and Jude Bloomfield (Cambridge: Cambridge University Press, 1987).

1. An Excess of Citizens

1. José Gardoño, interview by author, March 18, 2015, Thermal, California, digital recording.
2. Jorge Castañeda, planned speech, August 1978, Caja 119B, Expediente 19, Archivo General de la Nación, Fondo Porfirio Muñoz Ledo. Information on when it was presented from James Daniel, "Mexico: America's Newest Problem?," *Washington Quarterly* 3, no. 3 (1980): 96.
3. See Kelly Lytle Hernández, *Migra! A History of the U.S. Border Patrol* (Berkeley: University of California Press, 2010), 84–88; Lawrence A. Cardoso, *Mexican Emigration to the United States, 1897–1931: Socio-economic Patterns* (Tucson: University of Arizona Press, 1980), 96–118; Mercedes Carreras de Velasco, *Los mexicanos que devolvió la crisis, 1929–1932* (Tlatelolco: Secretaría de Relaciones Exteriores, 1974); Alfonso Fábila, *El problema de la emigración de obreros y campesinos mexicanos* (Mexico City: Talleres Gráficos de la Nación, 1929); and Moisés González Navarro, *Los extranjeros en México y los mexicanos en el extranjero, 1821–1970* (Mexico City: Colegio de México, 1993 and 1994).
4. This does not mean that there was a monolithic "Mexican state" that uniformly followed these new guiding principles but rather that those in charge of migration in Mexico altered their position.
5. Jorge Castañeda, planned speech.

6. Some scholars speak of a "policy of no policy." See Juan Gómez-Quiñones, "Mexican Immigration to the U.S. and the Internationalization of Labour, 1848–1980: An Overview," in *Mexican Immigrant Workers in the U.S.*, edited by Antonio Ríos-Bustamante (Los Angeles: Chicano Studies Research Center Publications, UCLA, 1981), 33; and Alexandra Délano, *Mexico and Its Diaspora in the United States* (Cambridge: Cambridge University Press, 2011), 105–107.

7. Douglas S. Massey, Jorge Durand, and Nolan J. Malone, *Beyond Smoke and Mirrors: Mexican Immigration in an Era of Economic Integration* (New York: Russell Sage Foundation, 2002), 45.

8. Francisco Alba, *La población de México: Evolución y dilemas* (Mexico City: El Colegio de México, 1977); José Angel Hernández, *Mexican American Colonization during the Nineteenth Century: History of the U.S.-Mexico Borderlands* (Cambridge: Cambridge University Press, 2012), 40; Víctor Manuel García Guerrero, *Proyecciones y políticas de población en México* (Mexico City: El Colegio de México, 2014); and *Los grandes problemas de México, Tomo I, Población*, edited by Brígida García and Manuel Ordorica (Mexico City: El Colegio de México, 2010).

9. David FitzGerald, *A Nation of Emigrants: How Mexico Manages Its Migration* (Berkeley: University of California Press, 2009), 39; and Lytle Hernández, *Migra!*, 86.

10. Quoted in FitzGerald, *A Nation of Emigrants*, 39.

11. Quoted in Lytle Hernández, *Migra!*, 86.

12. "Ley de Migración de 1926," *Diario Oficial de la Federación*, March 13, 1926, Archivo General de la Nación.

13. "Ley General de Población de 1936," *Diario Oficial de la Federación*, August 29, 1936, Archivo General de la Nación. For more on questions of assimilability, see Pablo Yankelevich and Paola Chenillo Alazraki, "La arquitectura de la política de inmigración en México," in *Nación y extranjería: La exclusión racial en las políticas migratorias de Argentina, Brasil, Cuba y México*, edited by Pablo Yankelevich (Mexico City: Universidad Nacional Autónoma de México, 2009), 219–220.

14. Manuel Gamio, *Mexican Immigration to the United States: A Study of Human Migration and Adjustment* (Chicago: University of Chicago Press, 1930), 138, 172–173.

15. Lytle Hernández, *Migra!*, 86–87.

16. FitzGerald, *A Nation of Emigrants*, 43.

17. Ibid., 44.

18. Kelly Lytle Hernández, " 'Persecuted Like Criminals': The Politics of Labor Emigration and Mexican Migration Controls in the 1920s and 1930s," *Aztlán: A Journal of Chicano Studies* 34, no. 1 (2009): 225.

19. Ibid., 227.

20. Ibid., 230.

21. Pablo Mares, cited in Manuel Gamio, *The Mexican Immigrant, His Life-Story: Autobiographic Documents* (Chicago: University of Chicago Press, 1931), 2.

22. Kelly Lytle Hernández, *Migra! A History of the U.S. Border Patrol*, Kindle ed. (Berkeley: University of California Press, 2010), 94.

23. Secretaría de Relaciones Exteriores, *La migración y protección de mexicanos en el extranjero: Labor de la Secretaría de Relaciones Exteriores en Estados Unidos de América y Guatemala* (Mexico City: Secretaría de Relaciones Exteriores, 1928), 5.

24. Quoted in Lytle Hernández, *Migra!*, 93.

25. Gamio, *Mexican Immigration to the United States*, 176.

26. George J. Sánchez, *Becoming Mexican American: Ethnicity, Culture, and Identity in Chicano Los Angeles, 1900–1945* (New York: Oxford University Press, 1993), 216. See also Abraham Hoffman, *Unwanted Mexican Americans in the Great Depression: Repatriation Pressures, 1929–1939* (Tucson: University of Arizona Press, 1974); Carreras de Velasco, *Los mexicanos que devolvió la crisis;* and Fernando Saúl Alanís Enciso, *Que se queden allá: El gobierno de México y la repatriación de mexicanos en Estados Unidos, 1934–1940* (Tijuana: El Colegio de la Frontera Norte, 2007), 25. Alanís Enciso argues that Mexican officials did not actively try to repatriate Mexicans during the Great Depression as is commonly believed, but he agrees that "the Cardenista initiatives had to do with an idea, developed since the beginnings of the twentieth century in official channels, that Mexicans who resided outside the country would populate Mexico and contribute to its development through the knowledge and habits they acquired abroad" (author's translation).

27. Mae M. Ngai, *Impossible Subjects: Illegal Aliens and the Making of Modern America* (Princeton, NJ: Princeton University Press, 2004), 72.

28. Quoted in Sánchez, *Becoming Mexican American*, 217.

29. Deborah Cohen, *Braceros: Migrant Citizens and Transnational Subjects in the Postwar United States and Mexico* (Chapel Hill: University of North Carolina Press, 2011), 25.

30. Ibid., 26.

31. For a detailed description of the binational nature of Operation Wetback and an extended timeline of such actions, see Kelly Lytle Hernández, "The Crimes and Consequences of Illegal Immigration: A Cross-Border Examination of Operation Wetback, 1943 to 1954," *Western Historical Quarterly* 37, no. 4 (2006): 421–444.

32. They generally relocated to the interior only migrants who came from states far away from the border.

33. "Repatriación de Millones de Braceros," *ABC*, June 12, 1954, 1.

34. Lytle Hernández, *Migra!*, Kindle ed., 187.

35. Membership card of Nicolás Sánchez Baroso, Alliance of National Workers of Mexico in the United States, Archivos de la Secretaría de Relaciones Exteriores, México, Topográfica: TM-153–2.

36. Verne A. Baker, "Braceros Farm for Mexico," *Americas* 5, no. 9 (1953): 3–5, 30–31.

37. Other strategies included the support of large-scale, irrigated, mechanized, chemical-dependent agricultural techniques, as well as investments in the construction of highways and farm-to-market roads. With much government support, total irrigated land expanded from one to four million hectares from 1941 to 1964. David A. Sonnenfeld, "Mexico's 'Green Revolution,' 1940–1980: Towards an Environmental History," *Environmental History Review* 16, no. 4 (1992): 48.

38. Cynthia Hewitt de Alcántara, *Modernizing Mexican Agriculture: Socioeconomic Implications of Technological Change, 1940–1970* (Geneva: United Nations Research Institute for Development, 1976), 23. See also Angus Lindsay Wright, *The Death of Ramón González: The Modern Agricultural Dilemma* (Austin: University of Texas Press, 2005); Joseph Cotter, *Troubled Harvest: Agronomy and Revolution in Mexico, 1880–2002* (Westport: Praeger, 2003); Verónica Castillo-Muñoz, "Historical Roots of Rural Migration: Land Reform, Corn Credit, and the Displacement of Rural Farmers in Nayarit Mexico, 1900–1952," *Mexican Studies* 29, no. 1 (2013); and Gilberto Aboites Manrique, *Una mirada diferente de la revolución verde: Ciencia, nación y compromiso social* (México: Plaza y Valdés, 2002).

39. Casey Walsh, "Eugenic Acculturation: Manuel Gamio, Migration Studies, and the Anthropology of Development in Mexico, 1910–1940," *Latin American Perspectives* 31, no. 5 (2004): 119.

40. Lytle Hernández, "The Crimes and Consequences of Illegal Immigration," 426.

41. Cohen, *Braceros,* 24.

42. For example, in 1960, 74 percent of workers in Michoacán labored in the primary sector (mostly in agriculture), while in the country as a whole, only 54 percent of workers labored in this sector. VIII Censo General de Población 1960, "Población económicamente activa, por posición en la ocupación, rama de actividad y grupos de edad," accessed February 14, 2017, http://www.beta.inegi.org.mx/proyectos/ccpv/1960/default.html.

43. Quoted in FitzGerald, *A Nation of Emigrants,* 50.

44. Ibid., 50–51.

45. Rosemary Thorp, "A Reappraisal of the Origins of Import-Substituting Industrialisation, 1930–1950," *Journal of Latin American Studies* 24, no. 1 (1992): 181–195.

46. Steven J. Bachelor, "Toiling for the 'New Invaders': Autoworkers, Transnational Corporations, and Working-Class Culture in Mexico City, 1955–1968," in *Fragments of a Golden Age: The Politics of Culture in Mexico since 1940,* edited by Gilbert M. Joseph, Anne Rubenstein, and Eric Zolov (Durham, NC: Duke University Press, 2001), 277; Gilbert M. Joseph and Jürgen Buchenau, *Mexico's Once and Future Revolution: Social Upheaval and the Challenge*

of Rule since the Late Nineteenth Century (Durham, NC: Duke University Press, 2013), 155–156; and Jefferson Cowie, *Capital Moves: RCA's Seventy-Year Quest for Cheap Labor* (Ithaca, NY: Cornell University Press, 1999), 112. For earlier investments in Mexico's northern region, see Rachel St. John, *Line in the Sand: A History of the Western U.S.-Mexico Border* (Princeton, NJ: Princeton University Press, 2011).

47. Francisco Alba and Joseph E. Potter, "Population and Development in Mexico since 1940: An Interpretation," *Population and Development Review* 12, no. 1 (1986): 53.

48. Bachelor, "Toiling for the 'New Invaders,'" 273–275.

49. Ibid., 274.

50. VIII Censo General de Población 1960, "Población económicamente activa."

51. México, *Programa Nacional Fronterizo* (México: PRONAF, n.d.), 11–12, 19, 22, 27; Antonio J. Bermúdez, *El rescate del mercado fronterizo: Una obra al servicio de México* (México: Ediciones Eufesa, 1966), 37–38.

52. Bermúdez, *El rescate del mercado fronterizo,* 21, 138.

53. *Tijuana, B.C., Programa Nacional Fronterizo* (México: PRONAF, n.d.), sección II.

54. Cohen, *Braceros,* 91–92.

55. Hipólito Burrola Ruiz, interview by Anais Acosta for the Smithsonian's exhibit, *Bittersweet Harvest,* November 12, 2005, El Paso, Texas, transcription in author's possession.

56. After that they fell as a result of Operation Wetback. Manuel García y Griego and Mónica Verea Campos, *México y Estados Unidos frente a la migración de indocumentados* (Mexico City: Coordinación de Humanidades, M.A. Porrúa, 1988), cuadro (table) 2.

57. Ibid., cuadro 1.

58. Cowie, *Capital Moves,* 110.

59. Lawrence Douglas Taylor Hansen, "The Origins of the Maquila Industry in Mexico," *Comercio Exterior* 53, no. 11, (2003): 8–9.

60. Letter from Pedro Barraza Ríos to Presidente Gustavo Díaz Ordaz, August 9, 1965, Archivo General de la Nación, Fondo Gustavo Díaz Ordaz, Volumen 4 (149–148).

61. Memorandum from Lic. Joaquín Cisneros M. to C. Lic. Luis Echeverría, Secretario de Gobernación, Palacio Nacional, June 22, 1965, Archivo General de la Nación, Fondo Gustavo Díaz Ordaz, Volumen 4 (149–148).

62. Fernando España, "Via Crucis del BRACERO," *Avance,* May 28, 1965, 2.

63. "Es muy posible la Contratación de Braceros," *Baja California,* March 24, 1965, 2.

64. Cowie, *Capital Moves,* 112.

65. Bachelor, "Toiling for the 'New Invaders,'" 277; Joseph and Buchenau, *Mexico's Once and Future Revolution,* 155–156; and Cowie, *Capital Moves,* 112.

66. Quoted in Bermúdez, *El rescate del mercado,* 53.

67. Hansen, "The Origins of the Maquila Industry in Mexico," 9–10; and Jorge Carrillo and Alberto Hernández, *Mujeres fronterizas en la industria maquiladora* (Mexico City: Consejo Nacional de Fomento Educativo, 1985), 83.
68. Quoted in Cowie, *Capital Moves,* 111.
69. Rosalío Valdés, interview, April 23, 1982, cited in Cruz Arcelia Tanori Villa, *La mujer migrante y el empleo* (Mexico City: Instituto Nacional de Antropología e Historia, 1989), 29.
70. Cowie, *Capital Moves,* 119.
71. Speech by Dra Guillermina Valdes Villalva, "El sector social de la industria fronteriza," to Miguel de la Madrid, April 1982, Caja 376, Expediente 80, Archivo General de la Nación, Fondo Porfirio Muñoz Ledo.
72. Calculated from Cowie, *Capital Moves,* 117; Instituto Nacional de Estadística y Geografía, "Población total, por sexo y número de localidades, por entidad federativa y municipio," IX Censo General de Población 1970, cuadro 3, accessed July 30, 2015, http://www3.inegi.org.mx/sistemas/tabuladosbasicos/default.aspx?c=16763&s=est.
73. Roberto Newell and Luis Rubio, *Mexico's Dilemma: The Political Origins of Economic Crisis* (Boulder, CO: Westview Press, 1984), 111.
74. Jeffrey Bortz, "The Effect of Mexico's Postwar Industrialization on the U.S.-Mexico Price and Wage Comparison," in *U.S.-Mexico Relations: Labor Market Interdependence,* edited by Jorge Bustamante, Clark Reynolds, and Raúl Hinojosa Ojeda (Stanford, CA: Stanford University Press, 1992), 217–218.
75. Miguel Ángel Centeno, *Democracy within Reason: Technocratic Revolution in Mexico* (University Park: Pennsylvania State University Press, 1994), 183.
76. Francisco Alba, "Responses to Migration: Mexico's 1982 Economic Crisis," *University of Texas Papers,* 1224, accessed January 3, 2010, http://www.utexas.edu/lbj/uscir/binpapers/v3c-2alba.pdf.
77. Centeno, *Democracy within Reason,* 8–9. From 1940 to 1970, the Mexican economy expanded between 6 and 7 percent annually in real terms. See Manuel Gollás, "México, crecimiento con desigualdad y pobreza (de la sustitución de importaciones a los tratados de libre comercio con quien se deje)," *Centro de Estudios Económicos,* no. 3 (México: Colegio de México, 2003).
78. Alba and Potter, "Population and Development in Mexico since 1940," 60.
79. Alianza de Braceros Nacionales de México, "Boletín de Orientación Mensual," November 15, 1970, Archivos de la Secretaría de Relaciones Exteriores, México, Topográfica: TM-153–2.
80. Alba and Potter, "Population and Development in Mexico since 1940," 59.
81. Quoted in Matthew Gutmann, *Fixing Men: Sex, Birth Control, and AIDS in Mexico* (Berkeley: University of California Press, 2007), 110.
82. Matthew Connelly, *Fatal Misconception: The Struggle to Control World Population* (Cambridge, MA: Harvard University Press, 2008); Matthew Connelly, "Seeing Beyond the State: The Population Control Movement and the Problem of Sovereignty," *Past and Present* 193, no. 1 (December 2006):

197–233; and Gabriela Soto Laveaga, "'Let's Become Fewer': Soap Operas, Contraception, and Nationalizing the Mexican Family in an Overpopulated World," *Sexuality Research and Social Policy* 4, no. 3 (2007): 20.

83. Judith Adler Hellman, *Mexican Lives* (New York: New Press, 1994), 1–2.

84. Vernon M. Briggs, "Migration as a Socio-political Phenomenon" (paper presented at the Conference on Border Relations, La Paz, Mexico, February 28, 1980), accessed September 13, 2017, http://digitalcommons.ilr.cornell.edu /briggsII.

85. Jorge A. Bustamante, "Las propuestas de política migratoria de los Estados Unidos y sus repercusiones en México," *Foro Internacional* 18, no. 3 (1978): 529.

86. For a list of these studies and a critique of these views, see Jorge Durand and Douglas S. Massey, "Mexican Migration to the United States: A Critical Review," *Latin American Research Review* 27, no. 2 (1992): 3–42; and Jorge Durand, Emilio A. Parrado, and Douglas S. Massey, "Migradollars and Development: A Reconsideration of the Mexican Case," *International Migration Review* 30, no. 2 (1996): 423.

87. Durand and Massey, "Mexican Migration to the United States"; and Durand, Parrado, and Massey, "Migradollars and Development," 424.

88. García y Griego and Verea Campos, *México y Estados Unidos frente a la migración de indocumentados,* cuadro 2, 118–121.

89. This strategy has been described by scholars as one of "benign omission" and as a "policy of no policy." Juan Gómez-Quiñones, "Mexican Immigration to the U.S. and the Internationalization of Labour, 1848–1980: An Overview," in *Mexican Immigrant Workers in the U.S.,* edited by Antonio Ríos-Bustamante (Los Angeles: Chicano Studies Research Center Publications, UCLA, 1981), 33; García y Griego and Verea Campos, *México y Estados Unidos frente a la migración de indocumentados,* 145–147; Jesús Tamayo and Fernando Lozano, "Mexican Perceptions on Rural Development and Migration of Workers to the United States and Actions Taken, 1970–1988," in *Regional and Sectoral Development in Mexico as Alternatives to Migration,* edited by Sergio Diaz-Briquets and Sidney Weintraub (Boulder, CO: Westview Press, 1991), 368; and Alexandra Délano, *Mexico and Its Diaspora in the United States* (Cambridge: Cambridge University Press, 2011), 105–107.

90. Antonio Córdoba (pseudonym), interview by author, January 2, 2010, Tzintzuntzan, Michoacán, digital recording.

91. Between 1971 and 1976, public investment increased by 266 percent in real terms. Louise E. Walker, *Waking from the Dream: Mexico's Middle Classes after 1968* (Stanford, CA: Stanford University Press, 2013), 49.

92. Tamayo and Lozano, "Mexican Perceptions on Rural Development," 368.

93. Ibid., 371.

94. Interactive map, CONAVI, accessed February 3, 2017, http://www.conavi .gob.mx/php/mapa_interactivo/busqueda_avanzada/historicos _viviendas/mapa_interactivo.php.

95. Rose J. Spalding, "State Power and Its Limits: Corporatism in Mexico," *Comparative Political Studies* 14, no. 2 (1981): 144.

96. Viviane Brachet Marquez, "El Estado benefactor mexicano: Nacimiento, auge y declive (1823–2000)," in *Pobreza, realidades y desafíos en México y el mundo,* edited by Julio Boltvinik and Araceli Damián (México D.F.: Siglo XXI Editores, 2004), 254–256.

97. Stephen R. Niblo, *Mexico in the 1940's: Modernity, Politics, and Corruption* (Wilmington, DE: Scholarly Resources, 1999), 188; and Hellman, *Mexican Lives,* 118–124.

98. "Vivir en Tierra Extraña," *El Sembrador,* no. 2, May 1, 1983, found in the personal archives of Guadalupe Guillermina Sandoval Meléndrez, Nochistlán, Zacatecas.

99. Bustamante, "Las propuestas de política migratoria de los Estados Unidos," 528.

100. Letter from Manuel Cusul Ávila to Señor Presidente don Gustavo Dias [*sic*], Ordaz, January 5, 1965, Mexicali, Baja California, Archivo General de la Nación, Fondo Gustavo Díaz Ordaz, Volumen 4 (149–148).

101. Gutmann, *Fixing Men,* 107; and Walker, *Waking from the Dream,* 60.

102. Rodolfo Echeverría, cited in "Diario de los Debates de La Cámara de Diputados del Congreso de los Estados Unidos Mexicanos XLIX Legislatura," November 27, 1973, Ley General de Población, 22.

103. Unpublished booklet, Coordinación Nacional, "Plan Nacional de Planificación Familiar—Síntesis," October 28, 1977, Caja 105, Expediente 25, Archivo General de la Nación, Fondo Porfirio Muñoz Ledo; and Soto Laveaga, " 'Let's Become Fewer,' " 19–33.

104. The government's discourse targeting rural women was explicit. Officials argued, for instance, that "to a great extent, Mexico's demographic dynamic originates" in the "rural environment." Unpublished booklet, Coordinación Nacional, "Plan Nacional de Planificación Familiar—Síntesis."

105. Paul VI, "Encyclical Letter *Humanae Vitae* of the Supreme Pontiff Paul VI," *Libreria Editrice Vaticana,* July 25, 1968, accessed February 13, 2012, http://www.vatican.va/holy_father/paul_vi/encyclicals/documents/hf_p -vi_enc_25071968_humanae-vitae_en.html.

106. Gutmann, *Fixing Men,* 111.

107. Ibid.

108. Laura Briggs, *Reproducing Empire: Race, Sex, Science, and U.S. Imperialism in Puerto Rico* (Berkeley: University of California Press, 2002); Annette B. Ramírez de Arellano and Conrad Seipp, *Colonialism, Catholicism, and Contraception: A History of Birth Control in Puerto Rico* (Chapel Hill: University of North Carolina Press, 1983); and Margarita Ostolaza Bey, *Política sexual en Puerto Rico* (Río Piedras: Ediciones Huracán, 1989), 74–97.

109. Pánfilo Orozco Álvarez, cited in "Diario de los Debates," de La Cámara de Diputados del Congreso de los Estados Unidos Mexicanos XLIX Legislatura," November 27, 1973, Ley General de Población.

110. Juan Guillermo Figueroa-Perea, "Avances y retos en la incorporación del enfoque de género en políticas de salud reproductiva," *Salud Pública de México* 49 (2007): 172.

111. Cited in Figueroa-Perea, "Avances y retos en la incorporación del enfoque de género," 173.

112. "Ley General de Población de 1947," *Diario Oficial de la Federación*, December 27, 1947, Article 13, III, Archivo General de la Nación (emphasis added).

113. "Ley General de Población de 1974," *Diario Oficial de la Federación*, January 7, 1974, Article 76, I, Archivo General de la Nación (emphasis added).

114. "Ley General de Población de 1974," *Diario Oficial de la Federación*, Article 3, VIII.

115. "Ley General de Población de 1947," *Diario Oficial de la Federación*, Article 13, IV.

116. Lytle Hernández, " 'Persecuted Like Criminals,' " 231.

117. "Diario de los Debates," de la Cámara de Diputados del Congreso de los Estados Unidos Mexicanos XLIX legislatura, November 27, 1973.

118. "Ley General de Población de 1974," *Diario Oficial de la Federación*, Article 138.

119. George Frank, "Baja Governor to Keep Heat on Alien Smugglers," *Los Angeles Times*, June 16, 1979, A1, 6.

120. "Ley General de Población de 1947," *Diario Oficial de la Federación*, Article 4.

121. "Ley General de Población de 1974," *Diario Oficial de la Federación*, Article 32.

122. Ibid., Article 37.

123. Yankelevich and Chenillo Alazraki, "La arquitectura," 197–219.

124. Alejandro Mújica Montoya, cited in "Diario de los Debates de La Cámara de Diputados del Congreso de los Estados Unidos Mexicanos XLIX Legislatura," November 27, 1973, Ley General de Población.

125. "Ley General de Población de 1974," *Diario Oficial de la Federación*, Article 138.

126. María Cristina García, *Seeking Refuge: Central American Migration to Mexico, the United States, and Canada* (Berkeley: University of California Press, 2006), 45–48.

127. For example, they disagreed on how to deal with Guatemalan refugees. See García, *Seeking Refuge*, 49.

128. Samuel Moyn, *The Last Utopia: Human Rights in History* (Cambridge, MA: Belknap Press, 2012).

129. Victor M. Salinas, "Seguirán Emigrando a EU, 'No Podemos Ponerles Grilletes,' " *Ultimas Noticias*, August 27, 1976, p. 1.

130. Department of State, Notes, "Establishment of Commissions to Study Mexican Illegal Alien Problem," January 3, 1975, Freedom of Information Act Request, Department of State, Case No. 200908069, 9.

131. Ibid.

132. "Proyecto de agenda—Reunión de la Comisión Binacional México-Estados Unidos de América," attached to Telefacs from EMBAMEX EUA to RELMEX-C. Secretario Bernardo Sepúlveda, March 29, 1983, Archivos Secretaría de Relaciones Exteriores, México, Tercera Reunión Binacional, Topográfica III-7803–3.

133. Gregorio Casillas, interview by author, October 7, 2009, Aguascalientes, digital recording.

134. Frank del Olmo, "Mexico Bars Alien Airlift," *Los Angeles Times,* June 1, 1976, A3.

135. Secretaría de Relaciones Exteriores, "Boletín de Prensa," July 22, 1976, Archivos Secretaría de Relaciones Exteriores, México, Topográfica: BI-436–2 Third Part.

136. Wayne King, "U.S. to Bus Illegal Aliens Far Back Inside Mexico," *New York Times,* August 26, 1983, A10.

137. Memorandum, "Meeting between Mexican and U.S. Representatives to Discuss the Bracero Problem," October 28, 1969, Freedom of Information Act Request, NRC2007048843, 123.

138. Government document, "El Problema de los Trabajadores Migratorios," 1970s, Archivos Secretaría de Relaciones Exteriores, México, Topográfica BI-436–2, Parte 2, 48.

139. Alan Riding, "Mexicans Are Vexed by U.S. Migrant Plan," *New York Times,* August 28, 1977, 15.

140. "Proyecto de Agenda—Reunión de la Comisión Binacional México-Estados Unidos de América," attached to Telefacs from EMBAMEX EUA to RELMEX-C. Secretario Bernardo Sepúlveda, March 29, 1983, Archivos Secretaría de Relaciones Exteriores, México, Tercera Reunión Binacional, Topográfica III-7803–3.

141. Memorandum, "Meeting between Mexican and U.S. Representatives," 123.

142. Stanley Meisler, "Mexico Drops Goal of Migrant Pact with U.S.," *Los Angeles Times,* October 24, 1974, A25; and Luis Echeverría Álvarez, "Quinto Informe que rinde al H. Congreso de la Unión el C. Presidente de la República," 84, Archivo General de la Nación.

143. Meisler, "Mexico Drops Goal of Migrant Pact," A25.

144. Boxes from CONSULMEX, El Paso, Texas, from 1955 to 1994. Not stored with a particular "topográfica."

145. J. Craig Jenkins, "Push / Pull in Recent Mexican Migration to the U.S.," *International Migration Review* 11, no. 2 (1977): 183.

146. Letter from Epifanio Quintín to Cónsul General José Inés Cano, March 30, 1969, Archivos de la Secretaría de Relaciones Exteriores, México, Topográfica: TM-153–1.

147. Letter from Epifanio Quintín to Dirección General de Asuntos de Trabajadores Migratorios, Secretaría de Relaciones Exteriores, June 15, 1969, Archivos de la Secretaría de Relaciones Exteriores, México, Topográfica: TM-153–1.

148. Letter from Feliciano García Ramos, Director General de la Dirección General de Asuntos de Trabajadores Migratorios, to Epifanio Quintín, August 12, 1969, Archivos de la Secretaría de Relaciones Exteriores, México, Topográfica: TM-153–1.

149. Summary of Meeting, "Reunión del Grupo de Acción Sobre Relaciones Fronterizas México-Estados Unidos," 7–8, Archivos Secretaría de Relaciones Exteriores, México, Segunda Reunión Binacional, Topográfica: III-7803–2.

150. "La Nueva Oficina Consular Abierta," *San Ysidro Reminder,* August 1978, Archivos de la Secretaría de Relaciones Exteriores, México, Detención Mexicanos Indocumentados, Topográfica: PAC-F-130–25.

151. Summary of Meeting, "Reunión del Grupo de Acción Sobre Relaciones Fronterizas México-Estados Unidos," 7–8.

152. Presidencia de la República, Coordinación General de Estudios Administrativos, *Guía Básica de Servicios al Público y Trámites Ante la Administración Pública Federal* (México, 1980), 42.

153. Summary of the discussion by Ann L. Craig, rapporteur, "Mexican Immigration: Elements of the Debate in the United States and Mexico," June 1979, 11–12, Archivos de la Secretaría de Relaciones Exteriores, México, Topográfica: III-6350–1 (3a).

154. Ellen L. Lutz, *Derechos humanos en México: ¿Una política de impunidad?* (Mexico City: Editorial Planeta Mexicana, 1992).

155. Castañeda, planned speech.

156. Ibid.

157. Marlise Simons, "Washington Drops In on 'the Last Domino,'" *New York Times,* April 17, 1983, 180.

158. García, *Seeking Refuge,* 49.

159. For more on technocrats, see Centeno, *Democracy within Reason*; Miguel Ángel Centeno and Lorenzo Meyer, "La prolongada transición Mexicana: ¿Del autoritarismo hacia dónde?," *Revista de Estudios Políticos* 74 (1991): 363–387; and Juan Lindau, "Technocrats and Mexico's Political Elite," *Political Science Quarterly* 111, no. 2 (1996): 295–322.

160. This perception was cited as the reason why Mexico would not renew the Bracero Program. Wayne A. Cornelius and Sergio Aguayo, "La migración ilegal mexicana a los Estados Unidos: Conclusiones de investigaciones recientes, implicaciones políticas y prioridades de investigación." *Foro Internacional* 18, no. 3 (1978): 417.

161. The main occasion when Echeverría spoke about undocumented migration occurred during his 1975 State of the Union Address.

162. Mónica Verea, *Entre México y Estados Unidos: Los indocumentados* (Mexico City: El Caballito S.A., 1982), 147.

163. "Datos a incluir en los discursos del Presidente de la República en Washington, D.C (Mayo de 1984)," Archivos de la Secretaría de Relaciones Exteriores, México, Topográfica: III-7803–4.

164. "Entrevista Reagan—De La Madrid—Trabajadores Migratorios," Archivos de la Secretaría de Relaciones Exteriores, México, Topográfica: III-7803–4.

165. Proyecto de Agenda—Reunión de la Comisión Binacional México-Estados Unidos de América, attached to Telefacs from EMBAMEX EUA to RELMEX-C. Secretario Bernardo Sepúlveda, March 29, 1983, Archivos de la Secretaría de Relaciones Exteriores, México, Tercera Reunión Binacional, Topográfica III-7803–3.

166. Riding, "Mexicans Are Vexed by U.S. Migrant Plan," 15.

167. Documentos de Consulta para la Comisión Binacional, Washington, April 17, 1984, 14, Archivos de la Secretaría de Relaciones Exteriores, México, Topográfica: III-7803–4.

168. Political theorist Hannah Arendt argues that "to be uprooted means to have no place in the world, recognized and guaranteed by others; to be superfluous means not to belong to the world at all." Hannah Arendt, *Totalitarianism: Part Three of the Origins of Totalitarianism* (Orlando, FL: Harcourt, 1976), 173.

2. *"A Population without a Country"*

1. "Letters to *The Times*: Saxbe's Views on Illegal Aliens," *Los Angeles Times*, November 8, 1974, B6; and Ronald J. Ostrow, "Saxbe Calls Illegal Aliens a U.S. Crisis," *Los Angeles Times*, October 31, 1974, A1.

2. For further theorizations on the standing of workers, see Guy Standing, "The Precariat: From Denizens to Citizens?" *Polity* 44, no. 4 (2012): 588–608; David Harvey, *A Brief History of Neoliberalism* (Oxford: Oxford University Press, 2005); Saskia Sassen, *Cities in a World Economy*, 4th ed. (Thousand Oaks, CA: Pine Forge Press, 2012).

3. Manuel Jiménez, interview by author, August 6, 2013, South San Francisco, California, digital recording.

4. Wendy Rodríguez, interview by author, March 16, 2015, Palm Desert, California, digital recording.

5. Mae Ngai, *Impossible Subjects* (Princeton, NJ: Princeton University Press, 2004), 258.

6. Ibid., 227–264.

7. Ibid.

8. Statement of Sam Ervin in United States Senate, 89th Congress, *Immigration: Hearings before the Subcommittee on Immigration and Naturalization of the Committee on the Judiciary, United States Senate, Eighty-Ninth Congress on S. 500 to Amend the Immigration and Nationality Act, and for Other Purposes, Part 1* (Washington, DC: U.S. Government Printing Office, 1965).

9. Charles Bartlett, "Immigration Bill Stumbling Block," *Boston Globe*, August 24, 1965, 10.

10. Ibid.

11. Statement of Jacob Javits in United States Senate, 89th Congress, *Immigration*, 7.

12. Statements of Philip Hart and Nicholas Katzenbach in United States Senate, 89th Congress, *Immigration*, 29.

13. Statement of Nicholas Katzenbach in United States Senate, 89th Congress, *Immigration*, 14.

14. Quoted in Ngai, *Impossible Subjects*, 250.

15. Statement of Paul Douglas in United States Senate, 89th Congress, *Immigration*, 166.

16. George H. Gallup, *The Gallup Poll: Public Opinion, 1935–1971,* vol. 3 (New York: Random House, 1972), 1953.

17. Timothy J. Henderson, *Beyond Borders: A History of Mexican Migration to the United States* (Malden, MA: Wiley-Blackwell, 2011), 104–105.

18. Kitty Calavita, *Inside the State: The Bracero Program, Immigration, and the I.N.S.* (New York: Routledge, 2010), 176.

19. Robert Forward, "Log 72: El Presidente," *Adam-12,* season 1, episode 8, directed by Phil Rawins, aired November 9, 1968 (Los Angeles, CA: Universal Studios Home Entertainment, 2005), DVD.

20. Quoted in Ana Elizabeth Rosas, *Abrazando el Espíritu: Bracero Families Confront the U.S.-Mexico Border* (Berkeley: University of California Press, 2014), 67.

21. Jesús Hernández Medrano, interview by Anais Acosta, July 28, 2005, Salinas, California, oral history interview for the Smithsonian's Bracero History Project Records Bittersweet History, transcription in author's possession.

22. David G. Gutiérrez, *Walls and Mirrors: Mexican Americans, Mexican Immigrants, and the Politics of Ethnicity* (Berkeley: University of California Press, 1995), 198–199.

23. Yanek Mieczkowski, *Gerald Ford and the Challenges of the 1970s* (Lexington: University of Kentucky Press, 2005), 4.

24. Thomas Borstelmann, *The 1970s: A New Global History from Civil Rights to Economic Inequality* (Princeton, NJ: Princeton University Press, 2012), 61.

25. Michael B. Katz, *In the Shadow of the Poorhouse: A Social History of Welfare in America* (New York: Basic Books, 1986), 285.

26. Bill Clark, State of Texas House of Representatives, Austin, Texas, Position on Immigration, Box 13, Folder 5, Ruben Bonilla Collection, 1973–1984, General Counsel (1981–1984), LULAC Archives, Benson Library, University of Texas at Austin.

27. Richard L. Strout, "U.S.-Mexico Alien Problem Increases," *Christian Science Monitor,* December 14, 1976, 3.

28. "Too Many Mexicans," *Baltimore Sun,* December 20, 1976, A14.

29. "Population and the American Future," Report of the Commission on Population Growth and the American Future, chap. 13, accessed June 19, 2017, http://www.population-security.org/rockefeller/013_immigration.htm.

266   NOTES TO PAGES 56-59

30. See Thomas Adams, "The Servicing of America: Political Economy and Service Work in Postwar Southern California" (PhD diss., University of Chicago, UMI Publishing, 2009), 192–193.
31. Calculated from Manuel García y Griego and Mónica Verea, *México y Estados Unidos frente a la migración de indocumentados* (Mexico City: Coordinación de Humanidades, M.A. Porrúa, 1988), cuadro 2, 119–121.
32. Douglas S. Massey, Jorge Durand, and Nolan J. Malone, *Beyond Smoke and Mirrors: Mexican Immigration in an Era of Economic Integration* (New York: Russell Sage Foundation, 2002), 59.
33. Manuel Jiménez, interview.
34. Massey, Durand, and Malone, *Beyond Smoke and Mirrors,* 61.
35. Statement of Leonard F. Chapman in United States House of Representatives, 94th Congress, *Illegal Aliens: Hearings before the Subcommittee on Immigration, Citizenship, and International Law of the Committee on the Judiciary, House of Representatives, Ninety-Fourth Congress, First Session on H.R. 982 and Related Bills, Illegal Aliens* (Washington, D.C.: U.S. Government Printing Office, 1975), 26.
36. Harry Bernstein, "Illegal Aliens Cost U.S. Jobs—Marshall," *Los Angeles Times,* December 2, 1979, A1.
37. Letter from Andrew J. Biemiller, Director, Department of Legislation AFL-CIO, to Mr. César Chávez, President, United Farm Workers of America, AFL-CIO, November 21, 1975, UFW Information and Research Department Papers, Box 18, Folder 3, UFW Archives, Walter P. Reuther Library, Wayne State University.
38. Friedrich A. von Hayek, "Inflation and Unemployment," *New York Times,* November 15, 1974, 37.
39. Philip W. McKinsey, "Nixon's 'Full Employment' New Definition," *Christian Science Monitor,* January 3, 1974, 9.
40. Leonard Sloane, "Business People Economists, U.S. at Odds over Full Employment," *New York Times,* July 26, 1978, D2.
41. Jefferson Cowie, *Stayin' Alive: The 1970s and the Last Days of the Working Class* (New York: New Press, 2010), 270.
42. Ibid., 282.
43. Gallup Organization, *The Gallup Study of Attitudes toward Illegal Aliens,* June 1976, found in Box 9, Folder "Illegal Aliens—Domestic Council Committee, (3)" of the Richard D. Parsons Files at the Gerald R. Ford Presidential Library, 15.
44. Ibid.
45. George H. Gallup, *The Gallup Poll: Public Opinion 1935–1971,* vol. 3 (New York: Random House, 1972), 1953; and George H. Gallup, *The Gallup Poll: Public Opinion, 1972–1977,* vol. 2 (Wilmington, DE: Scholarly Resources, 1978), 1050.
46. Gutiérrez, *Walls and Mirrors,* 179–205; and David G. Gutiérrez, "Sin Fronteras?": Chicanos, Mexican Americans, and the Emergence of the Con-

temporary Mexican Immigration Debate, 1968–1978," *Journal of American Ethnic History* 10, no. 4 (1991): 24.

47. Gutiérrez, *Walls and Mirrors,* 198–199.
48. Ibid., 199.
49. Jacquelyne J. Jackson, "Illegal Aliens: Big Threat to Black Workers," *Ebony,* April 1979, 33–40.
50. Bayard Rustin, "Facts about Illegal Aliens," *Oakland Post,* February 2, 1979, 2.
51. Otero, "Immigration Policy: Drifting toward Disaster," *AFL American Federationist* 88, no. 2 (February 1981): 2.
52. Although articles never brought up the issues together, they both appeared regularly in the federation's literature. See, for example, ibid.; and "Runaway U.S. Plants Seek Low Wages in Mexico,"*AFL-CIO News Services,* November 22, 1967, William L. Kircher Papers, Walter P. Reuther Library, Wayne State University, Box 5, Folder 9.
53. José Juárez, interview by author, March 21, 2015, Van Nuys, California, digital recording.
54. For the development of this idea, see Saskia Sassen, *The Mobility of Labor and Capital: A Study in International Investment and Labor Flow* (Cambridge: Cambridge University Press, 1988).
55. Ibid.
56. Leslie Sklair, *Assembling for Development: The Maquila Industry in Mexico and the United States* (Boston: Unwin Hyman, 1988), 79. The company produced some of the lighter components in some of its plants in Hong Kong and Korea and the heavier ones in Mexico.
57. Christian Zlolniski, *Janitors, Street Vendors, and Activists: The Lives of Mexican Immigrants in Silicon Valley* (Berkeley: University of California Press, 2006), 26.
58. See Adams, "The Servicing of America," chaps. 2 and 5.
59. United States Senate, 98th Congress, "Part I: Trade and the Structural Adjustment Process," *Hearings before the Subcommittee on Economic Stabilization of the Committee on Banking, Finance and Urban Affairs, House of Representatives, Ninety-Eighth Cong., 2nd Sess.,* June 8, 12, 14, and 28, 1984 (Washington, DC: U.S. Government Printing Office, 1984), 61.
60. Interview with Robert Lyons by Mary Ann White, July 23, 1984, "Interview no. 665," Institute of Oral History, University of Texas at El Paso, accessed March 7, 2013, http://digitalcommons.utep.edu/cgi/viewcontent.cgi?article=1682&context=interviews.
61. William Claiborne, "Factory-Oriented Buffalo Is Plagued by Hard Times," *Washington Post,* December 13, 1974, A1.
62. See Adams, "The Servicing of America," 183.
63. Manuel Jiménez, interview.
64. Martin Gilens, *Why Americans Hate Welfare: Race, Media, and the Politics of Antipoverty Policy* (Chicago: University of Chicago Press, 1999), 122.

65. Annelise Orleck, *Storming Caesars Palace: How Black Mothers Fought Their Own War on Poverty* (Boston: Beacon Press, 2005), 3. The image of the black "welfare queen" was so violent and widely distributed that it has led historians to focus strictly on the cultural connotations of blacks as welfare abusers and even to argue that "by the 1970s the figure of the black solo mother had come to epitomize welfare dependency." Nancy Fraser and Linda Gordon, "A Genealogy of Dependency: Tracing a Keyword of the U.S. Welfare State," *Signs* 19, no. 2 (1994): 309–336.

66. Gallup Organization, *Gallup Study of Attitudes toward Illegal Aliens,* 16–17.

67. "Illegal Aliens Here on Welfare Said to Cost Millions," *New York Times,* February 22, 1972, 17; and "Aliens' Abuse of Welfare Cited: Cost Is $72 Million Yearly in Five States," *Los Angeles Times,* November 14, 1977, B1.

68. Studies cited in Wayne A. Cornelius, "Mexican Migration to the United States: Causes, Consequences, and U.S. Responses," paper prepared for the Brookings Institution–El Colegio de México Symposium on Structural Factors Contributing to Current Patterns of Migration in Mexico and the Caribbean Basin, June 28–30, 1978, Washington, DC, found in Archivo General de La Nación, Grupo Documental Porfirio Muñoz Ledo, Volumen 382, Expediente 36.

69. Vic M. Villalpando et al., *A Study of the Socioeconomic Impact of Illegal Aliens on the County of San Diego* (San Diego: County of San Diego Human Resources Agency, 1977), 57.

70. Kelly K. Richter, "Uneasy Border State: The Politics and Public Policy of Latino Illegal Immigration in Metropolitan California, 1971–1996" (PhD diss., Stanford University, 2014).

71. Ibid., 73.

72. Bruce Keppel, "County to Sue U.S. over Aliens: Hopes to Recover Costs of Medical Services," *Los Angeles Times,* July 20, 1977, D1.

73. Villalpando, *Socioeconomic Impact of Illegal Aliens,* 178.

74. Agapito Rodríguez, interview by author, January 3, 2009, Las Ánimas, Zacatecas, digital recording.

75. Anaberta Reinaga, interview by author, March 16, 2015, Coachella, California, digital recording.

76. "Estatutos del Comité de Beneficencia de los Angeles California, Bajo los Auspicios del Consulado General de Mexico [*sic*]," Capítulo I, uncataloged archives, La Casa del Mexicano, Los Angeles, California.

77. Letter from Juan G. Franco to Comité de Beneficencia Mexicana, Mexican Welfare Commttee [*sic*], December 5, 1967, Los Angeles, California, uncataloged archives, La Casa del Mexicano, Los Angeles, California.

78. "Casos Presentados En La Comisión de Auxilios de la Beneficencia," uncataloged archives, La Casa del Mexicano, Los Angeles, California.

79. Calculated from "Casos Presentados en la Comisión de Auxilios de la Beneficencia Mexicana," April–December 1970, uncataloged archives, La Casa del Mexicano, Los Angeles, California.

80. Leo C. Wolinsky, "Officials Fear Economic Impact of Illegal Aliens," *Los Angeles Times,* July 9, 1978, SG5.

81. Joseph Nalven, *Impacts and Undocumented Persons: The Quest for Useable Data in San Diego County, 1974–1986* (San Diego: Institute for Regional Studies of the Californias, San Diego State University, 1986), 39.

82. Immigration Coalition, "Position Paper on Immigration Reform," revised February 23, 1977, Bert Corona Papers, 1923–1984, Stanford University, M0248, Box 12, Folder 3.

83. "Illegal Alien Mother of 8 Wins Delay of Deportation," *Los Angeles Times,* November 27, 1985.

84. Karen Benker, quoted in Elena R. Gutiérrez, *Fertile Matters: The Politics of Mexican-Origin Women's Reproduction* (Austin: University of Texas Press, 2008), 52.

85. See, for example, Wayne Kings, "Mexican Women Cross Border So Babies Can Be U.S. Citizens," *New York Times,* November 21, 1982, 1; "One Day on the Border," *Los Angeles Times,* April 1, 1984, A1; and "Born on Border, Twins Left Behind by Mexican Mother: Woman Believed from Well-Off Family Is Returned to Homeland, Leaves Babies as American Citizens," *Los Angeles Times,* July 8, 1977, C24.

86. Kings, "Mexican Women Cross Border," 1.

87. Maria Suárez Oliva (pseudonym), interview by author, February 17, 2009, Nochistlán, Zacatecas, digital recording.

88. Statement of B. F. Sisk in United States House of Representatives, 93rd Congress, *Western Hemisphere Immigration: Hearings before the Subcommittee No. 1 of the Committee on the Judiciary, House of Representatives, Ninety-Third Congress, First Session on HR 981, Western Hemisphere Immigration,* March 28, 29; April 12; June 6, 7, 13, and 14, 1973 (Washington, DC: U.S. Government Printing Office, 1973).

89. United States Select Commission on Western Hemisphere Immigration, *Report of the Select Commission on Western Hemisphere Immigration* (Washington, D.C.: U.S. Government Printing Office, 1968), 13.

90. In United States House of Representatives, 94th Congress, *Western Hemisphere Immigration: Hearings before the Subcommittee on Immigration, Citizenship and International Law of the Committee on the Judiciary, House of Representatives, Ninety-Fourth Congress, First and Second Sessions on H.R. 367, H.R. 981, and H.R. 10323* (Washington, DC: U.S. Government Printing Office, 1976). Widely varying statistics on legal Mexican migration were cited. All estimates were above 45,000.

91. Ibid.

92. James Strom Thurmond in United States Senate, 94th Congress, *Hearings before the Subcommittee on Immigration and Naturalization of the Committee on the Judiciary, United States Senate, Ninety-Fourth Congress, Second Session on S. 3074 to Amend the Immigration and Nationality Act, and for Other Purposes* (Washington, DC: U.S. Government Printing Office, 1976), 21.

93. Ibid.
94. Statement of AFL-CIO in United States Senate, 94th Congress, Second Session, *Immigration 1976: Hearings before the Subcommittee on Immigration and Naturalization of the Committee of the Judiciary,* United States Senate, 144.
95. Ibid., statement by Melanie Wirken, 221.
96. Statement of Paul Sarbanes, 94th Congress, First and Second Sessions, *Western Hemisphere Immigration: Hearings before the Subcommittee on Immigration, Citizenship and International Law of the Committee on the Judiciary,* House of Representatives, 126.
97. Austin T. Fragomen, "1976 Amendments to Immigration & Nationality Act," *International Migration Review* 11, no. 1 (Spring 1977): 96.
98. The preference system gave first preference to unmarried sons and daughters under twenty-one years of age of U.S. citizens; second preference to spouses and unmarried sons and daughters of aliens with permanent resident status; third preference to professionals whose services were sought by U.S. employers; fourth preference to married children of U.S. citizens; fifth preference to the brothers and sisters of U.S. citizens twenty-one years or older; sixth preference to skilled and unskilled workers in short supply; and seventh preference to refugees.
99. As Mae Ngai argues, migrants' impossible placement began in the 1920s. Ngai, *Impossible Subjects.* This position was much reinforced with the passage of the Hart-Celler and Eilberg Acts.
100. Son Spencer, "Immigration Agents Step Up Action against Illegal Entry," *Newport Daily News,* June 11, 1973, 2.
101. Daniel Tichenor, *Dividing Lines: The Politics of Immigration Control in America* (Princeton, NJ: Princeton University Press, 2001), 229.
102. James Strong, "Hiring of Illegal Aliens Denounced," *Chicago Tribune,* March 27, 1975, N8.
103. "Job Rise Is Linked to Curb on Aliens," *New York Times,* September 22, 1974, 52.
104. Massey, Durand, and Malone, *Beyond Smoke and Mirrors,* 56; and Timothy J. Dunn, *The Militarization of the U.S.–Mexico Border, 1978–1992: Low-intensity Conflict Doctrine Comes Home* (Austin: University of Texas Press, 1995), 35.
105. Massey, Durand, and Malone, *Beyond Smoke and Mirrors,* 57.
106. Ibid., 58.
107. Ibid.
108. Tiliberto Rodríguez, interview by author, August 12, 2013, South San Francisco, California, digital recording.
109. Pamphlet, "Resolution on Immigration Issues," and Greater Los Angeles Community Agency, "News Release," Contact Jean McDowell, found in Bert Corona Papers, 1923–1984, M0248, Box 12, Folder 3.
110. Talk by Juan Arzube, "Illegal Aliens—Refugees from Hunger," date cut off, Bert Corona Papers, 1923–1984, M0248, Box 14, Folder 12.

111. Caso 44, "Casos Presentados en la Comisión de Auxilios de la Beneficencia," Basilio Ortega e Imelda Ortega, January 26, 1971, signed by
Bertha Aguilera, uncataloged archives, La Casa del Mexicano, Los Angeles, California.

112. Report, "Al Comité de Beneficencia Mexicana Reporte de las Actividades
de Carlos Chávez Vicepresidente en Ausencia del Sr. Luis Hermosillo, Presidente," July 13, 1970, uncataloged archives, La Casa del Mexicano, Los
Angeles, California.

113. Caso 15, "Uvaldo [*sic*] Rosas," Comité de Beneficencia Mexicana, June 20,
1970, signed by Bertha Aguilar, uncataloged archives, La Casa del Mexicano, Los Angeles, California.

114. Evan Maxwell, "Raids to Hit Aliens Holding Desirable Jobs," *Los Angeles
Times,* April 23, 1982, 1; and Chico C. Norwood, "INS Raids: Will They Help
or Hinder Black Community?" *Los Angeles Sentinel,* May 6, 1982, A2.

115. Larry Stammer, "INS Ends Raids on Illegal Aliens; 6,000 Seized in Week-
Long Project," *Los Angeles Times,* A30; Maxwell, "Raids to Hit Aliens," 1.

116. Maxwell, "Raids to Hit Aliens," 1.

117. "5,635 Rounded Up in Job Raids, INS Reports," *Los Angeles Times,* May 6,
1982, A2.

118. Larry Stammer and Victor M. Valle, "Most Aliens Regain Jobs after Raids:
Survey Contradicts INS Findings That Sweeps Succeeded," *Los Angeles Times,*
August 1, 1982, A1.

119. Information Letter, "¡Action Alert! From the National Council of La Raza:
Action Needed to Oppose INS Raids and Damaging Amendments to
Immigration Bill," May 11, 1982, National Council of La Raza Records,
Stanford University, M0744, RG:5, Box 58, Folder 4.

120. Letter from Congressman Edward R. Roybal to the Honorable William
French Smith, Attorney General of the United States, May 4, 1982, National Council of La Raza Records, Stanford University, M0744, RG:5, Box
58, Folder 4.

121. Memorandum from Angela Bean to Helen C. Gonzales and Richard Fa-
rardo, "Re: Preliminary Survey of INS Abuses," August 31, 1984, National
Council of La Raza Records, Stanford University, M0744, RG:5, Box 398,
Folder 11.

122. Ibid.

123. Ibid.

124. Even immigration officials noted the fact that "American citizens do not
carry any documentation proving that they are citizens" and that "physical methods which used to be used to identify suspected aliens, such as
clothing and jewelry . . . are no longer accurate means of identifying aliens."
Minutes from the Advisory Committee to District Director Washington
District Office, Immigration and Naturalization Service, June 15, 1982,
National Council of La Raza Records, Stanford University, M0744, RG:5,

Box 59, Folder 11. Memorandum from Angela Bean to Helen C. Gonzales and Richard Farardo, "Re: Preliminary Survey of INS Abuses."

125. Memorandum from Angela Bean to Helen C. Gonzales and Richard Farardo, "Re: Preliminary Survey of INS Abuses."

126. Ibid.

127. International Committee on Immigration and Public Policy, pamphlet, "A Special Appeal," the National Chicano Conference, Bert Corona Papers, 1923–1984, Stanford University, M0248, Box 14, Folder 1. For information on the conference, see Gutiérrez, *Walls and Mirrors*, 179.

128. Statement of Melanie J. Wirken in United States House of Representatives, 94th Congress, *Western Hemisphere Immigration*, 211.

129. Statement of Ben Burdetsky, in United States House of Representatives, 94th Congress, *Western Hemisphere Immigration*, 91.

3. The Intimate World of Migrants

1. Works that focus on Mexican queer migrants include Mireya Loza, *Defiant Braceros: How Migrant Workers Fought for Racial, Sexual, and Political Freedom* (Chapel Hill: University of North Carolina Press, 2016), 88–91; Lionel Cantú Jr., *The Sexuality of Migration: Border Crossings and Mexican Immigrant Men*, edited by Nancy A. Naples and Salvador Vidal-Ortiz (New York: New York University Press, 2009); and Héctor Carrillo, "Sexual Migration, Cross-Cultural Sexual Encounters, and Sexual Health," *Sexuality Research and Social Policy Journal of NSRC* 1, no. 3 (2004): 58–70. For works on Mexican migrant women, see Vicki Ruiz, *From Out of the Shadows: Mexican Women in Twentieth-Century America* (New York: Oxford University Press, 1998); and Pierrette Hondagneu-Sotelo, *Doméstica: Immigrant Workers Cleaning and Caring in the Shadows of Affluence* (Berkeley: University of California Press, 2007).

2. For some work on those who remained, see Ana Elizabeth Rosas, *Abrazando el Espíritu: Bracero Families Confront the US-Mexico Border* (Berkeley: University of California Press, 2014).

3. See, for example, Cantú, *The Sexuality of Migration*, 131–133. Similarly, in "Sexual Migration, Cross-Cultural Sexual Encounters, and Sexual Health," Héctor Carrillo looks at Mexican migrants in California to help explain "sexual migration," the theory that sexuality has directly and indirectly motivated individuals' international relocation.

4. For theorizations of oral history, its problems, and some of the ways it can be used, see Daniel James, *Doña María's Story: Life History, Memory, and Political Identity* (Durham, NC: Duke University Press, 2000); Peter Winn, "Oral History and the Factory Study: New Approaches to Labor History," *Latin American Research Review* 14, no. 2 (1979): 130–140; Jeffrey L. Gould and Aldo A. Lauria-Santiago, *To Rise in Darkness: Revolution, Repression, and Memory in El Salvador, 1920–1932* (Durham, NC: Duke University Press, 2008); Alessandro Portelli, *The Death of Luigi Trastulli, and Other Stories:*

Form and Meaning in Oral History (Albany: State University of New York Press, 1991); and Luisa Passerini, *Fascism in Popular Memory: The Cultural Experience of the Turin Working Class,* translated by Robert Lumley and Jude Bloomfield (Cambridge: Cambridge University Press, 1987).

5. For more about the oral histories and the methodology used, see Appendix A.

6. Jorge Durand, Douglas S. Massey, and Emilio A. Parrado, "The New Era of Mexican Migration to the United States," *Journal of American History* 86, no. 2 (1999): 519.

7. Douglas S. Massey, Jorge Durand, and Nolan Malone, *Beyond Smoke and Mirrors: Mexican Immigration in an Era of Economic Integration* (New York: Russell Sage Foundation, 2002), 67.

8. Jorge Durand, Douglas S. Massey, and René M. Zenteno, "Mexican Immigration to the United States: Continuities and Changes," *Latin American Research Review* 36, no. 1 (2001): 110–114.

9. Douglas Massey, Rafael Alarcón, Jorge Durand, and Humberto González, *Return to Aztlán: The Social Process of International Migration from Western Mexico* (Berkeley: University of California Press, 1987), 123.

10. Francisco Alba and Joseph E. Potter, "Population and Development in Mexico since 1940: An Interpretation," *Population and Development Review* 12, no. 1 (1986): 58–59.

11. Jorge Zavala (pseudonym), interview by author, August 24, 2009, Napa Valley, California, digital recording.

12. Sergio Zendejas Romero, "Comentario: La Otra Cara del Problema Campesino," in *Las realidades regionales de la crisis nacional: XI Coloquio de Antropología e Historia Regionales,* edited by Jesús Tapia Santamaría (Zamora, Mich.: El Colegio de Michoacán, 1993), 77–79.

13. Rodolfo Garza (pseudonym), interview by author, August 25, 2009, Napa Valley, California, digital recording.

14. Rosalía Laris Rodríguez (pseudonym), interview by author, January 2, 2009, Las Ánimas, Zacatecas, digital recording. While in the period between 1960 and 1964, 30 percent of village jobs involved the lumber trade, in the years between 1970 and 1974 only 7.5 percent did. Richard Mines, *Developing a Community Tradition of Migration to the United States: A Field Study in Rural Zacatecas, Mexico, and California Settlement Areas* (San Diego: Center for U.S.-Mexican Studies, UC San Diego, 1981), 86.

15. Clemente Lomelí, interview by author, January 2, 2009, Las Ánimas, Zacatecas, digital recording.

16. Aurora Garza (pseudonym), interview by author, August 25, 2009, Napa Valley, California, digital recording.

17. Rafael Ruano (pseudonym), interview by author, March 17, 2015, Thermal, California, handwritten notes.

18. Rodrigo Hernández (pseudonym), interview by author, August 16, 2007, Tangancícuaro, Michoacán, handwritten notes.

19. Ibid.
20. Massey, Alarcón, Durand, and González, *Return to Aztlán*, 200.
21. Everardo Camacho, interview by author, June 24, 2015, Palo Alto, California, digital recording.
22. Gregorio Casillas, interview by author, October 7, 2009, Aguascalientes, digital recording.
23. Raúl Pérez (pseudonym), interview by author, August 6, 2013, South San Francisco, California, digital recording.
24. Ibid.
25. Ibid.
26. Ibid.
27. Agustín Barragán, interview by author, August 16, 2009, Los Angeles, digital recording.
28. Jorge Zavala, interview by author.
29. For a more detailed analysis of seasonal migration patterns, see Zaragosa Vargas, *Labor Rights Are Civil Rights: Mexican American Workers in Twentieth-Century America* (Princeton, NJ: Princeton University Press, 2005).
30. Manuel Jiménez, interview by author, August 6, 2013, South San Francisco, California, digital recording.
31. Ibid.
32. Antonio Córdoba (pseudonym), interview by author, January 2, 2010, Tzintzuntzan, Michoacán, digital recording.
33. Rafael Montañez (pseudonym), interview by author, August 24, 2009, Napa Valley, California, digital recording.
34. Massey, Durand, and Malone, *Beyond Smoke and Mirrors*, 63.
35. Ibid.
36. Ibid., 66.
37. Manuel Jiménez, interview by author; and Feliciana Ramírez, interview by author, August 6, 2013, South San Francisco, California, digital recording.
38. Ibid.
39. Ellwyn R. Stoddard, "A Conceptual Analysis of the 'Alien Invasion': Institutionalized Support of Illegal Mexican Aliens in the U.S.," *International Migration Review* 10, no. 2 (1976): 162.
40. Lamar B. Jones, "Alien Commuters in United States Labor Markets," *International Migration Review* 4, no. 3 (1970): 68.
41. Ibid., 67.
42. Massey, Durand, and Malone, *Beyond Smoke and Mirrors*, 106.
43. Everett Holles, "Mexicans Mass at Tijuana for Stab at Border," *Pacific Stars and Stripes*, August 11, 1977, 8.
44. For more on the region, see Lawrence A. Herzog, "Politics and the Role of the State in Land Use Change: A Report from San Diego, California," *In-*

ternational Journal of Urban and Regional Research 7, no. 1 (1983): 5, 97; and Hikmat A. Al-Ani, B. R. Strain, and H. A. Mooney, "The Physiological Ecology of Diverse Populations of the Desert Shrub *Simmondsia chinensis,*" *Journal of Ecology* 60, no. 1 (1972): 43.

45. Everett Holles, "Mass of Migrants in Drive to Enter US," *Kennebec Journal,* August 12, 1977, 15.

46. Robert Reinhold, "Bones Found on Mexicans' Desert Path to U.S. Jobs," *New York Times,* September 26, 1985, A20.

47. "3 Mexican Sisters Die in Family Trek across Desert," *Los Angeles Times,* September 6, 1985, SD A4.

48. Paul L. Montgomery, "Illegal Aliens Pose Ever-Deepening Crisis," *New York Times,* October 17, 1971, 58.

49. Ibid.

50. Ibid.

51. "Nos Quemaron, Colgaron, y Escaparon: Los Braceros Torturados," *Excelsior,* August 23, 1976, clipping found in Archivos Secretaría de Relaciones Exteriores, México, Topográfica BI-437–1, Parte 4.

52. Rodolfo Acuña, *Occupied America: A History of Chicanos,* 2nd ed. (New York: Harper and Row, 1981), 177–178.

53. Manuel Jiménez, interview.

54. See Octavio Paz, *The Labyrinth of Solitude: Life and Thought in Mexico,* trans. Lysander Kemp (New York: Grove Press, 1962), 39–40; and Joseph Carrier, *De los Otros: Intimacy and Homosexuality among Mexican Men* (New York: Columbia University Press, 1995), 16–17. For understandings of sexuality in a more recent period and in other locales, see Rodrigo Parrini Roses, *Panópticos y laberintos: Subjetivación, deseo y corporalidad en una cárcel de hombres* (Mexico City: El Colegio de México, 2007); and Rodrigo Parrini Roses, *Los contornos del alma, los límites del cuerpo: Género, corporalidad y subjetivación* (Mexico City: Universidad Nacional Autónoma de México, Programa Universitario de Estudios de Género, 2007).

55. See Appendix BI for methodology.

56. See Appendix BII for methodology.

57. This explanation brings out Lionel Cantú's important argument that queer theory should not expunge economic understandings of migration. Cantú, *The Sexuality of Migration,* 7–8.

58. Enrique Plazas (pseudonym), interview by author, December 6, 2009, Santa Fe de la Laguna, Michoacán, digital recording.

59. Ibid.

60. David Aldame, interview by author, August 16, 2007, Tangancícuaro, Michoacán, digital recording.

61. Ibid.

62. Angel Arias (pseudonym), interview by author, August 16, 2007, Tangancícuaro, Michoacán, digital recording.

63. Mario Melendrez (pseudonym), interview by author, January 4, 2010, Tzintzuntzan, Michoacán, digital recording.

64. Diego Perea (pseudonym), interview by author, January 3, 2010, Patambicho, Michoacán, digital recording.

65. Ibid.

66. Ibid.

67. Antonio Corona (pseudonym), interview by author, July 27, 2007, Santa Fe de La Laguna, digital recording. The sexual reality of Michoacán seems to have changed. Younger queer men describe that they now have to pay "straight" or "real" men to penetrate them. Often they blame this change on sexual liberation by arguing that as women were more open to engaging in sexual activities before getting married, men stopped paying gay men to use them as sexual release and started charging them for it. Such an argument undermines the idea that women's sexual liberation and gay liberation are always tied up.

68. Felipe Ramírez (pseudonym), interview by author, August 20, 2007, Santa Fe de la Laguna, Michoacán, digital recording.

69. Cited in Siobhan B. Somerville, "Queer Loving," *GLQ: A Journal of Lesbian and Gay Studies*, 11, no. 3 (2005): 335–370.

70. "Sex perversion" was listed separately from "rape" and "lewd act with child." Table 33A-1975, "Offense, Ethnic Group and Time Served in Prison—Male Felons Paroled for the First Time 1975," Special Collections, Stanford University, California Prisoners-Felons Released from Prison, Bert Corona Records, MO248, Box 13, Folder 22.

71. Ibid. Twenty-four men were classified as "white," six as "black," and three as "other."

72. Mario Melendrez, interview.

73. Leonel J. Castillo, interview by Oscar J. Martínez, "Interview no. 532," 1980, Institute of Oral History, University of Texas at El Paso.

74. Angel Arias (pseudonym), interview.

75. Teresa Villarreal (pseudonym), interview by author, December 1, 2009, Pátzcuaro, Michoacán, digital recording.

76. Elena Arceo (pseudonym), interview by author, February 25, 2009, Nochistlán, Zacatecas, digital recording.

77. Massey, Durand, and Malone, *Beyond Smoke and Mirrors*, 53.

78. Ibid., 55.

79. Ibid.

80. Durand, Massey, and Zenteno, "Mexican Immigration to the United States," 114

81. "Table A-4b: Percentage of Men and Women in Different Age Classes, by Place," in Mines, *Developing a Community Tradition of Migration to the United States*, 167.

82. The number of incidents was unrecorded, as most women who entered illegally feared reporting sexual abuse to the authorities.

83. Laura Mazos (pseudonym), interview by author, August 2, 2007, Ruiz Cortines, Tangancícuaro, digital recording.

84. Ibid.

85. Sara R. Curran and Estela Rivero-Fuentes, "Engendering Migrant Networks: The Case of Mexican Migration," *Demography* 40, no. 2 (2003): 292.

86. Jorge Carrillo and Alberto Hernández, *Mujeres fronterizas en la industria maquiladora* (México City: SEP-CEFNOMEX, 1985), 59–61 and 117, mentioned in Cruz Arcelia Tanori Villa, *La mujer migrante y el empleo* (Mexico City: Instituto Nacional de Antropología e Historia, 1989), 59–61.

87. José Magaña, interview by author, June 30, 2007, Santa Fe de la Laguna, Michoacán, digital recording.

88. Massey, Durand, and Malone, *Beyond Smoke and Mirrors*, 129.

89. María Reyes, interview by author, August 6, 2013, South San Francisco, California, digital recording.

90. Talía Herrera (pseudonym), interview by author, August 2, 2007, Ruiz Cortines, Tangancícuaro, Michoacán, digital recording.

91. Luis Herrera (pseudonym), interview by author, August 2, 2007, Ruiz Cortines, Tangancícuaro, Michoacán, digital recording.

92. The original reads: "Si fueren á California, / Les encargo, compañeros, / que no se crean de las pollas, / mejor vivan de solteros. / Si el marido va á cantina, / á parrandas ó al billar, / y si su mujer lo sabe / ante el juez se va á quejar." From Merle Edwin Simmons, *Mexican Corrido as a Source for Interpretive Study of Modern Mexico, 1870–1950* (Bloomington: Indiana University Press, 1957), 437.

93. Ana Beltrán (pseudonym), interview by author, July 14, 2005, Santa Fe de la Laguna, Michoacán, digital recording.

94. Gail Mummert, "Mujeres de migrantes y mujeres migrantes de Michoacán: Nuevos papeles para las que se quedan y las que se van," in *Movimientos de población en el occidente de México,* edited by Thomas Calvo and Gustavo López (Michoacán: El Colegio de Michoacán, 1988), 285.

95. Laura Mazos, interview.

96. Eloísa Arroyo (pseudonym), interview by author, July 5, 2007, Tzintzuntzan, Michoacán, México, digital recording.

97. Ana Beltrán, interview.

98. Laura Mazos, interview.

99. Although analyzing a more recent period, Malia Kanaiaupuni came to a similar conclusion in "Reframing the Migration Question: An Analysis of Men, Women, and Gender in Mexico," *Social Forces* 78, no. 4 (2000): 1317–1318.

100. Ana Beltrán, interview.

101. María Suárez Oliva (pseudonym), interview by author, February 17, 2009, Nochistlán, Zacatecas, México, digital recording.

102. Laura Mazos, interview.

103. Mae Ngai uses the term "impossible subjects" to describe undocumented migrants who were "simultaneously a social reality and a legal impossibility." Mae Ngai, *Impossible Subjects: Illegal Aliens and the Making of Modern America* (Princeton, NJ: Princeton University Press, 2004), 4–5. In the years between 1965 and 1986, undocumented Mexicans found themselves in an impossible situation on both sides of the border.

4. Normalizing Migration

1. José Minero Legaspi, "Que será mi pueblo," in *Perfiles de obsidiana* (Nochistlán, Zacatecas: Instituto Zacatecano de Cultura, Gobierno del Estado de Zacatecas, 1998).
2. José Minero Legaspi, "Nochistlán," in *Perfiles de obsidiana*, 65–68.
3. Ana Elizabeth Rosas, *Abrazando el Espíritu: Bracero Families Confront the US-Mexico Border* (Berkeley: University of California Press, 2014), 9.
4. See Roger Rouse, "Mexican Migration and the Social Space of Postmodernism," *Diaspora: A Journal of Transnational Studies* 1, no. 1 (1991): 12, 17.
5. For other studies of migration from Las Ánimas in the post-1986 period, see Luin Goldring, "Diversity and Community in Transnational Migration: A Comparative Study of Two Mexico-U.S. Migrant Circuits" (PhD diss., Cornell University, 1999); and *Impacts of Border Enforcement on Mexican Migration: The View from Sending Communities*, edited by Wayne Cornelius and Jessa Lewis (San Diego: Center for Comparative Immigration Studies at the University of California, San Diego, 2007). For a study of migration from Las Ánimas in the pre-1986 period, see Richard Mines, *Developing a Community Tradition of Migration to the United States: A Field Study in Rural Zacatecas, Mexico, and California Settlement Areas* (San Diego: Center for U.S.-Mexican Studies, UC San Diego, 1981).
6. For a detailed comparison between migration from Las Ánimas and migration from the town of Gomez Farías, Michoacán, see Goldring, "Diversity and Community in Transnational Migration."
7. María Reyes, interview by author, August 6, 2013, South San Francisco, California, digital recording.
8. Rosas, *Abrazando el Espíritu*, 5.
9. María Reyes, interview.
10. Letter from Jorge Medina to Esther Ortega (pseudonyms), no date and no envelope, Personal Files of Esther Medina, Las Ánimas, Zacatecas.
11. Letter from Jorge Medina to Esther Ortega (pseudonyms), October 20, 1981, Personal Files of Esther Medina, Las Ánimas, Zacatecas.
12. As evidenced from the postmarks on the letters.
13. Letter from Jorge Medina to Esther Ortega (pseudonyms), letter not dated but envelope stamped in San Francisco on October 20, 1981, Personal Files of Esther Medina, Las Ánimas, Zacatecas.

14. Letter from Jorge Medina to Esther Ortega (pseudonyms), July 29, 1981, Personal Files of Esther Medina, Las Ánimas, Zacatecas.

15. Ibid.

16. Esther Ortega (pseudonym), interview by author, January 2, 2009, Las Ánimas, Zacatecas, digital recording.

17. Jorge Medina (pseudonym), interview by author, January 2, 2009, Las Ánimas, Zacatecas, digital recording.

18. Esther Ortega, interview.

19. Card from Jorge Medina to Esther Ortega (pseudonyms) for Mother's Day, "Madrecita Felicidades en tu Día," no date but stamps on envelope (both on the U.S. side) were from April 20, 1985, and May 18, 1985, Personal Files of Esther Medina, Las Ánimas, Zacatecas. The only part of the Nochistlán stamp that is readable is the year.

20. Letter from Jorge Medina to Esther Ortega (pseudonyms), not dated but envelope stamped in Pacoima, California, on April 20, 1985, Personal Files of Esther Medina, Las Ánimas, Zacatecas.

21. Douglas S. Massey, Jorge Durand, and Nolan J. Malone, *Beyond Smoke and Mirrors: Mexican Immigration in an Era of Economic Integration* (New York: Russell Sage Foundation, 2002), 62.

22. Ibid.

23. Douglas S. Massey, Rafael Alarcón, Jorge Durand, and Humberto González, *Return to Aztlán: The Social Process of International Migration from Western Mexico* (Berkeley: University of California Press, 1990), 318.

24. Mines, *Developing a Community Tradition of Migration*, 62–63.

25. Rosario Montoya (pseudonym), interview by author, August 2, 2007, Ruiz Cortines, Michoacán, digital recording.

26. Pedro Capica, interview by author, August 15 and 25, 2007, Morelia, Michoacán, digital recording.

27. María Acosta, interview by author, July 3, 2007, Cañada del Herrero, Michoacán, digital recording.

28. Ibid.

29. "Vivir en Tierra Extraña," *El Sembrador* no. 2, May 1, 1983, Personal Archives of Guadalupe Guillermina Sandoval Melendrez, Nochistlán, Zacatecas.

30. Ibid.

31. "Noticias," *El Sembrador* no. 20, January 8, 1984, Personal Archives of Guadalupe Guillermina Sandoval Melendrez, Nochistlán, Zacatecas.

32. Pedro Rodríguez Lozano, *Ofrenda: Geografía, historia, hechos, costumbres y tradiciones del municipio de Nochistlán, Zac* (Zacatecas, Zac.: [s.l.], 1984), 198.

33. Ibid.

34. Ibid.

35. Most women I interviewed spoke of "respecting" their migrant husbands when describing their own comportment.

36. Ana Beltrán (pseudonym), interview by author, July 14, 2005, Santa Fe de la Laguna, Michoacán, digital recording.

37. Laura Mazos (pseudonym), interview by author, August 2, 2007, Ruiz Cortines, Tangancícuaro, Michoacán, digital recording.

38. Quoted in Gail Mummert, "Mujeres de migrantes y mujeres migrantes de Michoacán: Nuevos papeles para las que se quedan y las que se van," *Movimientos de población en el occidente de México,* edited by Thomas Calvo and Gustavo López (Michoacán: El Colegio de Michoacán, 1988), 284.

39. Mines, *Developing a Community Tradition of Migration,* 60–61.

40. Trino González, interview by author, August 6, 2013, South San Francisco, California, digital recording; and Mines, *Developing a Community Tradition of Migration,* 130.

41. When I walked with villagers around their towns, they sometimes pointed out particularly large houses, which they told me had been built during the early 1980s by those who were now residents of the United States. Conversations in Jalpa, Guadalupe Victoria, Jerez, Ruiz Cortines, Chavinda, and Tangancícuaro.

42. Neighbors of house owners, notes from conversation in front of the house.

43. Mines, *Developing a Community Tradition of Migration,* 120–124.

44. Ibid., 128.

45. Ibid., 127.

46. Manuel Jiménez, interview by author, August 6, 2013, South San Francisco, California, digital recording.

47. Ibid.

48. Mines, *Developing a Community Tradition of Migration,* 125.

49. Manuel Jiménez, interview.

50. Mines, *Developing a Community Tradition of Migration,* 65 and 70.

51. Roberto and Adriana are pseudonyms.

52. Lucio Rodríguez, interview by author, August 16, 2013, South San Francisco, California, digital recording.

53. Trino González, interview.

54. Ibid.; and Mines, *Developing a Community Tradition of Migration,* 72–73.

55. Mines, *Developing a Community Tradition of Migration,* 73.

56. Trino González, interview.

57. Uriel Rojas, interview by author, August 17, 2009, Los Angeles, California, digital recording.

58. Mines, *Developing a Community Tradition of Migration,* 77.

59. Trino González, interview.

60. Mines, *Developing a Community Tradition of Migration,* 75.

61. Ibid., 74.

62. Jorge Zavala, interview by author, August 24, 2009, Napa Valley, California, digital recording.

63. Ibid.

64. "Table A-4a: Percentage of Men and Women in Different Branches of the Village-Migrant Community," in Mines, *Developing a Community Tradition of Migration,* 166.

65. Mines, *Developing a Community Tradition of Migration,* 77.

66. Trino González, August 6, 2013, conversation, South San Francisco, California, handwritten notes.

67. Feliciana Ramírez, interview by author, August 6, 2013, South San Francisco, California, digital recording.

68. Lucio Rodríguez, interview.

69. Ibid.

70. Ibid.

71. Uriel Rojas, interview.

72. Ibid.

73. Jorge Medina, interview.

74. Original draft of *Mexican Immigration to the United States,* 79, sentences that did not make it into final printed version quoted in George Sánchez, *Becoming Mexican American: Ethnicity, Culture, and Identity in Chicano Los Angeles, 1900–1945* (New York: Oxford University Press, 1993), 85.

75. Gregorio Casillas, interview by author, October 7, 2009, Aguascalientes, digital recording.

76. Epigmenio Jiménez, interview by author, August 16, 2013, South San Francisco, California, digital recording.

77. Ibid.

78. Raúl Sánchez (pseudonym), interview by author, December 5, 2009, San Andrés, Michoacán, digital recording.

79. Ibid.

80. José Domingo Magaña, interview by author, July 28, 2007, San Andrés, Michoacán, digital recording.

81. For more on migrant women's domestic labor, see Pierette Hondagneu-Sotelo, *Doméstica: Immigrant Workers Cleaning and Caring in the Shadows of Affluence* (Berkeley: University of California Press, 2001).

82. John M. Crewdson, "Abuse Is Frequent for Female Illegal Aliens," *New York Times,* October 23, 1980, A18.

83. Ibid.

84. Ibid.

85. Eva Villalobos (pseudonym), December 5, 2009, San Andrés, Michoacán, digital recording.

86. Ibid.

5. Supporting the Hometown from Abroad

1. Gregorio Casillas, interview by author, October 7, 2009, Aguascalientes, digital recording.

2. Gregorio Castillas, interview by author, October 17, 2009, Jalpa, Zacatecas, digital recording.

3. From the revolutionary period, what is now called the PRI changed its name from Partido Nacional Revolucionario (PNR) to Partido de la Revolución Mexicana (PRM), and ultimately to the Partido Revolucionario Institucional (PRI).

4. For more on the history of the Mexican welfare state, see Moramay López-Alonso, *Measuring Up: A History of Living Standards in Mexico, 1850–1950* (Stanford, CA: Stanford University Press, 2012).

5. Michael Katz, *The Price of Citizenship: Redefining the American Welfare State* (Philadelphia: University of Pennsylvania Press, 2008), 9.

6. Stephen J. Pitti, *The Devil in Silicon Valley: Northern California, Race, and Mexican Americans* (Princeton, NJ: Princeton University Press, 2003), 62.

7. Emilio Zamora, *The World of the Mexican Worker in Texas* (College Station: Texas A&M University Press, 1993), 86–109; José E. Limón, "El Primer Congreso Mexicanista de 1911: A Precursor to Contemporary Chicanismo," *Aztlán: A Journal of Chicano Studies* 5 (1974): 85–117; and Devra Weber, *Dark Sweat, White Gold: California Farm Workers and the New Deal* (Berkeley: University of California Press, 1994), 61.

8. Kaye Lynn Briegel, "Alianza Hispano-Americana, 1894–1965: A Mexican American Fraternal Insurance Society" (PhD diss., University of Southern California, 1974); Geraldo Cadava, *Standing on Common Ground: The Making of a Sunbelt Borderland* (Cambridge, MA: Harvard University Press, 2013), 73; and Juan Gómez-Quiñones, *Política chicana: Realidad y promesa, 1940–1990* (Mexico D.F.: Siglo Veintiuno Editores, 2004), 90.

9. See, for example, Katrina Burgess, "El impacto del Three-for-One en la gobernanza local," in *El programa 3x1 para migrantes, ¿Primera politica transnacional en México?,* edited by Rafael Fernández de Castro, Rodolfo García Zamora, and Ana Vila Freyer (México D.F.: ITAM/UAZ/Miguel Angel Porrúa, 2006), 99–138; Robert Smith, *Mexican New York: Transnational Lives of New Immigrants* (Berkeley: University of California Press, 2006), 284–287; Luin Goldring, "The Mexican State and Transmigrant Organizations: Negotiating the Boundaries of Membership and Participation," *Latin American Research Review* 37, no. 3 (2002): 55–99; Carlos González Gutiérrez, "Fostering Identities: Mexico's Relations with Its Diaspora," *Journal of American History* 86, no. 2 (1999): 545–567; and Xóchitl Bada, *Mexican Hometown Associations in Chicagoacán: From Local to Transnational Civic Engagement* (New Brunswick, NJ: Rutgers University Press, 2014). Xóchitl Bada provides a powerful history but does not go into the years between 1965 and 1986.

10. Michael Peter Smith, "Transnationalism, the State, and the Extraterritorial Citizen," *Politics and Society* 31, no. 4 (2003): 469; and Alicia Schmidt Camacho, *Migrant Imaginaries: Latino Cultural Politics in the U.S.-Mexico Borderlands* (New York: New York University Press, 2008), 305.

11. Gregorio Casillas, interview, October 7, 2009.

12. Ibid. For a discussion of how the Mexican nation-state was not fully materialized, see Manuel Gamio, *Mexican Immigration to the United States: A Study of Human Migration and Adjustment* (Chicago: University of Chicago Press, 1930).

13. As discussed in Chapter 1, during the 1930s the Mexican government supported the return of migrants to Mexico in part with the hopes that they would help modernize the nation. George Sánchez, *Becoming Mexican American: Ethnicity, Culture, and Identity in Chicano Los Angeles, 1900–1945* (New York: Oxford University Press, 1993), 216.

14. David FitzGerald, *A Nation of Emigrants: How Mexico Manages Its Migration* (Berkeley: University of California Press, 2009), 106.

15. Gregorio Casillas, interview, October 7, 2009.

16. Ibid.

17. Ibid.

18. Douglas S. Massey and Emilio Parrado, "Migradollars: The Remittances and Savings of Mexican Migrants to the USA," *Population Research and Policy Review* 13, no. 1 (1994): 24–25.

19. This was the case even though, through the multiplier effect, the inflow of remittances probably stimulated economic activity both directly and indirectly and led to significantly higher levels of employment, investment, and income within specific communities and the nation as a whole. Jorge Durand, Emilio A. Parrado, and Douglas S. Massey, "Migradollars and Development: A Reconsideration of the Mexican Case," *International Migration Review* 30, no. 2 (1996): 423–444.

20. Douglas S. Massey, Jorge Durand, and Nolan J. Malone, *Beyond Smoke and Mirrors: Mexican Immigration in an Era of Economic Integration* (New York: Russell Sage Foundation, 2002), 59.

21. Jerry Gonzalez, " 'A Place in the Sun': Mexican Americans, Race, and the Suburbanization of Los Angeles, 1940–1980" (PhD diss., University of Southern California, 2009), 89. Gonzalez also describes how ethnic Mexicans moved to the suburbs of East Los Angeles. Some club activists followed these patterns, creating clubs in places such as Baldwin Park.

22. George Sánchez, " 'What's Good for Boyle Heights Is Good for the Jews': Creating Multiracialism on the Eastside during the 1950s," *American Quarterly* 56, no. 3 (2004): 633–666.

23. Ibid., 642.

24. Deborah Dash Moore, *To the Golden Cities: Pursuing the American Jewish Dream in Miami and L.A.* (New York: Free Press, 1994), 211; and Abraham Hoffman, "My Boyle Heights Childhood, Los Angeles 1940s & 50s," *Western States Jewish Quarterly* 20, no. 2 (2002).

25. Raúl Villarreal, interview by author, August 12, 2009, Los Angeles, digital recording; and Gregorio Casillas, interview, October 7, 2009.

26. Gregorio Casillas, interview, October 7, 2009. US$200 in 1965 had the same purchasing power as US$1,384 in 2010. "CPI Inflation Calculator," Bureau

of Labor Statistics, accessed February 23, 2017, https://www.bls.gov/data/inflation_calculator.htm.

27. Membership figures taken from each group's folder, uncataloged archives, La Casa del Mexicano, Los Angeles, California.

28. Drawn from Calendar of Events, "Luis Hermosillo Real Estate—Beneficencia," Clubs Sociales Amigos de Alexico D. Ortega, Parte I, "Informe Financiero Del Homenaje Ofrecido a el Sr. Alerico D. Ortega en la Casa del Mexicano, el día 8 de Septiembre de 1968"; and "Clubs Presentes en Asamblea General del Domingo 24 de Noviembre de 1968, Casa del Mexicano," all found in uncataloged archives, La Casa del Mexicano, Los Angeles, California.

29. La Casa archives confirm the existence of fourteen new groups. "Contrato de Renta" for each club and from handwritten note "Depósito Feb-18–81," uncataloged archives, La Casa del Mexicano, Los Angeles, California. Of course, not all groups met at La Casa or formed a part of this club culture. In 1968, for instance, only sixteen out of the twenty clubs that left archival records at the center celebrated their parties there. Calendar of Events, "Luis Hermosillo Real Estate—Beneficencia," uncataloged archives, La Casa del Mexicano, Los Angeles, California; María Elena Serrano, interview by author, August 15, 2009, Downey, California, digital recording; Raúl Villarreal, interview; Agustín Barragán, interview by author, August 16, 2009, Los Angeles, California, digital recording; and Rafael Hurtado, interview by author, August 8, 2009, Los Angeles, California, digital recording.

30. Estatutos del Club Social San Vicente, 2; Estatutos del Club Social Guadalupe Victoria, in Gregorio Casillas, personal archives, Jalpa, Zacatecas; and "Constitución," Estatutos del Club Social Hermandad Latina, in Raúl Villarreal, personal archives, Los Angeles, California.

31. Calculated from the yearly letters from a representative from El Comité de Beneficencia to the Department of Alcoholic Beverages, otherwise referred to as Alcoholic Beverage Control Department, informing of all the parties that were going to take place at La Casa, uncataloged archives, La Casa del Mexicano, Los Angeles, California.

32. Some parties ended much earlier—they started at 4:00 PM and ended at around 8:00 PM. By the 1980s, most parties ended around 1:30 or 1:45 AM. See yearly "Contrato de Renta" and annual letters from a representative from El Comité de Beneficencia to Department of Alcoholic Beverages, both in uncataloged archives, La Casa del Mexicano, Los Angeles, California.

33. Estimated from letters to the Department of Alcoholic Beverages and "Contrato de Renta" for 1971, both in uncataloged archives, La Casa del Mexicano, Los Angeles, California. Also estimated from Gregorio Casillas, interview, October 7, 2009.

34. Pamphlet titled "Gran Baile A Beneficio Del Orfanatorio dirigido por las Hermanas Dominicas en Tampico, Tamps," uncataloged archives, La Casa del Mexicano, Los Angeles, California.

35. Letter from Norma P. de Castro to Club Social Hermandad Latina, At: Sr: Presidente Raúl Villarreal, Cd. Lerdo, Dgo 6 de Feb 1984, in Raúl Villarreal, personal archives, Los Angeles, California; letter from Carlos V. Salas, President of the Fundación, to Luis H. Hermosillo, President of the Comité de Beneficencia, requesting space to celebrate their anniversary in February, November 14, 1968, uncataloged archives, La Casa del Mexicano, Los Angeles, California; and Antonio Galarza Viramontes, interview by author, October 5, 2009, Jalpa, Zacatecas, digital recording.

36. Gregorio Casillas, interview, October 17, 2009; and Luciano Solís, interview by author, October 17, 2009, Jalpa, Zacatecas, digital recording.

37. See, for example, the social aid organizations for women organized from 1890 to 1935 in the United States, discussed in Linda Gordon, *Pitied but Not Entitled: Single Mothers and the History of Welfare, 1890–1935* (New York: Free Press, 1994); and Hazel Carby, "Policing the Black Women's Body in an Urban Context," *Critical Inquiry* 18, no. 4 (1992): 738–755. For examples of social control in Mexican and Mexican American communities, see Ana Raquel Minian, "Indiscriminate and Shameless Sex: The Strategic Use of Sexuality by the United Farm Workers," *American Quarterly* 65, no. 1 (2013): 63–90; and Ana Elizabeth Rosas, *Abrazando el Espiritu: Bracero Families Confront the U.S.-Mexico Border* (Berkeley: University of California Press, 2014), 25, 196, 208.

38. Luciano Solís, interview.

39. Ibid.

40. Ibid.

41. Ibid.

42. Letter to Sr. Luis Córdova, Presidente del Club Teocaltiche, October 9, 1968, Los Angeles, California, folder with all information related to Club Social Teocaltiche Jalisco, uncataloged archives, La Casa del Mexicano, Los Angeles, California. Because only the first page of the letter survives in the archive, it is impossible to know who signed it; the letterhead indicates it was sent by members of the "Dispensario Popular, Hidalgo Num. 7 Teocaltiche, Jalisco."

43. Letter from Antonio Córdova S., Secretario del Patronato del Dispensario Popular, Teocaltiche, Jal., to Luis Córdova, February 16, 1970, folder with all information related to Club Social Teocaltiche Jalisco, uncataloged archives, La Casa del Mexicano, Los Angeles, California.

44. Letter to Sr. Luis Córdova, October 9, 1968.

45. Letter from Antonio Córdova S., February 16, 1970.

46. Ernesto Ríos González is listed as president of the Dispensario Popular in the letter from Antonio Córdova S., Secretario del Patronato del Dispensario Popular, February 16, 1970.

47. Letter from Antonio Solanes to Sr. Don Raúl Villarreal, Cd. Jiménez, Chihuahua, June 14, 1972, in Raúl Villarreal, personal archives, Los Angeles, California.

48. Gregorio Casillas, interview, October 17, 2009.

49. Raúl Villarreal, unpublished memoirs, in Raúl Villarreal, personal archives, Los Angeles, California.
50. Letter from J. Jesús Ortega (and eighteen other signatories) to Sr. Lic. Gustavo Díaz Ordaz, Presidente electo de la Rep. Mexicana, August 10, 1964, Los Angeles, California, Archivo General de la Nación, Fondo Gustavo Díaz Ordaz, Volumen 4 (148–149), México City.
51. Ibid.
52. Ibid.
53. Letter from Roberto L. Castro, president of the Club Social Fresnillo, to Comité de Beneficencia, November 30, 1970, uncataloged archives, La Casa del Mexicano, Los Angeles, California. In 1968, the exchange rate was 1 U.S. dollar=12.5 Mexican pesos. INEGI, Estadísticas históricas de México, 2009, Moneda y Banca, cuadro 18.2.
54. "Dispensario Popular—Inventario de Mercancías al 30 de Agosto de 1968," folder with all information related to Club Social Teocaltiche Jalisco, uncataloged archives, La Casa del Mexicano, Los Angeles, California.
55. Letter from Luis Córdova, president of the club, to "A Quien Corresponda," July 1, 1970, folder with all information related to Club Social Teocaltiche Jalisco, uncataloged archives, La Casa del Mexicano, Los Angeles, California.
56. Antonio Leyva Ayala to Molina and to members of the organization, September 4, 1975. In "Agradecimiento" Campaña en pro de la Rehabilitación Ortopédica del Camarguense L. Ayala, folder with all information related to Club de Camargo, uncataloged archives, La Casa del Mexicano, Los Angeles, California.
57. Ibid.
58. Gregorio Casillas, interview, October 17, 2009.
59. Charles Ramírez Berg, *Cinema of Solitude: A Critical Study of Mexican Film, 1967–1983* (Austin: University of Texas Press, 1992), 100–102.
60. For more on how the PRI portrayed the Revolution and its aftermath, see Gilbert M. Joseph, *Revolution from Without: Yucatán, Mexico, and the United States, 1880–1924*, rev. ed. (Durham, NC: Duke University Press, 2003), xxii.
61. Aguilar fully supported the clubs. He even donated US$10,000 to build La Casa del Zacatecano in Los Angeles, for clubs to meet and organize. María Elena Serrano, interview, August 15, 2009.
62. Luciano Solís, interview.
63. Gregorio Casillas, interview by author, October 18, 2009, Jalpa, Zacatecas, digital recording.
64. Letter from Arnulfo Vergara Ramírez, Presidencia Municipal de Jocotepec, Jal., and Gilberto Cuevas to H. Club Social "Jocotepec" [*sic*] Jal., July 2, 1968, folder with all information related to Club Social Jocotepec, uncataloged archives, La Casa del Mexicano, Los Angeles, California.
65. José Encarnación Bañuelos, interview by author, October 3, 2009, Jerez, Zacatecas, digital recording.

66. Letter from Ernesto Ríos G, Presidente Municipal de Teocaltiche, Jal., to C. Luis Córdova, Presidente del Club Teocaltiche, c. 1970s, folder with all information related to Club Social Teocaltiche, uncataloged archives, La Casa del Mexicano, Los Angeles, California.

67. Ibid.

68. Gregorio Casillas, interview, October 7, 2009.

69. Ibid.

70. Ibid.

71. Letter from Natalia Villaseñor to Carlos Chávez, Presidente de la Beneficencia Mexicana de Los Angeles, California, Cd. Obregón Sonora, June 22, 1970, uncataloged archives, La Casa del Mexicano, Los Angeles, California.

72. Activists who showed me diplomas given by city officials, including mayors: María Elena Serrano, Gregorio Casillas, Raúl Villarreal, Rafael Hurtado, Salvador Vázquez, and José Encarnación Bañuelos.

73. María Elena Serrano, interview, August 15, 2009.

74. Rafael Hurtado, interview.

75. Clubs also avoided interfering in U.S. politics so as not to lose their non-profit tax-exempt status. Rafael Hurtado, interview; and Raúl Villarreal, interview.

76. Antonio Galarza Viramontes (who was undocumented), interview; Raúl Villarreal, interview; and Gregorio Casillas, interview, October 7, 2009.

77. Raúl Villarreal, interview.

78. María Elena Serrano, interview, August 15, 2009.

79. Ibid.

80. Ibid.

81. Ibid. Serrano emphasizes that her hardships as president resulted not only from her sex but also from the fact that, at the "age of twenty-three," she had to "manage forty men," most of whom were much older than she was— thus their perception of her as a daughter or niece. Serrano's experience reflects how clubs also blurred age distinctions.

82. Luin Goldring, "Gender, Status, and the State in Transnational Spaces: The Gendering of Political Participation and Mexican Hometown Associations," in *Gender and U.S. Immigration: Contemporary Trends,* edited by Pierrette Hondagneu-Sotelo (Berkeley: University of California Press, 2003), 341.

83. *Pancho Villa y la Valentina,* dir. Ismael Rodríguez (Películas Rodríguez, 1960).

84. María Elena Serrano, interview by author, August 20, 2009, Downey, California, digital recording.

85. For more on the politics of *indigenismo,* see Raymond B. Craib, *Cartographic Mexico: A History of State Fixations and Fugitive Landscapes* (Durham, NC: Duke University Press, 2004); Mauricio Tenorio-Trillo, *Mexico at the World's Fairs:*

Crafting a Modern Nation (Berkeley: University of California Press, 1996); and Barry Carr, "The Fate of the Vanguard under a Revolutionary State: Marxism's Contribution to the Construction of the Great Arch," in *Everyday Forms of State Formation: Revolution and the Negotiation of Rule in Modern Mexico,* edited by Gilbert M. Joseph and Daniel Nugent (Durham, NC: Duke University Press, 1994), 326–352.

86. "Club Michoacano Dancing," in booklet titled "Plaza de la Raza Folklife Festival," in Salvador Vázquez, founding president of the club, personal archives, Los Angeles, California.

87. Letter from Silvia Conlife, General Manager Department of General Services and City Purchasing Agent, and Victor Gargurevich, Parade Director Los Angeles Street Scene Fair, to Mr. and Mrs. Salvador Vázquez, November 2, 1982, in Salvador Vázquez, founding president of the club, personal archives, Los Angeles, California.

88. Lynn Stephen, *Transborder Lives: Indigenous Oaxacans in Mexico, California, and Oregon* (Durham, NC: Duke University Press, 2007), 211.

89. Maria Suárez Oliva (pseudonym), interview by author, February 17, 2009, Nochistlán, Zacatecas, digital recording.

90. Gerardo Armas Domínguez (pseudonym), interview by author, February 13, 2009, Nochistlán, Zacatecas, digital recording.

91. María Elena Serrano, interview, August 15, 2009.

92. Gregorio Casillas, interview, October 7, 2009.

93. Vicki L. Ruiz, *From Out of the Shadows: Mexican Women in Twentieth-Century America* (New York: Oxford University Press, 1998), 103.

94. Gregorio Casillas, interview, October 7, 2009.

95. María Elena Serrano, interview, August 15, 2009; Gregorio Casillas, interview, October 7, 2009; and Raúl Villarreal, interview.

96. For a detailed description of this switch, see David G. Gutiérrez, *Walls and Mirrors: Mexican Americans, Mexican Immigrants, and the Politics of Ethnicity* (Berkeley: University of California Press, 1995), 179–205.

97. Daniel Nugent and Ana María Alonso, "Multiple Selective Traditions in Agrarian Reform and Agrarian Struggle: Popular Culture and State Formation in the *Ejido* of Namiquipa Chihuahua," in *Everyday Forms of State Formation,* edited by Joseph and Nugent, 245.

98. Antonio Galarza Viramontes, interview.

99. Gregorio Casillas, interview, October 7, 2009.

100. José Encarnación Bañuelos, interview.

101. List of clubs Raúl Villarreal joined in Raúl Villarreal, unpublished memoirs, in Raúl Villarreal, personal archives, Los Angeles, California; and Raúl Villarreal, interview.

102. "Constitución," Estatutos del Club Social Hermandad Latina, in Raúl Villarreal, personal archives, Los Angeles, California.

103. Raúl Villarreal, interview.

104. Statutes, "Estatutos del Club Social Guadalupe Victoria 1962," Article I, Los Angeles, California, September 5, 1963, in Gregorio Casillas, personal archives, Jalpa, Zacatecas.

105. Statutes, "Estatutos del Club Social San Vicente," Gregorio Casillas, personal archives, Jalpa Zacatecas.

106. Letter from David J. Jiménez, Presidente, and Ana María Ramírez, Secretaria, to Sr. Raúl González Galarza, Consul General de México, June 18, 1970, folder with all information related to Club Social Independencia, uncataloged archives, La Casa del Mexicano, Los Angeles, California.

107. Ibid.

108. Gregorio Casillas, interview, October 7, 2009.

109. We know that the Fundación began at the latest in February 1968. See letter from Carlos V. Salas, President of the Fundación, to Luis H. Hermosillo, President of the Comité de Beneficencia, requesting space to celebrate their February anniversary, November 14, 1968. The four clubs from Chihuahua that joined the Fundación were Club Social Hidalgo Chihuahuense, Club Social Avalos, Chih., Club Social Santa Bárbara, Chih., and Club Social Camargo, Chih. Uncataloged archives, La Casa del Mexicano, Los Angeles, California.

110. Letter from Estanislao Robles, Pte. Relaciones Públicas, to Muy Señores Nuestros, notifying the Fundación's change of directors, March 6, 1969, uncataloged archives, La Casa del Mexicano, Los Angeles, California.

111. Gregorio Casillas, interview, October 17, 2009.

112. Plan Piloto de la Federación de Clubs Sociales Zacatecanos (paper letterhead), in Gregorio Casillas, personal archive, Jalpa, Zacatecas.

113. Ibid.

114. Ibid.

115. "Invitación Federación de Clubs Mexicanos Unidos," in José Encarnación Bañuelos, personal archives, Jerez, Zacatecas.

116. Gregorio Casillas, interview, October 7, 2009.

117. María Elena Serrano, interview, August 15, 2009.

118. Raúl Villarreal, interview.

119. "Invitación Federación de Clubs Mexicanos Unidos," in José Encarnación Bañuelos, personal archives.

120. María Elena Serrano, interview, August 15, 2009; and Agustín Barragán, interview.

121. Goldring, "The Mexican State and Transmigrant Organizations," 77.

122. See Xóchitl Bada, "Reconstrucción de identidades regionales a través de proyectos de remesas colectivos: La participación ciudadana extraterritorial de comunidades migrantes michoacanas en el área metropolitana de Chicago," in *Organizaciones de Mexicanos en Estados Unidos: La política transnacional de la nueva sociedad civil migrante,* edited by Guillaume Lanly and M. Basilia Valenzuela (Guadalajara: Universidad de Guadalajara, 2004),

175–224; Xóchitl Bada, "Clubes de michoacanos oriundos: Desarrollo y membresía social comunitarios," *Migración y Desarrollo* 2 (2004): 82–103; Burgess, "El impacto del Three-for-One," 99–138; David FitzGerald, "Beyond 'Transnationalism': Mexican Hometown Politics at an American Labour Union," *Ethnic and Racial Studies* 27, no. 2 (2004): 228–247; Goldring, "The Mexican State and Transmigrant Organizations," 55–99; Carlos González Gutiérrez, "Decentralized Diplomacy: The Role of Consular Offices in Mexico's Relations with Its Diaspora," in *Bridging the Border: Transforming Mexico-U.S. Relations,* edited by Rodolfo O. de la Garza and Jesús Velasco (Lanham, MD: Rowman and Littlefield, 1997), 49–68; and González Gutiérrez, "Fostering Identities," 545–567.

123. Smith, "Transnationalism, the State, and the Extraterritorial Citizen," 469; and Schmidt Camacho, *Migrant Imaginaries,* 305.

6. The Rights of the People

1. Jamie Williams, "Children versus Texas: The Legacy of *Plyler v. Doe,*" April 27, 2011, 9, https://www.law.berkeley.edu/files/Children_v._Texas_Williams.pdf. See also Katherine Leal Unmuth, "25 Years Ago Tyler Case Opened Schools to Illegal Migrants," *Dallas Morning News,* June 11, 2007.

2. See, for instance, Alicia Schmidt Camacho, *Migrant Imaginaries: Latino Cultural Politics in the US-Mexico Borderlands* (New York: New York University Press, 2008); Zaragoza Vargas, *Labor Rights Are Civil Rights: Mexican American Workers in Twentieth-Century America* (Princeton, NJ: Princeton University Press, 2005); Stephen J. Pitti, *The Devil in Silicon Valley: Northern California, Race, and Mexican Americans* (Princeton, NJ: Princeton University Press, 2003); Vicki L. Ruiz, *Cannery Women, Cannery Lives: Mexican Women, Unionization, and the California Food Processing Industry, 1930–1950* (Albuquerque: University of New Mexico Press, 1987); and Neil Foley, *The White Scourge: Mexicans, Blacks, and Poor Whites in Texas Cotton Culture* (Berkeley: University of California Press, 1997).

3. See Samuel Moyn, *The Last Utopia: Human Rights in History* (Cambridge, MA: Harvard University Press, 2010).

4. Mae M. Ngai, *Impossible Subjects: Illegal Aliens and the Making of Modern America* (Princeton, NJ: Princeton University Press, 2004), 57.

5. Mario Lazcano, interview by author, March 17, 2015, Coachella, California, digital recording.

6. David G. Gutiérrez, *Walls and Mirrors: Mexican Americans, Mexican Immigrants, and the Politics of Ethnicity* (Berkeley: University of California Press, 1995), 179–205.

7. For grassroots organizations in the black civil rights movement, see John Dittmer, *Local People: The Struggle for Civil Rights in Mississippi* (Urbana: University of Illinois Press, 1994); and Charles M. Payne, *I've Got the Light of Freedom: The Organizing Tradition and the Mississippi Freedom Struggle* (Berkeley:

University of California Press, 1995). For legal efforts, see Michael J. Klarman, *From Jim Crow to Civil Rights: The Supreme Court and the Struggle for Racial Equality* (Oxford: Oxford University Press, 2004).

8. For some critiques of identity-based movements for rights or the dilemmas they bring up, see John D'Emilio, "After Stonewall," in *Making Trouble: Essays on Gay History, Politics and the University,* edited by John D'Emilio (New York: Routledge, 1992), 247; Cathy J. Cohen, "Punks, Bulldaggers, and Welfare Queens: The Radical Potential of Queer Politics?," *GLQ: A Journal of Lesbian and Gay Studies* 3, no. 4 (1997): 437–465; and Joshua Gamson, "Must Identity Movements Self-Destruct? A Queer Dilemma," *Social Problems* 42, no. 3 (1995): 390–407.

9. Some other organizations that fought for undocumented workers included the Texas Farm Workers (TFW), led by Antonio Orendain, but its strikes and marches were largely unsuccessful. In cities, the best-known group to support undocumented migrants was the Centro de Acción Social Autónomo (CASA). See Matt S. Meier and Margo Gutiérrez, *Encyclopedia of the Mexican American Civil Rights Movement* (Westport, CT: Greenwood Press, 2000), 172; Miriam Pawel, *The Crusades of Cesar Chavez: A Biography* (New York: Bloomsbury Press, 2014), 419; Laura Pulido, *Black, Brown, Yellow, and Left: Radical Activism in Los Angeles* (Berkeley: University of California Press, 2006); Ernesto Chávez, *"¡Mi Raza Primero!" (My People First!): Nationalism, Identity, and Insurgency in the Chicano Movement in Los Angeles, 1966–1978* (Berkeley: University of California Press, 2002); and Mario T. García, *Memories of Chicano History: The Life and Narrative of Bert Corona* (Berkeley: University of California Press, 1994), 286–287.

10. Lupe Sánchez, interview by Bruce Perry, no date or place, cassette tapes turned into digital recording, in author's possession; and Don Devereux, interview by author, February 12, 2014, Phoenix, Arizona, digital recording. For the type of citruses grown in the area, see Richard Morin, "Illegal Aliens Have Been Striking in Arizona Citrus Groves," *Washington Post,* October 27, 1977, A3.

11. Deposition of Manuel Marín Bernal, MCOP-Series II: Legal Files, MSS353, Box 25, Folder 31, Archives of Arizona State University, Tempe. (Folders for this collection differ from what is stated in container list.)

12. Don Devereux, interview.

13. Deposition of Manuel Marín Bernal.

14. Letter from César Chávez to John Conyers Jr., August 7, 1974, UFW Central Administration, Box 6, Folder 3, Walter P. Reuther Library, Wayne State University.

15. Frank Bardacke, *Trampling Out the Vintage: Cesar Chavez and the Two Souls of the United Farm Workers* (London: Verso, 2012), Kindle locations 10837–10838.

16. Lupe Sánchez, interview.

17. Ibid.

18. Don Devereux, interview.

19. Lupe Sánchez, interview.
20. Deb Preusch, interview by author, February 13, 2014, Pinos Altos, New Mexico, digital recording.
21. Maralyn Edid, *Farm Labor Organizing: Trends and Prospects* (Ithaca, NY: ILR Press, 1994), 62.
22. Jesús Romo, quoted in Morin, "Illegal Aliens Have Been Striking."
23. Don Devereux, interview.
24. Ibid.
25. Lupe Sánchez had already gone to Mexico for the UFW, but rather than trying to convince workers to come to strike, he had tried to get them to stay away from areas where a strike was going on. Lupe Sánchez, interview.
26. Ibid.
27. Ibid.
28. Don Devereux, interview.
29. Lupe Sánchez, interview.
30. Don Devereux, interview; and Jesús Romo, interview by Bruce Perry, no date or place, cassette tapes turned into digital recording, in the author's possession.
31. Don Devereux, interview.
32. Morin, "Illegal Aliens Have Been Striking."
33. Don Devereux, interview.
34. Helen Dewar Washington, "Employer Agrees to Aid 'Undocumented' Workers," *Washington Post,* January 31, 1979, A2.
35. Ibid.
36. Guadalupe Sánchez and Jesús Romo, "Organizing Mexican Undocumented Farm Workers on Both Sides of the Border," Working Papers in US-Mexican Studies, no. 27 (La Jolla, CA: University of California, San Diego, 1981), 9.
37. Programmatic Report, October 1982–April 15, 1983, MCOP-Series 4: Papers, MSS353, Box 73, Folder 15, Archives of Arizona State University, Tempe.
38. Don Devereux, "The Arizona Farm Workers Union: Building a Better Tomorrow," *Saturday Magazine of the Scottsdale Daily Progress,* October 1, 1983, 3–4.
39. Ibid. The Cooperativa also started a pig farm and a sewing cooperative, built a technical secondary school, and instituted a midwife training program with funds from the United States.
40. Ed Griffin, "The Real Immigration Reform: Help Mexican Workers at Home," *The Nation,* March 3, 1984, 250; and Devereux, "The Arizona Farm Workers Union."
41. Deposition of Manuel Marín Bernal.
42. Deposition of Cresencio Frías Leal, MCOP-Series II: Legal Files, MSS353, Box 25, Folder 24, Archives of Arizona State University, Tempe.
43. Deposition of Manuel Marín Bernal.

44. Deposition of Manuel Marín Bernal; and Deposition of Hilario Pacheco Suárez, MCOP-Series II: Legal Files, MSS353, Box 25, Folder 27, Archives of Arizona State University, Tempe.

45. Richard Morin, "Illegal Aliens Have Been Striking."

46. Peter Schey, interview by author, February 17, 2017, Los Angeles, California, digital recording.

47. Sandra Paiz, interview by author, March 17, 2015, Coachella, California, digital recording.

48. José Guadalupe Rodríguez, interview by author, March 17, 2015, Palm Desert, California, digital recording.

49. In 1973, Cleary won the Supreme Court case *Almeida-Sanchez v. United States,* which was not explicitly about immigration itself but influenced most future rulings on INS stops and searches. Cleary argued that it was a violation of the Fourth Amendment for roving patrols to conduct warrantless searches without probable cause on vehicles that were in the greater border region. The Court agreed and declared that Border Patrol officials could not infringe on people's privacy in the entire borderlands area in the same way that they could at the nation's ports of entry. *Almeida-Sanchez v. United States,* 413 U.S. 266 (1973).

50. Kevin R. Johnson, "How Racial Profiling in America Became the 'Law of the Land': *United States v. Brignoni-Ponce* and *Whren v. United States* and the Need for Rebellious Lawyering," *Georgetown Law Journal* 98 (2010): 1005–1077.

51. See *United States v. Brignoni-Ponce,* 422 U.S. 873 (1975).

52. Sandra Paiz, interview.

53. Cleary was here referring to his earlier victory *Almeida-Sanchez v. United States* (see note 49 above).

54. Supplemental Brief for Appellant, United States of America vs Felix Humberto Brignoni-Ponce, No. 73–2161, En Banc Submission, United States Court of Appeals for the Ninth Circuit, 4, found in MALDEF Records, M0673, Record Group 9, Box, 123, Folder 19; and *United States v. Brignoni-Ponce,* 422 U.S. 873, 875 (1975).

55. Supplemental Brief for Appellant, United States of America vs Felix Humberto Brignoni-Ponce, 4.

56. Brief of the Mexican American Legal Defense and Educational Fund, *Amicus Curiae,* in the Supreme Court of the United States October Term, 1974, 30, found in MALDEF Records, M0673, Record Group 9, Box 122, Folder 1.

57. Ibid., 31.

58. Quoted in Johnson, "How Racial Profiling in America Became the 'Law of the Land,'" 1018.

59. See ibid., 1024; Kristin Connor, "Updating *Brignoni-Ponce:* A Critical Analysis of Race-Based Immigration Enforcement," *New York University Journal of*

Legislation and Public Policy 11, no. 3 (2008): 567–620; and Victor C. Romero, "Racial Profiling: Driving While Mexican and Affirmative Action," *Michigan Journal of Race and Law* 6, no. 195 (2001): 195–207.

60. Quoted in Johnson, "How Racial Profiling in America Became the 'Law of the Land,'" 1022.

61. Justice Powell, opinion of the Court, delivered in *United States v. Martinez-Fuerte*, 428 U.S. 543, 545–567 (1976).

62. See Johnson, "How Racial Profiling in America Became the 'Law of the Land.'"

63. José Juárez, interview by author, March 21, 2015, Van Nuys, California, digital recording.

64. The union was the Chicago Leather Workers Union, Local 431, Amalgamated Meatcutters and Butcher Workmen of North America. In this case, there were two small firms that constituted a single integrated employer for purposes of the National Labor Relations Act. *Sure-Tan, Inc. and Surak Leather Company, Petitioners v. National Labor Relations Board*, 467 U.S. 883 (1984).

65. *NLRB v. Sure-Tan, Inc.*, 672 F.2d 592 (1982).

66. http://openjurist.org/672/f2d/592/national-labor-relations-board-v-sure-tan-inc, accessed September 2, 2014, *NLRB v. Sure-Tan Inc.*, 672 F.2d 592 (1982).

67. Ibid.

68. Ibid.

69. Ibid.

70. National Labor Relations Act of 1935 § 157, 29 U.S.C. § 151–169.

71. *NLRB v. Sure-Tan, Inc.*, 672 F.2d 592 (1982).

72. Ibid.

73. "Sure-Tan, Inc. and Surak Leather Co. and Chicago Leather Workers Union, Local 43L, Amalgamated Meat Cutters and Butcher Workmen of North America, AFL-CIO. Cases 13-CA-16117 and 13-CA-16229," *NLRB* 234, no. 190 (1978): 1190.

74. Ibid.

75. A flurry of diverse labor, community, and government organizations sent amici curiae briefs to the Court in support of the workers, including MALDEF, the Asian American Legal Defense and Education Fund (AALDEF), the Asian Law Caucus, the UFW, the AFL-CIO, the California Rural Legal Assistance Foundation, the National Immigration Project of the National Lawyers' Guild, and the California Labor Relations Board.

76. Brief for the National Labor Relations Board, Sure-Tan, Inc. and Surak Leather Company v. National Labor Relations Board, in the Supreme Court of the United States, October Term 1983.

77. *Sure-Tan, Inc. and Surak Leather Company, Petitioners v. NLRB*, 467 U.S. 883 (1984).

78. Joaquín Méndez, Jr., "One Step Forward, Two Steps Back: The Court and the Scope of Board Discretion in *Sure-Tan, Inc. v. NLRB*," *University of Pennsyl-*

vania Law Review 134, no. 3 (1986): 703–740; Linda S. Bosniak, "Exclusion and Membership: The Dual Identity of the Undocumented Worker under United States Law," *Wisconsin Law Review* 955 (1988): 955–1042; John W. Sagaser, "Rights without a Remedy—Illegal Aliens under the National Labor Relations Act: *Sure-Tan, Inc. and Surak Leather Company v. NLRB*," *Boston College Law Review* 27, no. 2 (1986): 407; and Michael J. Wishnie, "Emerging Issues for Undocumented Workers," *University of Pennsylvania Journal of Labor and Employment Law* 6 (2004): 497.

79. *Sure-Tan, Inc. and Surak Leather Company, Petitioners v. NLRB*, 467 U.S. 883 (1984).

80. Michael A. Olivas, *No Undocumented Child Left Behind: Plyler v. Doe and the Education of Undocumented Schoolchildren* (New York: New York University Press, 2012), 9–10.

81. Ibid., 17; and Guadalupe San Miguel Jr., *"Let All of Them Take Heed": Mexican Americans and the Campaign for Educational Equality in Texas, 1910–1981* (Austin: University of Texas Press, 1987).

82. Testimony from H. Loe, in MALDEF Records, M0673, Record Group 5, Carton 1497, Folder "Plyler v. Doe. Appendices to Supreme Court Brief."

83. A study conducted in Texas found that 89 percent of parents of undocumented children had no intention of going back to Mexico. "Plaintiff's Exhibit 207," E-43, in MALDEF Records, M0673, Record Group 5, Carton 1497, Folder "Plyler v. Doe. Appendices to Supreme Court Brief."

84. See Barbara Belejack, "A Lesson in Equal Protection," *Texas Observer*, July 13, 2007 (https://www.texasobserver.org/2548-a-lesson-in-equal-protection-the-texas-cases-that-opened-the-schoolhouse-door-to-undocumented-immigrant-children/), accessed September 23, 2017; Mary Ann Zehr, "Case Touched Many Parts of Community," *Education Week* 26, no. 39 (2007): 13; Katherine Leal Unmuth, "25 Years Ago Tyler Case Opened Schools to Illegal Migrants," *Dallas Morning News*, June 11, 2007, https://latinoedbeat.files.wordpress.com/2012/06/plylervdoe-1.pdf, accessed September 23, 2017; Michael A. Olivas, "The Story of Plyler v. Doe, the Education of Undocumented Children, and the Polity," in *Immigration Stories*, edited by David A. Martin and Peter H. Schuck (New York: Foundation Press, 2005); and Williams, "Children versus Texas."

85. Testimonies from H. Loe, J. Doe, F. Boe, and J. Roe, in MALDEF Records, M0673, Record Group 5, Carton 1497, Folder "Plyler v. Doe. Appendices to Supreme Court Brief"; and Williams, "Children versus Texas," 8.

86. Testimony of H. Loe; and "The Rights of Undocumented Alien Children," in MALDEF Records, M0673, Record Group 4, Box 127, Folder 8.

87. Testimony of J. Doe.

88. Testimony of J. Roe.

89. Paul Feldman, "Texas Case Looms over Prop. 187's Legal Future," *Los Angeles Times*, October 23, 1994. Name of McAndrews spelled with an "s" in his

testimony in MALDEF Records, M0673, Record Group 5, Carton 1497, Folder "Plyler v. Doe. Appendices to Supreme Court Brief"; and in Williams, "Children versus Texas."

90. In 1977, a local Houston attorney, Peter Williamson, filed the first challenge in the case *Hernandez v. Houston Independent School District,* but the district court and the court of civil appeals rejected his due process and equal protection arguments. *Hernandez v. Houston Independent School District,* 558 S.W.2d 121 (1977).

91. Peter Schey, interview.

92. Ibid.

93. Ibid.

94. Olivas, *No Undocumented Child Left Behind,* 15.

95. Ibid.

96. "Testimony Presented by Plaintiffs," 83, MALDEF Records, M0673, Record Group 9, Box 130, Folder 11.

97. *Plyler v. Doe,* Oral Argument, accessed February 2, 2014, http://www.oyez .org/cases/1980-1989/1981/1981_80_1538.

98. Ibid.

99. Peter Schey, interview.

100. Ibid.

101. James G. Murphy, "Equal Protection—Intermediate Scrutiny Applied to Texas Statute Denying Education to Undocumented Children—*Plyler v. Doe,*" *Wake Forest Law Review* 19 (1983): 307.

102. Justice Brennan, opinion of the Court, *Plyler v. Doe,* 457 U.S. 202, 220 (1982).

103. Williams, "Children versus Texas," 34.

104. José Islas Pérez, "Vivir en tierra extraña: Los 'norteños y sus derechos,'" *El Sembrador,* June 12, 1983, found in the personal archives of Guadalupe Guillermina Sandoval Meléndrez, Nochistlán, Zacatecas.

105. Ibid.

106. Tom Barry and Deb Preusch, *El otro lado: Una guía para los indocumentados* (Albuquerque: New Mexico People and Energy, 1980).

107. Tom Barry, interview by author, February 13, 2014, Pinos Altos, New Mexico, digital recording.

108. Deb Preusch, interview by author, February 13, 2014, Pinos Altos, New Mexico, digital recording.

109. Tom Barry, interview.

110. Barry and Preusch, *El otro lado;* and Tom Barry, interview.

111. From July 19–25, 1976, trade unionists in Mexico came together at the Jornada de Solidaridad con el Trabajador Mexicano Inmigrante en los EEUU (Conference of Solidarity with the Mexican Immigrant Worker in the United States). Although most attendees lived in Mexico, some CASA activists showed up. Similarly, in October 1977, U.S. activists held the First National Chicano / Latino Conference on Immigration and Public Policy in San Antonio. Organized primarily by the Texas La Raza Unida Party, it at-

tracted nearly 2,000 participants, including members from LULAC, MALDEF, and CASA.

112. "Bill of Rights," in "Conferencia en defensa de los derechos de los trabajadores indocumentados," in Secretaría de Relaciones Exteriores México, Departamento de Concentraciones, topográfica, III-7467–1 (1a).

113. Ibid.

7. A Law to Curtail Undocumented Migration

1. Photograph in Robert Pear, "President Signs Landmark Bill on Immigration," *New York Times,* November 7, 1986, A12. Weather found at "Weather History for KDCA—November, 1986," *Weather Underground,* accessed January 18, 2017, http://www.wunderground.com/history/airport/KDCA/1986/11/6/DailyHistory.html?&reqdb.zip=&reqdb.magic=&reqdb.wmo=ds.

2. The subcommittee that discussed employer sanctions first met in 1971. On August 3, 1972, Congressman Peter Rodino introduced the first major immigration bill seeking employer sanctions. The law that ultimately passed was called the Immigration Reform and Control Act, Pub. L. No. 99–603, 100 Stat. 3359 (codified as enacted in scattered sections of 8 U.S.C.).

3. Quoted in Pear, "President Signs Landmark Bill on Immigration."

4. Romano L. Mazzoli and Alan K. Simpson, "Immigration Reform, Round Two," *Cincinnati Post,* September 19, 2006, A15.

5. Douglas S. Massey and Katherine Bartley, "The Changing Legal Status Distribution of Immigrants: A Caution," *International Migration Review* 39, no. 2 (2005): 479; and Douglas S. Massey, "Immigration and the Great Recession," A Great Recession Brief, Russell Sage Foundation and Stanford Center on Poverty and Inequality, October 2012, accessed January 18, 2017, https://web.stanford.edu/group/recessiontrends/cgi-bin/web/sites/all/themes/barron/pdf/Immigration_fact_sheet.pdf.

6. Douglas S. Massey, Jorge Durand, and Nolan Malone, *Beyond Smoke and Mirrors: Mexican Immigration in an Era of Economic Integration* (New York: Russell Sage Foundation, 2002), 105–141.

7. Ibid.

8. Sandra Paiz, interview by author, March 17, 2015, Coachella, California, digital recording.

9. U.S. Congress Architecture found in "Marble," *Architect of the Capitol,* accessed May 27, 2017, https://www.aoc.gov/capitol-hill/architecture/marble.

10. For more on the broad shift in the push to curtail undocumented migration from left to right, see Rodney Benson, *Shaping Immigration News: A French-American Comparison* (Cambridge: Cambridge University Press, 2013), 73–78; Kelly Kelleher Richter, "Uneasy Border State: The Politics and Public Policy of Latino Illegal Immigration in Metropolitan California, 1971–1996" (PhD diss., Stanford University, 2014), 6; and Carolyn Wong, *Lobbying for*

Inclusion: Rights Politics and the Making of Immigration Policy (Stanford, CA: Stanford University Press, 2006), 9–10, 77.

11. See United States House of Representatives, 92nd Congress, *Amending the Immigration and Nationality Act, 92 H.R. 14831; 92 H.R. 16188 of the Committee on the Judiciary,* Report No. 92-1366, 2nd sess., August 1972.

12. United States House of Representatives, 93rd Congress, *Illegal Aliens: Hearings before Subcommittee No. 1 of the Committee on the Judiciary,* 1st sess., March 1973.

13. Statement of Joshua Eilberg, ibid., 2.

14. Statement of the AFL-CIO to United States House of Representatives, 94th Congress, *Illegal Aliens: Hearings before the Subcommittee on Immigration, Citizenship and International Law of the Committee on the Judiciary,* 1st sess., February and March 1975, 192.

15. Ibid., 193.

16. Testimony of Manuel Fierro, President of National Congress of Hispanic-American Citizens, to United States House of Representatives, 94th Congress, *Illegal Aliens,* 316.

17. Pamphlet, Bay Area Coalition against the Rodino Bill, "Un Llamado . . . / A Call . . . ," CASA archives, Stanford University, Special Collections, M0325, Box 32, Folder 12.

18. Ibid.

19. Adalberto Rodríguez, interview by author, March 18, 2015, Thermal, California, digital recording.

20. Ibid.

21. David G. Gutiérrez, *Walls and Mirrors: Mexican Americans, Mexican Immigrants, and the Politics of Ethnicity* (Berkeley: University of California Press, 1995), 179–205.

22. Quoted in ibid., 199.

23. Christine Marie Sierra, "In Search of National Power: Chicanos Working the System on Immigration Reform, 1976–1986," in *Chicano Politics and Society in the Late-Twentieth Century,* edited by David Montejano (Austin: University of Texas Press, 1999), 131–134.

24. Michael Cortés, Testimony on the Civil Rights Implications of Proposed Federal Policies concerning Undocumented Workers and Immigrants before the United States Commission on Civil Rights, November 14, 1978, National Council of La Raza Records, Stanford University, M0744, Record Group 5, Box 58, Folder 2.

25. Ibid.

26. Statement of Vilma Martínez to United States Senate and House of Representatives, 97th Congress, *Final Report of the Select Commission on Immigration and Refugee Policy: Joint Hearings before the Subcommittee on Immigration and Refugee Policy of the Senate Committee on the Judiciary and Subcommittee on Immigration, Refugees and International Law of the House Committee on the Ju-*

diciary, Ninety-Seventh Congress, First Session on the Final Report of the Select Commission on Immigration and Refugee Policy, May 1981 (Washington, DC: U.S. Government Printing Office, 1981), 149.

27. Nora Hamilton and Norma Stoltz Chinchilla, *Seeking Community in a Global City: Guatemalan and Salvadorans in Los Angeles* (Philadelphia: Temple University Press, 2001), 83.

28. Ibid.

29. María Elena Salazar, quoted in El Centro de Información Para Asuntos Migratorios y Fronterizos Del Comité de Servicio de los Amigos, "Indocumentados," *Boletín Informativo Sobre Asuntos Migratorios y Fronterizos* (1980): 9.

30. Ibid., 10.

31. Ibid., 9.

32. See, for instance, ILGWU's statements to United States Senate and House of Representatives, 97th Congress, *Immigration Reform and Control Act of 1982: Joint Hearings before the Subcommittee on Immigration, Refugees, and International Law of the Committee on the Judiciary, House of Representatives, and Subcommittee on Immigration and Refugee Policy of the Committee on the Judiciary of the Senate, United States Senate, Ninety-Seventh Congress, Second Session on H.R. 5872, S2222* (Washington, DC: U.S. Government Printing Office, 1982), 700–705; and to United States House of Representatives, 98th Congress, *Hearing on Employment Discrimination and Immigration Reform: Hearing before the Subcommittee on Employment Opportunities of the Committee on Education and Labor, House of Representatives, Ninety-Eighth Congress, First Session on H.R. 1510, to Revise and Reform the Immigration and Nationality Act and for Other Purposes,* May 1983 (Washington, DC: U.S. Government Printing Office, 1983), 242–243.

33. Statement of Vilma Martínez to United States Senate and House of Representatives, 97th Congress, *Final Report of the Select Commission on Immigration and Refugee Policy,* 156–157.

34. Wendy Rodríguez, interview by author, March 16, 2015, Palm Desert, California, digital recording.

35. Statement of Thomas S. Donahue, Secretary-Treasurer, AFL-CIO, to United States Senate, 99th Congress, *Immigration Reform and Control Act of 1985: Hearings before the Subcommittee on Immigration and Refugee Policy of the Committee on the Judiciary, United States Senate, Ninety-Ninth Congress, First Session on S. 1200 Bill to Amend the Immigration and Nationality Act to Effectively Control Unauthorized Immigration to the United States, and for Other Purposes* (Washington, DC: U.S. Government Printing Office, June 1985), 422.

36. Statement of AFL-CIO Executive Council on Illegal Aliens to United States House of Representatives, 94th Congress, *Illegal Aliens,* 197.

37. José Razo, "Las condiciones de trabajo de los indocumentados en Los Ángeles y San Diego," in *Boletín Informativo Sobre Asuntos Migratorios y Fronterizos,* El Centro de Información Para Asuntos Migratorios y Fronterizos Del Comité de Servicio de los Amigos (February–March, 1980): 9.

38. Rodolfo Rosales (pseudonym), quoted in "Testimonios," *Boletín Informativo Sobre Asuntos Migratorios y Fronterizos*, El Centro de Información Para Asuntos Migratorios y Fronterizos Del Comité de Servicio de los Amigos (July–August, 1979): 9.

39. Statement by Robert T. Thompson to United States Senate, 97th Congress, *The Knowing Employment of Illegal Immigrants: Hearing before the Subcommittee on Immigration and Refugee Policy of the Committee on the Judiciary, United States Senate, Ninety-Seventh Congress, First Session on Employer Sanctions*, September 1981 (Washington, DC: U.S. Government Printing Office, 1982), 96.

40. Arizona Cattle Growers' Association in United States Senate, 95th Congress, *S. 2252: Alien Adjustment and Employment Act of 1977: Hearings before the Committee on the Judiciary, United States Senate, Ninety-Fifth Congress, Second Session on S. 2252 to Amend the Immigration and Nationality Act, and for Other Purposes, Part 2*, September 1978, 200.

41. Ibid., 201.

42. Statement of George F. Sorn to United States Senate, 99th Congress, *Immigration Reform and Control Act of 1985*, 198.

43. Statement of Stephanie Bower to United States Senate, 97th Congress, *The H-2 Program and Nonimmigrants: Hearing before the Subcommittee on Immigration and Refugee Policy of the Committee on the Judiciary, United States Senate, Ninety-Seventh Congress, First Session on the H-2 Program and Nonimmigrants*, November 1981 (Washington, DC: U.S. Government Printing Office, 1982), 205.

44. Statement of Peter Allstrom to United States Senate, 97th Congress, *Temporary Workers: Hearing before the Subcommittee on Immigration and Refugee Policy of the Committee on the Judiciary, United States Senate, Ninety-Seventh Congress, First Session on a New Temporary Worker Program with Mexico*, October 1981 (Washington, DC: U.S. Government Printing Office, 1982), 144.

45. Antonio Hinojosa quoted in George Natanson, "Mexicans Still Waiting to Return to U.S. Jobs," *Los Angeles Times*, April 9, 1965, A4.

46. Manuel García y Griego and Mónica Verea, *México y Estados Unidos frente a la migración de indocumentados* (Mexico City: Coordinación de Humanidades, M.A. Porrúa, 1988), cuadro 2, 119–121.

47. Richter, "Uneasy Border State," 1.

48. Ibid., 54, and Nicholas Laham, *Ronald Reagan and the Politics of Immigration Reform* (Westport, CT: Praeger, 2000), 109–110.

49. Statement by Robert T. Thompson in United States Senate, 97th Congress, *The Knowing Employment of Illegal Immigrants*, 112.

50. Mario Lazcano, interview by author, March 17, 2015, Coachella, California, digital recording.

51. For more on Mexico's entrance to the GATT and reactions to it, see Dale Story, "Trade Politics in the Third World: A Case Study of Mexican GATT Decision," *International Organization* 36, no. 4 (1982): 767–768.

52. Ralph B. Evans, statement of the Chamber of Commerce of the United States "On: Immigration Reform" to Subcommittee on Immigration and Refugee Policy of the Senate, June 14, 1985, National Council of La Raza Records, M0744, Record Group 5, Box 400, Folder 3.

53. Ibid.

54. Ibid.

55. Ibid.

56. Gregorio Casillas, interview by author, October 7, 2009, Aguascalientes, digital recording.

57. Memorandum from Raul Yzaguirre, president of the National Council of La Raza to Congressional Hispanic Caucus, "On Immigration Reform Confidential—Not for Distribution," October 4, 1985, National Council of La Raza Records, MO744, Record Group 5, Box 107, Folder 12.

58. Sierra, "In Search of National Power," 148.

59. Handwritten notes, no title, subsection called "Sobre la amnistía— Elementos y Conclusiones," CASA Archives, M0325, Box 31, Folder 9.

60. Michael Cortés, Hispanic Ad Hoc Coalition on Immigration, "Response by Hispanics to Changes in Immigration Law Proposed by President Jimmy Carter," National Council of La Raza Records, M0744, Record Group 5, Box 58, Folder 2.

61. Statement of Joseph M. Trevino, "On S. 1200: The Immigration Reform and Control Act of 1985 before the Senate Judiciary Committee Subcommittee on Immigration and Refugees," June 17, 1985, National Council of La Raza Records, M0744, Record Group 5, Box 400, Folder 7.

62. Raul Yzaguirre, president of the National Council of La Raza, "On Immigration Reform and Control Act of 1982 S. 2222," before the Joint Hearings of the Senate Subcommittee on Immigration and Refugee Policy and House Subcommittee on Immigration, Refugees, and International Law, April 1, 1982, National Council of La Raza Records, M0744, Record Group 5, Box 58, Folder 4.

63. Michael Cornell Dypski, "Caribbean Basin Initiative: An Examination of Structural Dependency, Good Neighbor Relations, and American Investment," *Journal of Transnational Law and Policy* 12, no. 1 (2002–2003): 100.

64. Documentos de Consulta Para La Comisión Binacional, Washington, April 17, 1984, p. 15, Archivos de la Secretaría de Relaciones Exteriores, México, Topográfica III-7803–4.

65. Richter, "Uneasy Border State," 1.

66. Massey, Durand, and Malone, *Beyond Smoke and Mirrors*, 63.

67. Feliciana Ramírez, interview by author, August 6, 2013, South San Francisco, California, digital recording.

68. John M. Crewdson, "Violence, Often Unchecked, Pervades U.S. Border Patrol," *New York Times*, January 14, 1989, A1; and Frank del Olmo, "Crackdown on Border Bandits," *Los Angeles Times*, October 26, 1976, B3.

69. María Cristina García, *Havana USA: Cuban Exiles and Cuban Americans in South Florida, 1959–1994* (Berkeley: University of California Press, 1996), 46.

70. United States Select Commission on Immigration and Refugee Policy, *U.S. Immigration Policy and the National Interest: The Final Report and Recommendations of the Select Commission on Immigration and Refugee Policy with Supplemental Views by Commissioners* (Washington, DC: U.S. Government Printing Office, 1981), 4–5.

71. For a history of how the border became militarized in practice after 1978, see Timothy Dunn, *The Militarization of the U.S.-Mexico Border, 1978–1992: Low Intensity Conflict Doctrine Comes Home* (Austin: Center for Mexican American Studies, University of Texas, Austin, 1996).

72. For instance, an article from the *Washington Star-News* that became additional material for the 1975 hearings suggested that the border be "tighten[ed] up" by using "the sensors, which are Vietnam war surplus devices planted in the major foot trails to detect movement." Michael Satchell, "The Biggest Hole in the Dike," *Washington Star-News*, November 18, 1972, cited in United States House of Representatives, 94th Congress, *Illegal Aliens*, 68.

73. Statement of Leonard F. Chapman to United States House of Representatives, 94th Congress, *Illegal Aliens*, 34.

74. Ibid., 34.

75. Testimony of William Smith to United States Senate and House of Representatives, *Joint Hearing before the Subcommittee on Immigration, Refugees and International Law of the House Committee on the Judiciary and the Subcommittee on Immigration and Refugee Policy of the Senate Committee on the Judiciary*, 97th Congress 1st sess., July 30, 1981, 6.

76. Massey, Durand, and Malone, *Beyond Smoke and Mirrors*, 85.

77. Senator Simpson, Congressional Record—Senate, May 23, 1985, cited in United States Senate, 99th Congress, *Immigration Reform and Control Act of 1985*, 493–494.

78. Ibid., 494.

79. Statement by Michael V. Durando to United States Senate, 99th Congress, *Immigration Reform and Control Act of 1985*, 184.

80. Statement of Arnoldo S. Torres to United States Senate, 99th Congress, *Immigration Reform and Control Act of 1985*, 103.

81. Statement of Raul Yzaguirre to United States Senate, 99th Congress, *Immigration Reform and Control Act of 1985*, 160.

82. Statement of Alan C. Nelson to United States Senate, 99th Congress, *Immigration Reform and Control Act of 1985*, 437, 442.

83. While seeming ignorance about migrants' actual movement drove much of the congressional discourse on "population," some witnesses did address the circularity of migration. They often did so, however, as a way of insisting that migrants and their families be excluded from national

belonging. See, for instance, Statement of Barry Chiswick to United States Senate, 99th Congress, *Immigration Reform and Control Act of 1985*, 40–41.

84. Douglas S. Massey and Audrey Singer, "New Estimates of Undocumented Mexican Migration and the Probability of Apprehension," *Demography* 32, no. 2 (1995): 210.

85. Statement of Dr. M. Rupert Cutler to United States Senate, 99th Congress, *Immigration Reform and Control Act of 1985*, 295.

86. Senator Simpson, Congressional Record—Senate, May 23, 1985, cited in United States Senate, 99th Congress, *Immigration Reform and Control Act of 1985*, 494.

87. See John F. Kennedy, *A Nation of Immigrants* (New York: Harper and Row, 1964).

88. Statement of Thomas Donahue, United States Senate and House of Representatives, 97th Congress, *Final Report of the Select Commission on Immigration and Refugee Policy*, 101.

89. Ibid., 102.

90. Ibid.

91. Statement of Hank Brown to United States Senate, 98th Congress, *Immigration Reform and Control Act of 1983: Hearings before the Subcommittee on Immigration, Refugees, and International Law of the Committee on the Judiciary, House of Representatives, Ninety-Eighth Congress, First Session on H.R. 1510, Immigration Reform and Control Act of 1983* (Washington, DC: U.S. Government Printing Office, 1983), 143.

92. Statement of Ralph B. Evans of the Chamber of Commerce to United States Senate, 99th Congress, *Immigration Reform and Control Act of 1985*, 472.

93. Ibid., 472.

94. Manuel Jiménez, interview by author, August 6, 2013, South San Francisco, California, digital recording.

95. P. Lussa, "Charlas de Sobremesa," *El Informador*, February 27, 1980, 4A.

96. Statement of John Tanton to United States House of Representatives, 94th Congress, *Illegal Aliens*, 277–278.

97. Statement of Martin D. Finn, M.D., to United States House of Representatives, 98th Congress, *Immigration Reform and Control Act of 1983: Hearing before the Subcommittee on Health and the Environment, Committee on Energy and Commerce, House of Representatives, Ninety-Eighth Congress, First Session on H.R. 1510, A Bill to Revise and Reform the Immigration and Nationality Act, and for Other Purposes* (Washington, DC: U.S. Government Printing Office, 1983), 108. See *Madrigal v. Quilligan*, decided in 1978.

98. Statement of Vilma S. Martínez to United States Senate and House of Representatives, 97th Congress, *Final Report of the Select Commission on Immigration and Refugee Policy*, 157.

99. Statement of Religious Leaders on Immigration Reform, signed by Bishop R. Cousin, African Methodist Episcopal Church, Bishop Anthony J. Bevilacqua,

Rabbi Alexander Schindler, Rev. Dr. Arie Brouwer, Rabbi David Saper-
stein, Rev. Daniel F. Hoye, Rev. William K. Duval, National Council of
La Raza Records, M0744, Record Group 5, Box 340, Folder 10.

100. Statement of George G. Higgins to United States House of Representatives,
94th Congress, *Illegal Aliens*, 300.

101. Statement of Ramón Andrada to United States Senate, 95th Congress, *S.
2252: Alien Adjustment and Employment Act of 1977*, 77.

102. Ibid.

103. Immigration Reform and Control Act of 1986, Pub. L. No. 99–603, §§ 301,
100 Stat. 3359, 3411. The H-2 program would thereafter be divided into
the H-2A program to import agricultural workers and the H-2B program
for nonagricultural, unskilled workers.

104. Immigration Reform and Control Act of 1986, Pub. L. No. 99–603, §§ 302,
100 Stat. 3359, 3417. The new law also provided a program by which replenishment workers (RAWs) could be brought into the United States. However,
because there were never labor shortages in the country, replenishment
farmworkers were never needed. See Debra L. DeLaet, *U.S. Immigration Policy
in an Age of Rights* (Westport, CT: Praeger, 2000), 132; and Laham, *Ronald
Reagan and the Politics of Immigration Reform*, 189.

105. Immigration Reform and Control Act of 1986, Pub. L. No. 99–603, §§ 201,
100 Stat. 3359, 3394.

8. The Cage of Gold

1. Personal notes from interview of Junior Adriano by Kainaz Amaria and
author, for National Public Radio, March 24 and 25, 2014, Anthony, Texas.

2. "Junior: A Video about Life in between, in His Words," *Borderland*, National
Public Radio, April 3, 2014, http://apps.npr.org/borderland/#_/junior.

3. Immigration Reform and Control Act of 1986, Pub. L. No. 99–603, 100 Stat.
3359 (codified as enacted in scattered sections of 8 U.S.C.).

4. "Junior," *Borderland*.

5. Douglas S. Massey, Jorge Durand, and Nolan Malone, *Beyond Smoke and
Mirrors: Mexican Immigration in an Era of Economic Integration* (New York: Russell Sage Foundation, 2002), 90.

6. Anaberta Reinaga, interview by author, March 16, 2015, Coachella, California, digital recording.

7. Ibid.

8. Immigration Reform and Control Act of 1986, Pub. L. No. 99–603, §§ 201,
100 Stat. 3395.

9. Estela Bogarín and Everardo Camacho, interview by author, June 24, 2015,
Stanford, California, digital recording.

10. Sandra Paiz, interview by author, March 17, 2015, Coachella, California,
digital recording.

11. Massey, Durand, and Malone, *Beyond Smoke and Mirrors*, 138.

12. "Foreign-Born Population, Hispanics," *Migration News* 5, no. 5 (1998), accessed September 29, 2017, https://migration.ucdavis.edu/mn/more.php?id =1514.

13. After IRCA, Mexican migrants started spreading beyond the Southwest to the rest of the United States. Massey, Durand, and Malone, *Beyond Smoke and Mirrors*, 126–128.

14. Marco Antonio Velarde, interview by author, March 16, 2015, Coachella, California, digital recording.

15. Andrés Delgado, interview by author, March 17, 2015, Thermal, California, digital recording.

16. Ibid.

17. Marco Antonio Velarde, interview.

18. Mirella Amador, interview by author, March 22, 2015, Los Angeles, California, digital recording.

19. Olga Juárez, interview by author, March 21, 2015, Van Nuys, California, digital recording.

20. Héctor Rodríguez, interview by author, March 16, 2015, Palm Desert, California, digital recording.

21. Wendy Rodríguez, interview by author, March 16, 2015, Palm Desert, California, digital recording.

22. Sandra Paiz, interview.

23. Adalberto Rodríguez, interview by author, March 18, 2015, Thermal, California, digital recording.

24. José Juárez, interview by author, March 21, 2015, Van Nuys, California, digital recording.

25. Immigration Reform and Control Act of 1986, Pub. L. No. 99–603, §§ 201, 302, 100 Stat. 3359, 3394, 3417.

26. Pedro Pérez (pseudonym), interview by author, March 17, 2015, Coachella, California, digital recording; and Mario Pérez (pseudonym), interview by author, March 17, 2015, Coachella, California, digital recording.

27. Josefina Cruz (pseudonym), interview by author, March 21, 2015, Los Angeles County, California, digital recording.

28. Fernando Gutiérrez (pseudonym), interview by author, March 23, 2015, Los Angeles, California, digital recording.

29. CONEVAL (Consejo Nacional de Evaluación de la Política de Desarrollo Social), "Evolución de la pobreza por dimensión de ingreso en México, 1992–2014," accessed August 18, 2015, http://www.coneval.gob.mx/Medicion /EDP/Paginas/Medicion-por-ingresos-1990–2012.aspx.

30. Ibid.

31. Banco de México, "Tipos de cambio y resultados históricos de las subastas CF102—Tipos de cambio," *Sistema de Información Económica*, accessed October 2, 2015, http://www.banxico.org.mx/SieInternet/consultarDirector ioInternetAction.do?accion=consultarCuadro&idCuadro=CF102&sector =6&locale=es.

32. Philip L. Martin, "Mexican Migration to the United States: The Effect of NAFTA," in *International Migration: Prospects and Policies in a Global Market,* edited by Douglas S. Massey and J. Edward Taylor (Oxford: Oxford University Press, 2004), 120–130.

33. Janet Reno, "Consider NAFTA a Border Control Tool: Immigration: Expansion of Job Opportunities in Mexico Is the Only Long-Term Answer," *Los Angeles Times,* October 22, 1992, accessed February 16, 2017, http://articles .latimes.com/1993-10-22/local/me-48356_1_illegal-immigrants.

34. Philip Martin, "Economic Integration and Migration: The Case of NAFTA," *UCLA Journal of International Law and Foreign Affairs* 3, no. 2 (1998–1999): 429.

35. Amy Clark, "Is NAFTA Good for Mexico's Farmers?," *CBS,* July 1, 2006, accessed February 10, 2017, http://www.cbsnews.com/news/is-nafta-good -for-mexicos-farmers/.

36. Eduardo Zepeda, Timothy A. Wise, and Kevin P. Gallagher, *Rethinking Trade Policy for Development: Lessons from Mexico under NAFTA* (Carnegie Endowment for International Peace, Policy Outlook, December 2009), 5. Accessed June 26, 2017, http://ase.tufts.edu/gdae/policy_research/Carnegie.html.

37. Griselda Mendoza, cited in Shasta Darlington and Patrick Gillespie, "Mexican Farmer's Daughter: NAFTA Destroyed Us," *CNN Money,* February 9, 2017, accessed May 29, 2017, http://money.cnn.com/2017/02/09/news /economy/nafta-farming-mexico-us-corn-jobs/.

38. Francisco Perea (pseudonym), interview by author, October 17, 2009, Jalpa, Zacatecas, personal handwritten notes.

39. Calculated from numbers in Massey, Durand, and Malone, *Beyond Smoke and Mirrors,* 131.

40. Gonzalo Bueno (pseudonym), interview by author, March 21, 2015, Los Angeles County, California, digital recording.

41. Enrico A. Marcelli and Wayne A. Cornelius, "The Changing Profile of Mexican Migrants to the United States: New Evidence from California and Mexico," *Latin American Research Review* 36, no. 3 (2001): 105–131.

42. Massey, Durand, and Malone, *Beyond Smoke and Mirrors,* 134.

43. José Guadalupe Rodríguez, interview by author, March 17, 2015, Palm Desert, California, digital recording.

44. Josefina Cruz, interview.

45. Gonzalo Bueno, interview.

46. Fernando Gutiérrez, interview.

47. Gonzalo Bueno, interview.

48. Kevin R. Johnson, "Drivers Licenses and Undocumented Immigrants: The Future of Civil Rights Law?," *Nevada Law Journal* 5, no. 213 (2004): 213–239.

49. Gonzalo Bueno, interview.

50. José Gardoño (pseudonym), interview by author, March 18, 2015, Thermal, California, digital recording.

51. The literal translation is "man of the home."

52. Josefina Cruz, interview.

53. Marc Rosenblum and Lang Hoyt, "The Basics of E-Verify, the U.S. Employer Verification System," *Migration Policy Institute,* July 13, 2011, accessed June 20, 2017, http://www.migrationpolicy.org/article/basics-e-verify-us -employer-verification-system. The program changed its name to E-Verify in 2007.

54. Josefina Cruz, interview.

55. Fernando Gutiérrez, interview.

56. Educators for Fair Consideration, "Fact Sheet on Undocumented Students," *Freedom University Georgia,* accessed June 26, 2017, http://www.freedomu-niversitygeorgia.com/facts-and-figures.html.

57. Fernando Gutiérrez, interview.

58. Bill Ong Hing and Kevin R. Johnson, "The Immigrant Rights Marches of 2006 and the Prospects for a New Civil Rights Movement," *Harvard Civil Rights–Civil Liberties Law Review* 42, no. 96 (2007): 1–2; Oscar Avila and Antonio Olivo, "A Show of Strength; Thousands March to Loop for Immigrants' Rights," *Chicago Tribune,* March 11, 2006, accessed May 27, 2017, http://articles.chicagotribune.com/2006-03-11/news/0603110130_1 _immigration-debate-pro-immigrant-illegal-immigrants; and Teresa Watanabe and Hector Becerra, "500,000 Pack Streets to Protest Immigration Bills," *Los Angeles Times,* March 26, 2006, accessed May 27, 2017, http:// articles.latimes.com/2006/mar/26/local/me-immig26.

59. See Walter Nicholls, *The DREAMers: How the Undocumented Youth Movement Transformed the Immigrant Rights Debate* (Stanford, CA: Stanford University Press, 2013).

60. Julieta Garibay, blog post, "DREAMer Julieta Garibay Says 'I Will No Longer Tolerate Injustice,'" *Freedom from Fear Award,* January 24, 2011, accessed June 10, 2017, http://www.freedomfromfearaward.com/dreamer-julieta -garibay-says-%E2%80%9Ci-will-no-longer-tolerate-injustice-%E2% 80%9D/.

61. Undocumented youth could avoid deportation as long as they had continuously resided and attended school in the country, had not been convicted of a felony or major misdemeanor, and did not pose a threat to national security or public safety. *U.S. Citizenship and Immigration Services,* accessed September 9, 2016, http://www.uscis.gov/humanitarian/consideration -deferred-action-childhood-arrivals-daca.

62. Greg Price, "Even Republicans Want Dreamers to Stay in America and be Citizens, New Poll Shows," *Newsweek,* September 29, 2017, accessed September 29, 2017 http://www.newsweek.com/dreamers-republicans-america -citizens-674335.

63. The term "through no fault of their own" became broadly popularized and was used by Paul Ryan, Barack Obama, and even Donald Trump. See "Statement of DACA Program," https://www.speaker.gov/press-release/statement -daca-program; Kevin Liptak, "Obama Slams Trump for Rescinding DACA,

Calls Move 'Cruel,'" http://www.cnn.com/2017/09/05/politics/obama-daca /index.html; and Twitter comment by Donald Trump, https://twitter.com /realdonaldtrump/status/908278070611779585?lang=en (all accessed September 29, 2017).

64. *Plyler v. Doe*, 457 U.S. 202, 220 (1982).

65. Xóchitl Bada, *Mexican Hometown Associations in Chicagoacán: From Local to Transnational Civic Engagement* (New Brunswick: Rutgers University Press, 2014), 25; David FitzGerald, *A Nation of Emigrants: How Mexico Manages Its Migration* (Berkeley: University of California Press, 2009), 56; Nicholas De Genova and Ana Y. Ramos-Zayas, *Latino Crossings: Mexicans, Puerto Ricans, and the Politics of Race and Citizenship* (New York: Routledge, 2003), 41.

66. Salvador Vázquez, interview by author, August 17, 2014, Monterey Park, California, digital recording.

67. FitzGerald, *A Nation of Emigrants*, 56.

68. Ibid., 57.

69. Hanako Taniguchi, "Reducción de requisitos aumenta solicitudes de voto en el extranjero: IFE," *CNNMéxico*, January 11, 2012, accessed August 17, 2015, http://mexico.cnn.com/nacional/2012/01/11/reduccion-de-requisitos -aumenta-solicitudes-de-voto-en-el-extranjero-ife.

70. Roberto Suro and Gabriel Escobar, "Pew Hispanic Center Survey of Mexicans Living in the U.S. on Absentee Voting in Mexican Elections," *Pew Research Center*, February 22, 2006.

71. Ibid.

72. David FitzGerald, "150 Years of Transborder Politics: Mexico and Mexicans Abroad," in *A Century of Transnationalism: Immigrants and Their Homeland Connections*, edited by Nancy Green and Roger Waldinger (Chicago: University of Illinois Press, 2016), 121; and David Gutiérrez, Jeanne Batalova, and Aaron Terrazas, "The 2012 Mexican Presidential Election and Mexican Immigrants of Voting Age in the United States," *Migration Policy Institute*, April 26, 2012, accessed June 2, 2017, http://www.migrationpolicy.org/article/2012-mexican -presidential-election-and-mexican-immigrants-voting-age-united-states.

73. José Juárez, interview by author, March 21, 2015, Van Nuys, California, digital recording.

74. Immigration Reform and Control Act of 1986, Pub. L. No. 99–603, §§ 301, 100 Stat. 3411.

75. David Griffith, *American Guestworkers: Jamaicans and Mexicans in the U.S. Labor Market* (University Park: Pennsylvania State University Press, 2006), 153–178.

76. Fernando Tapia (pseudonym), telephone interview by author, July 25, 2015, digital recording.

77. Ibid.

78. Mary Bauer, "Close to Slavery: Guestworker Programs in the United States," *Southern Poverty Law Center*, accessed September 29, 2017, https://www.

splcenter.org/sites/default/files/d6_legacy_files/downloads/Close_to _Slavery.pdf, 2; and "Impact Report 2013," Centro de los Derechos del Migrante, Inc., accessed September 29, 2017, http://www.cdmigrante.org/wp -content/uploads/2013/12/Impact-Report_2013-1.pdf, 1.

79. Adarely Hernández, telephone interview by author, July 24, 2015, digital recording. For more on family members' position on H-2 visas, see Griffith, *American Guestworkers*, 153–178.

80. Raúl Pérez (pseudonym), telephone interview by author, August 8, 2015, digital recording.

81. Ibid.

82. Adarely Hernández, interview.

83. Raúl Pérez, interview (emphasis added).

84. Bauer, "Close to Slavery," 22.

85. Fernando Tapia, interview.

86. Jimena Herrera (pseudonym), telephone interview by author, June 23, 2015, digital recording.

87. Raúl Palafox (pseudonym), telephone interview by author, August 7, 2015, digital recording.

88. Ibid.

89. Adarely Hernández, interview.

90. Alicia Schmidt Camacho, "Migrant Melancholia: Emergent Discourses of Mexican Migrant Traffic in Transnational Space," *South Atlantic Quarterly* 105, no. 4 (2006): 831–861.

91. Author handwritten notes, summer 2007, Tarímbaro.

92. José Luis Sierra, "Tomb of the Unknown Migrant," *New America Media*, November 9, 2011, accessed September 29, 2017, http://newamericamedia.org /2011/11/tomb-of-the-unknown-migrant.php.

93. Ibid.

Afterword

1. "Full text: Donald Trump Announces a Presidential Bid," *Washington Post*, June 6, 2015, accessed February 10, 2017, https://www.washingtonpost .com/news/post-politics/wp/2015/06/16/full-text-donald-trump -announces-a-presidential-bid/?utm_term=.89c6cb0e4525.

2. Philip Bump, "Here's What Donald Trump Said in His Big Immigration Speech, Annotated," *Washington Post*, August, 31, 2016, accessed February 10, 2017, https://www.washingtonpost.com/news/the-fix/wp/2016 /08/31/heres-what-donald-trump-said-in-his-big-immigration-speech -annotated/?utm_term=.10f875cfd733; Jeremy Diamond, "Donald Trump: Birthright Babies Not Citizens," *CNN*, August 19, 2015, accessed February 10, 2017, http://www.cnn.com/2015/08/19/politics/donald-trump-birthright -american-citizenship; and Elizabeth Gurdus, "Trump: 'We Have Some Bad

Hombres and We're Going to Get Them Out,' " CNBC.com, October 19, 2016, accessed February 25, 2017, http://www.cnbc.com/2016/10/19/trump -we-have-some-bad-hombres-and-were-going-to-get-them-out.html.

3. Suzanne Gamboa, "Trump Claims in Debate Mexico 'Sends the Bad Ones' to U.S.," *NBC News,* August 6, 2015, accessed February 10, 2017, http://www .nbcnews.com/news/latino/trump-claims-debate-mexico-sends-bad -ones-u-s-n405661.

4. "Full Text: Donald Trump Announces a Presidential Bid"; and Michael A. Cohen, "The Big Winner of the GOP Debate: That 'Angry,' 'New York Values' Donald Trump," *Fox News,* January 17, 2016, accessed February 10, 2017, http://nation.foxnews.com/2016/01/17/big-winner-gop-debate-angry -new-york-values-donald-trump.

5. Ana Gonzalez-Barrera, "More Mexicans Leaving Than Coming to the U.S.," Pew Hispanic Center, November 19, 2015, accessed February 10, 2017, http://www.pewhispanic.org/2015/11/19/more-mexicans-leaving-than -coming-to-the-u-s/.

6. Between 1970 and 2014, the fertility rate in Mexico dropped from 6.8 to 2.2 births per woman. "Fertility Rate, Total (Births per Woman)," World Bank, accessed February 10, 2017, http://data.worldbank.org/indicator/SP .DYN.TFRT.IN?locations=MX.

Appendix A

1. I also conducted five phone interviews with particular migrants whose stories I wanted to learn more about but who I couldn't meet in person. Due to the difficulty of establishing the same type of personal relationship with these interviewees that I did with those I met in person, these phone interviews were less comprehensive. I was not always able to gather the same demographic information or details about everyday life as I did with in-person oral histories. For this reason, I have omitted these phone interviews from the tables in this appendix.

2. Oral History Association, "Principles and Best Practices for Oral History" (2009), accessed June 1, 2017, http://www.oralhistory.org/about/principles -and-practices.

3. Douglas S. Massey, Jorge Durand, and Nolan J. Malone, *Beyond Smoke and Mirrors: Mexican Immigration in an Era of Economic Integration* (New York: Russell Sage Foundation, 2002), 52–53, 66.

4. Jonathan Fox, "Reframing Mexican Migration as a Multi-ethnic Process," *Latino Studies* 4, no. 1 (2006): 40, accessed October 1, 2017, https:// escholarship.org/uc/item/4nn6v8sk.

5. Daniel James, *Doña María's Story: Life History, Memory, and Political Identity* (Durham, NC: Duke University Press, 2000); Peter Winn, "Oral History and the Factory Study: New Approaches to Labor History," *Latin American Research Review* 14, no. 2 (1979): 130–140; Jeffrey L. Gould and Aldo A. Lauria-

Santiago, *To Rise in Darkness: Revolution, Repression, and Memory in El Salvador, 1920–1932* (Durham, NC: Duke University Press, 2008); Alessandro Portelli, *The Death of Luigi Trastulli, and Other Stories: Form and Meaning in Oral History* (Albany: State University of New York Press, 1991); Elizabeth Tonkin, *Narrating Our Pasts: The Social Construction of Oral History* (New York: Cambridge University Press, 1992); and Luisa Passerini, *Fascism in Popular Memory: The Cultural Experience of the Turin Working Class,* translated by Robert Lumley and Jude Bloomfield (Cambridge: Cambridge University Press, 1987).

6. Oral History Association, "Principles and Best Practices for Oral History."
7. Luise White, Stephan F. Miescher, and David William Cohen, eds., *African Words, African Voices: Critical Practices in Oral History* (Bloomington: Indiana University Press, 2001); and Richard Roberts and Donald Moore, "Listening for Silences," *History in Africa* 17 (1990): 319–325.

Appendix B

1. Douglas S. Massey, Jorge Durand, and Nolan Malone, *Beyond Smoke and Mirrors: Mexican Immigration in an Era of Economic Integration* (New York: Russell Sage Foundation, 2002), 54.
2. See "Study Design," Mexican Migration Project, accessed October 1, 2017, http://mmp.opr.princeton.edu/databases/studydesign-en.aspx.
3. INEGI, "VIII Censo General de Población 1960," Tabulados, Area Geográfica: Zacatecas, Población, Población total y número de localidades, por municipio y tamaño de la localidad, según sexo, accessed October 1, 2017, http://www.beta.inegi.org.mx/proyectos/ccpv/1960/default.html.
4. INEGI, "IX Censo General de Población y Vivienda 1970," Tabulados, Area Geográfica: Zacatecas, Población, Población total por municipio y tamaño de la localidad, accessed October 1, 2017, http://www.beta.inegi.org.mx/proyectos/ccpv/1970/default.html.
5. INEGI, "XI Censo General de Población y Vivienda 1990," Tabulados, Area Geográfica: Zacatecas, Población, Población total por municipio y tamaño de la localidad, según sexo, accessed October 1, 2017, http://www.beta.inegi.org.mx/proyectos/ccpv/1990/default.html.

ACKNOWLEDGMENTS

All books are collaborative projects; this one was especially so. It is imbued with the memories of hundreds of individuals who shared their stories and personal collections with me. All of them inform this work, and it is they who inspired this project. In particular, I want to thank Gregorio Casillas, Sandra Paiz, María Elena Serrano, and Raúl Villarreal. The four of them spent entire weeks recounting their lives and sharing their archives. Ten years after I first began this work, I can only hope that it does justice to migrants' stories, to their courage and work, to the struggles they faced as a result of undocumented border crossing, and especially to their visions of a different future.

A wide circle of mentors helped shape this book. Stephen Pitti supported me beyond measure from the beginning of this project with intellectual rigor, kindness, and grace. George Chauncey was an encouraging and sharp reader who never failed to challenge me with his keen insights. Their mentorship throughout the years helped me grow as a person and as a scholar. I received infinite help from Alicia Schmidt Camacho, whose passion for and knowledge of the topic kept me afloat and motivated me even when the stories I wrote about were heartbreaking. Patricia Pessar taught me how to use and think about oral histories. Gilbert Joseph was always available to discuss Mexico's history and historiography. Matthew Jacobson, Mary Lui, and Joanne Meyerowitz encouraged my intellectual growth. Mae Ngai's support meant more to me than she can imagine. Her breathtaking book provided me with an exemplary model of migration history, and she kindly read this manuscript twice, giving me exceptional suggestions each time. Albert Camarillo welcomed and mentored me at Stanford University. A pioneer in Chicana/o history, he provided me with insightful comments and with direction.

A community of generous scholars read the entire manuscript with a sharp eye. I thank Geraldo Cadava, Al Camarillo, David Gutiérrez, Ramón Gutiérrez, David Montejano, and Mae Ngai for their rich and astute criticism. Their perceptive observations helped me to deepen my analysis and refine the focus of the book. James Campbell read through the manuscript twice and spent countless hours helping me to think about how to put the pieces of this puzzle together. Allyson Hobbs and Richard White challenged me to revise and improve this book far beyond what I thought was possible. I am grateful to Laura Briggs, Margaret Chowning, Raymond Craib, Brian DeLay, and Zephyr Frank for encouraging me to consider the broad questions in Latin American history and for helping me to think through my major arguments. I thank Julio Capó Jr., Gordon Chang, Raúl Coronado, Kathleen Frederickson, José David Saldívar, and Caroline Winterer for their brilliant suggestions about how to bring out migrants' voices and concerns. Although far from my field, Richard Roberts, Priya Satia, and Jun Uchida read the manuscript closely and provided me with sharp feedback. The book is more intellectually rigorous thanks to their enlightening insights.

For carefully reading large portions of the book and offering perceptive suggestions, I am indebted to Rodolfo Acuña, José Alamillo, Gabriela Arredondo, Jennifer Burns, Ernesto Chávez, Brian Distelberg, Silas Ellison, Estelle Freedman, María Cristina García, Jerry Gonzalez, Adam Goodman, Richard Griswold del Castillo, Nicole Guidotti-Hernández, Laura Gutiérrez, Steven Hahn, Tamar Herzog, Ben de Jesus, Emilio Kourí, Gabriela Soto Laveaga, Masha Lisak, David Lobenstine, Kelly Lytle Hernández, Simeon Man, Monica M. Martínez, Aaron Mertz, Julie Minich, Natalia Molina, María Montoya, Yumi Moon, Melanie Morten, Jocelyn Olcott, Pablo Piccato, Ana Elizabeth Rosas, George Sánchez, Edith Sheffer, Max Strassfeld, Mauricio Tenorio-Trillo, Julie Weise, Mikael Wolfe, Tiffany Yap, and Elliot Young. They were all extremely kind with their suggestions, and I often compelled them to read revised versions and to answer dozens of follow-up questions. I am deeply grateful for their support. *Undocumented Lives* is better thanks to feedback from the members of the Tepoztlán collective.

This book would not have been possible without the work of gifted research assistants Evelyn Anderson, Aaron Bae, María Guadalupe Bojórquez, Karen Camacho, Mateo Carrillo, David Albán Hidalgo, Jonatan Pérez, Katie Petway, and Chris Suh. They helped transcribe interviews, looked for sources, and checked footnotes. Jonatan and Karen immersed themselves in this project with me for two years.

A community of friends helped me conduct the research for this work. Joseph Fronczak spent six weeks with me during my first research trip in migrant communities in Michoacán. Eloísa Andjel, Donna Blumenfeld, David Holzman, Aaron Mertz, and Teresa Zerón came with me to different parts of Mexico's Central Plateau region. I am also indebted to the Zerón-Medina Laris family who allowed me to stay in their house in Michoacán and introduced me to priests and individuals from communities of high out-migration. El Padre Nacho in Angahuan played a key role helping me meet people in his community. Heather Ashby always supported my research travels within the United States. Tim Retzloff allowed me to stay with him and showed me around Flint. Aurora Camacho de Schmidt shared her history and provided me with invaluable sources. Miriam Powell sent me original oral history interviews conducted with AFW leaders. Deb Preusch and Tom Barry invited me to stay at their house in Pino Altos while I conducted interviews. Christian Paiz and Sandra

Paiz introduced me to their family and community members in the Coachella Valley, and Morelia Baltazar Ferreira let me stay at her house there. Omar Amador took me to his home in Los Angeles so that I could conduct oral history interviews with his parents and neighbors.

I am grateful to Susan Gzesh and Douglas Massey for all their support throughout the years. They helped me think about my methodology when I was conducting research and shared valuable sources and information that are now part of the book.

The book benefited greatly from suggestions I received from Xóchitl Bada, Marjorie Becker, Gabriela Cano, Patricia Fernández-Kelly, Mario García, Matt García, Pierrette Hondagneu-Sotelo, Florencia Mallon, Anne Martínez, Daniel Morales, José Moya, Andrés Reséndez, Marian Schlotterbeck, Amy Stanley, Marc Stein, Alexandra Minna Stern, Charles Walker, and Barbara Weinstein. It also benefited from conversations and support from Jennifer Brody, Paula Findlen, Angela García, Jonathan Gienapp, Tomás Jiménez, Paula Moya, Matthew Sommer, Laura Stokes, Kären Wigen, Ali Yaycioglu, and Steven Zipperstein. Tom Mullaney, my mentor in the History Department at Stanford, helped me plan the road to complete this book and supported me throughout. Over the years, Mike Amezcua, Noa Bar, Kathleen Belew, Dinah Berch, Joshua Berch, Zane Curtis-Olsen, Lori Flores, Kendra Froshman, Eva Gurría, Betty Hillman, Eli Kim, Ellen Klutznick, Drew Konove, Tala Manassah, Naomi Paik, Tim Retzloff, Sarah Rezny, Ximena Rubio, Ana Paola Ruiz, Raya Samet, Lisa Stern, Tim Stewart-Winter, Lisa Ubelaker, Zohar Weimun-Kelman, Jen Wellington, Teresa Zerón, and Azeret Zúñiga bestowed upon me their friendship and intellectual stimulation. At Stanford University, the History Department and the Center for the Studies of Race and Ethnicity provided me with an engaging community and a productive space to think about existing social problems.

I am deeply grateful for Joyce Seltzer's careful and unparalleled editing. Her thoughtful criticism pushed me to write a more engaging manuscript that was always centered in migrants' experiences. I also want to thank her wonderful team at Harvard University Press.

Like most historians, I have many people to thank for giving me access to the archives I needed. Adán Griego, Everardo Rodríguez, and Roberto Trujillo helped me access the archives at Stanford's Special Collections. At the Department of Homeland Security, Marian Smith helped me place a Freedom of Information Act request on immigration files. Multiple archivists from the Archivo General de la Nación, the Archivo de la Secretaría de Relaciones Exteriores, and the Presidencia Municipal de Nochistlán were also indispensable for the success of this project. Many of the archives I used, however, were kept in personal collections. For giving me access to their files, I want to thank José Encarnación Bañuelos, Gregorio Casillas, Don Devereux, María Elena Serrano, Salvador Vázquez, Raúl Villarreal, and individuals, priests, and government officials from the communities of Angahuan, Zitácuaro, Tangancícuaro, Morelia, San Andrés, Santa Fe de la Laguna, Cañada del Herrero, Tarímbaro, Tzintzuntzan, Ruiz Cortines, Pátzcuaro, and Zacán in Michoacán as well as Nochistlán, Las Ánimas,

Jalpa, and Jerez in Zacatecas. I also used the collections stored at La Casa del Mexicano in Los Angeles. Chapter 5 is an expanded version of *"De Terruño a Terruño*: Reimagining Belonging through the Creation of Hometown Associations," *Journal of American History*, Volume 104, Issue 1 (1 June 2017): 120–142. Published by Oxford University Press on behalf of the Organization of American Historians. Every effort has been made to trace copyright holders and to obtain their permission for the use of copyrighted material. Should omissions or errors be present, notification of any additions or corrections that should be incorporated in future reprints or editions of this book would be greatly appreciated.

This project benefited from generous financial assistance from many sources. From the Consejo Nacional de Ciencia y Tecnología I received a Beca CONACYT en el Extranjero, from Yale University I received a Leylan Fellowship in the Humanities, a MacMillan Center Research Grant, a research grant from the Fund for Lesbian and Gay Studies Research, and a Women, Religion and Globalization Fellowship. At Stanford University, I was supported by a Clayman Faculty Fellowship, a CCSRE Faculty Research Fellowship, and a Latin American Studies Conference fellowship. Thanks to support from the Donald D. Harrington Fellowship I spent the 2013–2014 academic year at the University of Austin, where I was able to work among an engaging community of scholars. For the invitation to participate in this fellowship, I thank Nicole Guidotti-Hernández.

A community of friends gave me the strength to write this book. Silas Ellison and Tiffany Yap provided me with countless hours of laughter and a loving family in San Francisco. Armando García, Allyson Hobbs, Monica M. Martínez, Aaron Mertz, and Adam Weissmann were constant sources of support. Julio Capó Jr., Kevin Fogg, and Carla Marcantonio spent hours working with me at writing retreats. Their support and friendship was essential to complete this project. There are few words that can describe everything Julio has done for me and for this book. Nicknamed "mi media naranja," Julio is not only my closest interlocutor but also one of my most important sources of happiness.

My two sisters, Nadia and Tamara, encouraged me with their love and enthusiasm. Reneé, Sarah, Batia, Moisés, Natasha and Jim eased the hard moments of research and writing. Melanie Morten was key in helping me start and finish this book. From coming with me on research trips, to hearing me repeatedly read the book out loud; from ensuring that I was up and writing every morning to staying up at night working with me, Melanie was a source of light and support without which I could not have written this work and much less so with a smile.

This book is dedicated, in part, to my parents. Their history, embedded in struggles for social justice, inspired me since my youth. My dad's interest in history motivated me to follow this path. His love and jokes helped to sustain my work. But no one deserves more praise and gratitude than my mother. My best friend since childhood, she has helped me to no end. She heard every idea I had, read multiple versions of this book, and cheered me up when things got tough. No list or description I write here can begin to depict the huge impact she has had on my life and scholarship.

INDEX

Absent sons *(hijos ausentes)*, 111–112, 236
Acosta, María, 110
Activism, 130; belonging fought for
through, 226, 232; as binational, 9,
153; of Chicano/as, 131, 147; of *clubes
sociales*, 125–127, 141, 155–156, 196,
225, 284n29; Comité de Beneficencia
Mexicana, 65, 72, 140, *144*; of communities, 131, 159, 240; DREAMers
promoting, 224; for education, 63–64,
126, 176; exclusion defied by, 141; as
grassroots, 160; hometowns supported
by, 130–131, 140; as local, 9; Maricopa
County Organizing Project, 159,
162–167, 206; for mobility, 161,
210–212; risks involved in, 9; roads and
highways used for, 158–159, 169–172,
180; socioeconomic status in, 142;
strategies for, 159; success of, 223; as
translocal, 9; for union rights, 9, 11,
136, 158–159, 162, 164, 169, 172–175,
181, 189, 193–194; by United States
social movements, 146; for voting
rights, 162, 225. See also *Clubes sociales;*
Constitutional rights; Migrant activism;
Unions
Adriano, Junior, 208–210, 236
African Americans: civil rights
movement of, 159; prejudice views
against, 146; as replaced, 59; unemployment of, 52; welfare mess blamed
on, 63
Agricultural development, 21–24, 57, 113,
193, 218; Green Revolution influence
on, 81; out-migration and, 23; tech-
niques of, 256n37; as unprofitable, 114.
See also Green Revolution; Irrigation;
Valle Bajo Río Bravo irrigation project
Agricultural goods, market prices for, 29
Aguilar, Antonio, 138
Aid distribution: behavioral restrictions
to, 133–134; protection through, 173;
qualifying for, 187–188; unemployment
assisted through, 197–198
Aid to Families with Dependent
Children, 63
Airlifting, 40
Aldame, David, 93
Alianza de Braceros Nacionales de
México en los Estados Unidos de
Norteamérica, 20–21, 29
All in the Family, 59
Allstrom, Peter, 193
Amador, Mirella, 213
American Federation of Labor and
Congress of Industrial Organizations
(AFL-CIO), 52, 57, 59–60, 69,
191–204
American Jewish Congress, 131
Amnesty *(la amnistía),* 59, 191, 214–215.
See also Immigration Reform and
Control Act; *Jaula de Oro;* Legalization
Anchor baby, stereotypes of, 8, 66–67
Andrada, Ramón, 206–207
Angelino organizations, 130
Las Ánimas, 83–86, 115, 120, 244;
baseball in, 118–119; correspondence
to, 107; interviews conducted in, 12;
land ownership in, 113; long-distance
partnerships in, 106, 108; mobility
patterns in, 87, 97, 105; wages in, 111,
114. See also Baseball team, Las Ánimas

Anti-foreign sentiments, of United States, 19
Apprehensions: by Border Patrol, 2, 14, 123, 170; by Immigration and Naturalization Service, 71–74, 83–87, 158, 174; statistics on, 4–6, 16, 25, 30–31, 56, 194, 251n6
Arendt, Hannah, 264n168
Arrowhead Ranch, 161, 164
Asphyxiation, 42
Assembly plants. See *Maquiladoras*
Austerity programs, 28, 197
Ávila Camacho, Manuel, 19–20
Ayala Domínguez, Jesús, 90

Baker, Verne, 21
Baltimore Sun, 56
Barragán, Augustín, 85
Barraza Ríos, Pedro, 25–26
Barry, Tom, 180
Baseball team, Las Ánimas, 118–119
Basic Guide of Services for the Public, 42
Bean, Angela, 74–75
Beauty pageants, 141–142
Belonging, 5, 75; acceptance and, 53–54; achieving of, 211, 214; activism fighting for, 226, 232; capacity for, 221; Catholic Church increasing feeling of, 120; *clubes sociales* establishing, 127, 140–142, 148, 156; communities denying, 80; communities renewing sense of, 133; experience of not, 10–11; family separation shaping, 78; gender and, 142–143; as geographic, 153; to hometowns, 104, 113; of indigenous people, 146; isolation associated with, 129; lack of, from circular migration, 49, 87–88, 210; Mexico denying migrant, 46, 78, 232; multiple visions of, 151–153; as partial, 104–105, 182; pressures inhibiting, 103; as primary migration concern, 203–204; race influencing, 145; recognizing of, 46; reinforcing of, 179; rooted in experience, 150; as rooted in "otherness," 150; sexuality and, 79; struggle for, 232; tragedy of not, 236; as transnational, 224; United States denying migrant, 46, 74, 78, 141, 202, 222; unwanted feeling and, 75. *See also* Activism; Constitutional rights; Space, sense of
Benker, Karen, 66

Bermúdez, Antonio, 24, 27
Binational U.S.-Mexico Commission, 45–46
Birth rates: slashing of, 34. *See also* Fertility; Oral contraceptives; Population; Sterilization
Blanco, Delores, 90
Boardinghouses, 115
Border checkpoints *(la linea),* 88–89, 115, 169
Border crossing: advocates for, 41; criminality from, 68; dangers of, 199, 210; deaths from attempted, 89–90, 110, 230–232; environmental elements of, 89; expensive process of, 210; increase in, 25, 195; mentality shift in, 5; safest ways of, 88; as severe problem, 19; violence of, 14, 62, 78, 95–96; violence preventing, 90. *See also Jaula de Oro*
Border enforcement: for human containment, 194; increase in, 90–91, 200, 202, 234
Border Industrialization Program (BIP), 27, 60, 98. See also *Maquiladoras; Programa Nacional Fronterizo*
Borderland cities, 76; as dangerous, 88; employment opportunities in, 115; unemployment in, 25–26
Border Patrol, 293n49; apprehensions by, 2, 14, 123, 170; fear of, 170; linewatch-hours increased, 71; Mexican officials joint operation with, 1–2; searches by, 84. *See also* Border enforcement; Immigration and Naturalization Service
Borrego Estrada, Genaro, 155
Boutilier v. Immigration, 95
Bracero Program, 4–5, 192–193; agricultural workers recruited by, 56; culture promoted by, 81; duration of, 20, 25, 252n9; end of, 3, 30–31, 41, 42, 109–110; gender inequality of, 97; renewal of, 26, 263n160. *See also* Guest-worker contracts
Bradley, Tom, 140
Bribes *(mordidas),* 24
Briggs, Vernon, 29–30
Brignoni Ponce, Felix Humberto, 170
Brown, Hank, 204
Brown v. Board of Education (1954), 176
Burdetsky, Ben, 76
Burrola Ruiz, Hipólito, 25
Bustamange, Jorge, 30, 33

Cage of Gold. See *Jaula de Oro*
Camacho, Everardo, 83, 211
Campos Salas, Octaviano, 26–27
Canadian migration, 69
Cantú, Lionel, 275n57
Capital movement, 60
Capital relocation, 197. *See also* Border
    Industrialization Program; *Maquila-
    doras;* Programa Nacional Fronterizo
Cárdenas, Cuauhtémoc, 225
Cardenas, Lázaro, 126
Carter, Jimmy, 45, 46, 165
Cartoon, illustrating exploitation, *190*
La Casa del Mexicano, 131–133, 142, 154,
    239
Casillas, Gregorio: background of, 150;
    childhood of, 128–129; extraterritorial
    welfare state built by, 236; geographic
    loyalty of, 121; government inactions
    recalled by, 39, 137; high school
    experience of, 147; isolation as
    motivation for, 129; lack of support for,
    196; money raised by, 131
Casillas Jaime, Gregorio, 128
Castañeda y Álvarez de la Rosa, Jorge,
    14–16, 43–44
Castillo, Leonel J., 95
Castro, Fidel, 200
Catholic Church, 18, 34, 247; communi-
    ties formation through, 120; Mexican
    officials rift with, 22; sense of be-
    longing increased by, 120
Central Labor Union, 27
Central Plateau region, 23, 38, 92, 105
Centro de Acción Social Autónomo
    (CASA), 147, 187, 291n9
Chamber of Commerce, U.S., 192,
    195–196, 204
Chapman, Leonard, 71, 200–201
Charrería (horsemanship), 119–120
Chávez, Cesar, 59, 161
Chicago Leather Workers Union, 173,
    294n64
Chicano/as: activism for, 131; *clubes
    sociales* engagement of, 147; identity
    development of, 188; radical organ-
    izations of, 187, 197
Children: deportation leaving abandoned,
    74; education rights for, 175–179; as
    immigration law circumvention, 70; of
    migrants, citizenship of, 65–67; as
    responsibility of women, 97–99
Christian Science Monitor, 56

Circular migration, 5–6, 9–10, 77, 91,
    302n83; as impermanent, 80; lack of
    belonging from, 49, 87–88, 210;
    lifestyles reconfigured through, 104,
    179, 184, 209; long-term compared to
    short-term, 18; permanent relocation
    compared to, 179, 184; shift to
    entrapment from, 226; transnational
    dimension of family and, 105–110;
    willingness towards, 209. See also *Jaula
    de Oro*
Citizenship, 252n19; benefits of, 47;
    through birth, 8; carrying of documen-
    tation for, 271n124; of children of
    migrants, 65–67; false claims of, 88;
    law for acquiring of, 190–191; migrants
    upholding national, 10; social clubs
    producing vision of civic, 148
Ciudad Juárez, unemployment in, 28
Civil rights, 157–158
Clark, Bill, 55
Cleary, John J., 169–172, 293n49
Clubes de oriundos (Hometown associa-
    tions), 125–130, 244–245
Clubes sociales (Social clubs): activism of,
    125–127, 141, 155–156, 196, 225,
    284n29; agents of, 133–135; attach-
    ments reflected in, 148–150; belonging
    established by, 127, 140–142, 148, 156;
    Casillas work in, 125; Chicano/as
    engagement in, 147; ethnic diversity of,
    131, 145–148; as extraterritorial
    welfare state, 136, 147; gender roles in,
    142–144; government relationship
    with, 139–140; history of, 244–245;
    hometowns represented in, *132;* joining
    together of, 153–154; purpose of,
    129–130, 140–142; responsibilities of,
    136–138; transnational perspective
    of, 152. *See also* Activism; specific
    types
Club Social Guadalupe Victoria, 125,
    129–131, 133–134; attachment
    demonstrated by, 148–149; clinic
    formation by, 138
Club Social San Vicente, 152–153
Comité de Beneficencia Mexicana
    (Mexican Welfare Committee), 65, 72,
    140, *144. See also* Activism
Commission on Population Growth and
    the American Future, 56
Communal lands *(ejidos),* 32–33, 138–139
Communism, 29, 201

Communities: alliances between, 159;
belonging denied by, 80; as binational,
235; Catholic Church strengthening,
120; communication maintained
within, 111; exclusion from, 123, 234;
fallen women in, 106; forming
translocal, 119; funds for betterment of,
128; gender roles presented in, 117–118;
history importance of, 240–241; migrant
benefits spreading through, 211;
migrants identifying with different
types of, 117–118, 124, 130, 148; of
migrants in United States, 115–116;
migrants pushed out of, 209; migration
decisions influenced by, 78, 124;
organizing strategies for, 130; physical
space of, 113–114; recognition from,
225; redefining of meaning of, 105,
110–112, 124, 125; renewed sense of
belonging in, 133; safety net for, 196;
state responsibility of improvement for,
135; strength in, 202; translocal
movement shaping, 104; transnational
dimension of, 105; unemployment in
industrial, 54–55; wars between, 121.
See also Belonging; Hometowns
Community Services Organization (CSO),
131
Comrie, Keith, 65–66
Concentrated Enforcement Program, 191
El Concilio Manzo, 72
Conditions, for migrant workers, 160
Constitutional rights, 45, 169, 171,
177–178, 217–218
Consumption, 52
Contract-worker agreements. *See*
Guest-worker contracts
Contributions, 202, 204
Conyers, John, 161
Córdova, Luis, 134–135
Correspondence: to Las Ánimas, 107;
relationship complexity increased by,
107–108; saving of, 239–240. *See also*
Love letters
Cortés, Michael, 188–189
Cosmopolitanism, 8, 78
Cotton farming, 22
Coyotes. See Smugglers
Criminalization: from border crossing,
68; of undocumented migrants, 18, 178
Cristeros, 18
Cuba, 200
Cusul Ávila, Manuel, 33

Daves, Larry, 176
Deaths: from border crossing attempts,
89–90, 110, 230–232; smugglers
causing, 90
Deferred Action for Childhood Arrivals
(DACA), 224
Delgado, Andrés, 212
Demand-side economics, 51
Department of Health, Education, and
Welfare, 186
Dependency, 185
Deportation: children left abandoned
from, 74; cost of, 2; family separation
from, 72–73; increase in, 39, 71; of
individuals multiple times, 87; limiting
of, 15; pay avoided through, 191;
process of, 86; risk of, 18, 160; support
for, 47, 161; threats of, 59; from
unionization, 175; violence in, 72
Desirable immigrants, 37
Detention centers, 86, 95
Devereux, Don, 161–162, 164, 291n10
Díaz Ordaz, Gustavo, 25–26, 33, 136
Domingo Magaña, José, 122–123
Douglas, Paul, 52
DREAMers, 224

Eastland, James, 53
Ebony, 59
Echeverría, Luis, 28–34, 41, 45, 263n161
Echeverría, Rodolfo, 33–34
Economic agents, as indispensable, 124,
125–126, 141
Economic dignity, 137
Economic restructuring, 258n77;
acceleration of, 217–218; of Mexican
government, 9; remittances influ-
encing, 109, 283n19
Education: access to, 122, 223; curric-
ulum inclusion of Mexican history,
147; for migrants, 64; as reason for
immigration, 176
Education rights, 175–179, 181
Eilberg, Joshua, 186
Eilberg Bill, 48, 70
Ejidos (communal lands), 32–33, 138–139
Embezzlement, 134
Emotional hardships, 213–214, 243
Employer sanctions, 190–194, 200–204,
216, 297n2; discrimination increased
through, 189; family separation from,
205; implementation of, 44; introduction of, 207; opposition to, 198; passage

of, as likely, 194; as strategy, 196; support for, 40, 185–187
Employment: borderland cities opportunities for, 115; falling rates of, 28; modernization influencing, 81; problems with hiring practices for, 192–196; for returned braceros, 26–27. *See also* Full employment; Unemployment
Encarnación Bañuelos, José, 139, 150
Enciso, Alanís, 255n26
English language, migrants lack of, 83, 108
Entrapment, 6, 199–200, 209–210, 219–222, 226. See also *Jaula de Oro*
Entry fees, 6
Entry points, unofficial, 88
Ervin, Sam, 50
Escape valve, undocumented migration as, for Mexican policymakers, 46, 217
Ethno-racial system, of Mexico, 50, 121, 146. *See also* Indigenous people, of Mexico
Exclusion, 2–3, 213; activism defying, 141; redrawing lines of, 145; as triple, 6
Extraterritorial welfare state, 9; Casillas building, 236; *clubes sociales* creating, 136, 147; government assistance and, 126; structures countered by, 156

Fairchild electronics company, 60–61
Family: circular migration and transnational dimension of, 105–110; connections of, 49–50, 101–103; division of labor within, 98; integrity of, as priority, 74; international mobility, gender, sexuality and, 103; preference system and, 70; pressure from, 8; redefining meaning of, 105, 124, 125; as resource, 240; reunification of, 205; transnational dimension of, 205; values of, 67
Family separation, 83; belonging shaped by, 78; from deportation, 72–73; as emotional, 87, 112, 236, 243; employer sanctions causing, 205
Farm Labor Alliance, 201
Farmworkers' Economic Development Corporation (FEDC), 166
Fears, 10, 170
Federación de Clubs Mexicanos Unidos, 142–143; inception of, 154; representation for, 155
Federal Defenders of San Diego, 168, 172

Fertility, 10; developing countries rates of, 29; as irrepressible, 49, 67, 75, 99–100, 185, 205; stereotype of excessive, 185; women, welfare and, 66. *See also* Birth rates
Finn, Martin, 205
First National Chicano / Latino Conference on Immigration and Public Policy, 75, 296n111
Form I-186, 88
Franco, Juan, 65
Friedman, Milton, 57–58
Friendship Festival, 1949, 130–131
Full employment, 58
Fundación Humberto Gutiérrez, 153–154, 289n109

Galarza Viramontes, Antonio, 130, 148–149
Gamio, Manuel, 17–18, 30, 120
Garibay, Julieta, 224
Gender: belonging and, 142–143; Bracero Program and inequality of, 97; discrimination of, in guest-worker contracts, 109; as factor for migration, 7–8; inequality, 93; international mobility, sexuality, family and, 103; migration role of, 78; as overlooked, 27; sexuality, labor and, 76, 92–93; undocumented migration probabilities per, 97
Gender roles: communities presenting, 117–118; influence of, 91–93; in social clubs, 142–144; of women, 7–8
General Agreement on Tariffs and Trade (GATT), 17, 195, 199
General Population Law (Ley General de Población), 16–17, 33–39
Geographic loyalties, 121, 150, 153
G.I. Forum, 54
Givens, James, 27
Goldring, Luin, 143
Goldwater, Barry, 161
González, Trino, 115–116
González Avelar, Miguel, 46
Gossip, 101–102, 112, 206
Great Depression, 19, 39, 48, 128
Green Revolution, 22, 29, 81. *See also* Agricultural development; Irrigation; Valle Bajo Río Bravo irrigation project
Guest-worker contracts, 3–4, 44, 192–193; concern for, 41; conditions

Guest-worker (*continued*)
    for, 56–57; decrease in, 25; defense of,
    20–21; gender discrimination in, 109.
    See also Bracero Program; H-2A
    program; H-2B program; H-2 program
Gutiérrez, Gustavo, 161

Harmful portrayal, 48
Hart, Philip, 51
Hart-Celler Act, 48–52, 68, 69
Hawkins, Augustus, 58
Hemispheric equity, 68–69
Hernández, Adarely, 227–229
Hernández, Emanuel, 82
Hernández Medrano, Jesús, 53
Hernández Serabia, Elsa Marina,
    170
*Hernandez v. Houston Independent School
    District*, 296n90
Hiding, 84
Hijos ausentes (absent sons), 111–112,
    236
Hinojosa, Antonio, 193
Hispanic lobby, 188
Hometown associations (HTAs). See *Clubes
    de oriundos*
Hometowns: activism supporting,
    130–131, 140; belonging to, 104, 113; in
    clubes sociales, 132; containment in, 100;
    improving life in, 127–129; leaving of,
    11, 25, 31, 62, 65; migrants pushed out
    of, 92; pressure from, 5, 80, 97–98, 124;
    queer life in, 94–96; redefining
    meaning of, 125; returning to, 76, 90,
    105, 111; sense of space change in,
    113–114; as shrinking, 8, 83; women
    obligation to, 78
Hopelessness, 136
Horsemanship *(charrería)*, 119–120
H-2A program, 228–229. *See also*
    Guest-worker contracts
H-2B program, 226–227. *See also*
    Guest-worker contracts
H-2 program, 192–193, 207, 210, 230,
    304n103. *See also* Guest-worker
    contracts
Humanae Vitae, 34
Human rights, 39, 198; commitment to,
    165; inability to assert, 75; of migrants,
    16, 41–44
Human Rights Watch, 43
Humphrey, Hubert, 58
Hurtado, Rafael, 140

Identity, 216
Identity-based movements, 159–160,
    291n8
Illegal Immigration Reform and Immi-
    grant Responsibility Act, 222
Immigration and Nationality Act of 1952,
    94–95, 252n10
Immigration and Nationality Act of 1965,
    3–4, 68
Immigration and Naturalization Service
    (INS), 25, 30–31; apprehensions by,
    71–74, 83–87, 158, 174; enforcement
    expansion of, 71; knowledge of
    whereabouts of, 84–85; power limita-
    tion of, 53; raids by, 72–76, 177. *See also*
    Border enforcement; Border Patrol
Immigration Coalition, 66
Immigration quotas, 51
Immigration Reform and Control Act
    (IRCA) (1986), 6, 182–186, 198,
    207–216, 304n104. *See also* Amnesty;
    Employer sanctions; H-2A program;
    H-2B program; H-2 program; *Jaula de
    Oro;* Legalization
Imperialism, 35
Import substitution industrialization, 23,
    28, 29
Indigenous people, of Mexico, 121–122,
    145–146. *See also* Tarascan language
Inequality, 10, 47
Infidelity, 99–102, 107
Inflation, 10, 28, 54, 57
Institutional Revolutionary Party (PRI),
    16, 46, 126, 138, 282n3
Internal migration, 128–129, 195
International Conference for the Full
    Rights of Undocumented Workers,
    180–181
International Ladies' Garment Workers'
    Union (ILGWU), 189–190
International Monetary Fund, 28
Invisibility, 11
Irrigation, 22, 166, 256n37. *See also*
    Agricultural development; Green
    Revolution; Valle Bajo Río Bravo
    irrigation project
Isolation, 129, 162, 229

Japanese American Citizens League
    (JACL), 131
Jaula de Oro (Cage of Gold), 6, 209,
    219–223, 235. *See also* Border enforce-
    ment; Circular migration

Javits, Jacob, 51
Jiménez, Epigmenio, 121
Jiménez, Manuel, 49, 56–57, 62–63, 86–88, 90, 114
Job stealing, 47, 60–62, 69, 73
Juárez, José, 60
Juárez, Olga, 213

Kissinger, Henry, 41

Labor, 4–5, 19–20; division of, within family, 98; as feminized, 61; gender, sexuality and, 76, 92–93; surplus labor force, 16, 44; United States standards of, 56
Labor certification, 70
Labor rights, 156–158, 167
Lazcano, Mario, 158, 195
Laziness, 64, 67, 114; stereotypes of, 63–64, 67
"League of Friendship, The" (La Liga de la Amistad), 118
League of United Latin American Citizens (LULAC), 54, 197
Leal, Ilda, 67
Legalization, 211–216. See also Amnesty; Immigration Reform and Control Act
Legal status, 113, 141, 190–191
Levya Ayala, Antonio, 137
Ley General de Población. See General Population Law
"Liga de la Amistad, La" (The League of Friendship), 118
Limitations, 25, 69
la línea (border checkpoints), 88–89, 115, 169. See also Border enforcement; Border Patrol; Smugglers
Local government relationships, 139
Lomelí, Clemente, 81–82
López, Alfredo, 157–158
López, José and Lidia, 157, 176, 178–179
López Mateos, Adolfo, 24
López Portillo, José, 45, 195
Los Angeles Times, 66, 67, 73
Love letters, 11, 107–108, 206, 236. See also Correspondence

MacGregor, Clark, 51
Machismo, 100
de la Madrid, Miguel, 45, 199
de la Madrid, Roberto, 36
Magaña, José, 98
El Malcriado, 54–55

Manhood, establishing, 82–83
Maquiladoras (Assembly plants), 26–28, 60, 195, 267n56. See also Border Industrialization Program; Programa Nacional Fronterizo
Mares, Pablo, 18
Maricopa County Organizing Project (MCOP), 159, 162–167, 206. See also Activism
Mariel boatlift, 200
Marín Bernal, Manuel, 160, 163, 166
Marriage, influence of, 79–83, 98
Marshall, F. Ray, 57
Martínez, Vilma, 176
Mazoli, Romano L., 183
Mazos, Raúl, 101
McAndrew, Michael, 176
McCarran-Walter Act, 37
Media: population problems reflected in, 55–56; protest coverage desired by, 161–162; undocumented migration attention from, 53
Medicaid, 63. See also Welfare
Memories, 80, 118, 241–243
Mendoza, Griselda, 218
Messersmith, George, 19
Mestizos, 17, 145
Mexican American Legal Defense and Educational Fund (MALDEF), 74, 157, 168, 176–177, 190–191; family reunification argued by, 205; seen as purist, 196
Mexican Department of Labor, 45
Mexican Department of Migration, 18–19
Mexicanidad, 120
Mexican independence, 17
Mexican Migration Project (MMP), 248
Mexican policymakers: blame from, 15–16; dual goals of, 19; ignorance of, 32; migration patterns influenced by, 235; migrations benefits focused on by, 30; one-dimensional solutions of, 206; silence desired by, 46; undocumented migration as escape valve for, 46, 217
Mexican Revolution, 16, 32, 50, 138, 144
Mexican Social Security Institute (IMSS), 32
Mexican Welfare Committee. See Comité de Beneficencia Mexicana
Mexico: acceptance of economic aid for, 198–199; austerity package for, 28; blamed for undocumented migration, 234; Central Americans inflow to, 44;

Mexico (*continued*)
  constitutional rights denied for,
  217–218; creation of jobs for, 136–137;
  economic independence of, 197;
  economic problems in, 28, 216–217;
  ethno-racial system of, 121; failure of
  government in, 136; funding from
  government of, 155–156; indigenous
  people of, 121–122; intolerable
  conditions of, 34, 75, 158, 166; Latin
  America connection with, 43; migrant
  activists taking on fiscal responsibilities
  of government of, 137–138, 156;
  migrant belonging denied by, 46, 78,
  232; migrants' desire to return to, 65;
  modernization of, 283n13; national
  economic independence of, 109;
  political switch in, 38; socioeconomic
  problems of, 3; structural changes for,
  140; wall between United States and,
  233–234
Mexico City, 29
Mexico National Center for Information
  and Work Statistics, 45
Mexico Secretariat of Foreign Affairs,
  18–19, 26, 36–39
Migradollars, 30
Migrant activism, 3, 156; government
  fiscal responsibility taken on by,
  137–138; recognition certificates for,
  140
Migration laws, 17
Migratory Workers Archives, 41
Million Dollar Theatre, 85
Minero Legaspi, José, 104–105
Miramontes, Asunción, 134
Mobility: activism for, 161, 210–212;
  expansion of, 211–212; gender,
  sexuality, family and international,
  103; patterns of, in Las Ánimas, 87, 97;
  range of, 103; restrictions on, 8–9,
  84–86, 221–222, 228–229; rights for,
  181; woman and local, 100–103.
  See also Translocal mobility
Modernization, 30; achieving, 44;
  employment influenced by, 81; of
  Mexico, 283n13; of migrants, 19, 22
Money: Casillas raising, 131; as factor in
  migration purpose, 8; flaunting of, 77;
  social clubs donating, 133, 137. See also
  Clubes sociales; Remittances
Montañez, Rafael, 87
Mordidas (bribes), 24

Moreno López, Mario, 74
Movement maps, 9, *85*
Movimiento Estudantil Chicano de
  Aztlán (MEChA), 147
Multiculturalism, 48
Muñoz H., Daniel, 26

National Association for the Advance-
  ment of Colored People, 59
National Center for Human Rights, 168
National Congress of Hispanic-American
  Citizens, 187
National Council of La Raza (NCLR), 188,
  196–198, 202
National Labor Relations Act (NLRA), 75,
  173, 181
National Labor Relations Board (NLRB),
  173–175
National Population Council (CONAPO),
  34
National Social Solidarity Program, 32
National Workers Conference on the
  Undocumented, 165
National Workers' Housing Fund Institute
  (INFONAVIT), 32
Naturalization, 94–95, 211
Nelson, Alan, 202
New York Times, 46, 67, 123
Ngai, Mae, 278n103
Nixon, Richard, 29, 58, 71
No Man's Land, 1, 3, 208
Nonmigrants, 7, 79, 240
Non-refoulement, 44
Normalization: of migration, 105–107,
  109; migration encouraged by, 124; of
  migratory process, 116, 121
North American Free Trade Agreement
  (NAFTA), 199, 217–218
Nostalgia, 145
Nuñez Ayala, José, 170

Oakland Post, 59
Obama, Barack, 224, 234
Oil, 28, 57, 97, 198–199
Operation Blockade, 231
Operation Gatekeeper, 231
Operation Jobs, 73
Operation Wetback, 39, 255n31
Oral contraceptives, 35. *See also* Birth
  rates; Fertility; Population; Sterilization
Oral histories, 12–13, 80; characteristics of
  interviewees for, 240–241; geographic
  locations of interviewees for, *242*

Orozco Álvarez, Pánfilo, 35
Ortega, Imelda, 72
Ortega, Jesús, 136–137
*Other Side, The: A Guide for the Undocu-
mented (El otro lado: Una guía para los
indocumentados)* (Preusch and Barry),
180
Out-migration: agricultural development
and, 23; benefits of, 30; development
model relationship with, 33; restricting
of, 19; support for, 8–9, 39, 44, 46,
75–76, 136

Pacheco Suárez, Hilario, 164, 167
Paiz, Sandra, 168, 170, 185, 211, 214
Pancho Villa y La Valentina (1958), 143–144
Parties *(pachangas)*, 117, 132–133, 284n32
Party of the Democratic Revolution
(PRD), 225
Paul VI (Pope), 34
Phillips, A. W., 57
Phillips curve, 57–58
Plyler v. Doe, 177–179, 182, 223
Policymakers: deliberations of, 7; human
rights interest of, 42–43; migrant
stereotypes promoted by, 9–10; migrant
world removed from, 77. *See also*
Mexican policymakers; U.S.
policymakers
Popular Socialist Party, 35
Population: control of, 185–186; immi-
gration quotas preventing increase in,
51; increase in, as detrimental, 28–29;
increase in, as future problem, 51; of
Mexico, as overflowing, 56; of migrants
after 1986, *215*; natural growth of, 17;
social order, unemployment and, 30.
See also Fertility; Oral contraceptives;
Sterilization
Poverty, 2; birth rate associated with, 66;
resources to alleviate, 126
Powell, Lewis, 171
Preference system, 37, 49, 68, 70,
229–230, 270n98
Preusch, Deb, 180
Programa de Inversiones Públicas para el
Desarrollo Rural (Public Investment
Program for Rural Development,
PIDER), 31–32
Programa Nacional Fronterizo
(PRONAF), 24, 27. *See also* Border
Industrialization Program;
Maquiladoras

Program for the Use of the Surplus Labor
Force. *See* Border Industrialization
Program
Promiscuity, label of, 66
Protections, denying of, 159
Protests: of migrants as risky, 158;
towards Sensenbrenner bill, 223–224
Public Investment Program for Rural
Development (Programa de Inversiones
Públicas para el Desarrollo Rural,
PIDER), 31–32

Queer men: dangers for, 95; economic
stability of, 92; in hometown life of,
94–96; identifying as, 244; migration
of heterosexual men compared to,
78–80, 92–96, 103, 244, 249; migration
statistics methodologies of, 247–249;
sexual activity paid for by, 276n67;
undocumented migration and, 78–80,
91–94, 219
Queer women, 94–96, 244
Quintín, Epifanio, 42

Racial hostility, 67–68
Racism, 50, 53, 71, 170; towards African
Americans, 146; belonging influenced
by, 145; denouncing of, 67; violence
from, 74
Ramírez, Feliciana, 87–88, 118,
199–200
Ramírez, Lorenzo, 23–24
Ramírez, Valentina, 143–144
Reagan, Ronald, 183–184, 194, 199, 201,
204
Red Cross, 135
Reinaga, Anaberta, 64, 211
Remittances, 17, 30, 102, 206; commodi-
ties purchased from, 113; dependence
on, 108, 244; different from money
sent by clubs, 131, 133–134; economic
restructuring influenced by, 109,
283n19; improvements through, 104;
as link to United States, 79; standard of
living improved through, 130. *See also*
Money
Reno, Janet, 217
Repatriation, 17, 20, 128, 255n26
Residency, 211
Reyes, María, 98–99, 106
Rights. *See specific types*
de los Ríos, María, 65
Ríos González, Ernesto, 135

Robles, Francisco, 173–174
Rockefeller Foundation, 22
Rodino, Peter W., 186, 297n2
Rodríguez, Adalberto, 187–188, 214
Rodríguez, Agapito, 64
Rodríguez, Héctor, 213
Rodríguez, José Guadalupe, 169, 220
Rodríguez, Lucio, 115, 118
Rodríguez, Ray, 151–152
Rodríguez, Tiliberto, 71
Rodríguez, Wendy, 49, 213
Rodríguez Lozano, Pedro, 111–112
Rojas, Uriel, 115–116, 119–120
Romero, Carlos Humberto, 44
Romo, Jesús, 161
Roos, Peter, 176
Rosas, Ubaldo, 72–73
Rustin, Bayard, 59

Salazar, María Elena, 189
Salinas de Gortari, Carlos, 217
Sánchez, Lupe, 161–163, 167, 292n25
Sánchez Baroso, Nicolás, 255n35
San Diego, California, 1
Sandinista rebels, 43–44
Sandoval, Renato, 53
San Francisco Examiner, 59
Santibáñez, Enrique, 17
Sarbanes, Paul, 70
Saxbe, William B., 47
Schey, Peter, 168, 177
Secretariat of Agriculture and Livestock, 39
Select Commission on Immigration and Refugee Policy, 200
Select Commission on Western Hemisphere Immigration, 68–69
El Sembrador, 111, 179
Sensenbrenner bill, 223–224
Serrano, María Elena, 140, 142–144, 147, 287n81
Service industry, migrants working in, 61
Sevilla, Charles M., 169
Sexual ideologies, 93–96, 99
Sexuality, 9, 275n54; belonging and, 79; gender, labor and, 76, 92–93; international mobility, gender, family and, 103; liberation of, 276n67; as migration factor, 7–8, 78, 91–96, 272n3. See also Queer men; Queer women
Sexual violence, 96, 97–98, 199, 276n82
Silence: following end of Bracero Program, 109–110; in histories, 245; Mexican

policymakers' desire for, 46; as strategy, 44–45; women experience of, 112
Silicon Valley, 60
Simpson, Alan K., 183, 201
Sisk, B. F., 68
Smith, William French, 201
Smugglers, 1–2, 14, 36, 71; deaths caused by, 90; fees for, 98; migrants hidden by, 89, 115; transporting and, 40; violence of, 231. See also Border enforcement; Border Patrol
Social clubs. See Clubes sociales
Social development programs, 16
Socialization, 77, 135
Social networks: expansion of, 8, 110; geographic extent of, 114–115; interview process facilitated by, 244; local pressures countered by, 124. See also communities
Social security, 49
Sodomy laws, 95
Solanes, Antonio, 135
Solís, Luciano, 134
Somoza Debayle, Anastacio, 43
Space, sense of, 78–80, 83, 113–114. See also Mobility
Spanish colonization, 145–146
Stagflation, 47
Stereotypes: advantage of racial, 172; of African Americans, 146; as election tool, 234; excessive fertility rates as, 185; of illegality, 65; laws backed by, 207; of laziness, 63–64, 67; of migrants, 9–10, 69, 192, 204, 236; welfare abuser as, 64, 72, 172, 234
Sterilization: as forced, 66; of women, 34–35. See also Birth rates; Fertility; Oral contraceptives; Population
Strikebreakers, 59
Strikes: laws for union, 162; success of, 164–165; trust needed for, 163
Supplemental Security Income, 63. See also Welfare
Surak, John, 173–174
Sure-Tan, Inc., 173
Sure-Tan, Inc. v. NLRB, 174–175
Surplus population, 42, 49, 71, 236
Survey on Emigration to the North and to the U.S., 45

Tanton, John, 205
Tarascan language, 122. See also Indigenous people, of Mexico

Tariffs, 26–27
Taxes, 63
Technocrats, 44, 263n159
Thurmond, Strom, 69
Los Tigres del Norte, 219, 222
Tijuana, 115; population growth of, 24;
  poultry farm in, 136
Tourism, 24, 53, 139, 243
Tovar, Hilda, 66
Trade liberalization, 209, 217
Traditions, maintaining of, 50, 145
Translocal mobility, 104–105
Trump, Donald, 224, 233–234

Undocumented migrants. See specific topics
Undocumented migrants' rights, 169–182
Undocumented migration. See specific topics
Unemployment, 9; of African Americans,
  52; alleviating of, 5; in borderland
  cities, 25–26; in Ciudad Juárez, 28; in
  industrial communities, 54–55;
  inflation slowed down by, 57; migrants
  as responsible for, 57, 186; minorities
  and, 52; population, social order and,
  30; rise in Mexican, 80–81; solutions to
  Mexican, 15, 197. See also Employment;
  Full employment
Unión de Mexicanos y Residentes en el
  Extranjero (UMRE), 136–137
Unions: activism for rights of, 9, 11, 136,
  158–159, 162, 164, 169, 172–175, 181,
  189, 193–194; American Federation of
  Labor and Congress of Industrial
  Organizations, 52, 57, 59–60, 69, 191,
  204; Central Labor Union, 27; Chicago
  Leather Workers Union, 173, 294n64;
  International Ladies' Garment
  Workers' Union, 189–190; laws for
  strikes of, 162; migrants' acceptance by,
  189; strikebreakers and, 59; Unión de
  Mexicanos y Residentes en el Extran-
  jero, 136–137; United Farm Workers,
  59, 131, 147, 160–161, 186. See also
  Maricopa County Organizing Project;
  Strikes
United Farm Workers (UFW), 54, 59, 131,
  147, 160–161, 186
United Nations, 29
United States (U.S.): anti-foreign
  sentiments of, 19; belonging of
  migrants denied by, 46, 74, 78, 141,
  202, 222; exclusion explained in, 2–3;
  labor shortages in, 19–20; labor

standards of, 56; laws against Mexican
  migrants in, 45–46, 48–52, 68–69, 74,
  78, 141, 171, 177–178, 202, 222;
  Mexicans denied constitutional rights
  by, 45, 171, 177–178; migrant communities in, 115–116; oral histories
  conducted in, 12–13; pharmaceutical
  imperialism in, 34–35; remittances as
  link to, 79; wages in, 113–114; wall
  between Mexico and, 233–234
United States Commission on Civil
  Rights, 188
United States v. Brignoni-Ponce (1975), 171
United States v. Martinez-Fuerte (1976), 172
U.S. policymakers: congressional debates
  expressions of, 48–52, 68, 69; immigration made difficult by, 76, 184–185,
  194, 198

Valle Bajo Río Bravo irrigation project,
  22. See also Agricultural development;
  Green Revolution; Irrigation
Velarde, Marco Antonio, 212
Vergara Ramírez, Arnulfo, 138–139
Villalobos, Rafael, 123
Villalobos, Sara, 123
Villarreal, Raúl, 135–136, 142, 150,
  154–155, 240
Villaseñor, Natalia, 140
Violence: avoiding of, 18; of border
  crossing, 14, 62, 78, 95–96; border
  crossing prevented by, 90; as control
  method, 99; in deportation, 72; of
  employers, 228–230; as institutional-
  ized, 43; within queer life, 94; from
  racism, 74; of smugglers, 231. See also
  Sexual violence
Voting rights, 162, 225

Wages, 86; increase in, 57–58, 212–213;
  in U.S., 113–114; women earning,
  100–101
Wall between Mexico and United States,
  233–234
Welfare, 9; abuse of, stereotype, 64, 72,
  134, 172; dependency on, 114; as
  government responsibility, 187; illegal
  claims for, 72; legitimate need for,
  72–73; as mess, 48–49, 63; reliance on,
  64–65; system for, 133; women,
  fertility and, 66. See also Comité de
  Beneficencia Mexicana; Extraterritorial
  welfare state

Welfare queen, 63, 268n65
Western Hemisphere Act of 1976. *See* Eilberg Bill
Wet line, 161
White progressives, 159, 168
White supremacy, 146
Williamson, Peter, 296n90
Wilson, June, 47
Wirken, Melanie, 76
Women: children as responsibility of, 97–99; as confined to homes, 8, 99–101; dangers for, 78; employment for, 27–28; fallen, 106; gender role of, 7–8; identity difficulties for, 106–107; local mobility of, 100–103; migrants' influence on, 6, 61–62; as obligated to hometowns, 78; respect for husbands by, 279n35; rural environment of, 260n104; sexual activity openness of, 276n67; sexual relations exchanged for work by, 229–230; silence experience of, 112; social club participation, 142–143; sold to employers, 122–123; sterilization of, 34–35; traditional activities of, 93; undocumented migration of, 79–80, 96–103; vulnerability of, 219; wages earned by, 100–101; welfare, fertility and, 66. *See also* Queer women
World Bank, 31

Yorty, Sam, 140, 151
Yzaguirre, Raúl, 202. *See also* National Council of La Raza (NCLR)

Zero Population Growth (ZPG), 69, 76, 205